Fractures in IP, Trade, and Health

Fractures in IP, Trade, and Health

Centering a Public Health Framework

SRIVIDHYA RAGAVAN
Professor of Law and Dean's Research Chair, Texas A&M University School of Law, Fort Worth, Texas, USA

SWARAJ PAUL BAROOAH
Senior Expert, SpicyIP, India

OXFORD
UNIVERSITY PRESS

OXFORD
UNIVERSITY PRESS

Oxford University Press is a department of the University of Oxford.
It furthers the University's objective of excellence in research, scholarship,
and education by publishing worldwide. Oxford is a registered trade mark of
Oxford University Press in the UK and in certain other countries.

Published in the United States of America by Oxford University Press
198 Madison Avenue, New York, NY 10016, United States of America.

Library of Congress Cataloging-in-Publication Data
Names: Ragavan, Srividhya author | Barooah, Swaraj Paul author
Title: Fractures in ip, trade, and health: centering a public health
framework / Srividhya Ragavan, Swaraj Paul Barooah.
Description: 1. | New York : Oxford university press, 2026. |
Includes bibliographical references and index.
Identifiers: LCCN 2025048990 (print) | LCCN 2025048991 (ebook) |
ISBN 9780197684054 hardback | ISBN 9780197684061 | ISBN 9780197684085 |
ISBN 9780197684078 epub
Subjects: LCSH: Intellectual property—International cooperation | Foreign trade
regulation—Health aspects | Public health—Law and legislation |
International trade—Law and legislation | Public health—International cooperation
Classification: LCC K3570 .R34 2026 (print) | LCC K3570 (ebook)
LC record available at https://lccn.loc.gov/2025048990
LC ebook record available at https://lccn.loc.gov/2025048991

DOI: 10.1093/9780197684085.001.0001

Printed by Integrated Books International, United States of America

The manufacturer's authorized representative in the EU for product safety is
Oxford University Press España S.A. of Parque Empresarial San Fernando de Henares,
Avenida de Castilla, 2 – 28830 Madrid (www.oup.es/en or product.safety@oup.com).
OUP España S.A. also acts as importer into Spain of products made by the manufacturer.

Note to Readers

This publication is designed to provide accurate and authoritative information in regard to the subject matter covered. It is based upon sources believed to be accurate and reliable and is intended to be current as of the time it was written. It is sold with the understanding that the publisher is not engaged in rendering legal, accounting, or other professional services. If legal advice or other expert assistance is required, the services of a competent professional person should be sought. Also, to confirm that the information has not been affected or changed by recent developments, traditional legal research techniques should be used, including checking primary sources where appropriate.

(Based on the Declaration of Principles jointly adopted by a Committee of the American Bar Association and a Committee of Publishers and Associations.)

MIX
Paper
FSC FSC® C183721

To my parents and my family, for making my world special
–Srividhya

To my parents, living embodiments of love, resilience, and service
–Swaraj

Contents

Figures

Tables

Acknowledgements

Events that affect the globe in a disruptive manner also have the strange capacity to betray realities while at the same time leading to coalitions and collaborations. Covid's sudden precipitation of hidden tensions between trade, intellectual property, and global health exposed by the brutality of the pandemic brought to the forefront many projects and collaborations that perhaps would have been otherwise unimaginable. This book is certainly one of them.

The differences in backgrounds, experiences, geographies, and time zones (a 13-hour time-zone difference is the worst!) were overcome by our mutual interests and desire to highlight the structural and systemic frailty of the IP, trade, and public health nexus that governs so much of our interconnected lives. The book explores and addresses distinct shifts and ruptures within the medicine-access debates and the global pharmaceutical patent regime. In focusing on issues affecting the international trade and patent system with inroads into health, this book delves into substantive legal issues, realistic impediments and concerns. To us, this book represents merely the beginning of a conversation that we hope to engage more with in dealing with these many fractures of global systems that seem to govern our lives.

We would like to start this book with a series of acknowledgements to those who made it possible with their academic expertise and in many other ways. At the outset, we are particularly grateful to and appreciate the inputs of several research associates. Thus, we thank Carolina Ulanoski, Arthur Harris, Nand Mehta, Victoria Alsina, and Annie Ye of Texas A&M School of Law; and Sunidhi Das of the National Law School of India University in Bangalore; Praharsh Gour of SpicyIP; Md Sabeeh Ahmad of Cambridge University; and Aarav Gupta of National Law University, New Delhi. Special thanks and gratitude to Niraj Seth, an attorney and consultant based out of New Delhi who is currently a doctoral candidate at the National University for Juridical Sciences, Kolkata. We also extend our sincere thanks to Anjali Tripathi of Jindal Global Law School for her enthusiastic work, thoughts, and suggestions helping us define the front and back covers for the book.

Each one of you provided excellent assistance during different stages of the manuscript before the submission of the final draft to the publisher.

We additionally extend a sincere note of thanks to our publisher, Oxford University Press, which supported this project from the beginning, in particular, Robert Coorvis and Lindsay Glick. The editorial team of Oxford University Press assisted us with unquestionable dedication throughout the different stages of production of this book. They provided us with the much-needed lifeline to our manuscript. We also want to thank Texas A&M University School of Law, and SpicyIP and our colleagues at our respective institutions for supporting the project.

Our families, as always, were there for us both. We thank them for their support and immense patience as we spent hours away from them while completing this book. As the book unfolded, so did our lives. We had each confronted different issues, both good and bad, involving the rigours and realities of everyday life. We feel indebted to our respective families' presence and support. You define what we do.

We thank our friends who supported us. Sri extends special thanks and gratitude to Mrs. Sowmya R. Rammohan, Hosur, India, for being a friend indeed when in need.

Last, but not least, we, the authors, are grateful for having had the opportunity to collaborate and create this book together. To us, this book is a testament to the possibility of cooperation between scholars from different backgrounds and from different parts of the world and of the ability to bring creativity and diversity together into the pursuit of important projects, such as the one that we hope this book represents.

Swaraj Paul Barooah
Srividhya Ragavan

Background

The disruptions in 2021 involving trade and supply chains revealed longstanding failures and imbalances in global public health.[1] Health and trade have existed in tension for a very long time. Intellectual property (IP) has been a central cause of the tension. While IP was touted to bring foreign direct investments and result in development, it also raised the prices for and thereby limited access to critical health-care products such as patented medicines in parts of the globe. Patent protection created strong monopolies in the pharmaceutical arena and caused drugs to be priced at their maximum market price, making them unaffordable in many countries. Unlike consumer products, for which demand is elastic and monopoly pricing may make affordability an inconvenience, the demand for pharmaceuticals is inelastic; unaffordable costs can have dire consequences. As the need for low-cost access to patented medicines increased, so did its conflict with the IP and trade regimes.

Considering these exacerbated tensions, we believe that, rather than seeking stopgap solutions, this conflict needs to be resolved holistically. Indeed, the fragility displayed by public-health systems during the pandemic has challenged the traditional theories under which optimal trade requires harmonized IP rules to be imposed and enforced. The assertion has been that such imposition of IP rules was needed to ensure optimal innovation.

To be clear, IP rights are limited legal mechanisms created to incentivize creativity, with the goal of promoting innovations that lead to long-term public benefit. The trade regime works to reduce barriers to global trade in goods and services as a means to fuel economic productivity. Overall, while international trade and IP have seemed to work in tandem, public health has remained uncomfortably incompatible. Efforts to protect public health have been construed as barriers to trade and innovation. While much has been written about the tension, attempts to reconcile these areas have been few and divisive.

[1] Sean McLain, Christopher M. Matthews, and Costas Paris, *Everywhere You Look, the Global Supply Chain Is a Mess,* Wall St. J., (Mar. 18, 2021), https://www.wsj.com (last visited Oct 20, 2025).

The unaddressed incompatibility between public health and trade became undeniable with the onset of Covid-19. The level of destruction unleashed by the pandemic on an unassuming globe has been a game changer. Notably, Covid-19 has caused the realization that a fragile public-health system could devastate global trade, and at its whim. In reality, even as the globe was struggling to come to terms with the impact that public health was having over our supply chains, trade came to an abrupt halt. The onset of Covid forced the globe to reckon with the imbalance directly by exacerbating the existing tensions between international trade and IP, on the one hand, and the fragile state of international public health, on the other.

In light of this background, the information from Covid-19 presented an opportunity for natural experimentation to help address barriers to accessing health care, identify solutions to sustaining innovation, and stimulate trade without leaving health care as a casualty at a national and global level. Information on how global trade is affected when local productivity is impaired by a fragile health-care system tends to be sparse.

A desirable future comprises a culture of health as a means to enable robust trade. Such a framework has strong developmental roots and a strong basis on arguments that require a reframing of the dialogue on *local* national public health as the starting point. Examining the causes that impact *local* public health and its effect on global trade will help identify the causes of the current barriers to accessing health care.

In this context, and contrary to conventional wisdom, we, the authors, assert that trade and public health can and should work in a symbiotic fashion, and that the way forward requires finding common platforms to tap into the synergies that connect trade and IP rights with public health. Global public health must be reworked without compromising trade and innovation. Indeed, trade and IP have been thought of as the framework for enabling innovations. But health demands have repeatedly forced violations/deviations and caused ruptures, exposing the gaps in our innovation system.

This foundational understanding—that robust public health in all parts of the globe could fuel trade in a sustainable manner—forms the underlying theme of the book. Exclusive trade and IP rights may lead not only to long-term trade losses, as productivity is adversely affected, but to denial of public health and loss of life.

The benefits to innovation and trade from robust global public health are real. This book raises and addresses a timely question: Does the world need a multilateral approach to trade that posits public health as its central theme or fulcrum, and can a policy discussion of better global health-care policies improve overall global productivity?

In order to address these questions effectively, the book begins with an examination of the historic negotiations that resulted in the patent regime outlined in the Agreement on Trade-Related Aspects of Intellectual Property Rights (TRIPS Agreement). It draws from a game-theory framework to broadly outline interactions between vested interests and parties with sovereign nations that have long characterized the trade regime. The book is set in the background of the Covid-19 pandemic, the onset of which underscored the globe's need to realign its approach to health-care access. It is now clear that optimal trade and innovation necessitate well-balanced global public health. Thus, a reexamination of the role of trade and IP vis-à-vis public health seems imminent and essential.

1

Health-Care Access as an International Game

1. Introduction—Public Health as Casualty to the Trade-IP Nexus

1.1 Pandemic Parables and a Fragile Alliance

History has but one constant, and that is change.[1] The year 2020 brought several changes, some predictable, such as with reference to climate studies and race relations,[2] but the most impactful change would unleash extraordinary disruption on an unsuspecting globe. By March 2020 it was clear that the world was being afflicted by an extraordinary phenomenon.[3] The onset of 2020 felt as if the Voldemort of viruses had descended upon and circled the globe,[4] as if the Dark Lord, who had perhaps disappeared after the Spanish-flu pandemic, had reappeared after years of hibernation only to bring even more widespread destruction in the form of the Covid-19 virus.[5]

To effectively address the global issues that the pandemic raised, global agreements between nations to deal with public-health crises inevitably became implicated. Such global agreements or accords, including those that were negotiated under the auspices of the World Trade Organization

[1] This section draws on an earlier article published in the *Seton Hall Law Review*. *See generally* Srividhya Ragavan & Swaraj Paul Barooah, "Historic Tensions Involving International Intellectual Property Protection of Medical Technology with Disastrous Public Health Consequences," 54 SETON HALL L. REV. 339 (2023), https://scholarship.shu.edu/shlr/vol54/iss2/1/ (last visited Oct. 20, 2025).

[2] *See, e.g.,* WORLD METEOROLOGICAL ORG., WMO-No 1264, STATE OF THE GLOBAL CLIMATE 2020, at 6 (2021), https://library.wmo.int/doc_num.php?explnum_id=10618; *see also* BLACK LIVES MATTER, BLACK LIVES MATTER: 2020 IMPACT REPORT 4 (2020), https://blacklivesmatter.com/wp-content/uploads/2021/02/blm-2020-impact-report.pdf (last visited Oct. 20, 2025).

[3] *See* Ivan Pereira & Arielle Mitropoulos, "A Year of COVID-19: What Was Going On in the US in March 2020," ABC NEWS (Mar. 6, 2021), https://abcnews.go.com/Health/year-covid-19-us-march-2020/story?id=76204691 (last visited Oct. 20, 2025); *see also* A. Perrella et al., *Editorial-COVID-19, More than a Viral Pneumonia*, 24 EUR. REV. MED. PHARMACOLOGICAL SCI. 5183, 5183–85 (2020).

[4] J. K. ROWLING, HARRY POTTER AND THE PRISONER OF AZKABAN 74–75 (1999).

[5] *Id.*

Fractures in IP, Trade, and Health. Srividhya Ragavan and Swaraj Paul Barooah, Oxford University Press.
 DOI: 10.1093/9780197684085.003.0001

(WTO), are another feature of history that affects the handling of pandemic questions. As the real impact of the pandemic-wrecked global supply chains emerged, it raised the question of whether responses to the global public-health challenge had been stymied on account of history's condemnation of a tense and uncomfortable alliance between trade and intellectual-property (IP) rights. The pandemic seemed to underscore the perception that public health remained a significant casualty of the alliance of trade with IP rights.[6]

Against this backdrop, this chapter discusses how years of trade negotiations resulted in creating a pharmaceutical pyramid. To do so, it alternates between discussions of the historical tensions that have prevailed between IP and trade and contemporary times to capture the consequences for public health. It will examine alliances and the resulting tensions that led to the creation of the WTO's trade-related IP accord, in the form of the TRIPS Agreement. The accord is significant for having aligned the interests of trade by fusing it with IP rights, but this fusion was achieved without fully reconciling or providing flexibility for nations to address the structural inequities inherent in the WTO system.[7]

The chapter traces how the failure to create international flexibilities by taking into account national structural inequities caused global health to be subordinated to trade concerns within a WTO system that has merely entrenched inequalities between member states.

1.2 Trade-Centric IP as Barrier to Public Health

In the mid-1990s, an attempt to ally international trade with IP laws led to the IP laws being substantively harmonized.[8] The Agreement on Trade-Related Aspects of Intellectual Property Rights, or TRIPS Agreement, which took effect in 1995, introduced intellectual-property law into the international trading system for the first time. However, harmonization left the Agreement embroiled in controversy because of tensions over the imbalance between

[6] *See* Srividhya Ragavan & Swaraj Paul Barooah, *Historic Tensions Involving International Intellectual Property Protection of Medical Technology with Disastrous Public Health Consequences*, 54 Seton Hall L. Rev. 339, 346 (2023), https://doi.org/10.60095/EQAN3083 (last visited Oct. 20, 2025).

[7] Marrakesh Agreement Establishing the World Trade Organization, Apr. 15, 1994, 1867 U.N.T.S. 154, 33 I.L.M. 1144 (1994); *see also* Agreement on Trade-Related Aspects of Intellectual Property Rights, Apr. 15, 1994, Marrakesh Agreement Establishing the World Trade Organization, Annex IC, 1869 U.N.T.S. 299, 33 I.L.M. 1197 (1994) [TRIPS Agreement].

[8] *Id.*

IP rights and access to health care.[9] Consequently, sovereign members could not effectively facilitate the preservation and protection of national public health.[10] In fact, trade realities came to dictate public health to an extent that efforts of member states to protect public health could be considered as—and were often construed as—a barrier to trade.[11]

As barriers to public health rose, the tense coexistence of trade with IP rights resulted in an era of arguably indiscriminate expansion of the scope of private rights,[12] which created new barriers to public health even as health-related innovations were surging.[13]

Global patent mechanisms, even when working alongside trade flexibilities such as the Declaration on TRIPS and Public Health signed in Doha, Qatar (Doha Declaration), were seen to be failing to create operationally friendly mechanisms to deal with a public-health crises.[14] Similarly, it was seen as unacceptable that amidst public-health crises, whether global or local, patent ideologues continued to support very limited exceptions to a patent owner's rights.[15] There was a strong hesitancy to impose

[9] TRIPS Agreement, *supra* note 7.

[10] *Id.* It is one of several agreements established as an Annex of the Agreement that established the WTO. The purpose of the TRIPS Agreement is to provide effective and adequate protection of IP rights to encourage global competition and reduce barriers to international trade. When the WTO was established, the signing of the TRIPS Agreement marked a distinguished effort to control worldwide deterrence of IP in international trade. TRIPS Agreement art. 1.1; *see also* Srividhya Ragavan, *World Trade Organization: A Barrier to Global Public Health?*, *in* Intellectual Property Law and Access to Medicines: TRIPS Agreement, Health, and Pharmaceuticals 25–26 (Srividhya Ragavan & Amaka Vanni eds., 2021).

[11] *See generally* Srividhya Ragavan, *World Trade Organization: A Barrier to Global Public Health?*, *in* Intellectual Property Law and Access to Medicines: TRIPS Agreement, Health, and Pharmaceuticals (Srividhya Ragavan & Amaka Vanni eds., 2021).

[12] *See, e.g.*, Michael Palmedo & Srividhya Ragavan, *The U.S. Posture on Global Access to Medication & the Case for Change*, 11 Indian J. Intell. Prop. L. 76, 80 (2020).

[13] *See generally* Srividhya Ragavan & Swaraj Paul Barooah, *Historic Tensions Involving International Intellectual Property Protection of Medical Technology with Disastrous Public Health Consequences*, 54 Seton Hall L. Rev. 339, 346 (2023), https://doi.org/10.60095/EQAN3083 (last visited Oct. 20, 2025).

[14] *See* Carlos M. Correa, *Will the Amendment to the TRIPS Agreement Enhance Access to Medicines*, S. Ctr., Jan. 2019, at 1, 2, https://www.southcentre.int/wp-content/uploads/2019/01/PB57_Will-the-Amendment-to-the-TRIPS-Agreement-Enhance-Access-to-Medicines_EN-1.pdf (last visited Oct. 20, 2025); *see also* World Trade Organization, Ministerial Declaration of 14 November 2001, WTO Doc WT/MIN(01)/DEC/1, 41 I.L.M. 746 (2002).

[15] Brook K. Baker, *The Cynical Connectedness of Gilead's Hepatitis C Pricing and Anti-Diversion Policies*, BodyPro (Jan. 16, 2015), https://www.thebodypro.com/article/the-cynical-connectedness-of-gileads-hepatitis-c-p (last visited Oct. 20, 2025); *see also* Brook Baker, United Nations Secretary-General's High-Level Panel on Access to Medicines, Background Paper: Existing and Prior Work, Initiatives and Proposals to Improve Innovation and Access to Health Technologies 10 (2016). Eminent domain has always been an exception to the acquisition of private property. The extension of the same principles to patent law has been much more controversial. *See generally* US Const., amend. V ("[N]or shall private property be taken for public use, without just compensation").

mandatory obligations to differentially price or license the patent, voluntarily or compulsorily.[16] Such rights are one form of IP rights meant to encourage innovation.

Textbooks define the goal of the patent system as a "patent bargain" for the public benefit, intended to encourage innovation. However, the gap between theory and practice has widened, as a patent owner's ability to reap profits has been criticized for being prioritized at the expense of the goals of the system.[17] This is more prevalent in the context of access to lifesaving medication that the patent system implicates through its innovation framework.

In fact, abject failings of the trade and IP regime with respect to prioritizing global public health had long been rationalized based on the utilitarian goal of "the greatest happiness of the greatest number."[18] In the context of the "free market," the utilitarian underpinnings operate on the assumption that society's preferences will make themselves heard. Increasingly, though, the gap between theory and practice has become harder to ignore in the context of public health. Even broadly, the "greatest number" benefiting from the trade regime has increasingly become a smaller number that happen to have a higher *preference-expressing power*. As the expression-interest of a few invested parties increased, it proportionately resulted in more countries and people becoming increasingly excluded from engaging in their own expression-interest.

Realistically, this glaring exclusion resulted in more people across the globe losing their ability to afford lifesaving medication covered by different forms of IP rights.[19] Over time, as states and institutions promoted free-market policies through their membership in the WTO, their ability to address the needs of their own societies—especially in the realm of health care—was reduced. The tensions between the trade regime that advocates for minimal

[16] Brook K. Baker, *The Cynical Connectedness of Gilead's Hepatitis C Pricing and Anti-Diversion Policies*, BodyPro (Jan. 16, 2015), https://www.thebodypro.com/article/the-cynical-connectedness-of-gileads-hepatitis-c-p (last visited Oct. 20, 2025).

[17] *See* Srividhya Ragavan, *Correlative Obligation in Patent Law: The Role of Public Good in Defining the Limits of Patent Exclusivity*, 6 J. Intell. Prop. & Ent. L. 47, 54 (2016), https://jipel.law.nyu.edu/vol-6-no-1-3-ragavan/ (last visited Oct. 20, 2025).

[18] Jeremy Bentham, An Introduction to the Principles of Morals and Legislation 8 (1789) (Bentham argues that the morality of an action should be judged by its contribution to the overall happiness of the greatest number of people, a principle that became central to utilitarian philosophy).

[19] *See* Carlos M. Correa, *TRIPS and Access to Drugs: Toward a Solution for Developing Countries Without Manufacturing Capacity*, 17 Emory Int'l L. Rev. 389, 404 (2003); *see also* Carlos M. Correa, *TRIPS Agreement and Access to Drugs in Developing Countries*, 3 Sur Int'l J. Hum. Rts. 25, 27 (2005).

trade barriers but embraces monopolistic IP rights for health-care products needed more balancing with local economic and social realities, for which the trade regime left limited scope.[20] Arguably, the resulting system has increasingly worked to protect the market against democratic protestations, including those relevant to public health.[21]

1.3 Putting Health Access First in the Trade-IP Paradigm

Against this backdrop of misplaced priorities, it should be recalled that, although IP rights have been present in various forms from as early as the 1400s, the alliance between trade and IP regimes is a relatively recent development.[22] Foundations of some of these rights can be traced to England's Statute of Monopolies in 1623 in its colonies, and these later slowly diffused to other European countries.[23]

Only during the Industrial Revolution did it become clear that the increase in international trade and commerce necessitated an international agreement to handle the coordination of IP rights protection across countries.[24] The Paris Convention for the Protection of Industrial Property of 1883 and the Berne Convention for the Protection of Literary and Artistic Works of 1886, by requiring common administrative frameworks and principles for patents and copyrights, were the first international attempts at international harmonization of IP laws.[25] Although there were proposals for more "substantive" harmonization, these did not gain traction at that time because of

[20] *See generally* Brian Manning & Srividhya Ragavan, *The Dispute Settlement Process of the WTO: A Normative Structure to Achieve Utilitarian Objectives*, 79 UMKC L. Rev. 1 (2010).

[21] Quinn Slobodian, Globalists: The End of Empire and the Birth of Neoliberalism 2–6 (2018).

[22] *See generally* Giulio Mandich, *Venetian Patents (1450–1550)*, 30 J. Pat. & Trademark Off. Soc'y 166, 171 (1948).

[23] Srividhya Ragavan, Patent and Trade Disparities in Developing Countries 1–29 (2012).

[24] *See WIPO—A Brief History*, World Intell. Prop. Org., https://www.wipo.int/about-wipo/en/history.html (last visited Oct. 24, 2025) ("[F]oreign exhibitors refused to attend the International Exhibition of Inventions in Vienna, Austria in 1873"); *see also* Srividhya Ragavan & Swaraj Paul Barooah, *Historic Tensions Involving International Intellectual Property Protection of Medical Technology with Disastrous Public Health Consequences*, 54 Seton Hall L. Rev. 339, 346 (2023), https://doi.org/10.60095/EQAN3083 (last visited Oct. 20, 2025).

[25] *See WIPO—A Brief History*, World Intell. Prop. Org., https://www.wipo.int/about-wipo/en/history.html (last visited Apr. 24, 2020). When the World Intellectual Property Office (WIPO) was created in 1967, the administration of these two treaties was transferred to the WIPO.

the differences in how IP rights were granted and regulated across different countries.[26]

Over time, with the deepening integration of world economies driven by globalization and consequent economic and technological challenges, IP laws became independently embroiled in a struggle to define the limits of the involved exclusivities, especially in the context of addressing the system's inability to deliver its purported objective.[27] More often than not, the seemingly indiscriminate expansion of private rights has been criticized for coming at the cost of "marginalization of other interests at the heart of the IP system," eventually leaving both the source and the recipient bereft of benefits that the system intended.[28]

Against this background, the onset of Covid-19 resulted in the convergence of the trade regime's disadvantages with that of the patent regime's failings. This chapter discusses the nuts and bolts of the alliance between trade and IP rights in order to help clarify how the wider trade regime came to affect public health, both beneficially and detrimentally.

To that end, this chapter analyzes the historic negotiations that resulted in the TRIPS patent regime by drawing from a framework of game theory to outline the specific types of interactions between nations and other vested interests that have characterized the trade regime. It further describes how the historical international negotiation on trade demonstrates how TRIPS norms came to become the threshold or floor for IP harmonization.

As a result of the tensions between trade and IP, what was originally a global health-equity question morphed into a global issue of health-care access. The discussions led to an examination of the existence of a pharmaceutical food chain. The chapter will end with a discussion of how Covid-19 has changed the game and forced us to rethink the global approach to health care. It considers whether it is time to realign the place of public health within the trade-and-IP paradigm, and concludes by asserting the need for a realignment of the role of health care within the trade and IP paradigm. To confront the contemporary challenges to global health, such a discussion seems timely and necessary.

[26] Frederick M. Abbott et al., International Intellectual Property in an Integrated World Economy 3 (4th ed. 2019).

[27] *See, e.g.*, Carlos M. Correa, *Interpreting the Flexibilities Under the TRIPS Agreement*, *in* Access to Medicines and Vaccines: Implementing Flexibilities Under Intellectual Property Law 1, 19 (Carlos M. Correa & Reto M. Hilty eds. 2021), https://www.southcentre.int/wp-content/uploads/2021/06/RP-132.pdf (last visited Oct. 20, 2025).

[28] Eva Hillberg, *The Terra Nullius of Intellectual Property*, 36 Ethics & Int'l Affs. 125, 128 (2022).

2. Evolution, Consolidation, and Imposition of IP Maximalism

2.1 Origin of IPs as Instruments of Industrialization

The question of repositioning health care within the trade-IP regime leads us to the historical evolution of IP norms prior to the TRIPS Agreement. These norms embodied distinct variations between countries, usually based on the then-prevailing state of technological development. Several countries preferred flexible IP regimes, calibrated to account for their economic-development needs and commensurate with their concurrent social development and efforts at poverty alleviation.

In the twentieth century, countries such as the United States, Switzerland, Germany, and Japan, some of them then in their own developing phase, embraced very flexible patent regimes based on industrial developments taking place at the time.[29] The flexible IP regime they adopted emphasized policies that promoted competition and access. In a later chapter we will highlight the need for such flexibility in view of local realities today.

The organic development of IP rights has historically been a story of countries using flexible IP norms to promote national development based on local realities. For instance, the fall of Constantinople to the Turks in AD 1453 caused artisans to move to the Roman Empire because of IP-like protections, and led to a peak of economic prosperity in Venice.[30] To establish and maintain preeminence in manufacturing, Venice adopted several measures,[31] including enacting laws prohibiting the out-migration of skilled artisans and the export of certain materials, as well as laws encouraging the immigration of skilled workers by providing a tax holiday for two years after their arrival in Venice.[32] Other measures included providing monopoly

[29] *See, e.g.*, Srividhya Ragavan, Patent and Trade Disparities in Developing Countries 20–22 (2012); *see also* Graham Dutfield & Uma Suthersanen, Harmonization or Differentiation in Intellectual Property Protection? The Lessons from History 7–14 (2004), https://live-quno2025.pantheonsite.io/wp-content/uploads/2016/06/Harmonisation-or-Differentiation.pdf (last visited Oct. 20, 2025).

[30] Edward C. Walterscheid, *The Early Evolution of the United States Patent Law: Antecedents (Part 1)*, 76 J. Pat. & Trademark Off. Soc'y 697, 703, 710 (1994); *see also* Christopher May, *The Venetian Moment: New Technologies, Legal Innovation and the Institutional Origins of Intellectual Property*, 20 Prometheus 159, 160 (2002).

[31] Edward C. Walterscheid, *The Early Evolution of the United States Patent Law: Antecedents (Part 1)*, 76 J. Pat. & Trademark Off. Soc'y 697, 708–09 (1994); *see also A Brief History of the Patent Law of the United States*, Ladas & Perry LLP (May 7, 2014), https://ladas.com/education-center/a-brief-history-of-the-patent-law-of-the-united-states-2/ (last visited Oct. 20, 2025); *see generally* Martin Adelman et al., Cases and Materials on Patent Law 12 (5th ed. 2018).

[32] Edward C. Walterscheid, *The Early Evolution of the United States Patent Law: Antecedents (Part 1)*, 76 J. Pat. & Trademark Off. Soc'y 697, 710 (1994).

rights to foreign artisans, in order to attract immigrants and encourage local industrialization.[33]

Continuing this trend of linking IP-like protection to industrial policy, Queen Elizabeth granted patents meant "to stimulate domestic production of both raw materials and a wide variety of manufactured goods previously imported from abroad."[34] England's focus was on acquiring superior technology to reduce imports.[35] Edward Walterscheid has written that the Crown wanted to "attain economic self-sufficiency, thereby gaining in power and strength not only within its own borders but also relative to other states."[36] Patents are acknowledged as having enabled England to achieve a level of self-sufficiency.[37] Thus, as in Venice, patent laws in England were used as a mechanism not to increase trade but rather to improve local industrialization.[38] Much later too, local working or manufacturing requirement was recommended by the Sir Edward Fry Commission of 1901 as the choice policy prescription when Britain considered policy choices to compete with the United States and Germany in large-scale industrial production. Thus, local manufacturing and locally working inventions have been choice policy prescriptions used by nations wanting to improve their industrial capacity.[39]

Other parts of Europe also adopted flexible approaches to IP, in order to strategically use them as instruments of industrialization. A rule prohibiting product patents for chemicals was first introduced in the German Patent Law of 1877 to stimulate research in alternative methods of producing a product.[40] Within the next thirty years, Germany's process patent regime enabled the growth of the chemical industry.[41] Indeed, at the end of World War I, a British Law Amendment Committee chaired by Lord Parker pointed

[33] *Id.*

[34] Edward C. Walterscheid, *The Early Evolution of the United States Patent Law: Antecedents (Part 2)*, 76 J. Pat. & Trademark Off. Soc'y 849, 855 (1994).

[35] *Id.*

[36] *Id.* at 856.

[37] Srividhya Ragavan, Patent and Trade Disparities in Developing Countries 5 (2012).

[38] Adam Mossoff, *Rethinking the Development of Patents: An Intellectual History*, 1550–1800, 52 Hastings L.J. 1255, 1261–62 (2001).

[39] Shri Justice N. Rajagopala Ayyangar, Report on the Revision of Patents Law 126–27 (1959), https://ipindia.gov.in/writereaddata/Portal/Images/pdf/1959-_Justice_N_R_Ayyangar_committee_report.pdf (last visited Oct. 20, 2025) (discussing how manufacturing locally was important for India's self-sufficiency) [Ayyangar Report].

[40] *Id.* at 58.

[41] *Id.* Prior to 1877, Germany followed the French model. Under the French statute of 1844, patents were granted to chemical products per se. German scientists and research workers attributed the failure of the French chemical industry to the French product patent system. The Ayyangar Committee favorably cited the German belief that the grant of a product patent per se to chemical products precluded alternative processes of production.

to the German patent system and favored process protection for chemicals, food, and medicine.[42] Consequently, the United Kingdom Patent and Design Act, 1919 was passed with the amendments recommended by Lord Parker, making England's policies comparable with those of Germany.[43]

Similarly, the preference for process over product patent was adopted in Sweden, Spain, and Japan, which did not allow product claims for articles of food or medicine, and Denmark's own system did not allow any patents on food.[44] Further, the 1957 Italian law prohibited patenting medicinal products.[45] The Ayyangar Committee Report also refers to another report filed by the UK's Sargent Committee to discuss the following recommendation to make food affordable in England:

> During the War, it became apparent that Great Britain was suffering from a lack of medicine and drugs, many of which were the subject of patent rights in this country. On the other hand, it was found that in many European countries (e.g., France, Germany, Switzerland) such substances were not capable of protection under the patent laws of those countries. In this state of things, it was considered expedient to modify to some extent the monopoly consequent on the existence of patent rights in regard to such substances.[46]

In response to these policy imperatives, Section 38A of England's Patents and Designs Amendment Act of 1919 introduced process patents and imposed restrictions on patent protection for food.[47] Further, Section 38B(2) introduced compulsory licensing of patents relating to food substances.[48]

Seeing the example of Germany and Italy, India sought to enable its pharmaceutical-manufacturing capacity. Establishing a local generic manufacturing industry has often been the first step to promoting innovation. Hence, India embraced the process patent regime to enable competition by providing room for several manufacturers to compete using process innovation. This resulted in a robust generic manufacturing capacity, and the resulting competition also made medication affordable. Brazil followed

[42] Patents and Designs Act, 1919, United Kingdom (9 & 10 Geo. 5. c. 80) *Id.* at 72, 75.
[43] *Id.* at 72–75.
[44] *Id.*
[45] *Id.*
[46] *Id.* at 98.
[47] *Id.*
[48] *See generally id.* at 73–99.

India's path and at once abrogated patent on pharmaceuticals as a pathway to creating manufacturing capacity successfully in order to enable universal health coverage.

Most developing countries encouraged the use of process patents for food, drug, and pharmaceutical products, as well as chemical processes.[49] This was the key flexibility to kick-start market competition in these critical sectors.[50] India, for instance, adopted the process patent regime after carefully considering its advantages and disadvantages, as described in the seminal Ayyangar Report.[51] That is, the process patent regime enabled more process innovations on the same product, thus leading to more engagement with pharmaceutical process innovation.[52] Thus, the process patent regime did not protect the product itself, but rather the method or process of making the product. The goal was that identical products could be produced by several manufacturers, each of which held a process patent. Protecting innovative processes encouraged innovation in the methods of making known products, although the lack of product patent protection stunts the research and development of new products.[53]

In sum, the developing nations either embraced the process patent regime or declined to institute a patent regime to cover pharmaceutical innovations. Both policies were choice actions created thoughtfully to enable these countries to promote more competition in this area, which resulted in the establishment of a robust domestic generic-drug industry in countries like India and Brazil.

In recent decades, the stance of developed nations toward IP norms shifted from historically evolved national flexibilities to global rigidity. The following discussion outlines the contrasting approaches and positions maintained by "developed" and "developing" countries regarding those norms prior to and

[49] For example, the India Patent Act, § 5 (1970) reads as follows:

> In the case of inventions: claiming substances intended for use, or capable of being used, as food or as medicine or drug, or relating to substances prepared or produced by chemical processes (including alloys, optical glass, semi conductors and inter metallic compounds), no patent shall be granted in respect of claims for the substance themselves, but claims for the methods or processes of manufacture shall be patentable.

[50] *See* Srividhya Ragavan, *Can't We All Get Along? The Case for a Workable Patent Model*, 35 Ariz. St. L.J. 117, 135–37 (2003) (discussing Indian and Brazilian law on patents).

[51] *See* Srividhya Ragavan, *Of the Inequals of the Uruguay Round*, 10 Marq. Intell. Prop. L. Rev. 273, 274 (2006) (discussing the Ayyangar Report).

[52] Srividhya Ragavan, *A "Patent" Restriction on Research & Development: Infringers or Innovators?*, 2004 U. Ill. J.L. Tech. & Pol'y 73, 74.

[53] *See id.*

during the negotiations.[54] These original postures led to the creation of the WTO, within which the IP-trade nexus was first solidified in an enforceable manner. Of interest is the contrast between (1) the positions adopted by developed nations on IP and trade norms for themselves during the time they were improving their technological capabilities, and (2) the positions they have advocated for other countries that are currently working to evolve their technological prowess.

2.2 The Foundational Shift to WTO

The story of this historical contrast begins with the failed attempts at creating an International Trade Organization in the post–World War II era.[55] As a consequence, from 1948 to 1994 the legal principles enshrined in the provisional GATT effectively served as the only multilateral governing instrument for international trade.[56] During this period, a series of multilateral negotiations (trade rounds) were convened to improve this system. Only during the eighth trade round (the Uruguay Round), held from 1986 to 1994, were the WTO and its constituent agreements, including the TRIPS Agreement, conceived.[57] This round of negotiations represents the first significant substantive harmonization of IP norms internationally, as well as the first time that international trade was linked with the international IP regime.[58]

Western pharmaceutical companies, increasing their investment in shaping harmonized global IP policies, began lobbying their national governments in the face of stiff competition from the generic industry. The immediate consequence was a move by the developed nations away from the World Intellectual Property Organization (WIPO) to ally instead with

[54] *See generally* Sylvia H. Chant & Cathy McIlwaine, Geographies Of Development in the 21st Century: An Introduction to the Global South 137 (2008). This terminology groups countries according to their socioeconomic indices, with "developed countries" generally referring to high-income countries, and "developing countries" referring to middle- and low-income countries, per their World Bank classification. The authors acknowledge that this terminology is contested. Variations include Western/Eastern countries, developed, developing (least developed countries), and global North/global South countries; more recently, "majority world/minority world" phraseology is finding more usage. Each of these terms has its own drawbacks and limitations; more significantly, there is not yet an uncontested phraseology that conveys the underlying idea. Thus, these terms will be used interchangeably through this book.

[55] *The GATT Years: From Havana to Marrakesh*, World Trade Org., https://www.wto.org/english/thewto_e/whatis_e/tif_e/fact4_e.htm (last visited Oct. 20, 2025).

[56] *Id.*

[57] *Id.*

[58] *Id.*

the WTO, a venue/forum regarded as more likely to impose "global IP standards" strategically.

The one-state-one-vote rule of the WIPO prevented developed countries from taking these proposals forward successfully within the system.[59] These concerns and pressures saw IP discussions moving away from the WIPO forum toward the trade forum via the GATT. The linking of IP to trade, among other factors, shifted the fora to the WTO, resulting in two institutionally derived benefits for developed countries, described below.

The first of these benefits was enhanced negotiating power, which caused bargaining parities to skew toward developed nations. In linking IP with trade, the dependence of developing countries on the markets of developed countries helped the latter to better exert pressure over IP matters.[60] In combination with the desire to belong to the global trading regime, the WTO presented both carrot and stick incentives for developing countries to accept changes to international IP norms. Further, since decisions at the WTO are generally made by consensus rather than by vote, bilateral pressure mechanisms and side deals were used to prevent formal objections, thus masking the true positions of member states.[61]

The second benefit was the institutional advantage, in the form of the WTO's dispute-settlement mechanism, which had more teeth than the redressal mechanisms under the Paris and Berne Conventions. The WTO system included compensatory or retaliatory actions, such as trade sanctions for a member state not submitting to the decisions of the Dispute Settlement Body (DSB).[62]

From its inception, the WTO had a significant feature that could perhaps be characterized as a flaw. The alleged juridical equality, though based on a per se theory of juridical equality and equal bargaining powers among the

[59] Peter Drahos & John Braithwaite, Information Feudalism: Who Owns the Knowledge Economy? 65 (2002).

[60] *See* Laurence R. Helfer, *Regime Shifting: The TRIPS Agreement and New Dynamics of International Intellectual Property Lawmaking*, 29 Yale J. Int'l L. 1, 16–17 (2004) (discussing effects of regime shifting and benefits to powerful actors).

[61] *See* Marrakesh Agreement Establishing the World Trade Organization art. 9.1, Apr. 15, 1994, 1876 U.N.T.S. 154. Consensus at the WTO is obtained when no member country makes a formal objection to a proposal.

[62] J. H. Reichman, *Enforcing the Enforcement Procedures of the TRIPS Agreement*, 37 Va. J. Int'l L. 335, 339 (1997) ("Taken together, the enforcement and dispute-settlement provisions of the TRIPS Agreement put teeth into the pre-existing intellectual property conventions"); *see also* Srividhya Ragavan & Brian Manning, *The Dispute Settlement Process of the WTO: A Normative Structure to Achieve Utilitarian Objectives*, 79 UMKC L. Rev. 1, 16 (2010).

signatory nations, was in reality indifferent to the presence of highly unequally posited parties.[63]

Academics decried the misconceived juridical equality.[64] Richard Steinberg, for instance, asserted that the WTO exacerbated the power disparities between states, often to the detriment of local realities, and showcased the issues caused when engaging in ideological affinity, disregarding the effects on local realities.[65] Others, such as Olufunmilayo Arewa, termed the global IP regime's "top-down approach" as catering to the interests and needs of the IP-rich states.[66] Similarly, Jerome Reichman decried the establishing of the WTO system as an effort "to rig a regime for short-term advantages" and predicted that it could "boomerang against those who pressed hardest for its adoption."[67] Yet others, such as Margaret Chon, asserted that the approach of the WTO failed to generate the full range of policy choices for both developed and developing countries to maximize global social welfare with respect to human-development needs such as education.[68]

Criticisms notwithstanding, the WTO, with a singular objective of facilitating global trade by reducing barriers that affect it, created sovereign international obligations packaged as negotiated agreements.[69] In

[63] Pascal Lamy, *The Place of the WTO and Its Law in the International Legal Order*, 17 Eur. J. Int'l L. 969, 972 (2006) (noting that "the WTO legal order respects, *inter alia*, the sovereign equality of states, good faith, international cooperation, and the obligation to settle disputes peacefully, not to mention the rules of interpretation of conventions which the Appellate Body, for example, applies without hesitation").

[64] Srividhya Ragavan, *World Trade Organization: A Barrier to Global Public Health?*, *in* Intellectual Property Law and Access to Medicines: TRIPS Agreement, Health, and Pharmaceuticals 25, 26 (Srividhya Ragavan & Amaka Vanni eds., 2021).

[65] Richard H Steinberg, *In the Shadow of Law or Power? Consensus-Based Bargaining and Outcomes in the GATT/WTO*, 52 Int'l Org. 339, 341 (2002) (asserting that trade rounds have been closed through power-based bargaining dominated by the European Community and United States); *see also* Chios Carmody, Fairness in WTO Law 11 (Nov. 10, 2013) (unpublished manuscript) (on file with the University College London Symposium on International Economic Law), https://www.google.com/url?sa=t&source=web&rct=j&opi=89978449&url=https://uwo.scholaris.ca/bitstreams/2bb9c477-0572-4846-b588-312451901715/download&ved=2ahUKEwjuivHvp7WQAxXTRmcHHXEUKN0QFnoECBoQAQ&usg=AOvVaw0NKUE84QdZAFCQR5cItD5I (last visited Oct. 20, 2025); Adam S. Chilton & Ryan W. Davis, *Equality, Procedural Justice, and the World Trade Organization*, 7 Intercultural Hum. Rts. L. Rev. 277, 280 (2012).

[66] Olufunmilayo B. Arewa, *Piracy, Biopiracy and Borrowing: Culture, Cultural Heritage and the Globalization of Intellectual Property* 79 (Case W. Rsrv. Univ. Sch. of L., Working Paper No. 1114, 2006), https://law.bepress.com/expresso/eps/1114/ (last visited Oct. 20, 2025).

[67] Jerome H. Reichman, *Intellectual Property in the Twenty-First Century: Will the Developing Countries Lead or Follow?*, 46 Hou. L. Rev. 1115, 1119 (2009).

[68] Margaret Chon, *Intellectual Property "from Below": Copyright and Capability for Education*, 40 U.C. Davis L. Rev. 803, 810–12 (2007).

[69] *See generally id.*

turn, these agreements generated sovereign commitments covering a wide range of subjects affecting trade, including—and specifically—with respect to IP rights.[70] The resulting tension between trade and IP rights increased as the scope of what fell within "intangible properties," especially patents, continued to expand, further altering the structure of international trade permanently.

Despite that, the United States and other developed countries could not achieve all of their goals via the TRIPS Agreement. The final TRIPS Agreement was based on consensus, which naturally involved compromises. Unfortunately, these compromises caused the WTO to become a forum for aggressive pursuit of new norms through a more normative enforcement of its rules, mostly disconnected from local realities and welfare issues that would be affected by the enforcement of the WTO norms. This, in turn, has arguably led to the collapse of the WTO as a fair venue for negotiating or pursuing negotiations on other issues relating to trade and IP rights, such as agriculture.

Nonetheless, by the end of 1995 112 countries had joined the WTO, for several reasons, such as the exertion of unilateral pressure mechanisms from the Special 301 process of the US Trade Representative (USTR),[71] experience and expertise asymmetries,[72] lack of bargaining parities,[73] and the desire to be a part of the global trade regime.[74] Hence, the developing and least-developed nations, hoping to partake in the new world of globalized trade that was opening with much-vaunted promises of improved economic growth for all members, were left with little choice but to join the WTO. The number of member countries today stands at 164.

Building upon this transformation, the WTO required that, to gain membership, nations must sign the TRIPS Agreement, alongside the General Agreement on Trade and Tariffs (GATT)[75] and the General Agreement on

[70] *See* Marrakesh Agreement Establishing the World Trade Organization art. 2, Apr. 15, 1994, 1876 U.N.T.S. 154.

[71] *See generally* Suzanne Zhou, *Challenging the Use of Special 301 Against Measures Promoting Access to Medicines: Options Under the WTO Agreements*, 19 J. Int'l Econ. L. 51 (2016).

[72] Peter Drahos, *Global Property Rights in Information: The Story of TRIPS at the GATT*, 13 *Prometheus* 6, 15 (1995), https://doi.org/10.1080/08109029508629187 (last visited Oct. 20, 2025).

[73] Srividhya Ragavan, *Of the Inequals of the Uruguay Round*, 10 Marq. Intell. Prop. L. Rev. 273, 274 (2006).

[74] *See* Press Release, World Trade Org., Overview of Developments in International Trade and the Trading System (Dec. 1, 1995), https://www.wto.org/english/news_e/pres95_e/ov11.htm (last visited Oct. 20, 2025).

[75] General Agreement on Tariffs and Trade, Apr. 15, 1994, Marrakesh Agreement Establishing the World Trade Organization, Annex 1A, 1867 U.N.T.S. 187.

Trade and Services (GATS),[76] thereby effectively linking IP with trade in an internationally significant manner.[77] The prolonged absence of an international trading regime after World War II encouraged quick and widespread membership in the WTO,[78] and the trade-centric IP norms in the TRIPS Agreement soon became the dominant international framework for IP norms.

Thus, with the institutionally derived systems in place, the stage was set for global progress with a trade-centric regime. There ensued a new economic world order, brought about by increased interdependence, cooperation, and trade, leaving other issues such as health care hanging in the balance.

2.3 The Ideological Bases of a Maximalist IP Approach

Pushing localized flexibilities in IP to the sideline, the developed countries advocated for an ideological affinity toward a more maximalist approach to IP which allowed them to take a stance tactically leveraging IP as part of international trade. The discussion below outlines a confluence of complex and intentional factors that contributed to the process whereby the decidedly controversial and minority opinions of developed nations morphed into international norms. How did an idealistic goal become an international legal reality resulting from the linking of IP with trade? To deal with this question, the discussion below highlights how governments were lobbied into shifting their postures on policy issues.[79]

A key element in the story of these lobbying efforts by the West was the leading role played by the US Advisory Committee on Trade Negotiations (ACTN), the USTR's body that advised on domestic industry interests, in linking trade with IP rights. Edmund Pratt, CEO and chairman of Pfizer,

[76] General Agreement on Trade in Services, Apr. 15, 1994, Marrakesh Agreement Establishing the World Trade Organization, Annex 1B, 1869 U.N.T.S. 183.

[77] *See generally* Srividhya Ragavan, *World Trade Organization: A Barrier to Global Public Health?*, *in* INTELLECTUAL PROPERTY LAW AND ACCESS TO MEDICINES: TRIPS AGREEMENT, HEALTH, AND PHARMACEUTICALS 25, 26 (Srividhya Ragavan & Amaka Vanni eds., 2021).

[78] *See* Srividhya Ragavan & Swaraj Paul Barooah, *Historic Tensions Involving International Intellectual Property Protection of Medical Technology with Disastrous Public Health Consequences*, 54 SETON HALL L. REV. 339, 346 (2023), https://doi.org/10.60095/EQAN3083 (last visited Oct. 20, 2025); *see also* Margaret Chon, *Intellectual Property "from Below": Copyright and Capability for Education*, 40 U.C. DAVIS L. REV. 803, 810–12 (2007).

[79] SUSAN K. SELL, PRIVATE POWER, PUBLIC LAW: THE GLOBALIZATION OF INTELLECTUAL PROPERTY RIGHTS 8 (2003) ("State-centric accounts of the Uruguay Round are at best incomplete, and at worst misleading, as they obscure the driving forces behind the TRIPS Agreement").

was also chairman of ACTN through most of the 1980s.[80] As the advisory committee relaying the interests of the industry, ACTN maintained that the industries most deserving of protection were those with big IP portfolios—pharmaceuticals, semiconductor chips, and copyright in icons like Mickey Mouse.[81]

ACTN soon took two actions toward achieving this goal. First, it created an IP Task Force; second, it created a special position within the USTR to ensure that IP remained a priority throughout the negotiations. John Opel, chairman of IBM (where, coincidentally, Pratt had worked for some eleven years before joining Pfizer),[82] headed ACTN's Task Force on IP.

As Drahos and Braithwaite note, the ACTN Task Force on IP released two sets of recommendations.[83] They included policies embraced by the USTR in its international negotiations, including the "No GATT Round without IP" position.[84] These were largely taken from a 1985 paper written by Jacques Gorlin, a former IBM consultant, outlining strategies for a trade-based approach to IP.[85] Notably, the paper recommended the use of "a carrot and stick approach," such as providing technical trainings to foreign IP officials while also strengthening unilateral trade pressure tactics outlined as part of Section 301 of the 1974 Trade Act. These processes also weaved in the Generalized System of Preferences outlined under GATT to link access to the US market with "improved" IP protection.[86]

To amplify the call for a trade-centric approach to IP, in early 1986 USTR sought to include the European, Japanese, and Canadian governments in the Uruguay Round. Recognizing the inefficiency of working through existing associations in these countries, the USTR worked through industry associations, which resulted in Opel and Pratt constituting the Intellectual Property Committee (IPC). The IPC included twelve CEOs from large corporations, including Bristol-Myers, CBS, Du Pont, General Electric, General Motors, Hewlett-Packard, IBM, Johnson & Johnson, Merck,

[80] *See* Peter Drahos & John Braithwaite, Information Feudalism: Who Owns the Knowledge Economy? 72 (2002); *see also* Mohan Kumar, Negotiation Dynamics of the WTO: An Insider's Account 36 (2018).

[81] *See* Peter Drahos & John Braithwaite, Information Feudalism: Who Owns the Knowledge Economy? 72 (2002).

[82] *See Duke Benefactor Edmund T. Pratt Jr. Dies*, Duke Today (Sept. 6, 2002), https://today.duke.edu/2002/09/prattobit0902.html (last visited Oct. 20, 2025).

[83] *See* Peter Drahos & John Braithwaite, Information Feudalism: Who Owns the Knowledge Economy? 115–16 (2002).

[84] *Id.*

[85] Sell, *supra* note 79, at 101.

[86] *Id.*

Monsanto, and Pfizer.[87] The IPC members, along with their peers from Europe and Japan, stressed that IP issues required involvement beyond governments because of the high costs of piracy and the large impact it could have on these firms in the future, owing to inadequate IP protections in other countries.

The IPC, in turn, lobbied its respective governments, leading to the eventual adoption of these ideas by the Europeans and Japanese at the Uruguay Round in September 1986.[88] In June 1988, this group released its "Basic Framework of GATT Provisions on Intellectual Property," which borrowed heavily from the substantive proposals of Gorlin's 1985 paper.[89] This proposal, which advocated minimum standards, national enforcement mechanisms, and dispute-settlement mechanisms, would eventually form the basis of the TRIPS Agreement.[90]

With the adoption of these industry-driven prescriptions in the TRIPS Agreement, the successful framing of IP harmonization as a trade issue coincided with a dramatic expansion of IP rights.[91] Indeed, the last three decades have witnessed the expansion of property rights to include a swath of intangible properties within its realm. Even the convergence of copyrights, patents, trademarks, geographical indications, designs, plant-variety protection, and so on (which had previously existed as separate legal instruments) under a common umbrella of "IPR" was primarily due to its incorporation as such under the TRIPS Agreement.[92]

These expansions included notable requirements for patent protection for inventions in all fields of technology, a minimum twenty-year duration,[93] protection for microorganisms and plant varieties,[94] expansions in copyright-protectable subject matter with a minimum copyright duration of fifty years,[95] criminal penalties for trademark and copyright infringement,[96]

[87] *Id.* at 2.
[88] *See* Peter Drahos & John Braithwaite, Information Feudalism: Who Owns the Knowledge Economy? 124 (2002); *see generally* Sell, *supra* note 79.
[89] *See* Sell, *supra* note 79, at 107.
[90] *See id.* Compromises such as Compulsory Licenses, preferential treatment for developing countries, and transition provisions were included to achieve consensus on the document.
[91] *See* Srividhya Ragavan, *World Trade Organization: A Barrier to Global Public Health?*, *in* Intellectual Property Law and Access to Medicines: TRIPS Agreement, Health, and Pharmaceuticals 27 (Srividhya Ragavan & Amaka Vanni eds., 2021).
[92] *See* Amy Kapcyznski, *The Access to Knowledge Mobilization and the New Politics of Intellectual Property*, 117 Yale L.J. 804, 821–24 (2008); *see also* TRIPS Agreement, *supra* note 7, art. 1.
[93] TRIPS Agreement, *supra* note 7, art. 27.1.
[94] *Id.* art. 27.3(b).
[95] *Id.* arts. 12, 14.
[96] *Id.* art. 61 ("Members shall provide for criminal procedures and penalties to be applied at least in cases of willful trademark counterfeiting or copyright piracy on a commercial scale").

and more.[97] Consequent to the broadening purview of IP rights, the timing coincided for the TRIPS Agreement to oversee the upward harmonization of IP norms.

As a result of its universal coverage, the TRIPS Agreement expanded the realm of IP to unprecedented levels. In addition to implementing minimum standards and mandating compliance with the substantive provisions of the Berne and Paris Conventions, it required compliance with select provisions of the Rome Convention on Neighboring Rights and the Washington Treaty on Integrated Circuit Designs.[98] More significantly, it required WTO member states to guarantee detailed enforcement procedures under their national laws and submit themselves to the decisions of the DSB.[99]

This combination of harmonization of substantive IP norms and its trade linkage meant that the TRIPS Agreement would go much further than the linkage between IP and trade of its predecessors, such as the North American Free Trade Agreement (NAFTA)[100] and the USTR's Special 301 Process, in its ability to affect IP norms.[101] The following discussion traces the specifics of the unique developments that led to the TRIPS Agreement standards becoming not only a general norm but also the floor for future norm-setting.

2.4 TRIPS as Floor and TRIPS-Plus as Ceiling: IP Maximalism

Amid the evolution of the increasingly inequitable global trade institutional mechanism, many countries considered to be "developing economies" at the time of the TRIPS Agreement were (re)molding transplanted IP laws introduced as part of empire-building and colonization by key developed countries.[102] Indicatively, prior to the TRIPS Agreement, more than forty

[97] *See generally* Bryan Mercurio, *TRIPS-Plus Provisions in Ftas: Recent Trends*, *in* Regional Trade Agreements and the WTO Legal System 215 (Lorand Bartels & Frederico Ortino eds., 2006).

[98] J. H. Reichman, *Compliance with the TRIPS Agreement: Introduction to a Scholarly Debate*, 29 Vand. J. Transnat'l L. 363, 366 (1996).

[99] *Id.*

[100] North American Free Trade Agreement, Dec. 17, 1992, 32 I.L.M. 289; *see also* 48 C.F.R. § 25.405 (2022).

[101] Section 182 of the Omnibus Trade Act of 1974 is commonly referred to as "special 301" for the enforcement of IP rights. Trade Act of 1974, Pub. L. No. 93-618, § 182, 88 Stat. 1978, 2041 (1975) (codified as amended at 19 U.S.C. § 2242 (1974)).

[102] Peter Drahos, *Developing Countries and International Intellectual Property Standard-Setting*, 5 J. World Intell. Prop. 765, 772–73 (2002); *see generally* Ayyangar Report, *supra* note 39 (forming the basis for India's much-discussed 1970 Patent Law wherein patent laws of various countries were examined, along with the feasibility for such regimes in less-developed countries such as India).

countries did not grant patent protection for pharmaceutical products.[103] During the TRIPS Agreement negotiations, India, Spain, Brazil, Mexico, and Peru advocated that patent terms be left to the discretion of their states.[104] Developing countries did not view the TRIPS Agreement as favorable to their interests, with its widening of patent subject-matter scope, the addition of new rights to the global IP regime, and the required minimum standards, resulting in a maximalist approach of duration and basic features.[105]

Notably, prior to undertaking these sweeping obligations as part of the TRIPS Agreement, developing countries had started raising concerns at WIPO diplomatic conferences between 1980 and 1984, demanding revisions to the Paris Convention to make it more favorable to their domestic interests, such as health and agriculture.[106] Over time, developed countries, led by the United States, successfully resisted these revisions.

Claiming the superiority of a maximalist IP ideology, developed nations predicted a world order in which they would export knowledge capital to countries that established a minimum level of IP protection and thereby prompt a trade cycle that would generate investments.[107] Thus, the idea of mandatory international minimum standards of protection was floated particularly by the United States, Europe, and Japan—carefully calibrated as beneficial for their economic interests.[108] These countries also saw the reliance

[103] *See WTO and the TRIPS Agreement*, World Health Org., https://web.archive.org/web/20150311165543/http://www.michaelbaileyassociates.com:80/news/pharmaceutical/what-do-patent-expirations-mean-for-the-pharma-industry; *see also The TRIPS Agreement and Developing Countries*, UNCTAD, https://unctad.org/system/files/official-document/ite1_en.pdf (last visited Oct. 24, 2025).

[104] *See* Simon Lester & Huan Zhu, *Rethinking the Length of Patent Terms*, 34 Am. U. Int'l L. Rev. 787, 797 (2019); *see also* Josh Lerner, *150 Years of Patent Protection*, 7 Am. L. & Econ. Rev. 221, 221–25 (2002) (discussing historical patent lengths). Additionally, Australia, and New Zealand historically had shorter patent terms and therefore advocated patent terms of fifteen and sixteen years, respectively, while certain developed countries, including the United States, advocated for a duration of more than twenty years.

[105] *See generally* Srividhya Ragavan, Patent and Trade Disparities in Developing Countries (2012).

[106] Laurence R. Helfer, *Regime Shifting: The TRIPS Agreement and New Dynamics of International Intellectual Property Lawmaking*, 29 Yale J. Int'l L. 1, 20 (2004); *see also* Nagesh Kumar, *Intellectual Property Rights, Technology and Economic Development: Experiences of Asian Countries*, 38 Econ. & Pol. Wkly. 209, 210 (2003). ("The top 10 countries account for as much as 84 percent of global resources spent on R and D activity annually, they control 94 percent of the technological output in terms of patents taken out in the US, and receive 91 percent of global cross-border royalties and technology license fees.").

[107] Srividhya Ragavan, *World Trade Organization: A Barrier to Global Public Health?*, *in* Intellectual Property Law and Access to Medicines: TRIPS Agreement, Health, and Pharmaceuticals 27 (Srividhya Ragavan & Amaka Vanni eds., 2021).

[108] Generally, "stronger" IP protections include more expansive exclusion rights. It should be clarified, though, that the rhetorical value of "stronger" has no normative usage here, as it is now well established that countries require different IP norms depending on various socioeconomic variables.

on the International Court of Justice prescribed by the Paris Convention as an inadequate enforcement mechanism because of its dependence on voluntary cooperation.[109]

Finally, a substantial part of the rising gross domestic product (GDP) in developed countries was owed to IP-heavy industries, even while their capacity to rival manufacturing centers in newly developing economies of Asia was declining. It was therefore in the interest of the developed economies to press this comparative advantage internationally.[110] Ruth Okediji captures the underlying sentiment behind the massive lobbying that took place:

> It is important to emphasize that the integration of IP and trade in that multilateral trade context was not solely or even primarily to curtail piracy in global markets, although this was certainly an important issue. The more vital role of the trade context for IP was the consolidation of a domestic reconditioning of the basis of comparative advantage in order to exploit both factor endowments and to adjust to the new division of labor evident in the global economy. To secure these ends, a new multilateral order was necessary to: provide coherence in the global IP framework; decrease the dependence of effective protection on the vagaries of political relations; capture the static gains of the multiple bilateral agreements already in place; and legitimize the economic imperative of unilateralism.[111]

The TRIPS Agreement, as the most important international framework for IP norms, by mandating minimum standards, more often than not served as a floor in practice.[112] That is, very few of the TRIPS Agreement flexibilities have been actually used in reality.[113] Despite the oft-repeated touting of flexibilities, after twenty-five years of the TRIPS Agreement the international

[109] *See* Anthony D. Sabatelli, *Impediments to Global Patent Law Harmonization*, 22 N. Ky. L. Rev. 579, 592 (1995). The ICJ's jurisdiction was based on the consent of States, making the voluntary cooperation of States mandatory for effective enforcement or dispute settlement.

[110] *See* Ruth Okediji, *Back to Bilateralism? Pendulum Swings in International Intellectual Property Protection*, 1 U. Ottawa L. & Tech. J. 125, 138 (2003); *see also* Peter K. Yu, *Currents and Crosscurrents in the International Intellectual Property Regime*, 38 Loy. L.A. L. Rev. 323, 356 (2004).

[111] *See* Okediji, *supra* note 110, at 135.

[112] *See* Yu, *supra* note 110, at 357; *see also* Henning Grosse Ruse-Khan, *Time for a Paradigm Shift? Exploring Maximum Standards in International Intellectual Property Protection*, 1 Trade L. & Dev. 56, 62 (2009) (exploring the possibilities of reversing this equation by identifying and examining rationales for a ceiling or maximum standards in international IP protection).

[113] *See* Sisule F. Musungu & Cecilia Oh, The Use of Flexibilities in TRIPS by Developing Countries: Can They Promote Access to Medicines? 7–12 (2006).

IP regime has failed to take the needs, interests, and local realities of poorer nations into consideration.[114]

Nevertheless, the relative recapture of the multilateral process by developing countries through the Doha Declarations led to developed countries modifying their own approach. An era that sidestepped multilateral impediments ensued, with a renewed focus on bilateral and regional agreements. This saga bolstered the TRIPS Agreement, emphatically morphing it into the threshold or "floor" of international IP norm-setting.

Soon, various free-trade agreements (FTAs), bilateral agreements, and unilateral pressure mechanisms denied the effective exercise of TRIPS flexibilities due to further upward harmonization through "TRIPS Plus" provisions, which, in turn, resulted in the strengthening of the TRIPS Agreement as the floor or threshold for negotiating IP rights.[115] As Ruth Okediji notes, "Rather than signal an end to the aggressive unilateralism that characterized pre-Uruguay Round IP strategies, the new bilateralism is rightly viewed as a means to roll back both substantive and strategic gains of the TRIPS Agreement for developing countries."[116]

Interestingly, despite the careful balance required for appropriate calibration of copyright and patent regimes vis-à-vis a welfare paradigm, the evolution of IP flexibilities has not taken place at the same rate as, or in a manner commensurate with, the expansion of market control rights for rights holders. Instead, more rights have steadily been identified and strongly pushed. Some examples include requiring test-data exclusivity periods rather than test-data protection, easing the standard of patentability, limitations or prohibitions on pre-grant oppositions, and patent linkages that tie marketing approval with patent status.

As commentators have noted, a rights-centric approach has been encouraged in various FTAs by an interpretation of the most-favored-nation clause in TRIPS Agreement. Consequently, TRIPS-Plus obligations

[114] *See* Michele Boldrin & David K. Levine, Against Intellectual Property Monopoly 245 (2008). These claims are borne out by history as well. For instance, several developed countries which now advocate for strong patent protection did not provide for product patent protection for chemicals/pharmaceuticals till very late in their own technological development trajectories, such as Japan (1976), Germany (1967), Switzerland (1977), and Sweden (1978).

[115] Yu, *supra* note 110, at 363; *see also* Mercurio, *supra* note 97; *see generally* Peter Drahos, *BITS and BIPS: Bilateralism in Intellectual Property*, 4 J. World Intell. Prop. 791 (2001); Rosemary J. Coombe, *Fear, Hope, and Longing for the Future of Authorship and a Revitalized Public Domain in Global Regimes of Intellectual Property*, 52 DePaul L. Rev. 1171, 1177 (2003) (describing the "growing tendency" of the United States and Europe to press developing countries to accede to bilateral treaties with higher IP protection).

[116] *See* Okediji, *supra* note 110, at 129.

have been extended to WTO members who are not members of that FTA. At the same time, the trade concessions and favorable trading terms are carefully limited to parties of the FTA by relying on the exception to the nondiscrimination rule in GATT Article XXIV (allowing discrimination in trade concessions contained in bilateral agreements/FTAs). This has further nudged WTO members to join FTAs and bilateral agreements and to more voluntarily accept trade terms that have maximalist IP norms, including those that impair access to medicines. In contrast, flexibilities have been left ambiguous and discretionary, while hard and soft pressure to limit their usage remains.[117]

Reflecting these trends, various bilateral and multilateral trade agreements used what are labeled as TRIPS-Plus measures to further expand copyright- and patent-protection levels. Multilateral approaches such as the Regional Comprehensive Economic Partnership (RCEP) and even the failed Trans-Pacific Partnership Agreement (TPP) seemed to target TRIPS-Plus measures.[118] Several bilateral and broader trade agreements included maximized IP norms through negotiations with individual countries. For example, commentators have noted that the TRIPS-Plus copyright norms under the Trans-Pacific Partnership Act are meant to build further upon already existing TRIPS-Plus bilateral agreements, such as the Australia-US FTA and the Singapore-US FTA.[119]

Lack of transparency is a common area of concern in the negotiation of these mega-trade deals, during which the only basis for public deliberation often stems from leaked drafts. This is relevant in view of the massive public protests against earlier trade agreements that sought to maximize IP norms, such as the proposed Anti-Counterfeiting Trade Agreement (ACTA) and the suspended EU-India FTA. It had been speculated that the RCEP's IP provisions would meet the same fate as the ill-fated TPP provisions.[120]

However, in stark contrast, after significant pushback from developing countries, including India's opting out of the agreement altogether, the final

[117] *See* Christopher S. Mayer, *The Brazilian Pharmaceutical Industry Goes Walking from Ipanema to Prosperity: Will the New Intellectual Property Law Spur Domestic Investment?*, 12 Temp. Int'l & Comp. L.J. 377, 378–80 (1998).

[118] *Regional Comprehensive Economic Partnership (RCEP) Agreement*, Ass'n Se. Asian Nations, https://asean.org/our-communities/economic-community/integration-with-global-economy/regional-comprehensive-economic-partnership-rcep/ (last visited Oct. 20, 2025); *see also* Trans-Pacific Partnership, art. 1, Feb. 8, 2016, 18 U.S.T. 1127.

[119] Free Trade Agreement, U.S.-Sing., May 6, 2003, Hein's No. KAV 6376, https://ustr.gov/trade-agreements/free-trade-agreements/singapore-fta (last visited Oct. 20, 2025).

[120] RCEP, *supra* note 118.

draft did not introduce TRIPS-Plus provisions negatively impacting access to medicines. Leaked drafts indicate that, unlike trade agreements for which countries like the United States set the agenda, there was no single dominating power in the RCEP but rather a multitude of diverse members who mounted internal resistance to controversial proposals, including an extension of maximalist IP norms to areas of public health.

Interestingly, on the question of public participation, Kelsey notes that, although actual protests were muted, "joint civil society initiatives across the participating countries, presence at negotiations, and sharing of analysis based on available information clearly influenced some delegations and were reflected in the final text."[121] It seems clear that, despite the lack of transparency in these negotiations, "imposed" public participation can play an influential role in bringing some balance to trade deals that affect public health.

3. The Big Pharma Game: Lobbying, Negotiations, and Power Play

3.1 The Prelude

This part analyzes the patterns of interaction between WTO members on trade and IP to outline a larger strategic pattern that has resulted in relegating global public health to the background. These interactions are offered as a lens through which to understand the dynamics between parties with divergent and vested interests, which are often different from the goals of the larger system. Further, the inevitable involvement of powerful third-party stakeholders, such as pharmaceutical-industry lobbyists, has influenced relationships among member states.

While private interests necessarily interject themselves into public-policy debates today, the discussion focuses on their effects on health-care-access issues. Whether the outcome of such influence marred health-care-related goals—that is, whether private revenue maximization caused an extent of divergence from the larger system-oriented goals of consumer protection, health-care equity and access, and improving innovation—is the question.

[121] Jane Kelsey, *RCEP: Nothing to See and Everything to See*, Afronomics Law at 1, 4–5 (Feb. 15, 2021), https://www.afronomicslaw.org/category/analysis/rcep-nothing-see-and-everything-see (last visited Oct. 20, 2025).

Such questions are raising concerns about the need for a new framework to reposition health-care access as important for global trade and productivity. The discussion below analyzes how these influences have generated a predictable pattern of reactions to health-care-related issues, including during Covid-19, when there was a global request for access to vaccines and related products.

To fully capture the predictability of trade negotiations and their outcomes, this part draws upon basic game-theory concepts to show that invested players, such as corporations, strategize in anticipating the moves of different member nations, or, alternatively, that they lobby powerful nations to generate predictable outcomes beneficial to their vested interests. In analyzing such negotiations, this part highlights that different players have created outcomes that are "on paper" wins for global trade but nevertheless have proved unsustainable by adversely affecting global public health. The extent to which the goals of member states coincide or conflict with parties with divergent but vested interests informs the analysis.

Thus, the larger objective has always been to determine an appropriate balance between trade interests with welfare necessities such that trade obligations does not affect each member's local welfare commitments. That balance, is typically the saddle point which should bring together competing interests. Nevertheless, it is hard to create a perfect or even a good balance between trade and welfare obligations on account of competing and often, contrasting interests. Such competing interests are characterized by typical expectations of each member state (or player, in this case). In turn, that results in tweaks and changes from the larger package of trade negotiations/bargains. Meanwhile, each member's assessment of the reactions of one or more coalition(s) of players, and the bargaining parity of either an individual member or a coalition of members, play a role not just in the outcome but also in determining what the member believes it can successfully generate from the negotiations, as discussed below.

3.2 Generic Drugmakers: New Player in the Old Game

One such emerging player in the game, traditionally dominated by Big Pharma, is the generic-drug industry, whose advent unleashed the dynamics that resulted in a pharmaceutical food chain, to be discussed in section 4 of this chapter. After the TRIPS Agreement, the introduction of generics following the expiry of patents presented a unique opportunity for countries like India with indigenous capacity in generic-drug manufacturing, resulting in reduction of the cost of the medication.[122]

The year was 1963, and the United States had recently adopted the Drug Amendments of 1962 that resulted from hearings on drug prices in the US Senate.[123] The breaking news from the *Wall Street Journal* was an issue that would fit well in the post-TRIPS Agreement decades: drug companies were reporting fewer research breakthroughs but higher profits. Drug prices were so high that in 1961, Tennessee Democratic Senator Estes Kefauver, as Chairman of the US Senate Committee on Drug Prices (Kefauver Committee), compared drug prices in countries that grant patents with prices in countries that do not grant them.[124] The committee's findings that India's drug prices were among the highest in the world, because India fully relied on imported medication, matched the findings of India's own 1959 Report on the Revision of the Patent Laws, that fewer patents, especially in the pharmaceutical sector, would be more desirable for India![125] At that time, India did not produce bulk drugs locally, so the central government imported them under the Drugs Act of 1940.[126] The report resulted in the amendment of the 1970 Indian Patent Act to disallow product patents, thus paving the way for more production of generic pharmaceuticals by India's then-burgeoning pharmaceutical industry.

Internationally, many developing countries did not allow product patent protection for drugs, and thus companies producing generic drugs (which either copied innovative medications or created process changes over them) remained the primary source of pharmaceutical products.[127] In India, for

[122] *See* Gerard T. Vondeling et al., *The Impact of Patent Expiry on Drug Prices: A Systematic Literature Review*, 16 APPL. HEALTH ECON. HEALTH POLICY. 653, 659 (2018).

[123] Michelle Meadows, *Promoting Safe and Effective Drugs for 100 Years*, FDA CONSUMER MAG. (2006); Daniel C. Morgan & Samuel E. Allison, *The Kefauver Drug Hearings in Perspective*, 45 SW. SOC. SCI. Q. 59, 66–67 (1964) (discussing the impact of the Kefauver-Harris Drug Amendments of 1962 on the pharmaceutical industry and the regulation of drugs in the United States); *see also 2 Drug Companies Deny Price Fixing*, N.Y. TIMES (Aug. 13, 1963), https://www.nytimes.com/1963/08/13/archives/2-drug-companies-deny-price-fixing.html (last visited Oct. 20, 2025).

[124] ELLEN F.M. 'T HOEN, THE GLOBAL POLITICS OF PHARMACEUTICAL MONOPOLY POWER 15 (2009).

[125] AYYANGAR REPORT, *supra* note 39.

[126] Abhijit Dey et al., *Pharmaceutical Marketing in India: A Macroscopic View* (Nov. 2001); *see also* Srividhya Ragavan, *Of the Inequals of the Uruguay Round*, 10 MARQ. INTEL'L PROP. L. REV. 273 (2006).

[127] Prior to the TRIPS Agreement, about fifty countries did not grant patent protection to pharmaceutical products at all, and some also excluded pharmaceutical processes. RESOURCE BOOK ON TRIPS AND DEVELOPMENT: UNCTAD-ICTSD 353, 365 (2005); *see generally* SISULE F. MUSUNGU & CECILIA OH, THE USE OF FLEXIBILITIES IN TRIPS BY DEVELOPING COUNTRIES: CAN THEY PROMOTE ACCESS TO MEDICINES? 9 (2006) (discussing transition periods to implement pharmaceutical

example, after the Ayyangar Committee's report of 1959 undertook a detailed study of the effect of patents on drug prices across the world, the government took multiple steps to promote indigenous manufacturing of medicines. This approach would be championed through the laws and amendments that were to come in the next few decades. These measures included the 1970 Patents Act, which prohibited product patents on food, medicines, and chemical inventions.[128]

The patent legislation enabled India to innovate on different processes to produce patented products, which is also how Western nations got on the innovation bandwagon. For instance, the German Patent Law of 1877 denied patents to articles of food and medicinal products, though processes for their preparations remained patentable.[129] Similarly, in 1954 Switzerland amended its laws, which had excluded inventions relating to medicines, medicinal mixtures, and food products from patentability but allowed patenting for manufacturing processes.[130] Likewise, only in 1978 did Italy provide patent protection for pharmaceutical products.[131]

However, the impetus for India's move to establish a generic-drug industry was the prevalence of epidemic diseases, which accounted for 5.1 percent of total mortality at the time.[132] The country's first Five-Year Plan (1951–1956) recorded that India was then the world's largest reservoir of epidemic diseases.[133] Coming out of centuries of oppressive British colonization, poverty was also at its peak in India. Around 50 percent of its population was living in poverty and unable to afford the cost of drugs.[134] Life expectancy was consequently low because of diseases.

product patent protection for developing countries); Ernst-Ulrich Petersmann, *International Competition Rules for Private Business: A Trade Law Approach for Linking Trade and Competition Rules in the WTO–The Institutional and Jurisdictional Architecture*, 72 CHI.-KENT L. REV. 545, 563 (1996) (noting underdeveloped intellectual-property rights laws); UNCTAD SECRETARIAT, THE TRIPS AGREEMENT AND DEVELOPING COUNTRIES 62 (1996) (discussing implications for developing countries from implementing pharmaceutical product patent protection).

128 Damanjeet Ghai, *Patent Protection and Indian Pharmaceutical Industry*, INT'L J. PHARM. SCIS. REV. & RSCH., July–Aug. 2010, at 43, 43–45 (discussing how the 1970s patent policy affected the Indian pharmaceutical industry).

129 AYYANGAR REPORT, *supra* note 39, at ¶ 58.

130 *Id.* at ¶ 95.

131 Studio Legale Sutti, *IP and the Pharmaceutical Industry in Italy (Patents and Supplementary Protection)*, MONDAQ (Nov. 5, 1997), https://www.mondaq.com/italy/trademark/6296/ip-and-the-pharmaceutical-industry-in-italy-patents-and-supplementary-protection (last visited Oct. 20, 2025).

132 GOV'T OF INDIA, PLAN. COMM'N, THE FIRST FIVE YEAR PLAN 197–98.

133 *Id.*

134 Press Release, *India Shows Mixed Progress in the War Against Poverty*, WORLD BANK (Aug. 26, 1997), https://web.archive.org/web/20010914042714/http://www.worldbank.org/html/extdr/

In essence, establishing a generic-drug industry was the result of a realization of the limits of both IP rights broadly, and patents more particularly, in promoting competition in pharmaceuticals, which were critical to national development. Interestingly, as mentioned earlier, one of the forerunners of the idea of appreciating the limits of patents was Germany, a country that would later protect Pfizer Inc. during the Covid-19 pandemic in 2021 by supporting the corporation's refusal to provide or make vaccines available voluntarily at low cost.[135] The reasoning behind Germany's product-patent prohibition law of 1877 was later used in Lord Parker's recommendations, which resulted in similar patent laws in England in 1919.

Taking the German and British experience into consideration, the Indian government acted swiftly to address its urgent public-health and economic issues and signed an agreement with the United Nations Children's Fund (UNICEF) in 1951 to locally manufacture penicillin and other antibiotics via the newly created Hindustan Antibiotics Limited (HAL).[136] The founding of HAL in 1954 to manufacture low-cost generic drugs in turn led to the founding of Cipla, the company that would lower the cost of AIDS medication from US$15,000 to US$350 during the AIDS epidemic a few decades later.[137] As several scholars have documented, these developments would transform India into a generic manufacturing powerhouse over the decades that followed.[138]

India's first move in 1954 to develop an indigenous drug industry by establishing HAL would dramatically change the status of health-care access in India, as was expected.[139] From 1970 to 2000, the Indian pharmaceutical industry grew from a mere ₹100 million to ₹70 billion (or approximately US $2 billion).[140] By 2000, there were around 24,000 pharmaceutical units

extme/1449.htm; *see also India Achievements and Challenges in Reducing Poverty*, A World Bank Country Study (Jun. 1997), https://documents1.worldbank.org/curated/en/232941468756917265/pdf/multi-page.pdf (last visited Oct. 24, 2025).

135 *See supra* notes 48–52 and accompanying text.

136 Nasir Tyabji, *Gaining Technical Know-How in an Unequal World: Penicillin Manufacture in Nehru's India*, 45 Tech. & Culture 331, 345 (2004), https://mpra.ub.uni-muenchen.de/84236/ (last visited Oct. 20, 2025).

137 Martin Khor, *The Man Who Saved Millions with Cheap Medicines*, S. Cntr. (July 5, 2013), https://www.southcentre.int/question/the-man-who-saved-millions-with-cheap-medicines/ (last visited Oct. 20, 2025).

138 *See, e.g.*, Ghai, *supra* note 128, at 44 (noting that India has become a major player in the international generic-drugs market).

139 Ministry of Chemicals and Fertilizers, *Hindustan Antibiotics Limited*, Dep't Pharm., https://pharma-dept.gov.in/hindustan-antibiotics-limited (last visited Oct. 20, 2025).

140 Shondeep Banerji, *The Indian Intellectual Property Rights Regime and the Trips* Agreement, *in* Intellectual Property Rights in Emerging Markets 47, 80, 94 n.33 (Clarisa Long ed., 2000).

licensed in India,[141] and of the 465 bulk drugs used in India before the TRIPS Agreement, approximately 425 were manufactured locally. The Indian industry was slowly emerging as a world leader in the production of several bulk drugs,[142] pharmaceutical products that conform to specified pharmacopoeia or other standards or regulations. When the Indian generic-drug industry dramatically created alternatives, it shifted the conversations on health care globally. This was a game changer. Beyond developing indigenous pharmaceuticals, India was poised to grow as a major player in the international generic-drugs market even at the time of signing the TRIPS Agreement. The establishing of generic-drug companies from the 1950s to the 1970s was India's first significant pushback against Big Pharma.

Like India, Brazil also replicated the originally West German–US model of using a "weak" IP system to develop indigenously.[143] The Brazilian government abolished patent protection for pharmaceutical products in 1969. The objective was to create a stronger domestic pharmaceutical industry in the face of dominant multinational competitors. Brazil likewise started by producing generic versions of the drugs in developed nations. For AIDS drugs alone, Brazil would claim a total savings of US$490 million.[144] In 1971, in order to provide medicines for the poor, Brazil totally abrogated patent protection for pharmaceutical manufacturing processes. The state-owned Central de Medicamentos was created, and a master plan was carved for the implementation of the 1971 policy under the direct supervision of

[141] It is interesting to note that of 24,000 units, only 300 were large scale, and the remaining 23,700 were in the small- and medium-scale sector. *See* N. Lalitha, *Drug Policy 2002: Prescription for Symptoms*, ECON. & POL. WEEKLY, Jan. 2022, at 3102–04, https://www.epw.in/journal/2002/30/commentary/drug-policy-2002prescription-symptoms.html (last visited Oct. 20, 2025).

[142] The "Indian industry has emerged as a leader for the production of bulk drugs like sulphamethoxazole and ethambutol. Indian production accounts for nearly 50% of the world's production. Several companies, like Ranbaxy, Dr Reddy's, and Cipla, have the potential to become billion-dollar companies within the next few years." Ghai, *supra* note 128, at 44; *see* Martin J. Adelman & Sonia Baldia, *Prospects and Limits of the Patent Provisions in the TRIPS Agreement: The Case of India*, 29 VAND. J. TRANSNAT'L L. 507 (1996) (arguing that strong IP protection will be in India's interest given its infrastructure in pharmaceutical production). However, as Dreyfuss and Lowenfeld point out, the same data has been used by Reichman to argue that "free-riding is a way for a developing economy to accumulate the skills and capital necessary to become innovative"; *see also* Rochelle Cooper Dreyfuss & Andreas F. Lowenfeld, *Two Achievements of the Uruguay Round: Putting TRIPS and Dispute Settlement Together*, 37 VA. J. INT'L L. 275 (1997) (referring to *A Scholarly Debate*, *supra* note 98, at 363); *see also* Sajeev Chandran, Archna Roy, & Lokesh Jain, *Implications of New Patent Regime on Indian Pharmaceutical Industry: Challenges and Opportunities*, J. INTELL. PROP. RTS., July 2005, at 269, 270.

[143] *See* Christopher S. Mayer, *The Brazilian Pharmaceutical Industry Goes Walking from Ipanema to Prosperity: Will the New Intellectual Property Law Spur Domestic Investment?*, 12 TEMP. INT'L & COMPAR. L.J. 377, 378 (1998).

[144] *Id.*

the President.[145] Notably, the plan revived state-owned laboratories and vested preferential treatment to incentivize local companies to manufacture pharmaceuticals domestically without threatening the growth of private and domestic firms.[146] The fact that Brazil did not provide any patent protection till 1994 enabled the development of a domestic generic-drug industry.

Despite the emergence of the generic-drug industry, pushing unrealistic prices disconnected from the market or a country's GDP and nonchalance toward public-health crises that left countries grappling for solutions are both strategic mistakes that Big Pharma has had a propensity to repeat. If pharmaceutical companies had instead appreciated the role of volume sales, given that the two parties do not have completely opposing interests and that all parties have interests that are vested in one or more outcomes, pharmaceutical access could have assumed a more cooperative posture even if the outcome would be more variable—but it did not.

Faced with the new realities, as Peter Drahos notes, the Western pharmaceutical companies that had dominated the industry until that period were suddenly faced with the unexpected arrival of a new player: the generic manufacturers.[147] Whether due to fear of potential loss of burgeoning developing-country markets or concern that low-cost generics manufacturers would gradually develop innovative capacity, the Western companies increased their investment as players to shape global policies by engaging with their national governments.

3.3 The Uruguay Game and the Nash Solution of TRIPS Agreement

Before the Doha Declaration of 2001, the pharmaceutical industry saw the Uruguay Round as an opportune moment to deal with the generic-drug industries of developing countries that were quickly gaining the potential for loosening their strong grip on the market. The generic-drug industry was showing the capacity to become a fixture in the pharmaceutical industry, carving and occupying its own individual space. Patent monopolies had largely enabled pharmaceutical industries to become dominant globally, and

145 *Id.* at 379 n.22.
146 *Id.* at 380 n.25.
147 Peter Drahos, *Developing Countries and International Intellectual Property Standard-Setting*, 5 J. World Intell. Prop. 765, 772–73 (2002).

the generic-drug industry threatened to disrupt this dominance, as it was showing a remarkable potential to fill the gap in the market that Big Pharma could not cater to—a "gap" representing about three-fourths of the global population.

Thus, the Uruguay Round negotiations, which culminated in the TRIPS Agreement, remain, in significant part, a story of pharmaceutical companies pushing back against a generic-drug industry that seemed to be poised for growth.[148] These historical events represent the first instance that resulted in shaping the global pharmaceutical industry, by creating a hierarchy or pyramid that firmly places generics and biosimilar manufacturers below innovators of both chemical drugs and biologics.

During the early stage of growth in generics in the 1980s, the IPC was set up in the United States under the leadership of Edmund Pratt, CEO of Pfizer, along with the CEOs of twelve other companies.[149] Through most of the 1980s, Pratt served as the chairman of the ACTN. In that capacity, Pratt advised Congress that the industries most deserving of protection were those with big IP portfolios, such as pharmaceuticals, semiconductor chips, and copyright (which included companies such as Walt Disney).[150] Industry counterparts in Europe and Japan likewise lobbied their respective governments, and the ultimate result was the 1988 "Basic Framework of GATT Provisions on Intellectual Property."[151]

Continuing with its coordinated lobbying efforts, the IPC greatly enabled developed countries led by the United States to use their bargaining parity to successfully resist the arguably more pragmatic approach advocated by developing countries. The idea of instituting a mandatory minimum standard owes to the pharmaceutical lobby's particular craftiness in creating a commitment and strong belief in the superiority of the IP ideology.[152] The lobby had carefully ensured that pharmaceutical IP was left undistinguished from other utility patents. The United States, Europe, and Japan carefully

[148] *See* Srividhya Ragavan & Swaraj Paul Barooah, *Historic Tensions Involving International Intellectual Property Protection of Medical Technology with Disastrous Public Health Consequences*, 54 Seton Hall L. Rev. 339, 346 (2023), https://doi.org/10.60095/EQAN3083 (last visited Oct. 20, 2025).

[149] Sell, *supra* note 79, at 2. The other corporations were Bristol-Myers, CBS, Du Pont, General Electric, General Motors, Hewlett-Packard, IBM, Johnson & Johnson, Merck, Monsanto, and Pfizer.

[150] *See* Peter Drahos & John Braithwaite, Information Feudalism: Who Owns the Knowledge Economy? 72 (2002).

[151] *See id.* at 123; *see* Sell, *supra* note 79.

[152] Peter Drahos & John Braithwaite, Information Feudalism: Who Owns the Knowledge Economy? 10 (2002).

calibrated how strong IP would be beneficial for their economic interests by including patents on lifesaving medicines along with consumer and utility patents.[153] These nations extended to pharmaceutical products their general belief that member states' GDPs would increase if their IP-heavy industries had the rest of the globe as a market, and advocated that it was in their economic interest to support IP as a strategy to benefit from their comparative advantage internationally.[154]

In fact, at the time of the TRIPS Agreement negotiations, more than forty countries did not grant patent protection for pharmaceutical products.[155] Many developing countries wanted patent provisions to be left to their individual discretion,[156] and most viewed the TRIPS Agreement as lacking a balanced mechanism to promote innovation.[157] Considering this initial reluctance in the developing world, the culmination of the Uruguay negotiations in the signing of the TRIPS Agreement is perhaps reminiscent of John Nash's game-theory solution—that although there may be some level of utility for each of the players associated with every possible outcome, it can still lead to inequity.[158] That is, while each country's specific choice of policy or utility reflects its own preferences, this can still lead to an inequitable outcome because of a lack of parity. To take a simple illustration: Between a rich kid and a poor kid trying to divide a sum of US$50, the threat of reaching no agreement at all could cause the poor kid to accept $10, thus giving the rich kid more utility—an imperfect and inequitable result, although even the poor kid arguably gains some utility. The Nash solution, therefore, while "utilitarian," can still lead to unfair or inequitable outcomes, especially as these situations compound. The signing of the TRIPS Agreement remains a perfect example.

Following from this inequitable Nash-like game-theory perspective, the net result of these historical negotiations was the expansion of property rights to include intangible ones to fit into the larger trade agenda. To

[153] *See* Josh Lerner, *150 Years of Patent Protection*, 7 Am. L. & Econ. Rev. 221, 231 (2002).
[154] *See* Okediji, *supra* note 110, at 128; *see also* Yu, *supra* note 110, at 356.
[155] *WTO and the Trips Agreement*, *supra* note 103.
[156] *See* Lester & Zhu, *supra* note 104, at 797. For further discussion on historical patent lengths, *see* Josh Lerner, *150 Years of Patent Protection*, 7 Am. L. & Econ. Rev. 221, 221–25 (2002).
[157] *See* Srividhya Ragavan, Patent and Trade Disparities in Developing Countries 69 (2012).
[158] *See generally Two-person Variable-Sum Games*, Encyc. Britannica, https://www.britannica.com/science/game-theory/Two-person-variable-sum-games (last visited Oct. 20, 2025) The prisoner's dilemma could perhaps be seen as a well-recognized example of a Nash solution that is not equitable—in welfare-economic term, not *Pareto optimal*.

date, these negotiations remain one of the most nuanced and consequential developments of this century. In forcing the trade regime to include intangible property, the world negotiated a harshly forced accord that has affected global public health detrimentally. The dysfunctional arrangement has resulted in segregation into those with access to medication and those without such access—what Jesse Bump has accurately called modern-day colonialization.[159] The result was the creation of a fractious division in a globe already divided on the basis of gender, religion, caste, and race.

At this stage, the game was noncooperative, multifaceted, and global. Several events precipitated a divide between the so-called "innovators," the "copycats," and the "consumers" of pharmaceutical products. On one side were global corporate actors lobbying the developed countries; on the other were civil-society groups and consumer groups that seemed more aligned with local realities. Indeed, the structural paradigms of trade and the TRIPS Agreement would invigorate the next set of actors on both sides of the globe.[160]

3.4 The Doha Fightback

Constrained by the gradual rise of the developing nations led by the global generic powerhouse of India, the efforts of the United States and Europe at the 1999 WTO Seattle Ministerial Conference to introduce new clauses to the agreement under the WTO (relating to investment, competition, government procurement, labor, and environmental standards) backfired.[161] Moreover, developing countries have alleged that the United States and Europe conducted secretive "green room" meetings meant to manipulate the WTO process,[162] and such perceptions led developing countries to preemptively deny consensus to any declaration made at the Conference.[163] The collapse of the 1999 Ministerial Round signified the invigoration of developing

[159] *See generally* Jesse B. Bump et al., *Political Economy of Covid-19: Extractive, Regressive, Competitive*, BMJ, Jan. 22, 2021, at 1 ("The political economy of covid-19 reflects longstanding patterns of resource extraction linked to racial discrimination, marginalisation, and colonialism.").

[160] *Id.* at 3.

[161] *Id.* at 2.

[162] *See generally* Kent Jones, *Green Room Politics and the WTO's Crisis of Representation*, *in* 9 PROGRESS DEV. STUD. 349, 355 (2009).

[163] *See Africa, Caribbean and Latin America Protest No Democracy in WTO*, THIRD WORLD NETWORK, https://twn.my/title/deb5-cn.htm (last visited Oct. 20, 2025).

countries as a group and brought their goals to the forefront of the multilateral process.

While the developing countries pushed back at Seattle, the globe was experiencing the first public-health impact of the ill-fated alliance. HIV/AIDS unfolded as a public-health crisis on an unprecedented scale. Soon, the lack of access to patent-protected medications had resulted in millions of people in developing countries being affected by the epidemic. By this time, academics and civil-society groups within developing countries had coalesced around common concerns, especially regarding the effect of the TRIPS Agreement on public health, at a time when it was highly unusual for non-trade bodies to add their input to trade-related concerns.[164]

Remarkably, these coalitions led to other international institutions—the World Health Organization (WHO), the Joint United Nations Programme on HIV/AIDS (UNAIDS), and various regional organizations—adding their voice to the debate on the TRIPS Agreement and public health. In 2001, the WHO adopted two resolutions addressing TRIPS-related concerns, resolutions that brought public-health issues to the forefront.[165]

While the game for a share of the global market, which began with the establishment of the generic-drug industry, is ongoing, the signing of the Doha Declaration is the first instance of pushback from poorer nations seeking more health equity. It is also the first instance in which an epidemic changed the WTO rules of the game, causing member states to (re)negotiate an equitable outcome. At this time, any focus on public health would upset the fragile balance that the signing of the TRIPS Agreement represented. Nevertheless, the realities of an epidemic caused a paradigm shift.

Meanwhile, the number of member states—players in the game—had quadrupled by the time of the Ministerial Conference in Doha, and the AIDS crisis had provided a preview of a world dependent on patent profits and led to the realization that the consequences were not confined to AIDS medication.[166]

164 *See* Amy Kapcynzski, *The Access to Knowledge Mobilization and the New Politics of Intellectual Property*, 117 Yale L.J. 803, 821–24 (2008); *see also* Ellen 't Hoen, *TRIPS, Pharmaceutical Patents, and Access to Essential Medicines: A Long Way From Seattle to Doha*, 3 Chi. J. Int'l L. 27, 48–49 (2002).

165 *See* World Health Organization [WHO], Assembly Res. A54.10, *Scaling up the Response to HIV/AIDS* (2001), https://apps.who.int/gb/ebwha/pdf_files/WHA54/ea54r10.pdf (last visited Oct. 20, 2025); *see also* World Health Organization [WHO], Assembly Res. A54.11, *WHO Medicines Strategy* (2001), http://www.cptech.org/ip/health/who/wha54.11.pdf (last visited Oct. 20, 2025).

166 Ellen F. M. 't Hoen, The Global Politics of Pharmaceutical Monopoly Power 29 (2009).

As Andrew Chetley would note, access to medication was not a new issue for the poorer world, which had depended on the West for pharmaceutical innovation.[167] But the development of the generic-drug industry provided an alternative and created the "pharmacy of the world" in the form of India's generic-drug industry, and the TRIPS regime threatened it.[168]

The game, however, was different this time, as not only member states but other players such as patient groups and nongovernmental organizations became invested in the outcome, for various reasons. Because Article 30 of the TRIPS Agreement permitted limited exceptions to the monopoly rights of the patent holders, poorer countries pushed for more flexibility.[169] One such exception that members sought to bolster was already present in the TRIPS Agreement: compulsory licensing, allowing for mandatory acquisition of the patent under limited circumstances.[170] At the time, Article 31 required member states to seek the consent of the patent holder to license compulsorily except "[i]n the case of national emergency or other circumstances of extreme urgency," in which case the patent holder was to be notified as soon as is reasonably practical.[171]

Interestingly, Article 31 was what game theorists would call a saddle point in a perfect-information world. It was clear that poorer countries could use the exception in an exigency. But information is imperfect by nature, causing developed and developing nations to differ on when the Article 31(b) exception can be invoked. Developing nations with lower per capita income wanted to use compulsory licensing to balance the adverse effects of trade on public health by providing access to otherwise unaffordable medications. Developed nations, however, construed compulsory licensing as a derogation from the TRIPS Agreement.[172]

In the end, the public-health exception presented both common and conflicting interests for the member states, thus making it into a noncooperative variable-sum game. This, in turn, made it harder to find a viable solution. By June 2001, when a special session of the TRIPS Council heard the views of

[167] *See generally* ANDREW CHETLEY, A HEALTHY BUSINESS?: WORLD HEALTH AND THE PHARMACEUTICAL INDUSTRY 11–12 (1990).

[168] 'T HOEN, *supra* note 166, at 78.

[169] TRIPS Agreement art. 30.

[170] David K. Tomar, *A Look into the WTO Pharmaceutical Patent Dispute Between the United States and India*, 17 WIS. INT'L L.J. 579, 592–93 (1999).

[171] TRIPS Agreement art. 31(b).

[172] Sean Flynn et al., *An Economic Justification for Open Access to Essential Medicine Patents in Developing Countries*, 37 J.L. MED. & ETHICS 184, 185 (2009); Haochen Sun, *A Wider Access to Patented Drugs Under the TRIPS Agreement*, 21 BOS. U. INT'L L.J. 101, 107 (2003).

several member countries on issues relating to IP and access to medicines, a more agreeable format was reached.[173]

Further, the outcome at Doha was credited to an unrelated event that caused a fear of an epidemic: a domestic anthrax scare in the United States in 2001. In response, the US government considered the right to compulsorily license medication to deal with a public-health scare (which ultimately resulted in fewer than a dozen deaths from anthrax).[174] In doing so, the United States essentially negated its objections to developing nations' use of compulsory licenses to address the HIV/AIDS crisis in their respective countries.[175]

As part of the Doha negotiations, India assumed a leadership position and filed a detailed submission to the Negotiating Group on TRIPS, outlining what developing countries feared would be the consequences of patents over access to medication and, in turn, over their national socioeconomic development.[176] The Fourth WTO Ministerial Conference, held in Doha in 2001, acknowledged these concerns of the developing world, leading to the adoption of the Doha Declaration.[177]

The Doha Declaration noted that the TRIPS Agreement could and should be interpreted in a manner supportive of WTO members' right to protect public health, including the promotion of access to medicines for all.[178] It seemingly resulted in a more equitable outcome.[179] For instance, in recognizing the "gravity of the public health problems," Paragraph 3 of the Doha Declaration specified that prices of medication should not impede access in developing nations,[180] and advocated restraint when members

[173] Cecilia Oh, *U.S. Opposed to Moves to Address Public-Health Concerns About TRIPS*, Third World Network, https://twn.my/title/twr131f.htm (last visited Oct. 24, 2025).

[174] *Id;* Responding to a small number of anthrax patients who contracted the disease from unknown sources that were then alleged as being circulated by terrorists, the US Department of Health and Human Services (HHS) sought a workable solution. Interestingly, the one offered was to compulsorily license the anthrax medication, Cipro, unless the patent owner, Bayer AG Corporation, lowered its selling price. Divya Murthy, *The Future of Compulsory Licensing: Deciphering the Doha Declaration on the TRIPS Agreement and Public Health*, 17 Am. U. Int'l L. Rev. 1299, 1302 n.12 (2002).

[175] *Id.* at 1314 n.81.

[176] *Standards and Principles Concerning the Availability Scope and Use of Trade-Related Intellectual Property Rights*, World Trade Org. (July 10, 1989), https://docs.wto.org/gattdocs/q/UR/GNGNG11/W37.PDF (last visited Oct. 20, 2025).

[177] Doha Declaration, *supra* note 14; *see also* 't Hoen, *supra* note 164, at 48–49

[178] *Id.*

[179] *The Doha Declaration Explained*, World Trade Org., https://www.wto.org/english/tratop_e/dda_e/dohaexplained_e.htm (last visited Oct. 20, 2025).

[180] Fredrick M. Abbott, *The Doha Declaration on the TRIPS Agreement and Public Health and the Contradictory Trend in Bilateral and Regional Free Trade Agreements*, Quaker United Nations Off. (2004).

exercise such rights to promote public health.[181] Paragraph 6 encouraged members with the capacity to manufacture generic drugs, such as India, Thailand, and Brazil, to do so, while countries lacking such capacity were encouraged to find a viable solution.[182] Soon, the Council for TRIPS began working with the poorer nations to negotiate Article 31*bis*, which would facilitate importation of compulsorily licensed medication from countries that house manufacturing facilities.[183]

While the ratification of the Doha Declaration seemed like the conclusion of a long-drawn-out game resulting in a cooperative effort toward health equity, in fact neither group trusted the other to fully cooperate. Developed nations focused on indirectly forcing countries to ignore negotiated exceptions. Moreover, the onerous nature of the Article 31*bis* procedure defeated the overall objective.

Eventually, the Doha Declaration and Article 31*bis* were caught in the middle of what seemed like the classic game-theory prisoner's dilemma, wherein neither party trusted the other to operate together to achieve a stated goal. The net result from the lack of consensus has seemingly delayed all efforts to create more equitable access to health care leading up to, during, and after the pandemic.[184] The fallout of this was witnessed during the Covid-19 pandemic when the procedural burdens of Article 31*bis* caused poorer countries to seek a waiver of IP rights instead of using existing flexibilities.[185]

3.5 Generics Push Back for a Place in the Pharmaceutical Pyramid

Several remarkable instances mark the pushback for access to medication and the counter-lobbying to promote high-priced pharmaceuticals, which

[181] Doha Declaration, *supra* note 14, at ¶ 4 ("[T]he TRIPS Agreement does not and should not prevent members from taking measures to protect public health.").

[182] *Id.* at 6.

[183] World Trade Organization, *Implementation of Paragraph 6 of the Doha Declaration on the TRIPS Agreement and Public Health*, WTO Doc. WT/L/540 (Sept. 2, 2003), https://docs.wto.org/dol2fe/Pages/SS/directdoc.aspx?filename=Q:/WT/L/540.pdf&Open=True (last visited Oct. 20, 2025); On December 6, 2005, as part of the proceedings of the Hong Kong Ministerial Declaration, the WTO members made the amendment permanent to the TRIPS Agreement. *See* World Trade Organization, *Amendment of the TRIPS Agreement*, WTO Doc. WT/L/641 (Dec. 8, 2005), https://www.wto.org/english/tratop_e/trips_e/wtl641_e.htm (last visited Oct. 20, 2025); *see also* Press Release, World Trade Organization, Members OK Amendment to Make Health Flexibility Permanent (Dec. 6, 2005), https://www.wto.org/English/news_e/pres05_e/pr426_e.htm (last visited Oct. 20, 2025).

[184] *TRIPS Agreement and Access to Drugs in Developing Countries*, *supra* note 19, at 5.

[185] *See generally* Frederick M. Abbott, *The WTO Medicines Decision: World Pharmaceutical Trade and the Protection of Public Health*, 99 Am. J. Int'l L. 317, 343 (2005).

has remained radical and unrealistic. Nationally, some countries pushed back the efforts, such as in the case of Bayer's famed Sorafenib, a drug used to treat advanced liver and kidney cancer, to extend the life of a patent.[186] Wielding the patent's market power without any restraint, Bayer priced the drug at ₹280,428 per month (approximately US$ 4,500 per month at the time).[187] At that time, and even in 2023, an Indian employee earning ₹280,428 per month would consider himself very, *very* well-employed. In fact, the average living wage for a family per annum in India is approximately this amount, even in 2021.[188] The price was nearly five times higher than the median annual income in India, although the highlight remains to be the visceral reaction of the US when a compulsory license was issued for the drug in India.[189] *Sorafenib* created a have-not of the haves!

The generic pushback culminated in a landmark legal challenge when a petition finally landed in the chamber of Justice Prabha Sridevan at the Intellectual Property Appellate Board (hereinafter "the Board") after the then Patent Controller General, Mr. P. H. Kurien, ordered Sorafenib to be compulsorily licensed, on the grounds that the patent owner was not catering to the demands of the market in India.[190] At that time, India had approximately 20,000 patients with liver cancer and 9,000 patients with kidney cancer. Bayer, which received its patent for Sorafenib Tosylate (sold as Nexavar) in 2008, provided unclear and sometimes contradictory information regarding its imports and sales figures to India for several years.[191] There was no evidence or claims of local manufacture. In the years 2008 to 2010, a negligible amount of Sorafenib was imported into India for sale by Bayer, with sales averaging 1,500–2,200 drug units each year.[192] In fact, no

[186] Radhieka Pandeya & Manish Ranjan, *Delhi HC Turns Down Bayer's Patent Claims*, LiveMint (Feb. 10, 2010, at 12:02 IST), https://www.livemint.com/Home-Page/yGWj16xgG45IeHEIOGig7M/Delhi-HC-turns-down-Bayer8217s-patent-claims.html (last visited Oct. 20, 2025); *see also* Bayer Corporation v. Natco Pharma Ltd., Order No. 45/2013 (Intellectual Property Appellate Board, Chennai) (India).

[187] Soumyadeep Bhaumik & Tamoghna Biswas, *From Outlier to Trendsetter*, 184 Canadian Med. Ass'n J. E635, E635 (2012).

[188] *Average Income of Indian Family is Rs 23,000 per Month: Survey*, India.com (Nov. 5, 2022, at 10:10 IST), https://www.india.com/business/average-income-of-indian-family-is-rs-23000-per-month-survey-5725299/ (last visited Oct. 20, 2025).

[189] Srividhya Ragavan, *Patients Win Over Patents*, The Hindu (July 21, 2016), https://www.thehindu.com/opinion/op-ed/patients-win-over-patents/article4482469.ece#google_vignette (last visited Oct. 20, 2025).

[190] *See Bayer Corporation v. Natco Pharma Ltd.*, Order No. 45/2013 (Intellectual Property Appellate Board, Chennai) (India).

[191] Shamnad Basheer and Rupali Samuel, Bayer's Nexavar and the "Working" of Compulsory Licensing: Mind the Patent (Information) Gap! 15–16 (April 2015), https://spicyip.com/wp-content/uploads/2015/04/Report-on-Bayer-for-writ-Finalized.pdf (last visited Oct. 20, 2025).

[192] *Id.* at 8.

importation was recorded in 2008—a year when Bayer recorded a worldwide profit of over US$678 million.[193] The compulsory license was granted to Natco, an Indian company.

Statutorily, under the Indian laws, an application for the grant of a compulsory license on a patent can be made under Section 84(1) of the Patent Act, 1974, by any interested person, to the Controller, within three years from the date of the grant of the patent.[194] The grounds for granting the license was not satisfying "reasonable" requirement of the public with respect to the patented invention, its unavailability to the public at a "reasonably" affordable price, or its non-working within India. Section 84(6) of the Act provides that the Controller, in considering such an application, shall take into account factors such as the nature of the invention; the time since the patent was granted; measures taken by the patentee or his licensee to make full use of the invention; the ability of the applicant to work the invention to the public advantage; his capacity to undertake risk in providing capital and working the invention if the application is granted; prior efforts made by the applicant to obtain a license from the patentee on "reasonable" terms; and its success or failure within a "reasonable" time period.[195] Section 84(7) of the Act deems that "reasonable" requirements of public are not satisfied under certain circumstances such as refusal of the patentee to grant a license on "reasonable" terms and not-working the patented invention in the territory of India on a commercial scale to the fullest extent "reasonably" practicable.[196] The focus is on the encouragement for local working/manufacturing of new inventions and on ensuring marketability of the invention by licensing it using "reasonable" terms. Both local manufacturing and reasonable terms for marketing are contentious issues in today's pharmaceutical access to medication issues within the trade regime.

Hence, in sum, the statutory standard of "reasonability" under Section 84 of the 1974 Indian Patent Act includes the quantity of the patented invention supplied by the patentee as a proportion of its total public demand and affordability of its price; the terms and conditions on which, and the time period within which, the voluntary license was (un)successfully offered by the patentee; and the extent of working of the patented invention in India on commercial scale (local working). Such local working was the key for

[193] *Id.* at 5.
[194] *See* Patent Act, 1970, § 84(1) (India).
[195] *Id.* § 84(6).
[196] *Id.* § 84(7).

countries to enable technology transfer and become less import-dependent. The term "working" is construed to create local manufacturing or production or "working" in such a manner that there is a reduced dependency on importing over time. The underlying idea is that a certain amount of knowledge of the technology will be imbibed in the importing nation. In contemporary times, innovators in some fields have resisted local working or manufacturing on the grounds that such knowledge that will be passed is critical know-how that is distinct from patents and hence, is susceptible to independent protection.

Consistent with the letter and spirit of the provisions of the 1970 Patent Act, the Board in *Bayer Corporation v. Natco Pharma Ltd.* (2013)[197] held that the patentee, Bayer, had failed the test of "reasonableness" as laid down under Section 84(1) and upheld the grant of compulsory license for the patented invention, Sorafenib Tosylate, to the applicant, Natco.

Justice Prabha Sridevan's bold decision to sustain the compulsory license interpreted the term "reasonable" by carefully highlighting the ability to purchase and positing public interest right at the heart of patent issues in India. Specifically, the Board applied a standard of reasonableness in terms of both quantity and price. With regard to quantity, it stated that only commercial and not philanthropic sales ought to be considered. As to price, it held that reasonableness of affordability needs to be seen from the viewpoint of the public, and must consider the purchasing capacity of an average patient in India. What is relevant is the market price of the patented invention being charged in India, not the cost incurred in research and development, the price charged for the invention in other countries, and not the prices charged for similar products manufactured by competitors of the patentee. The public interest, and not the interest of the applicant of the compulsory license or that of the patentee, ought to be the deciding factor. Regarding the efforts by Natco to obtain a voluntary license from Bayer on reasonable terms, the Board noted that such an effort was indeed made by Natco, which offered to make available the drug at less than ₹10,000 per month if the license was granted. But the offer was rejected by Bayer; hence, Natco was not legally obliged to make another request, and the requirement of law was fully met.

In line with such domestic efforts to assert public interest through the invocation of TRIPS-permitted flexibilities at the national level, when Brazil

[197] *See Bayer Corporation v. Natco Pharma Ltd.*, Order No. 45/2013 (Intellectual Property Appellate Board, Chennai) (India).

implemented a law in 1996 establishing a "local working" requirement that would have allowed compulsory licensing if a patent had not been worked in the territory of Brazil, the United States initiated dispute-settlement proceedings in *DS199: Brazil—Measures Affecting Patent Protection.* Similarly, India has been repeatedly placed on USTR's Special 301's "priority watchlist" for using TRIPS-permitted flexibilities such as utilizing its legislation to deny frivolous patents and for its single usage of the compulsory license regime, while also having referred to multilateral agreements such as the TPP as positive developments.

Reinforcing the recurring trend of crackdowns against the legitimate use of TRIPS-permitted flexibilities, other forms of soft pressure include the United States and Switzerland hinting at bringing a "non-violation" complaint against India to the WTO for the same legislative provision meant to deny frivolous patents. Non-violation complaints, which have been under moratorium for some time now, would allow countries to approach the WTO's dispute-settlement mechanism, wherein a WTO member alleges that there has been an impairment of benefits despite no actual violation of the TRIPS Agreement.[198] Interestingly, some authors have observed that developing countries could conversely argue that there has been a systemic violation of the structure and purpose of the TRIPS Agreement by enforcing TRIPS-Plus measures.[199] Such an argument could be a segue to potentially filing a WTO dispute against the use of the non-violation compliant. Nevertheless, the current state of international power dynamics is such that the question remains academic and seems unlikely to emerge into the WTO arena.

Continuing with the unwarranted and persistent pressure, the pharmaceutical industry's lobbying effort translated on August 2, 2013, into a request from the chairman of the US Senate Committee on Finance and the House Committee on Ways and Means to the US International Trade Commission to institute an investigation of India's trade practices.[200] Similarly, the Special 301 Reports of the USTR in 2012 and 2013 specifically identified the Bayer

[198] Swaraj Paul Barooah, *US, Switzerland Take Out WTO Gun for India's Sec 3(d); Point at Foot*, SpicyIP (June 17, 2015), https://spicyip.com/2015/06/us-switzerland-take-out-new-wto-gun-for-indias-sec-3d-point-at-foot.html (last visited Oct. 20, 2025).

[199] Susy Frankel, *Challenging TRIPS-Plus Agreements: The Potential Utility of Non-Violation Disputes*, 12 J. Intl. Econ. L. 1023, 1041 (2009).

[200] Trade, Investment, and Industrial Policies in India: Effects on the U.S. Economy, Inv. No. 332–543, USITC Pub. 4501 (Dec. 2014) (Final) (requesting information on issues relating to trade, investment, and industrial policies in India, with particular reference to its effects on the US economy and US jobs); *see also* 19 U.S.C. § 1332(g).

decision as "concerning."[201] Interestingly, the decision continued to be cited in the Special 301 reports as late as 2020.[202]

The United States established a pattern of hostile response against Colombia's use of negotiated flexibilities in the interest of public health, similar to that of its Indian response, after Colombia passed Resolution 2475 of 2016 on June 17, 2016, to issue a compulsory license to lower the price of Novartis AG's Imatinib, a leukemia drug marketed as Glivec.[203] At that time, the cost of 400 mg of Glivec in Colombia amounted to US$15,000 per patient per year and represented nearly twice the average annual income of Colombians.[204] In May 2016, the USTR, citing Resolution 2475, indicated that funds intended for a peace accord with Paz Colombia could be at risk.[205] The USTR's response caused the House Democrats to express serious concern over the USTR's actions.[206] A letter, addressed to the USTR

[201] Request for Public Comment and Announcement of Public Hearing, 79 Fed. Reg. 421 (Jan. 3, 2014); *see also* Ronald Kirk, 2012 Off. U.S. Trade Representative Special 301 Report 35 (2012); Demetrios Marantis, 2013 Off. U.S. Trade Representative Special 301 Report 38 (2013).

[202] Robert E. Lighthizer, 2020 Off. U.S. Trade Representative Special 301 Report 50.

[203] Andrew Goldman, *Colombia Issues Public Interest Declaration to Lower Price of Glivec*, Knowledge Ecology Int'l (June 15, 2016), https://www.keionline.org/23119 (last visited Oct. 20, 2025); *see also* Ministry of Health and Social Protection, *Resolution No. 2475 of June 14, 2016*, https://www.keionline.org/wp-content/uploads/2017/08/colombia-ministerio-de-salud-resolution-2475-14-june-2016.pdf (last visited Oct. 20, 2025); *see generally* Ministerio de Salud y Protección Social, *Solicitud de una declaración de interés público en el acceso al medicamento imatinib bajo condiciones de competencia* (Nov. 24, 2014), https://www.minsalud.gov.co/sites/rid/Lists/BibliotecaDigital/RIDE/VS/MET/Solicitud-de-una-declaracion-en-el-acceso-al-medicamento-IMATINIB.pdf (last visited Oct. 20, 2025).

[204] Andrew Goldman, Andrea Carolina Reyes Rojas, & Dr. Francisco Rossi, *Background FAQ on Glivec (imatinib) Compulsory License in Colombia*, Knowledge Ecology Int'l, https://www.keionline.org/book/background-faq-on-glivec-imatinib-compulsory-license-in-colombia (last visited Oct. 20, 2025).

[205] *Excerpts from the August 24 Announcement of a Final Peace Accord Between the Colombian Government and the FARC*, Colom. Peace, https://colombiapeace.org/excerpts-from-the-august-24-announcement-of-a-final-peace-accord-between-the-colombian-government-and-the-farc/ (last visited Oct. 20, 2025). The conflict with FARC ended after more than fifty years. Unfortunately, Paz-Columbia was never implemented because the deal was rejected in a referendum; *see also* Sibylla Brodzinsky, *Colombia Referendum: Voters Reject Peace Deal with see also Farc Guerrillas*, Guardian (Oct 3, 2016, at 7:10 ET), https://www.theguardian.com/world/2016/oct/02/colombia-referendum-rejects-peace-deal-with-farc (last visited Oct. 20, 2025); Stephanie Burgos, *Does Colombia Really Have to Choose Between Poverty and Public Health*, Oxfam (May 23, 2016), https://politicsofpoverty.oxfamamerica.org/does-colombia-really-have-to-choose-between-peace-and-public-health/ (last visited Oct. 20, 2025).

[206] Andrew Goldman, *15 House Dems Press USTR to Clarify Position on Compulsory Licensing of Cancer Drug Patent in Colombia*, Knowledge Ecology Int'l (May 26, 2016), https://www.keionline.org/23097 (last visited Oct. 20, 2025); *see* Zachary D. Carter, *Colombia Fears U.S. May Reject Peace Plan to Protect Pharma Profits*, Huffington Post (May 11, 2016), https://www.huffpost.com/entry/colombia-gleevec_n_5733d4ece4b077d4d6f224ee (last visited Oct. 20, 2025); Carolyn Y. Johnson & Karen DeYoung, *Dispute with Swiss Drugmaker Has Colombian Officials Worried About U.S. Peace Funding*, Wash. Post (May 18, 2016), https://www.washingtonpost.com/business/

Ambassador, Michael Froman, asserted that the United States would detract from its obligations as a signatory to the TRIPS Agreement and the Doha Declaration, which expressly authorize the use of such licenses in the same situations for which it was used by Colombia.

During that time, one of the current authors, writing with Brook Baker and Sean Flynn, asserted the following with respect to the 2013 Special 301 report:

> [T]hese judgments were considered, and their Special 301 implications were fully evaluated last year. And India's status remained on the priority watch list. Importantly, nothing has happened since the last Special 301 Report to justify a further downgrading of India's status as a Priority Foreign Country, even assuming that the [sic] USRT's original concerns about these decisions are warranted. That the concerns are not warranted is a point highlighted in later sections of this statement.[207]

Nevertheless, the Nexavar compulsory licensing decision was featured again in the 2014 Special 301 report.[208]

In a separate study, Michael Palmedo notes that during the same eleven-year period, the USTR remained very responsive to requests from Big Pharma. On average, 83 percent of the countries prioritized by the Pharmaceutical Research and Manufacturers of America (PhRMA) through its listing recommendations were included in the Special 301 Report.[209] He adds that in 2016 and 2017, for instance, all of the countries PhRMA prioritized were included in the report. The number of these countries that the USTR added as a Priority Foreign Country (PFC), Priority Watch List country (PWL), or Section 306 country varied from a low of 46 percent in 2009 to a high of 65 percent in 2011 and has averaged 53 percent

economy/dispute-with-swiss-drugmaker-has-colombian-officials-worried-about-us-peace-funding/2016/05/18/6f1903ee-1c5e-11e6-8c7b-6931e66333e7_story.html (last visited Oct. 20, 2025).

[207] Srividhya Ragavan, Sean Flynn, & Brook Baker, *Comment Letter on Special Review of Countries That Do Not Provide Adequate Protection of Intellectual Property Rights*, REGULATIONS.GOV (Mar. 8, 2014), https://www.regulations.gov/comment/USTR-2013-0040-0092 (last visited Oct. 20, 2025).

[208] MICHAEL B. G. FROMAN, 2014 OFF. U.S. TRADE REPRESENTATIVE SPECIAL 301 REP. 37, https://ustr.gov/sites/default/files/USTR%202014%20Special%20301%20Report%20to%20Congress%20FINAL.pdf (last visited Oct. 20, 2025).

[209] Michael Palmedo, *Unilateral Norm Setting Using Special 301*, *in* INTELLECTUAL PROPERTY LAW AND ACCESS TO MEDICINES: TRIPS AGREEMENT, HEALTH, AND PHARMACEUTICALS 274, 282 (Srividhya Ragavan & Amaka Vanni eds., 2021).

over the last eleven years. The relentless pushback from PhRMA continued post-Covid-19.[210]

These events showcase the constant and unrealistic pushback to creation of meaningful access using negotiated flexibilities that remained even as the globe was facing a pandemic. The realities of a teetering global health-care structure boiled over during the Covid-19 crisis, causing poorer countries to seek alternatives. As Amaka Vanni would say, by the time Covid-19 happened, "a fault line can be traced in the TRIPS regime between developed and developing nations at the interface of IP and access to medication."[211] This fault line can be seen running through diverse issues, each of which represents one more strategy affecting the larger game of access to medication.

3.6 Health Equity Morphs into a Global Health-Care Problem

The issue of pharmaceutical access was initially a health-equity question.[212] That is, the rhetoric was that parts of the globe have no access to medication that is available to the rest of the globe. Such health-equity questions were amplified over time, as access to medication became a global issue. The evolution of health equity into a health-care access issue became unavoidable when countries that housed innovative pharmaceutical industries, and thus had available medications, found that these medications were unaffordable and hence inaccessible to a segment of their population.

The United States is a great example of how a country which houses Big Pharmaceutical companies that innovates has nevertheless struggled to address policy prescriptions that balances availability with access. The Hatch-Waxman statute and the Biologics Price Competition statute are examples of effort to enact policies that create pathways for the entry of generic or biosimilar drugs, as the case is, with other statutes and regulations, such as patent laws, that promote innovation.[213] In August 2021, for instance,

[210] *Id.* at 281.

[211] Srividhya Ragavan & Amaka Vanni, Introduction to Intellectual Property Law and Access to Medicine: TRIPS Agreement, Health, and Pharmaceuticals (Srividhya Ragavan & Amaka Vanni eds., 2021).

[212] This section draws on an earlier article titled published one of the coauthors, Srividhya Ragavan, *Make America Healthy: Reducing High Pharmaceutical Prices Without Reducing Innovation*, 77 SMU L. Rev. 787 (2025).

[213] Drug Price Competition and Patent Term Restoration Act of 1984, Pub. L. No. 98-417, 98 Stat. 1585 (1984) (enacted on September 24, 1984, and amended the Federal Food, Drug, and Cosmetic Act (21 U.S.C. § 355) and patent laws (35 U.S.C. §§ 156, 271). *See also* Biologics Price Competition

President Biden's administration considered drug prices as an issue to include in the Democrats' US$3.5 trillion social-policy bill to allow Medicare to negotiate lower prices.[214] The increase in drug prices has impacted both treatment and cure of all diseases, particularly in poorer countries. In 2025, the Trump administration too worked with innovator pharmaceutical companies to lower prices.[215]

Note that, against this background of rising global and domestic concern over drug prices, pharmaceutical prices in more developed economies, such as and especially in the United States, had been under scrutiny even before the Uruguay Round was negotiated. In fact, less than a year after the passage of the Drug Amendments Act of 1962, which dealt with safety and efficacy issues, the Federal Trade Commission (FTC) ruled that six drug companies conspired to rig bids to fix the price of tetracycline, raising the question of why drug companies reported higher profits but lower innovation.[216]

During that same period, investigations in the *Fortune* magazine detailed that thirteen of the twenty largest drug companies were among the fifty largest industrial corporations in the United States, based on profitability according to the rate of return on sales.[217] Similarly, the Kefauver Committee focused on whether the prices of drugs in the United States were high by comparing gross profits, net profits, and foreign market prices.[218] While the Kefauver Committee's findings remain distinctive, they highlighted huge price markups for drugs while taking "price to druggist" as a percent of direct factory costs. For example, the report noted exceptional markups of drug prices over their cost of production; examples included prednisone (for arthritis), 1891 percent; reserpine (for hypertension), 6,270 percent; tetracycline (antibiotic), 1,557 percent; and neprobamate (mild tranquilizer), 927 percent.[219] The Kefauver Committee found that prices of medications

and Innovation Act of 2009 (BPCIA), Pub. L. No. 111-148, § 7001, 124 Stat. 119, 804 (2010) (enacted on March 23, 2010, as part of the Affordable Care Act, it amends the Public Health Service (PHS) Act to create an abbreviated approval pathway for biosimilar biological products).

[214] Jonathan Weisman, *Biden Presses Congress to Move on Price Controls for Prescription Drugs*, N.Y. Times (Aug. 12, 2021), https://www.nytimes.com/live/2021/08/12/us/politics-news (last visited Oct. 20, 2025).

[215] Sydney Lupkin, *Trump struck deals with 16 drug companies. But they're still raising prices this year*,NPR KERA *available at* https://www.npr.org/2026/01/16/nx-s1-5678915/trumprx-pharma-drug-price-deals-list-prices (January 16, 2026).

[216] Morgan & Allison, *supra* note 123.

[217] *Id.* at 61.

[218] *Id.*

[219] *Id.*

were invariably lower outside of the United States when comparing prices of drugs in the United States with those in other countries.[220] As the study by Morgan and Allison highlights, "Eli Lilly's penicillin, V-Cillin, was illustrative. It sold in other countries for far less than it did in Indianapolis, where it is manufactured."[221]

Such concerns over inflated drug pricing were a natural consequence of a maximalist IP policy regime. These trends continued as the underlying assumption was that a maximalist IP policy is essential to promote innovation. In turn, the number of patents that protected a drug increased over time. For example, in the year 2022, the ten top-selling drugs in the United States had an average of 140 patent applications and 74 granted patents apiece.[222] As Table 1 depicts, the top-selling drug in the United States in the year 2021, AbbVie's Humira, which treats arthritis, had 311 patent applications and 165 granted patents to its credit as of that year, creating a patent thicket that shielded the drug from competition for nearly forty-three years.[223] Further, between 2013 and 2020, the list price of Humira rose by 141 percent—more than doubling in less than eight years![224] As of 2025, Humira sells at a sky-high list price of US$90,000 per annum.[225] The next-best-selling drug, Merck's Keytruda, which treats cancer, has a patent thicket consisting of 180 patent applications and 78 granted patents, and these are expected to block generic competition for nearly thirty-seven years.[226] It sells at a staggering list price of US$200,000 for a year's dosage.[227] For context, American households earned a median annual income of US$85,810 in the

[220] *Id.* at 62.
[221] *Id.*
[222] I-MAK, OVERPATENTED, OVERPRICED CURBING PATENT ABUSE: TACKLING THE ROOT OF THE DRUG PRICING CRISIS 5 (2022), https://www.i-mak.org/wp-content/uploads/2023/01/Overpatented-Overpriced-2023-01-24.pdf (last visited Oct. 20, 2025); *see also Contra* ADAM MOSSOFF, HUDSON INSTITUTE, UNRELIABLE DATA HAVE INFECTED THE POLICY DEBATES OVER DRUG PATENTS 2–4 (2022), https://s3.amazonaws.com/media.hudson.org/Mossoff_Unreliable%20Data%20Have%20Infected%20the%20Policy%20Debates%20Over%20Drug%20Patents.pdf (last visited Oct. 20, 2025).
[223] *See Investigating the Pharmaceutical Industry's Drug Patenting Practices*, I-MAK, https://www.i-mak.org/2025/02/21/investigating-the-pharmaceutical-industrys-drug-patenting-practices/#:~:text=206%20patent%20applications%20have%20been,by%20the%20U.S.%20patent%20system (last visited Oct. 20, 2025).
[224] *See* Skylar Jeremias, *Despite Steep Discounts, Humira Biosimilars Are Priced More Than Original Originator Price*, CNTR. BIOSIMILARS (July 17, 2023) https://www.centerforbiosimilars.com/view/despite-steep-discounts-humira-biosimilars-are-priced-more-than-original-originator-price (last visited Oct. 20, 2025).
[225] *See Drug Patenting Practices*, *supra* note 223.
[226] *See id.*
[227] *See id.*

year 2024, per the World Bank statistics—less than half of the annual cost of Keytruda![228] The third top-selling drug in the United States, a cure for multiple myeloma, owned by Celgene and brand-named Revlimid, carries a list price of approximately US$18,000 per twenty-eight-day cycle in 2025, or US$234,643 per year; a patent thicket formed of 206 patent applications and 117 granted patents lends the drug a patent shield against generic competition for nearly forty-three years.[229] Once again, for a comparative context, to truly appreciate these numbers, the average annual expenses of an American household (a housing unit with one or more people living in it) in the year 2023, as provided by the US Bureau of Labor Statistics, stood at US$77,280—one-third of the annual cost of Revlimid![230]

Table 1.1 below succinctly summarizes these hard facts about America's top three best-selling drugs to help understand how the US patent system is being misused by the Big Pharma for their own myopic commercial ends, leaving American patients suffering from life-threatening diseases penniless.

Another research from *Blood* noted that the biggest barrier to treating acute myeloid leukemia (AML) in India is cost.[231] The cost of the drug Idhifa, or Enasedinib, used to treat AML, was a whopping ₹2.3 million (US$30,000) for a month's supply in India.[232] The patent is held by the biotechnology company Celgene, owned by Bristol Myers Squibb (BMS), and the drug was not even registered for sale in India in 2020. The drug was approved by the FDA in 2017 and sold globally at a cost of approximately US$28,000. Notably, BMS was one of the thirty-nine major drug companies involved in a lawsuit against the government of South Africa over a 1997 statute that used the negotiated TRIPS flexibilities to lower the cost of the drugs by compulsorily licensing them. The result was a swathe of national welfare issues resulting from poor public health, which became exacerbated in light of the AIDS epidemic. Amidst this, the pharmaceutical company faced a global public-relations crisis for its posture in the face of a public health crisis. BMS not only refused to lower the cost of AIDS medication but it prevailed on the United States to exert pressure using trade terms to prevent institution of

[228] *GDP Per Capita (Current US$)–United States*, World Bank, https://data.worldbank.org/indicator/NY.GDP.PCAP.CD?locations=US (last visited Oct. 20, 2025).

[229] *See Drug Patenting Practices*, *supra* note 223.

[230] *BLS Report*, U.S. Bureau of Lab. Stat. (Dec. 2024), https://www.bls.gov/opub/reports/consumer-expenditures/2023/ (last visited Oct. 20, 2025).

[231] Chepsy C. Philip et al., *Acute Myeloid Leukemia: Challenges and Real World Data from India*, 124 Blood 3685 (2014).

[232] *Idhifa Prices, Coupons, Copay Cards & Patient Assistance*, Drugs.com, https://www.drugs.com/price-guide/idhifa (last visited Oct. 20, 2025).

Table 1.1 The three top-selling drugs in the United States (2021 US sales).

Drugs	**Humira**	**Keytruda**	**Revlimid**
Ranking, US sales in 2021	1	2	3
Drugmaker	AbbVie	Merck	Bristol Myers Squibb (Celgene)
Primary Condition Treated	Arthritis	Cancer	Multiple myeloma
Number of Patent Applications Filed (as of 2021)	311	180	206
Number of Patents Granted (as of 2021)	165	78	117
List Price (as of 2025)	US$90,000 per annum	US$ 200,000 per annum	US$234,643 per annum (based on the standard list price of US$18,000 per cycle of 28 days)
Patent Protection (Number of Years Generic Competition Has Been Blocked)	43.3 years	37.3 years	43 years

Source: Data from I-MAK (2025) *Investigating the Pharmaceutical Industry's Drug Patenting Practices* under a Creative Commons Attributions 3.0 Unported Deed (CC BY 3.0).

any policy prescription such as compulsory licensing or other exception to its patent rights as being in violation of the trade regime's prescription. The realities on the ground in South Africa in light of the egregiousness of the price and the posture of the trade regime, eventually resulted in South Africa asserting its rights resulting in lowering the cost of AIDS medication. BMS continues its presence in South Africa albeit in a different avatar—Celgene.

Reflecting the broader concern that these specific instances raise, the value of the social-benefit component, from a pure legal-theory perspective, has continued to diminish and has ceased to be an integral part of the larger IP regime, particularly patents. The health-care game played by the trade regime's rules seems "rigged" and reeks of inequity. The systemic issues of inequity and exclusiveness leading to lack of access begin at the stage of research and development. It is dominated by market interest, to the extent that it has become increasingly dissociated with public-health ends.[233]

[233] Rhiannon Osborne & Hayfaa Chalabi, *Global Vaccine Apartheid–A Rigged System Ripe for Reimagining*, SHADO (Sept. 4, 2021), https://shado-mag.com/articles/opinion/global-vaccine-apartheid-a-rigged-system-ripe-for-reimagining/ (last visited Oct. 20, 2025).

In that, the pandemic remains significant for highlighting how much the rhetoric around patent laws has moved away from the goals of the system and has instead taken on a more rights-centric approach to patent protection.[234]

Thus, the relentless games of Big Pharma come at the cost of real lives. Covid-19 exacerbated the issue, causing the Biden administration to call on Congress for measures to lower drug prices.[235] The request for a waiver from IP, in hopes for a more egalitarian system, is the latest pushback by poorer countries in response to Covid-19, and perhaps it will be the beginning of changes to ensure that medications are accessible.[236]

4. The Pharmaceutical Food Chain

4.1 Correlated Market with Distributed Capacities

In the context of growing inequities and reaction against a rights-centric IP regime, recent years have seen a change in the pharmaceutical industry, clearly showcasing the presence of a correlated market. For example, in 2011 developed countries such as France, Germany, Italy, and Canada saw relative stagnation in their pharmaceutical markets, and the US pharmaceutical market actually regressed.[237] Soon after this, pharmaceutical sales growth in developing-emerging countries shot up.[238] As the patent terms of several blockbuster drugs expired, more generic drugs, as well as more upselling of local generic drugs, have contributed to the shift.[239]

[234] Srividhya Ragavan, *Correlative Obligation in Patent Law: The Role of Public Good in Defining the Limits of Patent Exclusivity*, 6 N.Y.U. J. INTELL. PROP. & ENT. L. 47, 50 (2016).

[235] Press Release, The White House, Fact Sheet: President Bid Calls on Congress to Lower Prescription Drug Prices (Aug. 12, 2021), https://bidenwhitehouse.archives.gov/briefing-room/statements-releases/2021/08/12/fact-sheet-president-biden-calls-on-congress-to-lower-prescription-drug-prices/ (last visited Oct. 20, 2025).

[236] Peter Coy, *What Game Theory Says About China's Strategy*, N.Y. TIMES (Sept. 13, 2021), https://www.nytimes.com/2021/09/13/opinion/game-theory-china.html (last visited Oct. 20, 2025).

[237] Maya Tanoury & Zouhair Attieh, *The Influence of Emerging Markets on the Pharmaceutical Industry*, CURRENT THERAPEUTIC RSCH., April 14, 2017, at 19, 20. https://www.sciencedirect.com/science/article/pii/S0011393X16300984 (last visited Oct. 20, 2025); *see also What Do Patent Expirations Mean for the Pharma Industry?*, MICHAEL BAILEY ASSOCS., https://web.archive.org/web/20150311165543/http://www.michaelbaileyassociates.com:80/news/pharmaceutical/what-do-patent-expirations-mean-for-the-pharma-industry.

[238] *See id.* ("Between 2015 and 2020, pharma sales growth estimates scored higher in emerging countries than in developed countries"); *see also* Booz & Company, *Pharma Emerging Markets 2.0*, PWC (2013), https://www.scribd.com/document/309347896/Strategyand-Pharma-Emerging-Markets-2-0 (last visited Oct. 20, 2025).

[239] *See* Srividhya Ragavan, *Make America Healthy: Reducing High Pharmaceutical Prices Without Reducing Innovation*, 77 SMU L. Rev. 787, 790 (2025).

Despite the emergence of generic drugs, the patent system requires the pharmaceutical industry to be capital- as well as risk-intensive. This limits the number of countries that can support a robust domestic pharmaceutical manufacturing base. It means that such countries seeking to access cheaper products will always be net importers of generic medicines from other exporting countries. All of this leaves the globe, with a "pharmaceutical pyramid". The pharmaceutical food chain consists of innovative chemical and biological at one level with the biosimilars, and generics products as the natural next level to close the gap in pharmaceutical affordability and to ensure access.

4.2 Generic Drugs: Pharmacy of the UnEquals

The negotiations and the resulting restructuring of the health-care industry have resulted in the pharmaceutical food chain, which is good for the consumer. At the lower end of the pharmaceutical food chain lie off-patent or non-patented generic drugs, small-molecule bioequivalent medications created to be the same as patented brand-name drugs "in dosage form, safety, strength, route of administration, quality, performance characteristics, and intended use,"[240] but whose selling prices typically do not account for the cost of drug discovery.

Generic drugs do not have patents on their active ingredient,[241] and chemical drugs are often easier to replicate post-patent.[242] Thus, when a patent expires, the drug's formula would be known, the clinical trials would have been completed by the innovator, and the generic maker's "only requirement is to demonstrate to regulators that its version is as good and effective in humans as the original."[243] Chemical bioequivalents are made

[240] *Generic Drugs: Questions & Answers*, US Food & Drug Admin. (Mar. 16, 2021), https://www.fda.gov/drugs/frequently-asked-questions-popular-topics/generic-drugs-questions-answers#q1 (last visited Oct. 20, 2025).

[241] Srividhya Ragavan, *A "Patent" Restriction On Research & Development: Infringers Or Innovators?*, 2004 U. Ill. J. L. Tech. & Pol'y 73, 84 (noting that new processes for producing generic drugs may be patentable, but the active ingredient is not).

[242] Additionally, and significantly, the patent application provides the exact composition of the chemicals and the process of manufacture involved in the disclosures as part of the patent bargain. *See id.* at 78 ("Product-by-process claims describe the product by defining the process of production.").

[243] Ranit Mishori, *Why Are Generics Cheaper Than Brand-Name Medications?*, Wash. Post (July 11, 2011), https://www.washingtonpost.com/national/health-science/why-are-generic-drugs-cheaper-than-brand-name-ones/2011/07/05/gIQAwZdL9H_story.html (last visited Oct. 20, 2025).

either by using a different process or by using a bioequivalent compound of the patented product to create a therapeutic substitute.[244] Generics embody the same active pharmaceutical ingredients (APIs) as the original version; hence, a prescription for a brand-name drug can usually be satisfied by substituting a generic drug.[245] In other words, patients can expect the same therapeutic outcome from the generic drug as from the branded pharmaceutical.[246]

Despite an equivalent therapeutical efficacy, generics cost less than branded drugs, for two reasons. First, they enter the market after the patent expires. That is, the patent specification of the branded drug guides the generic manufacturer with the exact composition of the chemicals and the process of manufacture, such that the APIs can be used to create a therapeutic substitute of the patented drug at the expiration of the patent term. The expiration of the patent term also signifies the end of the monopolistic market power granted by the patent, which is the period during which the protected material can benefit from monopoly pricing.[247] When the patent term ends, the material falls into the public domain, and multiple competitors enter the market, which increases competition, driving down the cost/price to the benefit of consumers.[248]

Second, in most countries, the approval process for a generic version is less rigorous than that for the innovator's version. In the United States, for instance, generics are considered exact copies of the original drug, and hence undergo a shorter approval process by the FDA. The FDA's role, under the Drug Price Competition and Patent Term Restoration Act of 1984, is to institute checks and balances to ensure that generics are safe and enter the market after the patent on the brand-name drug expires.[249]

[244] C.-P. Milne & L. A. Cabanilla, *Orphan Drugs and Generics*, *in* Comprehensive Medicinal Chemistry II 667 (John B. Taylor & David J. Triggle eds., 2007); *see also* Srividhya Ragavan, *A "Patent" Restriction On Research & Development: Infringers Or Innovators?*, 2004 U. Ill. J. L., Tech. & Pol'y 73, 86 (explaining the significance of creating efficient patent procedures for generic drugs for economic growth and encourage domestic innovation in developing countries).

[245] *See Generic Drug Facts*, U.S. Food and Drug Admin. (Nov. 11, 2021), https://www.fda.gov/drugs/generic-drugs/generic-drug-facts (last visited Oct. 20, 2025).

[246] *Id.*

[247] 35 U.S.C. §154.

[248] *See* Srividhya Ragavan, Patent and Trade Disparities in Developing Countries 35–45 (2012).

[249] *See* Drug Price Competition and Patent Term Restoration Act of 1981, Pub. L. No 98-417, 98 Stat. 1585, 1585–88 (1984) (codified in relevant part at 21 U.S.C. § 355 and 35 U.S.C. § 271(e)) [Hatch-Waxman Act]; 21 U.S.C. § 355; *see also* Ravi Gupta et al, *Generic Drugs in the United States: Policies to Address Pricing and Competition*, 105 Clinical Pharmacology & Therapeutics 329, 329–30 (2019) (discussing the role of the FDA in the approval process for generic drugs).

In order to ensure safety, the FDA allows the generics to use the clinical trial data submitted by the innovator of the patented drug.[250] That is, the FDA does not require generic applicants to repeat animal and clinical (human) studies that are required of the brand-name medicines in order to demonstrate safety and effectiveness.[251] Generic manufacturers only submit details of the manufacturing process, so as to inform how the drug combines the APIs to demonstrate safety and reliability to the FDA.[252] This relieves generic manufacturers of the associated costs to pass that benefit onto consumers by pricing it low.

4.3 Biologics and Biosimilars: The Next Big Game

Biologic medicines are medical treatment options that are sourced biologically, from active substances made of protein, and derived from humans, animals, or microorganisms.[253] Biologics are used to treat a variety of medical conditions—such as cancer, through immunotherapy to inhibit the growth of cancerous cells.[254] For instance, Avastin, a biologic used for cancer treatment, is based on a living substance, bevacizumab, which is a humanized antibody (a type of protein that plays a vital role in the body's immune response) derived from mice.[255] Amgen, Eli Lilly, GlaxoSmithKline, and Pfizer are among the biologic makers with the highest market share in the US biologic market.[256]

A *biosimilar* is the therapeutic equivalent of a biologic in terms of its biological activity and its efficacy, safety, and immunogenicity profile.[257] The similarity arises because of a common living substance, mainly proteins, used in both biosimilars and biologics.[258] For instance, the biosimilar

[250] 35 U.S.C. § 112 (discussing disclosures. Patent protection is granted by the government in exchange for disclosing how to make and use the invention so that when it falls into public domain, third parties can manufacture it). *See also* 21 U.S.C. §§ 355, 360.

[251] *Generic Drugs: Questions & Answers*, *supra* note 240.

[252] *See* 21 U.S.C. §§ 355(b)(2), (j).

[253] *Biosimilar Medicines: Overview*, EUR. MEDS. AGENCY, https://www.ema.europa.eu/en/human-regulatory-overview/biosimilar-medicines-overview (last visited Oct. 20, 2025).

[254] *Id.*

[255] *See* Amber R. Watson, *All About Avastin*, HEALTHLINE (Jan. 20, 2022), https://www.healthline.com/health/drugs/avastin#what-it-is (last visited Oct. 20, 2025).

[256] *Biologic Market–Growth, Trends, COVID 19 Impact, And Forecasts (2023–2028)*, MORDOR INTEL., https://www.marketresearch.com/Mordor-Intelligence-LLP-v4018/ (last visited Oct. 20, 2025).

[257] *Biosimilar Medicines: Overview*, *supra* note 253.

[258] *Id.*

Zirabev is based on the active substance bevacizumab, the same common biologic source found in the biologic Avastin.[259]

Biosimilars are not exact copies or replicas of biologics, because of the natural variability of living substances, but they are similar in embodying the same common protein and have comparable therapeutic efficacy based on immunogenicity and cytotoxicity.[260] While biosimilars can be prescribed as a substitute for their respective reference product/biologic, they are not interchangeable unless they are specifically approved as such.[261] Biologics with an "interchangeable" designation can be auto-substituted at the pharmacy level.[262]

Ensuring compliance with good clinical and manufacturing-process norms, as well as the maintenance of safety, efficacy, and quality, entails the submission of preclinical, pharmacodynamic, and pharmacokinetic studies, repeat-dose toxicity, and clinical trial studies. Phase III results are mandatory for approval of biologics in most countries, whereas for "similar biologics," quality-comparability studies must be satisfactory.[263] In addition, pharmacovigilance as well as risk-management plans must be instated to ensure appropriate reporting and follow-up of adverse events in the post-marketing scenario.

Further, because of the particular nature of biologics, compliance with biosafety requirements as well as the involvement of specialized bodies such as Genetic Engineering Appraisal Committees are essential in the case of genetically modified microorganisms. Similarly, Recombinant DNA Advisory Committees should be involved in the case of rDNA-based products.

4.4 Generics vs. Biosimilars

Given the complex regulatory requirements outlined above, biosimilars differ significantly from generics in terms of production, costs, and approval timelines. Unlike generics, mass production is more challenging for biosimilars because they are large, complex molecules that are produced

[259] *Zirabev*, Eur. Meds. Agency, https://www.ema.europa.eu/en/medicines/human/EPAR/zirabev (last visited Oct. 20, 2025).

[260] Biosimilar Medicines: Overview, *supra* note 253.

[261] *Id.*

[262] US Food & Drug Admin., Considerations in Demonstrating Interchangeability With a Reference Product Guidance for Industry: Guidance for Industry (2023); *see also* US Food & Drug Admin., Biosimilar Product Regulatory Review and Approval, https://www.fda.gov/files/drugs/published/Biosimilar-Product-Regulatory-Review-and-Approval.pdf (last visited Oct. 20, 2025).

[263] Ramesh Jois et al., *Similar Biologics in India: A Story of Access or Potential for Compromise?*, 152 Indian J. Med. Res. 456, 560–64 (2020) (noting India, US, EU and WHO guidelines on approval of biosimilars).

in living cells rather than by classical chemical processes.[264] In the United States, the Biologics Price Competition and Innovation Act of 2010 (BPCIA), which deals with regulatory approvals for biosimilars, created an abbreviated approval process for biosimilars.[265] The process is nevertheless cumbersome compared to that for generics, as the former involves more research. Biosimilars are also less cost-effective than generics.[266] For comparison, while generic drugs (chemical origin) require an investment of approximately US$2 million to US$3 million and can be approved in two to three years, biosimilars can cost between US$100 million and US$200 million and typically take eight to ten years for approval.[267]

4.5 Access to Biologics and Biosimilars

Given the high regulatory and cost barriers to biosimilar development, other countries, unlike the United States, especially in Europe, have been more successful in making biosimilars available. Enabling biosimilars is a way to balance access with innovation. For instance, Europe's first biosimilar, Sandoz's somatotropin's biosimilar, Omnitrope, was approved in 2006.[268] Following this, the European Union (hereinafter the *EU*) also established a framework for their recognition and approval in a manner that balanced biosimilar development with biologic innovation.[269] As of 2018, the EU had approved more than forty biosimilars, as opposed to a mere fifteen in the United States.[270]

Similarly, developing countries, particularly India, have ramped up their expertise in biologics, with a keen eye on the cost of the medication.

[264] *What Are Biosimilars and How Do They Expand Treatment Options for Patients?*, PFIZER (Sept. 28, 2022), https://www.pfizer.com/news/articles/what_are_biosimilars_and_how_do_they_expand_treatment_options_for_patients (last visited Oct. 20, 2025) (noting that biologics are products of years of R&D and involve long gestation periods that entail a tedious and costly regulatory approval process); *see also Comparison of the Cost of Development of Biological and Biosimilars*, GENERICS & BIOSIMILARS INITIATIVE (Nov. 3, 2022), https://gabionline.net/reports/comparison-of-the-cost-of-development-of-biologicals-and-biosimilars (last visited Oct. 20, 2025) [hereinafter *Cost of Development of Biosimilars*].

[265] Hannah Koyfman, *Biosimilarity and Interchangeability in the Biologics Price Competition and Innovation Act of 2009 and FDA's 2012 Draft Guidance for Industry*, 32 BIOTECHNOLOGY L. REP. 238, 238–45 (2013), (discussing the BPCIA's regulatory framework for biosimilars and interchangeable, which is still subject to interpretation given the complexity of biologics); 42 U.S.C. § 262(k).

[266] *Cost of Development of Biosimilars*, *supra* note 264.

[267] *Id.*

[268] *Biosimilar Medicines: Overview*, *supra* note 253.

[269] *Id.*

[270] Ying Chen et al., *What's Next for Biosimilars in Emerging Markets?*, MCKINSEY & CO. (Apr. 1, 2019) https://www.mckinsey.com/industries/life-sciences/our-insights/whats-next-for-biosimilars-in-emerging-markets (last visited Oct. 20, 2025).

Until 2020, India had approved about sixty biologics.[271] A study by Chen, Lehmann, and Silva notes that seventy biologics are marketed in India, and more than forty are marketed in China.[272]

In light of these developments across developed and developing countries, the contemporary food chain shows an industry that has changed considerably since 1992, when the TRIPS Agreement was negotiated. The larger question pondered is whether health issues of a global scale, fueled by trade and interconnected with technology, independently provide a reason to reconsider the global public-health framework.

5. Conclusion: From Misalignment to Realignment

A comprehensive appreciation of historical events alongside contemporary developments remains crucial to understanding the main factors that influenced the formulation of today's normative framework, as well as the alliances that defined health as a subset of the larger trade and IP agenda. The history of the tension-filled alliance between trade and IP shows an ever-expanding set of IP norms in trade agreements. Concerted efforts by various stakeholders have led to an ironic constant of change in the "framing" of IP, shifting it from "trade" to invoking "public health," "human rights," "postcolonialism," "access to knowledge," and "users' rights."

Unfortunately, none of the changes have satisfactorily captured the expansionist tendencies of the trade regime to the detriment of health. Instead, they have contributed to a level of expansionism with a corresponding reduction in limitations and flexibilities for the local and national governments that tend to be first responders in a health-care crisis. The consequence is a trading system whose imbalance and distortions in the health-care area were exposed during the pandemic.

The need is for a systematic assessment of IP's position in health-care access in this fast-changing world. The next chapter deals with the question of realignment by discussing whether a new framework is needed or, alternately, whether the existing framework would sufficiently address the crisis of health care being left behind in a trading world.

[271] Ramesh Jois et al., *Similar Biologics in India: A Story of Access or Potential for Compromise?*, 152 Indian J.Med. Rsch. 456, 460 (2020) (discussing the regulatory guidelines for approval of similar biologics in India).

[272] *Id.*

2

Presumption-Risks: Impact of Local Realities on Patent Goals

1. Introduction: The Globalized IP Paradigm Disconnected from Realities

1.1 Global Harmonization of Laws

The inclusion of IP rights into the larger trade regime coincided with an era that witnessed advancements in information and communication technologies. As a result of globalization, there has been an increase in trade, involving significantly more cross-border movement of ideas, goods, and services. In turn, this has increased the push for greater harmonization of laws to further facilitate the flow of goods and services across borders, which has led to even more trade and development.

The trend toward harmonization of laws across borders was originally a response to the need for the domestic legal systems of member states to interface with one another more smoothly, in order to better reap the benefits of the trade regime. The assumption was that reduction or elimination of trade barriers would enable all member states to benefit from trade. Historically, when different jurisdictions apply different sets of laws to the same goods and services, the transaction costs for obtaining and enforcing corresponding rights in different countries increase. The drive to improve the efficiency of the trading system by reducing these transaction costs has led to a movement toward the harmonization of laws.[1]

[1] As many studies are now showing, the costs of the current model of harmonization are significant. Joseph E. Stiglitz, Economic Foundations of Intellectual Property Rights, 57 Duke L. J. 1693, 1701 (2008). Globalization may be more than the gains that can be achieved by it. *See* Kenneth C. Shadlen, *Harmonization, Differentiation, and Development: The Case of Intellectual Property in the Global Trading Regime, in* Knowledge in the Development of Economies: Institutional Choices Under Globalization 44 (Silvia Sacchetti & Roger Sugden eds., 2009). *See generally* Joseph E. Stiglitz, Globalization and Its Discontents 60–62 (2002).

Fractures in IP, Trade, and Health. Srividhya Ragavan and Swaraj Paul Barooah, Oxford University Press.
 DOI: 10.1093/9780197684085.003.0002

1.2 Shift Toward a Knowledge Economy

This movement toward harmonization has had two consequences: (1) a rise in knowledge intensity of economic activity, and (2) the increased globalization of economic affairs.[2] The shift toward a knowledge economy has had a defining and impactful role on IP. The protection and promotion of IP and the broadening of rights have taken on greater importance against the backdrop of globalization in the knowledge economy.

The knowledge economy has created a new order. The new trade regime has resulted in an explosion of talent capital, causing changes to traditional lifestyles. Although this has resulted in expanded development, the sustainability of the current model has been increasingly debated. With respect to health-care access in particular, questions about equitable redistribution and class divisions have increased.

1.3 Presumption Risks in the IP-Innovation Paradigm

In this new order, the different forms of IP, and particularly patents, have often been identified as a key driver of innovation per se, and especially technological innovation. An ever-increasing need for further economic development in certain parts of the world has also led to a call for the steady tightening of patent norms across the globe in order to enhance private property rights.

The call for strengthening the patent systems is based on an assumption, known as *presumption risk*, that stronger IP rights result in better innovations and thus stronger economies. International obligations, especially with reference to patents, are structured on the assumption that innovations are uniformly beneficial to every market. Especially in the health-care area, such an assumption is a presumption risk that can be easily negated.

This chapter exhaustively examines the historical role of patents in order to clarify the contemporary operational inefficiencies integral to the innovation framework and how they pose a constraint on global public health on account of such presumption risk.

[2] John Houghton & Peter Sheehan, *A Primer on the Knowledge Economy* 2 (Ctr. for Strategic Econ. Stud., Working Paper No. 18, 2000).

1.4 Local Realities as a Presumption Risk

One such presumption risk, termed as *local realities,* is outlined in this chapter as a factor that, although relevant to determining the efficiency of the outcome, is often either ignored or presumed as beneficial. "Local realities" refers to national and local issues impacting productivity and hence the society. The benefit for the local market is tied with local realities, which can engage with several factors such as per capita income, relevance of that innovation for that community (especially in the case of pharmaceuticals), and local cultural realities. From the perspective of health-care access, localized issues such as poverty, the ability to afford, weather, food habits, access to medications, and the types of diseases pervasive in the locality (for example, tropical diseases) can all affect the functionality of the system. The goal is to assert that local relevance dictated by the realities of that locale is significant to calculate an innovation's overall benefit to the market.

Local realities have economic, social, technological, and political dimensions, which together influence and in turn are influenced by national and local issues and laws. Social realities include the patterns, customs, usages, beliefs, and institutions that have a bearing on coexistence of human beings as part of a social community. Social beliefs and customs, social structure and hierarchy, social freedom and liberties, social inequalities, family and marriage, culture, languages, status of women, and education are all social realities that are not uniform across the globe.

Economic realities can be seen as both a cause and a product of social realities, and thus the term "socioeconomic realities" lies at the core of economic development in our age. Economic realities include demographic factors (such as sex ratios, age distribution, and workforce-participation rate), the size and speed of a country's economy measured in terms of GDP and economic growth, household-income distribution, income inequalities, the extent of relative and absolute poverty, prevalence and types of unemployment, the structure and sectoral composition of the economy, monetary and fiscal policies, savings and investment at the household and national levels, integration of the domestic economy with the world economy and its measures in terms of net export and level of remittances, the balance-of-payment situation, the state of public health, agricultural production and productivity, industrialization, and self-sufficiency.

Technological realities, which are closely linked to the innovation system, include factors such as the state of technology in a country; policies to encourage technology transfer, technical education, training, and skill-building; public expenditure on R&D and technical education; and the incentive system for inventors and laws regulating their rights.

Political realities include constitutional ideals and aspirations, the type and form of the government system (dictatorial or democratic), political stability and succession, governance mandates and priorities outlined in constitutional and policy documents, the strength and independence of political leadership, checks and balances against abuse of power, civil and political rights and liberties enjoyed by people, fairness and independence of the election system, and political awareness and activism by citizens.

An innovation's benefit or impact should be calculated considering local realities, the deference for which should be given using sufficient *flexibilities* and *exceptions*. The resulting balance can be expected to lead to more socially desirable outcomes while preserving the benefits of the monopoly in a manner that fulfills the historic conceptions of patents. Yet, much like the failed promises of the "trickle-down economy,"[3] the much vaunted "balance" of the international trade system with competing values, including public health, has not been realized. Rather, as the following chapters will discuss, whether it is the HIV/AIDS crisis of the past, the pandemic crisis of the present, or concerns about future crises, the biggest concern for health-equity advocates today is the need for appropriate limitations or availability of flexibilities to ensure that patent systems achieve their ordained goals.

1.5 Globalized Norms Based in Local Realities

This chapter underscores the importance of specific local realities and examines whether international treaties give sufficient flexibility to nations for accommodating the different ground-level realities that impact health-equity questions. In examining the patent system, especially its role in the trade regime, it reexamines how local realities can affect predicted outcomes.

Having made a case for considering a new framework to facilitate health-care access, this chapter asserts that any such framework should carefully consider how local realities can play a role in achieving the stated goals. In outlining the insufficiencies of the innovation system, it will emphasize that local realities can influence and produce outcomes at variance

[3] H. W. Arndt, The "Trickle-Down" Myth, ECON. DEV. & CULTURAL CHANGE, Oct. 1983, at 1–10.

with expectations created from theoretical bases. These policies have been instituted with the presumption that they will result in a uniform and predictable outcome with manageable differences, thus leading to development, trade, and innovation at a global level. This *presumption-risk* has impacted countries that have emulated standardized international norms without fully engaging and considering the impact of their local sociopolitical conditions.

The chapter further asserts that over time, especially as regards health-care access, the impact from one part of the globe tends to affect the rest either directly or indirectly, and that globalized norms should therefore accommodate for local realities.[4] It begins with a discussion of the core of patent theory, discussing how the basic patent framework was always connected with local realities relevant to its efficient outcomes. Next, it discusses the presumption risks that contemporary regimes associate with the patent regime, such that the presence of a patent is presumed to be beneficial whether or not the product is on the market.

2. Theoretical Underpinnings of Patents and Their Rootedness in Local Realities

2.1 The Social-Rights Theory

The core doctrinal and normative structures of patent law can best be elucidated through the writings of Thomas Jefferson.[5] In denying patent law's proprietary underpinnings in natural rights, Jefferson asserts that the exclusive rights to the profits from an invention are a direct return "for the benefit" that society will derive.[6] Jefferson describes the concept of stable ownership as a mere gift of social law as opposed to a natural right.[7] Jefferson indicates

[4] *See* Srividhya Ragavan, Patent and Trade Disparities in Developing Countries 28 (2012).

[5] *But see generally* Adam Mossoff, *Who Cares What Thomas Jefferson Thought about Patents—Reevaluating the Patent "Privilege" in Historical Context*, 92 Corn. L. Rev. 953, 956–59 (2007).

[6] Letter from Thomas Jefferson to Isaac McPherson (August 13, 1813), *in* 6 The Writings of Thomas Jefferson 175, 180–81 (H. A. Washington ed., 2017), https://www.gutenberg.org/cache/epub/55075/pg55075-images.html (last visited Oct. 20, 2025); Letter from Thomas Jefferson to James Madison (August 28, 1789), National Archives, https://founders.archives.gov/documents/Jefferson/01-15-02-0354 (last visited Oct. 20, 2025).

[7] *See* Adam D. Moore, *A Lockean Theory of Intellectual Property*, 21 Hamline L. Rev. 65, 108 n.5 (1997) (noting that Thomas Jefferson explicitly disavowed any natural-law underpinning of intellectual property rights).

that the exclusive monopoly rights of the patent owner are not a natural right but a mere encouragement to pursue socially useful ideas.[8]

The inherent dilemmas confronting patent policy and its flirtations with improving innovation are perhaps best captured by Jefferson in his letter to Isaac McPherson.[9] Jefferson, himself an inventor and a draftsman of the 1793 Patent Act,[10] outlined to McPherson in August 1813 the social and economic rationale of the patent system in the following words:[11] "Society may give an exclusive right to the profits arising from them, as an encouragement to men to pursue ideas which may produce utility, but this may or may not be done, according to the will and convenience of the society, without claim or complaint from anybody."[12]

The societal discretion outlined in Jefferson's conception of patents creates the impression of a contract, which posits society's benefit as the consideration for patent exclusivity. For Jefferson, however, products that can benefit from exclusive rights ought to be clearly distinguished from those that do not deserve or require such protection,[13] although he acknowledges the difficulties of making this distinction. Thus, the central schema of the patent system is to benefit society.

This concept of the primacy of the social-benefit component of patents has survived to date and remains an integral part of US patent law. For instance, during a speech delivered during the Centennial Celebration of the American Patent System in 1891, W. C. Dodge reiterated that our patent system is based on the idea of primarily benefiting the public and not the inventor.[14] The US Supreme Court has also endorsed the view that exclusivity is a self-imposed sufferance by society (designed as an award by the

[8] This section draws on an earlier article published by one of the co-authors; *See generally* Srividhya Ragavan, *Correlative Obligation in Patent Law: The Role of Public Good in Defining the Limits of Patent Exclusivity*, 6 N.Y.U. J. Intell. Prop. & Ent. L., 47 (2016).

[9] Graham v. John Deere Co., 383 US 1, 8–10 (1966).

[10] *See* P. J. Federico, *Operation of the Patent Act of 1790*, 18 J. Pat. & Trademark Off. Soc'y 237, 238 (1936); *see also Graham*, 383 US at 7.

[11] *See Graham*, 383 U.S. at 7–9.

[12] *Id.* at 9 n.2; *see also* Letter from Thomas Jefferson to Isaac McPherson, *supra* note 6, at 180–81.

[13] Letter from Thomas Jefferson to Isaac McPherson, *supra* note 6, at 181. ("Inventions . . . cannot, in nature, be a subject of property").

[14] James L. Ewin, *The Minor Innovations of the Century, in* United States Bicentennial Commemorative Edition of Proceedings and Addresses 478 (1892); *see also* Srividhya Ragavan, *Correlative Obligation in Patent Law: The Role of Public Good in Defining the Limits of Patent Exclusivity*, 6 N.Y.U. J. of Intell. Prop. & Ent. Law 47, 56 (2016); *see also* George Ticknor Curtis, A Treatise on the Law of Patents for Useful Inventions in the United States of America 1 (2d ed., 1854).

government to the inventor) intended to generate a greater public good.[15] In *Graham*, the Court echoed Jefferson's words, holding that "the patent monopoly was not designed to secure to the inventor his natural right in his discoveries. Rather, it was a reward, an inducement, aimed at bringing forth new knowledge."[16]

> Similarly, Margaret Chon has argued that James Madison, whose thinking significantly shaped US patent law, subscribed to the view that "the public good fully coincides with the claims of individuals."[17] Thus, the concept of the social-benefit component of patents seems to have survived into contemporary times. In sum, societal tolerance of a monopoly encourages the creation of more innovations that benefit society, whereas disclosures merely help make the knowledge public. Society will, for its own benefit, tolerate the patentee's exclusive right for the term of the patent.[18] Commissioner Coe of the US patent office later rephrased the concept of the trade-off as "giving the inventor a limited amount of protection [to] assure society of the benefits of his genius."[19] Therein lies the internal core of patent law, which relates the societal benefit to the vesting of exclusive rights.[20]

The TRIPS Agreement acknowledges societal benefits as a precondition to the grant of exclusive rights to the patentee under Article 30, which allows member states to provide for limited exceptions to the exclusive rights conferred by a patent.[21] For instance, India, under the 1974 Patent Act,

[15] Srividhya Ragavan, *Correlative Obligation in Patent Law: The Role of Public Good in Defining the Limits of Patent Exclusivity*, 6 N.Y.U. J. Intell. Prop. & Ent. L. 47, 56 (2016).

[16] *Graham*, 383 U.S. at 9. ("The grant of an exclusive right to an invention was the creation of society—at odds with the inherent free nature of disclosed ideas—and was not to be freely given. Only inventions and discoveries which furthered human knowledge, and were new and useful, justified the special inducement of a limited private monopoly").

[17] *See* Margaret Chon, *Postmodern "Progress": Reconsidering the Copyright and Patent Power*, 43 DePaul L. Rev. 97, 146 (1993); *see also* The Federalist No. 43, at 271–72 (James Madison) (Clinton Rossiter ed., 1961).

[18] *See* Dotan Oliar, *Making Sense of the Intellectual Property Clause: Promotion of Progress as a Limitation on Congress's Intellectual Property Power*, 94 Geo. L.J. 1771, 1816 (2006) (outlining "three considerations—the fact that the Framers would not adopt the intellectual property proposals in the plenary form in which they were made, the political makeup of the Convention, and the origin of the words in the Progress Clause as qualifiers of other powers —all contributing to one consistent story according to which the Progress Clause was intended to limit Congress's intellectual property power").

[19] U.S. Pat. and Trademarks Off., The Story of the American Patent System: 1790–1940 28 (1940).

[20] *Id.*

[21] TRIPS Agreement art. 30.

provides for a regime of "local working" requirement and the grant of compulsory licensing in the event of nonworking of a patent within the territory of India, as exceptions to the exclusive rights of a patent-holder over the patented invention.[22] Brazil introduced its local-working regime in its patent law in 1996 to allow for compulsory licensing if a patent does not get worked in its territory.[23]

Legal safeguards that mandate local working of a patented invention in exchange for the patentee's continued enjoyment of monopoly rights over the invention are intended to ensure that the benefits of such inventions flow to the society, which is burdened with the correlative duty to abstain from appropriation of such inventions for commercial exploitation. Initially used by the Western nations as instruments of industrialization and a means to gain self-sufficiency, as elaborated in Chapter 1, "society," under these provisions, denotes a definitely delineated territory with a homogeneous set of local socioeconomic and political realities.

2.2 The Natural Rights Theory

The role of public benefit in the context of the awarded exclusive rights has traditionally been a key part of discussions on patents. The importance of the public-benefit end, originally described by Jefferson, has been reiterated by other distinguished experts.[24] For instance, in 1892, William E. Simonds, commissioner of patents, reasoned in the first volume of the *Yale Law Journal* that the extent of *natural right* exclusivity in IP creations should be subject to limitations, such as the principle of necessity.[25] "Each original inventor of an improvement in the useful arts," Simonds stated, "has . . . the same kind of a title to the exclusive enjoyment thereof."[26] He further adds that "while the exclusive natural right to an invention is a correct thing in theory, its exercise is suppressed through necessity."[27]

[22] *See* The Patent Act, 1970, § 84, No. 39, Acts of Parliament, 1970 (India).

[23] *See* Law No. 9,279 of May 14, 1996 (Brazil), https://www.gov.br/inpi/en/services/patents/laws-and-regulations/laws-and-regulations/lpienglish.pdf (last visited Oct. 20, 2025).

[24] Letter from Thomas Jefferson to Isaac McPherson, *supra* note 6, at 180–81; *accord* Letter from Thomas Jefferson to James Madison, *supra* note 6. *E.g.* George Ticknor Curtis, Treatise on the Law of Patents for Useful Inventions in the United States of America 1 (2d ed., 1854).

[25] *See* William E. Simonds, *Natural Right of Property in Intellectual Production*, 1 Yale L.J. 16, 23 (1891).

[26] *Id.* at 23–24.

[27] *Id.* at 25.

Elsewhere, Simonds outlined that "in all forms of society all kinds of property are held under such conditions and limitations as society deems reasonable. Under the right of eminent domain, governments take private property for public use on suitable remuneration when public necessity and convenience demand.[28] It is therefore entirely reasonable that society should set a limit to the enjoyment of the natural right of property in intellectual productions."[29]

Three important points from Simonds are exemplary of early thinking about the limits of an inventor's rights.[30] First, early thinking on patents was pervaded by concerns about outcome—that is, the system's ability to achieve its preordained objectives—rather than the inventor's rights it created. Thus, even a natural-rights theorist like Simonds considered circumscribing patents to achieve the system's objective. Second, early developments in patent law frequently warranted interference with patent exclusivity if the patent system was not primarily functioning to ensure the flow of benefits to society. Thus, early thinking favored the concept of society tolerating the grant of certain rights to an inventor, as opposed to recognizing that the inventor earned these rights. Third, the obvious view through a societal lens dictates imposing adequate limitations if the end—the public-benefit objective—is not well-served.

These three points together demonstrate that the correlative duty is not a per se reward for the inventor's genius but instead a self-imposed toleration by the society, driven and dictated by the larger public benefit. An inventor can gain recognition and rights as a consequence of the invention, but any exclusivity in those rights is simply an intended by-product of the correlative duty that society willingly tolerates. From the perspective of the law of contracts, the correlative duty can be viewed as a consideration for the larger public benefit.

Although Simonds considered patents to be a natural right—unlike Jefferson, who posited patent rights as a social right—he nonetheless found that necessity could circumscribe the extent of the right. Simonds's background as the commissioner of patents perhaps influenced his conception of patents as a natural right. Yet both men seem to suggest that the operation of patent law and the exercise of exclusivity are circumscribed by the needs of

[28] *Id.*

[29] *Id.* at 23–24.

[30] *See* Robert P. Merges, Justifying Intellectual Property 32–33 (2011) (expounding fully Locke's theory of property and applying it to IP rights).

society.[31] Thus, interference with patent exclusivity to ensure societal benefit is seen as a legitimate exercise that serves the objectives of the system, and concerns about social outcomes, especially where lifesaving drugs are concerned, implicate the need to take account of local realities.

The TRIPS Agreement takes cognizance of these local realities as "necessities" in order to circumscribe the scope of exclusive rights of the patentee under Article 31(b), under which, in cases of national emergency, extreme urgency, or public noncommercial use, members have been provided with flexibility to allow the use of the subject matter of a patent without the prior authorization of the patent right-holder.[32] India, in Section 92 of the 1974 Patent Act, incorporated such flexibilities to allow any interested person to apply for a compulsory license in respect of any patent in force that is deemed necessary by the central government in such circumstances.[33] The United States itself, as a prelude to the Doha Declaration, had considered the right to compulsorily license medication to deal with a public-health emergency posed by a domestic anthrax outbreak that resulted in fewer than a dozen deaths.[34] Hence, even the most developed and innovative economies have admitted the need to circumscribe the limits of patent rights in the event of local necessities.

2.3 The Lockean Theory of Property

The broad encapsulation of the limits of patent rights also comports well with John Locke's theory of property. Locke conceives property rights as an entitlement to a person for exercising labor:[35]

> The same law of Nature that does by this means give us property, does also bound that property too. . . . As much as anyone can make use of to any advantage of life before it spoils, so much he may by his labor fix his property in. Whatever is beyond this is more than his share, and belongs to others. . . .[36]

[31] Srividhya Ragavan, *Correlative Obligation in Patent Law: The Role of Public Good in Defining the Limits of Patent Exclusivity*, 6 N.Y.U. J. INTELL. PROP. & ENT. L. 47, 58 (2016).
[32] *See* TRIPS Agreement art. 30.
[33] *See* THE PATENT ACT, 1970, § 92, No. 39, Acts of Parliament, 1970 (India).
[34] Cecilia Oh, *U.S. Opposed to Moves to Address Public-Health Concerns About TRIPS*, THIRD WORLD NETWORK, https://twn.my/title/twr131f.htm (last visited Oct. 20, 2025).
[35] JOHN LOCKE, TWO TREATISES OF GOVERNMENT 101 (Thomas Hollis ed., 1764).
[36] *Id.*

Thus, under the Lockean conception of property, property rights are secured only through the sweat of the creator's own brow, and these rights are subject to the *sufficiency* and *spoliation* obligations. The sufficiency restriction requires that one must leave "enough and as good" for others, which Locke asserts is an integral part of a just property regime.[37] The spoliation principle states that the creator may only appropriate as much as he or she can use, and may not claim ownership of so many natural resources that some spoil before they can be used.[38]

Locke's theory of sufficiency and spoliation goes further than Simonds's necessity theory and provides a clearer limitation to natural rights over property. In the patent context, Locke fully recognizes the rights of the inventor, but these rights are subject to sufficiency and spoilage limitations. Locke's implication is that the limited room for rights about property is because of an abundance of resources, and that it could change if those resources become limited. That is, an inventor's appropriation should be limited by need and not greed. Also, property holders are required to leave "enough and as good"—in other words, sufficient—for the public.[39] Locke repeatedly suggests that there is something morally wrong with distributions in which some people's property leaves others with very little.[40]

Therefore, the grant of patent rights cannot work to the detriment of the flow of social benefit. If it does, the sufficiency proviso will empower society to use the property for public benefit. Commenting on this, John Simmons would later say, "[T]he clear implication is that in later ages, when scarcity is a problem, there is room for doubt about . . . largeness of possession."[41] Largeness of possession has come to present a significant problem in the contemporary patent system.

It is imperative for contemporary patent regimes to be engaged with the foundational objectives of the system to achieve its goals. The "as good left in common for others" is a direct recommendation to carefully consider public need. For a sovereign nation, such consideration requires engaging with local realities. For instance, the resurgence of India's generic-drug industry

[37] George H. Smith, *John Locke: Some Qualifications in Locke's Theory of Property*, LIBERTARIANISM.ORG (Nov. 6, 2015), https://www.libertarianism.org/columns/john-locke-some-qualifications-lockes-theory-property (last visited Oct. 20, 2025).
[38] *Id.*
[39] Daniel M. Layman, *Sufficiency and Freedom in Locke's Theory of Property*, 17 EUR. J. POL. THEORY 152, 154 (2015).
[40] *Id.*
[41] A. JOHN A. SIMMONS, THE LOCKEAN THEORY OF RIGHTS 291–98 (1992).

was a direct outcome of the survey of its local socioeconomic realities after the country was liberated from the clutches of colonial rule in 1947. Notably, with around half of its population living in poverty, India was then the largest reservoir of epidemic diseases, which accounted for nearly 5.1 percent of the country's total mortality at the time.[42] These ground realities, and the findings of the 1959 Report on the Revision of the Patent Laws that India's drug prices were among the highest in the world, as a direct result of the nation's over-reliance on imported medicines, led to amendments to the 1974 Patent Act to disallow product patents and paved the way for India to become the pharmacy of the developing world, as was discussed in Chapter 1.[43]

The realities under these circumstances should also consider the constitutional mandate (Brazil's universal coverage mandate, for instance) and the access capacity of the population, and should enable innovation without compromising public health. An efficient innovation regime based on the facts of local life must consider such political realities as the strength of the rule of law, the willingness of political leadership to take tough decisions in the national interest, and civil and political rights enshrined and protected through a written constitution. It was in keeping with such political realities that in 1971 Brazil abrogated patent protection for pharmaceutical manufacturing processes in the interest of access to medicines for its poor citizens, and created a state-owned enterprise and a master plan for policy implementation, supervised directly by the president of the country.[44]

Enabling local innovation necessitates a careful calibration of protecting creators' rights in balance with contemporary needs, seeking to balance need with inventor's greed. *Need,* by definition, will be different for different members and will be determined by the local realities. For example, data on the state of public health and nutrition, collected through various initiatives

[42] *See* Edward C. Walterscheid, *The Early Evolution of the United States Patent Law: Antecedents (Part II)*, 76 J. Pat. & Trademark Off. Soc'y 849, 855 (1994); *see also* Gov't of India Plan. Comm'n, The First Five Year Plan 197–98; *see also* Rebecca Robboy & Durudee Sirichanya, *India Shows Mixed Progress in the War Against Poverty,* World Bank (Aug. 26, 1997), https://web.archive.org/web/20010913214707/http://www.worldbank.org/html/extdr/extme/1449.htm (last visited Oct. 20, 2025); *see also India Achievements and Challenges in Reducing Poverty,* A World Bank Country Study (Jun. 1997), https://documents1.worldbank.org/curated/en/232941468756917265/pdf/multi-page.pdf (last visited Oct. 24, 2025).

[43] N. Rajagopala Ayyangar, Report on the Revision of Patents Law 126–27 (1959), https://ipindia.gov.in/writereaddata/Portal/Images/pdf/1959-_Justice_N_R_Ayyangar_committee_report.pdf (last visited Oct. 20, 2025).

[44] *See* Christopher S. Mayer, *The Brazilian Pharmaceutical Industry Goes Walking from Ipanema to Prosperity: Will the New Intellectual Property Law Spur Domestic Investment?*, 12 Temp. Int'l & Compar. L.J. 377, 378 (1998).

and surveys by governmental and nongovernmental organizations, could help highlight localized health-care needs and serve as the Lockean limitation on exclusive rights of patentee to enable local innovation. In India, government-backed surveys such as the National Family Health Survey (NFHS) provide crucial public-health and nutritional data: infant, child, and maternal mortality rates; nutritional status of women and children; prevalence of nutritional deficiencies such as anemia; prevalence of obesity and other non-communicable lifestyle diseases; and so on—which serve as key policy inputs enabling the national government to improve national health-care access.

In essence, the value of a particular invention and the resultant innovation shouldn't be divorced from local realities but should instead be correlated with evidence-based needs and abilities or disabilities of the society to access that innovation, particularly innovation related to lifesaving drugs.

2.4 The Contractual Theory

In his classic treatise on patent law, George Curtis defined patents from a contractual standpoint as a "grant by the government, to the author of a new and useful invention, of the exclusive right, for a term of years, of practicing that invention."[45] Curtis reflected that the consideration for the grant "is the benefit to the society resulting from the invention."[46] From this perspective, which views patent law through the lens of contract law, an inventor is obligated by a patent to provide benefits to the public in exchange for the public's refrainment from appropriating the patented invention. Thus, the inventor's obligation translates into society's right to expect benefits from the invention.

Therefore, the law of contracts provides a fitting construct of the rights-duty paradigm. Contracts being private transactions, reposition patents as a government grant that confers exclusive rights for a limited period in exchange for the inventor disclosing the invention information which will enter the public domain upon the expiry of the patent term. Hence, the duty that is imposed on a party to the agreement becomes a voluntary undertaking by the inventor in exchange for the grant, and the privity involved

[45] George Ticknor Curtis, A Treatise on the Law of Patents for Useful Inventions in the United States of America 1 (2d ed., 1854).

[46] *Id.*

can be effectively used to impose a duty over the inventor in exchange for the correlative obligation. Such imposition becomes a functional aspect of the grant. The inconvenient factor, however, is figuring out the constituents of the imposed duty in each of these grants.

The contractual nature of patents is clearly outlined in the TRIPS Agreement, which confers certain exclusive rights to the patent-holder (under Article 28) in exchange for the fulfillment of certain correlative duties (laid out in Article 29), chiefly, the condition that the patent applicant could be required to disclose the invention and the best mode of carrying it out in a sufficiently clear and complete manner.[47] It clearly shows that patent rights aren't unconditional rewards granted to the patentees by governments, but rather conditional rights subject to the fulfillment of correlative duties by the patentees to disseminate information about their invention for the benefit of society. India's 1974 Patent Act succinctly lays out the duties of a patent-holder as a condition for the availability of exclusive rights over patented inventions, and the general principles applicable to working of a patented invention for the purpose of compulsory licensing in case of non-working, under Section 83, which include among others, commercial working of patented invention in India, contribution to the promotion of technological innovation, transfer and dissemination of technology, and promotion of public interest.[48]

2.5 The Imperative Theory

H.L.A. Hart, in alluding to Jeremy Bentham's conception of the law of contracts, differentiates the imposition of duty by way of the law of contract as being "'incomplete' in a more radical way than the law underlying the institution of property."[49] Part of the reason for the incomplete status is because acts that fall within the determination of the duty paradigm are left undefined. Hart himself suggests that "this open area may be restricted in a greater or lesser degree by the law's insertion of compulsory clauses into contracts, or by its refusal to recognize the validity of certain types of agreement." Thus, the general law of power of agency can insert regulations of

[47] *See* TRIPS Agreement art. 28–29.
[48] *See* The Patent Act, 1970, § 83, No. 39, Acts of Parliament, 1970 (India).
[49] H.L.A. Hart, Essays on Bentham 165, 209 (1982).

varying degrees. Using contracts as a mechanism would require the inventor to be brought within the scope of the duty created by general law limited by the constitutional mandate of the progress of science. Thus, the inventor falls into the exercise of the power of *imperation*—a power to "procure persons to act in conformity with a command . . . providing motivation influencing their will."[50]

The general imperative theory has its basis in the power of legislative and administrative bodies to create rules and regulations that result in increased effectiveness or efficiencies. In the context of patents, the power of imperative would be dependent on the exclusive rights granted under a contract limited by the regulations that seek to achieve the mandate of the Constitution.[51] Notably, the mandate of every constitution is tied to national needs and local realities, which tend to vary from country to country. India's constitution mandates that the state apply certain fundamental principles in its governance, which include, under Article 47, raising the level of nutrition and the standard of living of its people and improving public health.[52] These constitutional mandates led the post-independence Indian government to act swiftly to address its dire public-health and economic issues by establishing Hindustan Antibiotics Limited (HAL) in 1954 to manufacture antibiotics locally, as the foundational step toward building a robust domestic manufacturing industry for generic pharmaceuticals.

Similarly, Brazil's Constitution, under Article 5, grants a fundamental right to authors of industrial inventions of temporary privilege for their usage as well as protection of intellectual property rights, *subject to* the social interest and the priorities for technological and economic development of the country.[53] Article 6 grants a social right to health—a social interest to which the rights of authors in their IP creations under Article 5 could be conditioned.[54] These constitutional mandates were the philosophical underpinnings of the Brazilian polity that enabled the development of the domestic generic-drug industry by not providing for any patent protection till as late as 1994.

Thus, the principles and ideals laid down in countries' constitutional laws lie at the core of local political realities that influence not just a nation's

[50] *Id.* at 201.

[51] Srividhya Ragavan, *Correlative Obligation in Patent Law: The Role of Public Good in Defining the Limits of Patent Exclusivity*, 6 N.Y.U. J. INTELL. PROP. & ENT. L. 47, 77 (2016).

[52] *See* India Const. art. 47.

[53] *See* Constituição Federal [C.F.] [Constitution] art. 5 (Braz.).

[54] *Id.*, art. 6.

domestic laws bearing on its IP and trade regime but also its policies regarding industrialization and public health.

2.6 The Incentive Theory on Patents

Of the several theories that have been proposed to justify the patent system, the incentive theory is the most prevalent.[55] It is premised on the basis that patents serve as an incentive for inventors to disclose information that they otherwise would not. In exchange for the disclosure, the inventors receive a monopoly right for a certain period during which they are exclusively entitled to use the knowledge claimed by their patents.[56] This period of exclusive rights allows inventors, in the absence of competition, to recoup their investment costs along with some profits, and thus serves as an incentive to encourage new inventions.[57] In substance, patent rights can best be understood as exclusionary rights over knowledge or information. Information is thus central to patent rights.

In the economics of information, knowledge or information has the characteristics of "public goods." As noted by Paul Samuelson in his seminal 1954 article on public expenditure, public goods have two main characteristics: *non-rivalrousness* and *non-excludability*. These two characteristics are central to understanding the efficiency of patents as an incentive for innovation.[58]

The first characteristic relates to *rivalrousness* in the consumability of the good. For non-rivalrous goods, one person's consumption of the good does not extinguish another person's ability to consume the same good. It can be either an intangible good, such as information, or (to an extent) a tangible good, such as public roads. Therefore, in the case of non-rivalrous goods, another person can freely "consume" or "enjoy" the same "product," as there is no marginal cost associated with each additional person's consumption of that good. This contrasts with private goods, which can be consumed by one person to the exclusion of another.

[55] William Fisher, Theories of Intellectual Property 9–10 (2001).
[56] *See* Robert P. Merges, Justifying Intellectual Property 150 (2011) (discussing the role of proportionality).
[57] *Id.*
[58] Paul A. Samuelson, *The Pure Theory of Public Expenditure*, 36 Rev. Econ. & Stats. 387, 387 (1954); *see also* Suzanne Scotchmer, Innovation and Incentives 44–46 (2004).

The second characteristic relates to *non-excludability*. Excludability refers to the ease with which one person's use of a good excludes another person's use of the same good. Common examples that exhibit aspects of non-excludability include public parks, public roads, and light from lighthouses.

Hence, exclusivity rights tied with the grant of patent ought to incentivize the kind of innovation and disseminate the type of information that are closely correlated with the local needs of the society. If such rights incentivize innovation or disseminate information that is not relevant to the socioeconomic needs of the locale or that is in conflict with local political realities, then it leads to a mere presumption risk of the innovation benefiting the society without actually benefiting it. Such presumption risks transform patents from supposedly public goods to a bundle of private rights, with their characteristic excludability and rivalrousness, that erode the efficiency of the patent system to incentivize innovation for the larger public benefit.

3. Presumption Risk of Taking Patents as Proxy for Innovation

3.1 Innovation Inefficiencies of the Patent System

The dual characteristics of information goods (or information embedded in goods)—that they are non-rivalrous and non-excludable—mean that there are no marginal costs associated with each additional use or consumption of the goods. Since there are no marginal costs, it is more efficient to distribute information or knowledge goods freely than to charge for them. Thus, to restrict non-excludable goods, in the way that patent right excludes others from utilizing information covered by a particular patent, an external or state intervention is required. Once a good covered by a patent right enters the market, unless it is sold at a perfectly competitive price point, it will invariably result in excluding potential buyers who could have afforded the good if it had been priced competitively.

Consumability of private goods protected by patent monopolies is closely associated with the consumer *in that particular market*. Patent monopolies thus lead to an underutilization of knowledge, which inherently has a marginal cost of zero but is charged as at least a marginal cost because of state-granted exclusion rights. This is referred to as *static inefficiency*, and it leads to what is known as a *deadweight loss*.[59]

The deadweight loss of the patent system is deemed necessary because the system is viewed as an incentive to encourage innovation. In the health context, this deadweight loss is represented by deaths and other health losses due to exclusion rights. *Disability-adjusted life years* (DALYs)[60] represent the time lost when consumers who could have purchased a drug at production cost are unable to purchase the drug at its current sale price.[61]

Scholars and courts[62] have tended to associate the twin functions of the patent system as encouraging innovation (incentivizing) and disseminating information.[63] Over time, each of these outcomes has come to represent interrelated functions, whether they in fact perform such functions or not. Incentive is a deadweight that has contributed to the distortions and inefficiencies of the system.

In contemporary times, incentivization has become the basis for increasing effectiveness and efficiencies. While this theory and its underpinnings have flourished doctrinally, the empirical basis for implementing patent policy using these justifications as a basis—especially in comparison with other innovation systems—has been the subject of much debate. In the 1950s, Fritz Machlup famously noted in a report commissioned by the US Congress that there was insufficient evidence to justify creating a patent system if one had not already existed, as well as insufficient evidence to justify abolishing an existing system.[64] More than sixty years later, Mark Lemley noted that we

[59] Kenneth Arrow, *Economic Welfare and the Allocation of Resources for Invention*, *in* The Rate and Direction of Inventive Activity: Economic and Social Factors 609, 623 (1962). Suzanne Scotchmer, Innovation and Incentives 36 (2004).

[60] The metric currently used by the WHO to quantify the burden of disease is a Disability-Adjusted Life Year (DALY). *See Disability-adjusted Life Years (DALYs)*, World Health Org., https://www.who.int/data/gho/indicator-metadata-registry/imr-details/156 (last visited Oct. 20, 2025).

[61] *See generally* William W. Fisher & Talha Syed, A Prize System as a Partial Solution to the Health Crises in the Developing World 23–25 (2008), https://www.law.berkeley.edu/files/Fisher_Prizes12.pdf (last visited Oct. 20, 2025).

[62] Benjamin N. Roin, *The Disclosure Function of the Patent System (or Lack Thereof)*, 118 Harv. L. Rev. 2007 (2005); *see also* Timothy R. Holbrook, *Possession in Patent Law*, 59 SMU L. Rev. 123 (2006); *see also* Eldred v. Ashcroft, 537 U.S. 186, 227 (2003) (Stevens, J., dissenting). See also Sony Corp. of Am. v. Universal City Studios, Inc., 464 U.S. 417, 429 (1984). *See, e.g.*, Pfaff v. Wells Elecs., Inc., 525 U.S. 55, 63 (1998) (stating that the patent system should be thought of as "a carefully crafted bargain that encourages both the creation and the public disclosure of new and useful advances in technology, in return for an exclusive monopoly for a limited period of time").

[63] *See generally* U.S. Pat. & Trademarks Off., The Story of the American Patent System: 1790-1940 (1953). *See also* Roberto Mazzoleni & Richard R. Nelson, *The Benefits and Costs of Strong Patent Protection: A Contribution to the Current Debate*, 27 Res. Pol'y 273, 274–300 (1998).

[64] S. Rep. No. 85-236, at 32–33 (1958) (discussing four theses that are offered for patent protection: (i) the "natural-law" thesis; (ii) the "reward-by-monopoly" thesis; (iii) the "monopoly-profit-incentive" thesis; and (iv) the "exchange-for-secrets" thesis, and further elaborating on the last thesis

now have plenty of evidence on several different nuances of IP and yet are no closer to clear answers.[65] He adds that the picture painted by all this evidence is extraordinarily complex.[66] And despite the plethora of evidence, IP policy influencers still tend to fall into "faith-based" positions on the incentivization prowess of the patent system.

One such position was taken by Benjamin Butterworth, the US commissioner of patents in 1883–85 and 1897–98, who, while discussing the effects of the patent system on the United States, explained the essentials of exclusivity as "there would be very few inventions if others have the equal right, without the permission of the inventor and discoverer, to manufacture, use, and sell the thing invented or discovered."[67]

Viewing the above broadly from the perspective of an efficient legal framework, a legal system that confers or allows for the presence of equal or even comparable power (of exclusivity) on more than one holder cannot capture true innovations. Under these conditions, there may be too many substitutable products, which can effectively dilute the effect of the power of exclusivity. That is, too many power holders will neutralize the effect of exclusivity. In terms of rights and duties, the aggregation of the rights of the patent holder (as opposed to enlargement of the scope) can be disproportionate when compared to the correlative duty—a point that I describe as *over-protection*. In such situations, each patent holder's exclusivity is circumscribed by the presence of other players. The effect of this is that each of the patent holders will alter the norms relative to the others. In turn, this would lead to a rivalrous effect on competition in the market. As each power holder alters the norms, the rivalrous effect causes the power holders to consolidate their powers.

The best example of the above proposition is in software patents. As the number of patents on the same or similar technology increased, corporations increasingly tended to consolidate—that is, to accumulate software patents to create a portfolio. For instance, in 2011 Apple, Microsoft, and RIM, calling themselves Rockstar Bidco, bought Nortel for its patent portfolio for US$4.5

that it works on the premise that in the absence of patent protection inventors would keep their inventions secret in order to prevent competitors from exploiting them).

[65] Mark A. Lemley, *Property, Intellectual Property, and Free Riding*, 83 Tex. L. Rev. 1031, 1065–69 (2005).

[66] *Id.*

[67] Letter from the Hon. Benjamin Butterworth, Commissioner of Patents, to the Cincinnati Convention of Inventors (Mar. 23, 1884).

billion, defeating Google's bid. In 2012 Google bought Motorola Mobility's patent for US$12.5 billion. Today each of these companies remains engaged in wars over different patent portfolios. Under these conditions, the market value from any single invention is limited. Consequently, the system tends to produce more patents, each with limited value as well as inventiveness.

Arguably, these conditions are most conducive to generating more patents, though their ability to promote the progress of science remains suspect; more research will be required to substantiate their claims. Indeed, whether the system incentivizes patents or creativity remains moot.

Similarly, a regime that indirectly promotes, say, egregious rights—another form of overprotection—by offering limited exceptions to the rights of the patent holder (for instance, no scope for compulsory licensing) results in an increased incentive to merely patent. Under such circumstances, excessive rights packages can lead to resentment at the system. The music industry's struggle to prevent downloading provides an example of disproportionate protection that has led to disobedience.

Arguably, the inventor's creative potential may also be short-circuited. A good example of this phenomenon would be the debates over the patenting of isolated genes. Justice Stephen Breyer in *Mayo v. Prometheus* (2012) opined that while the "promise of exclusive rights provides monetary incentives that lead to creation, invention, and discovery," such rights can also "impede the flow of information that might permit, indeed spur, invention. . . ."[68] Thus, largesse in the rights package can lead to two undesirable outcomes: first, by creating an imbalanced obligation and detrimentally affecting the benefits of exclusivity for the inventor, and second, by preventing the achievement of the targeted objective of the system.

Alternatively, a legal system that confers only limited powers on the patent holder will fail to capture all innovations. Thus, lack of adequate protection, or under-protection, can also act as a disincentive.

3.2 Operational Posture of Patents Delinked from Its Goals

The protection afforded by the patent system has clear economic objectives. By granting exclusive rights to the patent holder to use and sell the patented products, and legally preventing the appropriation of economically valuable

[68] Mayo Collaborative Servs. v. Prometheus Lab'ys, Inc., 566 U.S. 66, 92 (2012).

information by rivals without compensation, it seeks to promote investments in the creation of innovative products and processes and to maximize the patent holder's ability to commercialize his or her patent.[69] This, in turn, works to incentivize others to invest in innovative products or processes by proportionally adjusting the risks involved.[70]

Over time, scholarly discussions posit patents in such operational terms. The patent lattice, in its operational posture, is best defined as being conceived entirely in property terms, covered in a contractual blanket, and designed to capture the objectives of enhancing public benefit by incentivizing creativity. Such a framework has been essentially deployed to support the institutional notions and goals that the patent system is functioning to ultimately achieve its stated objectives.

Scholars, and indeed courts as well, suggest that such an operational construction has had the laudable impact of resulting in more patents. Patents are generally understood to denote innovation, which is understood as a public benefit. Thus, the operational conception of patents has the benefit of encapsulating patent law with the appealing sheen of producing public benefit.

Other scholars have stepped back further to examine innovation tradeoffs, comparing patents as one method of innovation against other methods such as prize systems and government funding.[71] In several sectors, reasonable returns on investment can be achieved to varying extents by non-patent-based mechanisms such as first-mover advantage, brand recognition, and need for the innovation at the local level.

Scholars have also demonstrated that granting strong patent rights tends to encourage activity that can be patented rather than innovative activity per se, even when the more innovative activity or activity associated with higher social welfare may be easier and cheaper to engage in.[72] The fault lines in international systems become brighter when they are divorced from local

[69] Keith E. Maskus, *Intellectual Property Rights and Economic Development*, 32 Case W. Rsrv. J. Int'l L. 471, 473 (2000), https://scholarlycommons.law.case.edu/jil/vol32/iss3/4/ (last visited Oct. 20, 2025).

[70] *Id.*

[71] *See* Dov Greenbaum, *Patent Sharing in Biotechnology*, *in* Patent Pledges: Global Perspectives on Patent Law's Private Ordering Frontier 65–66 (Jorge L. Contreras & Meredith Jacob eds., 2017); *see also Delink the Price of Drugs from the Cost of Research*, Health Impact Fund, https://healthimpactfund.org/en/ (last visited Oct. 20, 2025).

[72] Amy Kapcynzski & Talha Syed, *The Continuum of Excludability and the Limits of Patents*, 122 Yale L.J. 1900, 1942–43 (2013).

issues, which would have to be addressed first before fully graduating into the international regime.

For such reasons, crucial questions continue to plague all forms of IP rights, but particularly patents that can be lifesaving, such as pharmaceutical patents, and patents that can promote growth and development, such as computer-related technologies. Whether the current system of protection and regulation for pharmaceuticals yields the intended objectives of the system, such as public benefit and health equity, remains unclear. This question has become relevant from a perspective of both national and international norms.

The issue becomes exacerbated when considered in the context of contemporary technologies. It is unclear whether an increase in the number of patents and improved technological capabilities, such as the use of artificial intelligence (AI), have translated into any benefits in health-care access for the larger society. For instance, AI has enabled faster output of clinical trial information and better data, vastly benefiting pharmaceutical companies,[73] but whether these have resulted in better health-care access—as evidenced by, for example, innovation or access metrics—remains to be seen. The answers to these questions become critical as they continue to permit the trade-off of static inefficiencies and deadweight losses.

The key reason behind these unanswered questions is that the patent law has long suffered from lacking a realistic scale to measure its output, which has conveniently led the way for technical measures to become predicates of its outcome. Perhaps the heavy reliance on utilitarianism has resulted in an approach that measures success based on an aggregated outcome rather than individual outcomes.[74] As Shubha Ghosh has pointed out, a measure of success under the utilitarian theory would consider technical success first and consequences second.[75]

Scholars and even courts have expressed discontent over the outcome of the quality of innovation as well as the disclosure.[76] It is also unclear how

[73] Jonathan Kimball & Srividhya Ragavan, *AI (Re)Defining Pharmaceutical Exclusivities*, 41 Biotechnology L. Rep. 23 (2022).

[74] Shubha Ghosh, *Duty, Consequences, & Intellectual Property*, U. St. Thomas L.J. 801, 808 (2013).

[75] *Id.* at 807–808.

[76] *See* Sean B. Seymore, *The Teaching Function of Patents*, 85 Notre Dame L. Rev. 621, 641, 667–69 (2010) (asserting that the patent document should be readable if it is to fully perform its teaching function); *see also* Charles Duhigg & Steve Lohr, *The Patent Used as a Sword*, N.Y. Times (Oct. 7, 2012), https://www.nytimes.com/2012/10/08/technology/patent-wars-among-tech-giants-can-stifle-competition.html (last visited Oct. 20, 2025); *see also* Roin, *supra* note 62; In re Bilski, 545 F.3d 943, 1004 (Fed. Cir. 2008) (J. Mayer's dissent) (observing that the low threshold for patent eligibility has resulted in patents ranging from the somewhat ridiculous to the truly absurd).

to determine, as a policy measure, a specific contextual calibration for all innovations that equitably allows for recouping investment costs while providing adequate incentives to innovate without becoming excessive or insufficient, both of which are harmful. Specifically, the pharmaceutical industry has been loath to reveal actual investment and R&D costs, making it nearly impossible to perform this policy calculus.

A dissection of the iterative elements that form the operational aspect of the patenting system is essential to achieve the conceived end rather than just any end. That this exercise is bound to be self-reflective, especially in a capitalist system, is to be expected. That it may require weaving or even supplementing a more distributive notion to the system is conceded. Such an exercise promises to take us closer to a balance that can help achieve the original objectives of the system.

3.3 A Health-Care System Delinked from Local Realities

Achieving such a balance isn't a utopian dream. Several European nations with populations that are relatively well-off have strong socialized health-care systems, under which large amounts of government spending go into health care. These nations, by no coincidence, tend to have the healthiest populations in the world.[77]

Coincidentally, in the early 2020s the United States led the rest of the world in per-person spending on health care with an expenditure of US$10,931, while various Western European nations spent between approximately US$5,000 and US$10,000.[78] By comparison, the developing countries of Brazil, South Africa, and India have seen approximate health expenditures of

See generally Adam B. Jaffe & Josh Lerner, Innovation and Its Discontents: How Our Broken Patent System Is Endangering Innovation and Progress, and What to Do About It 170 (2002).

[77] *Healthiest Countries 2024*, World Population Rev., https://worldpopulationreview.com/country-rankings/healthiest-countries (last visited Oct. 20, 2025).

[78] *Current Health Expenditure per Capita (Current US$)–India*, World Bank Grp., https://data.worldbank.org/indicator/SH.XPD.CHEX.PC.CD?locations=IN&most_recent_value_desc=true (last visited Oct. 20, 2025); "The health expenditure estimates have been prepared by the World Health Organization under the framework of the System of Health Accounts 2011 (SHA 2011). The Health SHA 2011 tracks all health spending in a given country over a defined period of time regardless of the entity or institution that financed and managed that spending." *Metadata Glossary: Out-of-Pocket Expenditure (% of Current Health Expenditure)*, World Bank Grp., https://databank.worldbank.org/metadataglossary/world-development-indicators/series/SH.XPD.OOPC.CH.ZS (last visited Oct. 20, 2025) Data from 2019 was used to remove distortions due to Covid-19 effects.

merely US$850, US$551, and US$61, respectively![79] In the least-developed nations, where individual capacity to pay is much lower on average and there is often no health-care coverage at all, per capita spending has been even lower.

Overall, the structure can be seen as a pyramid, in which developed economies tend to provide better health care with varying levels of access than those in developing economies, which, in turn, have health-care and varying levels of access that tend to be better than those in the least-developed economies.

Arguably, higher health-care expenditure does not equate to better health-care access, affordability, or even outcomes. These figures indicate that more money is being spent on health for reasons that may be varied. Nevertheless, taking a wide range of local realities into consideration can result in increasing the per-unit impact of the expenditure.

Besides the impact of health expenditure, another important factor in equitable health-care access is the quality of innovation, which is typically defined by the measure of innovation. But innovation goals have also failed because of a lack of appropriate *fit* or *need*. For a country undergoing a crisis involving the Ebola virus, for example, a breakthrough in throat-cancer treatment would have little relevance or impact.

Moreover, the dissemination function of a patent serves little purpose when dissociated from the *need*. A country that has an Ebola-virus crisis gets little benefit from the dissemination of the throat-cancer patent information. Even if the throat-cancer drug ranks high in the innovation index, the drug will have low impact in the Ebola-infested country. The dissemination function will not be satisfied unless the innovation index can translate into useful dissemination in the form of immediate or future transfer of technology, embody the promise of distribution, and facilitate access. Otherwise, the drug is like a shining beacon on top of a mountain with no use for the population that lives in the dark valley surrounding it. Hence, the dissemination function should be associated with local realities to ensure that the needs of those localities are fulfilled.

[79] *Global Health Expenditure Database*, World Health Org., https://apps.who.int/nha/database (last visited Oct. 20, 2025) (choose "2019" from the Years dropdown; then choose "Brazil", "India", and "South Africa" from the Countries dropdown; then, under the Indicators dropdown, click "INDICATORS" then "AGGREGATES" then "Current Health Expenditure (CHE) per Capita in US$").

There are strong arguments that the patent system is governed more by geopolitical importance than by policy priorities, and thus does not seriously attempt, or perhaps even allow for, the necessary adjustments.[80] The so-called flexibilities and exceptions within the patent regime exist to ensure that a balance is maintained, but they have often been relegated to mere textual usage, with threats of sanctions and other methods of geopolitical pressure applied to countries that may choose to use them.[81] Flexibilities and exceptions are meant specifically to cater to the needs of a particular member state, especially in view of its needs for health-care access and food security. The inherent assumption is that disruptions in one part of the globe can have global effects.

Thus, flexibilities and exceptions are always tailored to social needs, with a close nexus to local realities. The need to cater to public-health issues *locally* by creating adequate flexibilities and exceptions should be the first step toward fulfilling *global* international obligations.

3.4 Skewed Rights–Duties Paradigm

IP law, particularly patent law, is arguably a gross misfit within the traditional property regime. Real property, for example, rarely permits absolute ownership, since it is regularly subject to public-interest considerations, eminent domain being one example of public-interest intrusion on private property rights. Unlike real-property law, in which the components of ownership and the ensuing exclusivity establish societal orderliness, the patents paradigm is considered as the natural means to the larger public-benefit end. As such, the establishment of exclusive privileges is predicated as the direct by-product of patent law's shared roots with property law.[82]

[80] *See* Swaraj Paul Barooah, *India's Pharmaceutical Innovation Policy: Developing Strategies for Developing Country Needs*, 5 Trade L. & Dev. 150, 166 (2013). It may be more accurate to say that powerful actors prevent the optimal usage of IP policy levers.

[81] Michael Palmedo & Srividhya Ragavan, *The U.S. Posture on Global Access to Medication & The Case for Change*, 11 Indian J. Intell. Prop. L. 76, 80–81 (2020).

[82] James Bessen & Michael J. Meurer, Patent Failure: How Judges, Bureaucrats, and Lawyers Put Innovators at Risk 30–70 (2008) (asserting and outlining the ways in which patent laws do not work well with property rights). *See also* Joseph E. Stiglitz, *How Intellectual Property Reinforces Inequality*, N.Y. Times (July 14, 2013), https://archive.nytimes.com/opinionator.blogs.nytimes.com/2013/07/14/how-intellectual-property-reinforces-inequality/ (last visited Oct. 20, 2025) ("[T]here are alternatives. Advocates of intellectual property rights have overemphasized their role in promoting innovation. Most of the key innovations—from the basic ideas underlying the computer, to transistors, to lasers, to the discovery of DNA—were not motivated by pecuniary gain. They were motivated by the quest for knowledge").

In any case, the prevailing notions of patents as an extension of property rights has led to construing patents in terms of their "rights" rather than obligations. Further, the lack of a measure of correlative duty corresponding to the rights has contributed to a skewed rights-vs.-duties paradigm of patents. The contemporary view of patent law focuses on the institutions granting a bundle of exclusive (negative) rights, the gaining of which in itself satisfies the twin objectives of encouraging innovation and dissemination of information.[83]

Such a construct dampens the presence of a corresponding (as opposed to correlative) duty and posits the grant of patent entirely within a rights paradigm—thus, the self-serving absoluteness of the protection for the rights regime, within which is deposited a presumed fulfillment of the corresponding duty to discharge the innovation and dissemination objectives of the larger system. Perhaps the corresponding duty arises from the overlay of the law of contracts on top of theories of intellectual-property law. The characteristic feature of contract law, on which IP is heavily based, imposes corresponding obligations or responsibilities on the rights holder.[84]

Shubha Ghosh couches this concept with more precision when he asserts that "while current IP law assumes the primacy of the rights of owners, emphasizing its attachment to the legal ownership, a nuanced consequentialism would recognize the place of the IP owner in a network of relationships that create duties and obligations."[85] Quoting Professor Sen, Ghosh asserts that sensitivity to the consequences of IP rights is sensitivity "to agencies and relations in evaluating what is happening in the world."[86] Thus, for the inventor's rights to be most effective, the invention (or the inventor) should ensure clarity of his obligation to generate an efficient correlative duty, which in turn will contribute toward achieving the ends of the system. Indeed, it amounts to recognition by society of the limits to the power it conferred on the inventor.

[83] H.L.A. Hart, Essays on Bentham, 165, 210 (1982). *See also* Wesley N. Hohfeld, *Some Fundamental Legal Conceptions as Applied in Judicial Reasoning*, 23 Yale L.J. 16, 32 (1913) (arguing that exclusion is considered important in property because it is "crucial to, and protects, a set of use privileges in relation to the res with which the owner is vested").

[84] Srividhya Ragavan, *Correlative Obligation in Patent Law: The Role of Public Good in Defining the Limits of Patent Exclusivity*, 6 N.Y.U. J. Intell. Prop. & Ent. L. 47, 77 (2016).

[85] Shubha Ghosh, *Duty, Consequences, & Intellectual Property*, 10 U. St. Thomas L.J. 801, 815 (2013).

[86] *Id.*

4. The Ground Realities of the Pharmaceutical Sector

4.1 Unique Challenges of the Pharma Sector

The scale and effects of presumption risk are particularly serious in the pharmaceutical sector, which is significantly unusual in at least four respects. First, pharmaceutical innovation has very high research and development (R&D) costs, and regulatory approvals are required before pharmaceuticals can be marketed, entailing expensive clinical trials.[87] Second, drug innovation is a comparatively risky activity entailing high investment with a small success ratio.[88] Third, it is relatively easy to reverse-engineer chemical medicines (although this becomes harder with biologics).[89] Fourth, the cost of (re)manufacturing as compared to inventing or discovering tends to be very low; this is especially true for generic drugs, but even biosimilars are less expensive to produce than biologics.[90]

In addition to the factors mentioned above, a variety of external factors—including insurance, absence of generics and biosimilars, evergreening (developing drugs that are therapeutically similar to patented drugs but with minor changes that make it eligible for a new patent), regulatory delays, supply-chain issues, selection of goods by third parties (doctors), and the need for the medication—may result in redundancy of any lead-time advantage or brand-recognition value that can be obtained from patents for inducing the purchase of goods.[91]

The case for stronger patents is premised on the argument that pharmaceutical investments result in socially desirable outcomes. But this argument ignores the fact that there is a level of certainty to recover the investment, generate a profit, and result in desirable outcomes relevant to the market. This seems to be supported by the data regarding pharmaceutical companies

[87] Alexander Schuhmacher, Markus Hinder, Nikolaj Boger, Dominik Hartl, & Oliver Gassmann, *The Significance of Blockbusters in the Pharmaceutical Industry*, NATURE REVS. DRUG DISCOVERY (Dec. 12, 2022), https://www.nature.com/articles/d41573-022-00213-z (last visited Oct. 20, 2025); *see also* David E. Adelman & K. L. DeAnglis, *Patent Metrics: The Mismeasure of Innovation in the Biotech Patent Debate*, 85 TEX. L. REV. 1677, 1679–80 (2007) (discussing the proliferation of low-quality patents that do not contribute to innovation or the public benefit).

[88] *Id. See* Aylin Sertkaya, Trinidad Beleche, Amber Jessup, & Benjamin D. Sommers, *Costs of Drug Development and Research and Development Intensity in the U.S., 2000–2018*, JAMA, June 28, 2024, at 1, 2, https://pmc.ncbi.nlm.nih.gov/articles/PMC11214120/ (last visited Oct. 20, 2025).

[89] Srividhya Ragavan, *Make America Healthy: Reducing High Pharmaceutical Prices Without Reducing Innovation* 77 SMU LAW REVIEW 787, 811–22 (2024).

[90] *Id.* at 811.

[91] *Id.* at 820.

centering their business strategy around patent rights, although the outcomes are often assumed rather than specifically measured relative to the market.

However, "all that these facts show, respectively, is that some mechanism is necessary to promote innovation in this sector and that those firms that dominate under the current system are dependent on the tools that brought them to dominance."[92] While such factors as branding strategies and product hopping can affect the market perception and value of a drug, exclusivity and the resulting monopoly are undoubtedly important factors in pharmaceutical pricing, and monopoly status typically helps in recouping investment costs. Whether exclusivity is the lone enabler for incentivization and innovation remains in question.

4.2 Challenges in Drug Pricing

While it is clear that the cost of R&D in pharmaceutical innovation is very large, the question of how large has been a notoriously difficult one to answer.[93] The question is particularly significant considering that pharmaceutical companies tend to claim that high R&D costs dictate the price of a product.[94] The lack of clarity on this issue is perhaps one reason for the lack of incentive to pursue region-specific diseases.[95]

Since pharmaceutical companies receive most of their revenue from the United States, Europe, and Japan, they focus their investment on these markets.[96] In the United States, pharmaceutical pricing is left to market

[92] Amy Kapczynski et al., *Addressing Global Health Inequities: An Open Licensing Approach for University Innovations*, 20 BERKELEY TECH. L.J. 1031, 1045 (2005).

[93] Joseph A. DiMasi et al., *The Price of Innovation: New Estimates of Drug Development Costs*, 22 J. HEALTH ECON. 151, 180–81 (2003) (estimating costs of a new drug to be $802 million). This study was challenged by Donald Light on a number of factors including response bias, sampling bias, and failure to account for government subsidies. Donald W. Light & Rebecca N. Warburton, *Extraordinary Claims Require Extraordinary Evidence*, 24 J. HEALTH ECON. 1030, 1031–32 (2005).

[94] For example, during the Kefauver hearings in the US Senate in 1959–1962, the industry's principal justification for its high prices on patented drugs was the high cost of R&D. Daniel C. Morgan & Samuel E. Allison, *The Kefauver Drug Hearings in Perspective*, 45 SW. SOC. SCI Q. 59, 66 (1964) (discussing the impact of the Kefauver-Harris Drug Amendments of 1962 on the pharmaceutical industry and the regulation of drugs in the United States); *see also 2 Drug Companies Deny Price Fixing*, N.Y. TIMES (August 13, 1963).

[95] *See generally* Amy Kapczynski et al., *Polymorphs and Prodrugs and Salts (Oh My!): An Empirical Analysis of "Secondary" Pharmaceutical Patents*, PLOS ONE (Dec. 5, 2012), https://journals.plos.org/plosone/article?id=10.1371/journal.pone.0049470 (last visited Oct. 20, 2025); Roger Collier, *Drug Patents: The Evergreening Problem*, 185 CAN. MED. ASS'N J. 385, 385–86 (2013) (discusses the practice of "evergreening" in the pharmaceutical industry, wherein drug companies make minor changes or improvements to existing drugs and then seek new patents to extend their monopolies).

[96] *See e.g.*, INTERNATIONAL MEDIA SUPPORT, IMS WORLD REVIEW (2009).

competition. But government grants favoring large companies can create private wealth in the form of broad patents and corporate-centric regulatory policies.[97]

The current state of the health-care market raises questions as to whether the supra-marginal pricing encouraged by exclusive patent rights results in an equivalent enhancement in innovation. This issue becomes more complex when the question is considered within a global paradigm of public health and welfare. While patents can lead to monopolies, the fact is that *any* supra-competitive pricing leads to deadweight loss, regardless of whether there is monopolistic power in the marketplace. In the context of medicines, this static inefficiency directly affects access to medicine, since it acts as a price barrier to needed health care and medication.[98]

Unlike consumer products, for which the elasticity of individual human needs may vary with affordability, the demand for pharmaceuticals is independent of affordability.[99] The effect of cost efficiency on the demand for medication is minimal, owing to the continued needs of patients and the lack of alternatives.[100] In markets with low per capita income, cost increases reduce affordability and worsen disease conditions, which in turn increase the demand for medication, thus raising the need to prioritize access.

Notably, patients rarely make decisions to purchase medications—especially life-saving drugs—except through intermediaries such as doctors and insurance companies. This naturally creates conflict-of-interest situations between the intermediaries and the beneficiaries. Both intermediaries and beneficiaries are thus invested in the system, along with other significant players such as hospitals, pharmaceutical companies, shareholders, and regulatory bodies.

Thus, a system that empowers and protects an increasing number of invested players, such as patent holders, intermediaries, and beneficiaries,

[97] Srividhya Ragavan & Swaraj P. Barooah, *Historic Tensions Involving International Intellectual Property Protection of Medical Technology with Disastrous Public Health Consequences*, 54 SETON HALL L. REV. 339, (2023).

[98] Srividhya Ragavan, *The Jekyll and Hyde Story of Internation Trade: The Supreme Court in* PhRMA v. Walsh *and the TRIPS Agreement*, 38 U. RICH. L. REV. 777, 798 (2004).

[99] *Id.* at 783. *See* Mary T. Griffin, *AIDS Drugs & the Pharmaceutical Industry: A Need for Reform*, 17 AM. J.L. & MED. 363, 367–69 (1991) (discussing the unique price and demand aspects of the pharmaceutical market).

[100] *See id.* at 370 ("Price competition is an integral part of the free-market enterprise system in this country, but not of the pharmaceutical industry."); *id.* at 372 (explaining how prices tend to increase when no treatment substitutes exist).

risks making patient welfare just one of several goals of the system rather than the main goal.

4.3 Blurred Pharma R&D Focus

Patents may arguably actively impede the rate of socially beneficial innovation. As discussed previously, it may be more beneficial for the innovator to invest less in new research than in "evergreening," developing therapeutically similar "me-too" drugs with a different active ingredient.[101] Additionally, the social value added by the me-too drug is disproportionately less than the private benefit that the innovator typically receives. A trend toward oligopolistic practices within therapeutic class levels also tends to ensure high rates of profits for the innovator.

Consequently, the patent system seems capable of distorting the direction of research and blurring the relevance of outcomes relative to the goals.[102] In any case, innovators will naturally direct their research toward patents that are likely to result in more profits. This is significant in areas such as pharmaceuticals, leading to a significant social loss owing to a lack of research focused on diseases prevalent in developing countries with "weaker" markets, rare diseases, and a bias toward maintenance drugs.[103] The profit incentive arguably encourages the development of more expensive therapeutically useful drugs, like biologics, even as the greater human need is for more efficient approaches to reducing the disease burden, both nationally and internationally.

Much has been written about resource allocation among competitive firms and the resulting inefficacies in allocating risks.[104] Resource waste as a

[101] Evergreening exists in several variant forms. Patenting of new dosing routines, of combinations with other drugs, and of esthers, ethers, metabolites, and more soluble versions of the same or similar compounds are all examples of methods for keeping the original product evergreened. *See* Sandeep Kanak Rathod, *Ever-Greening: A Status Check in Selected Countries*, 7 J. Generic Meds. 227, 229 (2010).

[102] Joseph E. Stiglitz, *Economic Foundations of Intellectual Property Rights*, 57 Duke L.J. 1693, 1706 (2008).

[103] Thomas Pogge, *The Health Impact Fund: Better Pharmaceutical Innovations at Lower Prices*, *in* Incentives for Global Health: Patent Law and Access to Essential Medicines 178, 184–85 (Thomas Pogge et al. eds., 2010).

[104] Earlier arguments by Scherer stated that different teams would take different paths to the same goal and that this method of risk allocation is inefficient. *See* Frederic M. Scherer, *Research and Development Resource Allocation Under Rivalry*, 81 Q. J. Econ. 359, 364–66 (1967). However, competitive firms that are not aware of each other's behavior cannot split risk in this manner, as they would not be working in tandem with each other. *See* William W. Fisher & Talha Syed,

consequence of overlapping secretive research activity, driven by the race to be the first to apply for patent rights, can lead to duplicative and wasteful research.[105] As a profit-maximization industry, drug companies naturally look to minimize costs while maximizing profits. However, the result may be to perversely incentivize the production of "me-too" or "evergreened" drugs, in which minor modifications are made to the chemical composition of an existing drug, which often results in a patent thicket.

Alternatively, multiple similar drugs exist within the same therapeutic class, including drugs that are chemically related or have an identical mechanism of action and drugs whose clinical outcomes are nearly identical to those of preexisting (popular) drugs.[106] There may be legitimate reasons to make different drugs within a therapeutic class, such as addressing multiple types of side effects or specific symptoms.[107] Nevertheless, the productivity of the pharmaceutical R&D sector, as measured by the number of therapeutically important new molecules brought to market per dollar spent on R&D, has seen a decline.[108] Such multidrug thickets can result in unjustified static inefficiency that is not balanced by a proportional increase in dynamic efficiency, thus representing a waste of resources. In all these cases, pharmaceutical companies, by already knowing the market-success indicators for drugs that demonstrate a particular therapeutic benefit, seek to allay the risk associated with coming up with new processes while ensuring that their new products still bring in revenues.

A Prize System as a Partial Solution to the Health Crises in the Developing World 14 n.29 (2008), https://www.law.berkeley.edu/files/Fisher_Prizes12.pdf (last visited Oct. 20, 2025). It has been argued that, even if competitive firms are aware of competitive behavior, duplication may still arise, since a particular path of research can still be seen as sufficiently more risk-averse than other paths that even when more than one firm chooses to take that path, they may have greater chances of success than if they take another path to drug discovery and development. *See generally* Michael Kremer & Rachel Glennerster, Strong Medicine: Creating Incentives for Pharmaceutical Research on Neglected Diseases 100–02 (2004).

[105] Steve P. Calandrillo, *An Economic Analysis of Property Rights in Information: Justifications and Problems of Exclusive Rights, Incentives to Generate Information, and the Alternative of a Government-Run Reward System*, 9 Fordham Intell. Prop. Media & Ent. L.J. 301, 329 (1998).

[106] *See generally* Jeffrey K. Aronson & A. Richard Green, *Me-Too Pharmaceutical Products: History, Definitions, Examples, and Relevance to Drug Shortages and Essential Medicines Lists*, 86 Brit. J. Clinical Pharmacology 2114 (2020), https://pmc.ncbi.nlm.nih.gov/articles/PMC7576625/ (last visited Oct. 20, 2025).

[107] *Id.* at 2115–16.

[108] Paul Grootendorst, *Patents, Public-Private Partnerships or Prizes: How Should We Support Pharmaceutical Innovation?* 2 Social and Economic Dimensions of an Aging Population Research Paper, Paper No. 250, 2009, https://ideas.repec.org/p/mcm/sedapp/250.html (last visited Oct. 20, 2025).

Most of the world's population, as well as much of the world's diseased population, lives in developing and least-developed economies.[109] Global populations have varying levels of purchasing capacity dependent on local socioeconomic factors—the local realities. Arguably, the harmonized patent regime perversely incentivizes the marketing of drugs that offer minimal or even negative social-welfare outcomes, in two ways.

First, the patent system, in its current form, works on the promise of recouping investments and generating a profit scaled to those investments, which naturally leads to a focus on research for products that can recoup these investment costs.[110] This especially leaves out diseases that are predominant in poorer economies. While the disease burden in the poorer nations is slowly shifting from communicable diseases to noncommunicable diseases, the former remain significantly present and concerning.[111]

Per the Global Health Estimates in 2019, communicable, maternal, perinatal, and nutritional conditions were responsible for 55 percent and 38 percent of all DALYs losses in low-income and lower-middle-income countries, respectively, but only 12 percent and 5 percent of DALYs losses in upper-middle-income and high-income countries, respectively.[112] Meanwhile, noncommunicable diseases account for 34 percent, 52 percent, 77 percent, and 85 percent of the DALYs lost for low-, lower-middle-, upper-middle-, and high-income countries, respectively.[113] This generally translates into very little, if any, investment or research directed toward poorer markets, as there is little scope for recoupment of investment, and therefore adequate

[109] UN TRADE & DEVELOPMENT, *UN Recognition of the Least Developed Countries*, https://unctad.org/topic/least-developed-countries/recognition#:~:text=Our%20technical%20cooperation%20helps%20developing,Brand%20materials (last visited Oct. 20, 2025). According to WHO's Global Health Observatory, at the end of 2007 low-income groups had a life expectancy of 57 and a healthy life expectancy of 49. At the same time, high-income populations had a life expectancy of 80 and a healthy life expectancy of 70. WHO's data-analyzer application available at *Global Health Estimates: Life Expectancy and Leading Causes of Death and Disability, The Global Health Observatory*, WORLD HEALTH ORGANIZATION, https://www.who.int/data/gho/data/themes/mortality-and-global-health-estimates (last visited Oct. 20, 2025).

[110] *See* ELLEN F. M. 'T HOEN, THE GLOBAL POLITICS OF PHARMACEUTICAL MONOPOLY POWER 81 (2009).

[111] *Global Health Estimates 2020: Deaths by Cause, Age, Sex, by Country and by Region, 2000–2019*, WORLD HEALTH ORG. (2020), https://www.who.int/data/gho/data/themes/mortality-and-global-health-estimates (last visited Oct. 20, 2025).

[112] *Global Health Estimates*, WORLD HEALTH ORG., https://www.who.int/data/global-health-estimates (last visited Oct. 20, 2025). There is a significant change in disease burden for the lower-income countries. In the year 2000, communicable, maternal, perinatal, and nutritional conditions were responsible for 72 percent, 57 percent, 21 percent, and 6 percent of the DALYs for the low-, lower-middle-, higher-middle-, and high-income countries, respectively. *Id.*

[113] *Id.*

incentive to make drugs for these markets rarely exists.[114] Though this problem manifests intranationally as well, the lack of incentives toward poorer market segments is seen more clearly when considering tropical diseases specific to countries in poorer regions.

The infamous example of a neglected disease in this aspect is tuberculosis (TB). According to the WHO, TB is the thirteenth-leading cause of death and the second-highest cause of death by infection worldwide, with an estimated 10.6 million cases in 2022.[115] This is all the more concerning when one realizes how little progress has been made on this front. For example, in 2007 there were an estimated 13.7 million chronic active cases and 1.8 million deaths worldwide, mostly in developing countries.[116] Today the WHO estimates that, on average, about 1.7 million people still die annually due to TB. Thus, although the disease was declared a global health emergency by the WHO in 1993, progress in treating it in the decades since has been very slow.[117]

Second, a focus on treatment has come at the cost of a lesser focus on prevention, such as by vaccinations and control of environmental factors. Preventive mechanisms have several positive spillover effects; however, since their benefit tends to be "invisible"—the absence of disease—it can be difficult to value.

For example, polio, one of the most dreaded infectious childhood diseases of the twentieth century, which mostly affected poor nations,[118] has still not been eradicated, even though two vaccines were created more than seventy years ago.[119] In fact, it has returned to many parts of the world, even as

[114] In general, the reason that the proportion of the disease burden is changing from communicable to noncommunicable diseases is due to the overall increase in life expectancy wherein noncommunicable diseases are more likely. Van Anh Le, *Thailand: Shooting Star for Access to Medicines Through Compulsory Licensing, in* INTELLECTUAL PROPERTY LAW AND ACCESS TO MEDICINE: TRIPS AGREEMENT, HEALTH, AND PHARMACEUTICALS 252, 267 (Srividhya Ragavan & Amaka Vanni eds., 2021).

[115] *Tuberculosis*, WORLD HEALTH ORG. (29 October 2024), https://www.who.int/news-room/fact-sheets/detail/tuberculosis (last visited Oct. 20, 2025).

[116] WORLD HEALTH ORG., WHO REPORT 2009: GLOBAL TUBERCULOSIS CONTROL 12 (2009), https://iris.who.int/server/api/core/bitstreams/9596bc0d-a12d-4bc9-bf0e-4c86f919bb22/content (last visited Oct. 20, 2025).

[117] *Id.* at 33. Indicatively, of the roughly 1,550 New Chemical Entities marketed worldwide between the years 1975 to 2004, only three were for tuberculosis; *see* Swaraj Paul Barooah, *OSDD Successfully Maps TB Genome*, SPICYIP (April 13, 2010), https://spicyip.com/2010/04/osdd-successfully-maps-tb-genome.html (last visited Oct. 20, 2025).

[118] *Poliomyelitis*, WORLD HEALTH ORG. (Oct. 24, 2023) https://www.who.int/en/news-room/fact-sheets/detail/poliomyelitis (last visited Oct. 20, 2025). Common effects included crippling, paralysis, and death. *Id.*

[119] *Id.* "Cases due to wild poliovirus have decreased by over 99% since 1988, from an estimated 350 000 cases in more than 125 endemic countries, to just two endemic countries (as of October 2023)." *Id.*

concerns have grown regarding the diminishing funding aimed at its eradication.[120] The two vaccines work differently, and both are still used today. Significantly, neither of the manufacturers patented their vaccines. According to one set of calculations, Jonas Salk, who developed the first vaccine, could have made US$2–2.5 billion had he patented his vaccine, and Albert Sabin, who developed the second, could have made US$5–6 billion.[121] As a relevant comparison, even after three to four decades of funding and work to reduce polio outbreaks, the Global Polio Eradication Initiative's (GPEI) 2022–2026 strategy for ending polio still required US$4.6 billion for its attempt to eradicate the disease. Successful eradication is expected to result in US$33.1 billion in health cost savings.[122]

Since polio cannot be cured but only prevented, there is no way of knowing precisely how many of the recipients of the vaccine directly benefited from it. Considering that it is an infectious disease, each potential carrier vaccinated represents future benefits for each potential polio victim. However, such networked benefits and unrealized potential harms are extremely difficult to quantify.[123]

Various studies have shown that the cost of insufficient prevention mechanisms such as vaccinations impacts not only population health but also health-care systems, the economy, and global public health.[124] Thus, eradication of an infectious disease, as a "public good," produces large benefits for society at large but results in little incentive for individual action. The WHO estimates that, in 2021, around 25 million children under the age of 1 did not receive basic vaccines.[125] One study shows, however, that,

[120] *Polio Eradication: Falling at the Final Hurdle?*, 400 LANCET 1079, 1079 (2022), https://www.thelancet.com/journals/lancet/article/PIIS0140-6736(22)01875-X/fulltext (last visited Oct. 20, 2025).

[121] *See How Much Money Did Jonas Salk Potentially Forfeit by Not Patenting the Polio Vaccine?*, FORBES (June 30, 2021), https://www.forbes.com/sites/quora/2012/08/09/how-much-money-did-jonas-salk-potentially-forfeit-by-not-patenting-the-polio-vaccine/ (last visited Oct. 20, 2025).

[122] Jaxx Artz, *World Leaders Pledge $2.6 Billion to End Polio at the World Health Summit*, GLOB. CITIZEN (Oct. 18, 2022), https://www.globalcitizen.org/en/content/world-leaders-pledge-to-eradicate-polio/ (last visited Oct. 20, 2025).

[123] *See* Gary S. Marshall, *Roots of Vaccine Hesitancy*, 66 S.D. MED. 52, 55 (2013). There are also surrounding issues such as convincing the public of the necessity to partake in a successful immunization program when the disease in question has already been largely, but not completely, eradicated. This is especially true when there is a risk or perception of risk attached to the vaccine.

[124] Paige M. Farrenkopf, *The Cost of Ignoring Vaccines*, 95 YALE J. BIOLOGY & MED. 265, 268 (2022), https://pmc.ncbi.nlm.nih.gov/articles/PMC9235251/ (last visited Oct. 20, 2025).

[125] "Of the 21 million, just under 60% of these children live in 10 countries: Afghanistan, Angola, the Democratic Republic of the Congo, Ethiopia, India, Indonesia, Nigeria, Pakistan, Sudan and Yemen." *Immunization Coverage*, WORLD HEALTH ORG. (July 15, 2024), https://www.who.int/news-room/fact-sheets/detail/immunization-coverage (last visited Oct. 20, 2025).

in low- and middle-income countries, US$52 is saved for every US$1 spent on immunization programs.[126]

The allocation of limited health resources among preventive and treatment measures can nonetheless be very complicated, raising questions about cost-effectiveness, discounted future returns, and the implicated ethical issues.[127] Cost-effectiveness pervades discussions of both prevention and treatment.[128]

A 2021 Compendium of WHO and other UN Guidance on Health and Environment estimated that around 24 percent of the world's deaths can be attributed to environmental risks to health, which are largely preventable.[129] Similarly, a few decades earlier, a 2006 WHO publication[130] undertook a systematic literature review, surveying over 100 experts worldwide to come out with a comprehensive report on the environmental burden of disease,[131] and notably reported that an estimated 24 percent of the global disease burden and 23 percent of all deaths could be attributed to environmental factors.[132]

In all, it is clear that there is sufficient literature on the interrelation between poverty and health, at both the individual and institutional level, to suggest that poverty is a major factor in the inability to modify these environmental conditions.[133] For instance, the diseases with the largest environmental

[126] *See* So Yoon Sim et al., *Return on Investment from Immunization Against 10 Pathogens in 94 Low- and Middle-Income Countries, 2011–30*, 39 HEALTH AFFS. 1343, 1349 (2020), https://www.healthaffairs.org/doi/10.1377/hlthaff.2020.00103 (last visited Oct. 20, 2025).

[127] Alan Williams, *Intergenerational Equity: An Exploration of the 'Fair Innings' Argument*, 6 HEALTH ECON. 117, 118–21 (1997).

[128] Ramanan Laxminarayan & Lori Ashford, *Using Evidence About "Best Buys" to Advance Global Health, in* FOUNDATIONS OF GLOBAL HEALTH: AN INTERDISCIPLINARY READER 93, 95 (Peter J. Brown and Svea Closser eds., 2019).

[129] *Compendium of WHO and Other UN Guidance on Health and Environment*, WORLD HEALTH ORG. (Sept. 3, 2021), https://www.who.int/tools/compendium-on-health-and-environment (last visited Oct. 20, 2025).

[130] Annette Prüss-Üstün & Carlos Corvalán, *Preventing Disease Through Healthy Environments: Towards an Estimate of the Environmental Burden of Disease*, WORLD HEALTH ORG. (2006), https://www.who.int/publications/i/item/9241593822?ua=1 (last visited Oct. 20, 2025).

[131] *Id.* at 8. The definition of "environment" used by the study was "all the physical, chemical and biological factors external to the human host, and all related behaviours, but excluding those natural environments that cannot reasonably be modified." It thus includes only those factors in the environment that are modifiable. *Id.* at 22.

[132] *Id.* at 9.

[133] Poverty and health (and other factors such as education) are both causes and effects in what is known as the "poverty cycle." *See generally* POVERTY AND HEALTH: A SOCIOLOGICAL ANALYSIS (John Kosa et al. eds., 1969) (examining and analyzing the many ramifications of the poverty-health complex); Adam Wagstaff, *Poverty and Health Sector Inequalities*, 80 BULL. OF THE WORLD HEALTH ORG. 97, 100 (2002); Ebrahim Shah, *Poverty, Inequality, and Health: An International Perspective*, 30 INT'L J. EPIDEMIOLOGY 1202, 1203 (2001). Both individual perspectives and institutional perspectives are examined in an analysis of 81 Participatory Poverty Assessment reports with over 40,000 participants in fifty countries around the world. DEEPA NARAYAN ET AL., VOICES OF THE POOR: CAN ANYONE HEAR US? 3 (2000).

contributions were diarrhea, lower respiratory infections, other unintentional injuries, and malaria.[134] Lack of sanitation alone contributes to about 10 percent of the global disease burden.[135]

Notably, developing countries were affected significantly more than developed countries by environmental burdens, almost fifteen times more per capita.[136] It is startling to see that, despite these in-depth studies, preventable deaths have not only failed to decrease but have actually increased by 1 percent—which is a testament to the clear disparity between "research" and "action."[137]

4.4 The New Poster Child of Pharma Patents Regime

The marketplace for drugs includes conventional drugs (that is, chemical drugs) and biologics and their equivalents, as well as generics and biosimilars. Of these, the pharmaceutical industry is increasingly focusing on biological drugs and personalized medicines.[138] Biologics represent a new frontier in

[134] About 94 percent of all cases of diarrhea are attributable to the environment, resulting in more than 1.5 million deaths annually. About 88 percent of all cases of diarrhea were attributable to factors related to "water, sanitation and hygiene." At least 42 percent of all lower respiratory infections were estimated as attributable to the environment in developing countries, while about 20 percent of these infections were similarly attributable to developed countries. It is estimated that about 42 percent of the global malaria burden could be prevented by environmental management. Not included in this measure is the use of insecticide-treated mosquito netting, which has been recognized as having a large impact on the reduction of malaria. Randomized trials of insecticide-treated mosquito nets in Africa have documented average reductions of 20 percent in all-cause under-age-5 mortality. *See* Annette Prüss-Üstün & Carlos Corvalán, *Preventing Disease Through Healthy Environments: Towards an Estimate of the Environmental Burden of Disease*, World Health Org. (2006), https://www.who.int/publications/i/item/9241593822?ua=1 (last visited Oct. 20, 2025).

[135] Duncan Mara et al., *Sanitation and Health*, PLOS Med., Nov. 16, 2010, at 1, 1–2 https://journals.plos.org/plosmedicine/article?id=10.1371/journal.pmed.1000363 (last visited Oct. 20, 2025) ("2.6 billion people in the world lack adequate sanitation" (i.e., the safe disposal of human excreta)); *Id.*; *Accord* Annette Prüss-Üstün et al., *Safer Water, Better Health: Costs, Benefits and Sustainability of Interventions to Protect and Promote Health*, World Health Org., at 7 (2008), https://iris.who.int/server/api/core/bitstreams/03059ecd-f3b9-49f8-9972-9cc81142fb6d/content (last visited Oct. 20, 2025).

[136] Annette Prüss-Üstün et al., *Safer Water, Better Health: Costs, Benefits and Sustainability of Interventions to Protect and Promote Health*, World Health Org., at 12 (2008). Infections like intestinal nematode infections, trachoma, and schistosomiasis, though not among the diseases causing the highest DALY loss, are 100 percent attributable to environmental conditions, with hygiene and sanitation being the largest common denominator. Dengue and Japanese encephalitis were estimated to be highly attributable to environmental factors. Chagas disease and lymphatic filariasis also had high environmental attribution rates.

[137] While national policy and, to an extent, individual responsibility are generally believed to play roles in the persistence of poverty, global institutional order is getting more attention as a participatory agent of this poverty. *See* Thomas Pogge, World Poverty and Human Rights 4 (2002).

[138] *See* Aylin Sertkaya, Trinidad Beleche, Amber Jessup, & Benjamin D. Sommers, *Costs of Drug Development and Research and Development Intensity in the U.S., 2000–2018*, JAMA, June 28, 2024,

medicine, going far beyond the capability of chemical-based drugs. Unlike small-molecule chemical drugs, biologics are more complex and usually much larger molecules, often comprising proteins, and may take the form of hormones, vaccines, allergenics, monoclonal antibodies, recombinant therapeutic proteins, gene and cellular therapies, or cytokines.[139] Biologics are highly sensitive to manufacturing and handling conditions, whereby even minor differences are capable of significantly changing the effect of a drug. Consequently, their development, production, and manufacturing processes, as well as quality and safety controls, are different from those of chemical drugs.

Several scholars "across faiths" agree that the biomedical industry is the main arena for patent rights.[140] The general sentiment seems to be that it is *here if anywhere* that the patent incentive is required in order to ensure adequate innovative activity.[141] The amount of time required, the high capital investment, and the high-risk factors involved make any argument against patents in this industry a "hard case." As critics have pointed out, though, while it is clear that stronger patent rights lead to more patenting activity, the correlation between stronger patent rights and genuine "innovation" is tenuous at best, even in the pharmaceutical sector.[142]

Biotechnology patents, which have become controversial on account of the access issues they create, represent an area where the disclosure requirement has been extensively used to define the rights and limits of patenting.[143]

at 1, 2, https://pmc.ncbi.nlm.nih.gov/articles/PMC11214120/ (last visited Oct. 20, 2025); *see also* J. A. DiMasi et al., *Research and Development Costs for New Drugs by Therapeutic Category: A Study of the U.S. Pharmaceutical Industry*, PHARMACOECONOMICS, Feb. 7, 1995, at 152, https://pubmed.ncbi.nlm.nih.gov/10155302/ (last visited Oct. 20, 2025).

[139] Favour Danladi Makurvet, *Biologics vs. Small Molecules: Drug Costs and Patient Access*, MED. DRUG DISCOVERY, Nov. 10, 2020, at 1, 1–2 (2021), https://www.sciencedirect.com/science/article/pii/S2590098620300622?via%3Dihub (last visited Oct. 20, 2025); *see also* Kristina M. Lybecker, *The Biologics Revolution in the Production of Drugs*, FRASER INST. June 2016, at 1, 3.

[140] *See, e.g.*, Joshua D. Sarnoff, *Abolishing the Doctrine of Equivalents and Claiming the Future After Festo*, 19 BERKELEY TECH. L.J. 1157, 1209 (2004).

[141] Joseph A. DiMasi et al., *Innovation in the Pharmaceutical Industry: New Estimates of R&D Costs*, J. HEALTH ECON. Feb. 12, 2016, at 1, 20–33 (2016); *see also* Olivier J. Wouters et al., *Estimated Research and Development Investment Needed to Bring a New Medicine to Market, 2009–2018*, JAMA, Mar. 2020, at 844.

[142] *See, e.g.*, Nancy Gallini & Suzanne Scotchmer, *Intellectual Property: When Is It the Best Incentive System*, INNOVATION POL'Y & ECON., Jan. 2002, at 51, 70.

[143] *See* Amy Maxmen, *The Great Gene-Patent Debate*, NATURE, July 20, 2012, at 1 https://www.nature.com/articles/nature.2012.11044 (last visited Oct. 20, 2025); Julia Carbone et al., *DNA Patents and Diagnostics: Not a Pretty Picture*, NATURE BIOTECHNOLOGY, Aug. 28, 2010, at 784; *see also* Mayo Collaborative Servs. v. Prometheus Labs., Inc., 566 U.S. 66, 86–87 (2012) ("The laws of nature at issue here are narrow laws that may have limited applications, but the patent claims that embody them nonetheless implicate this concern . . . [a]nd they threaten to inhibit the development of more

For instance, in the 1990s, a gradual lowering of standards in biotechnology inventions,[144] particularly in obviousness, as in *In re Deuel*,[145] resulted in an increase in biotechnology patent activity.[146] This resulted in a proliferation of IP rights in biomedical research.[147] As one court noted,

> Between 1990 and 1998, the total number of biotechnology patents granted to U.S. corporations has quadrupled. In contrast, between 1990 and 1998, the total number of patents issued increased by about sixty percent. This large disparity is cause for concern. It suggests that the biotechnology industry is using the relaxed non-obviousness standard to obtain genomic patents simply for corporate gain.[148]

The increase in patent activity was attributed to a regime that lowered thresholds, resulting in the patenting of basic biotechnology research materials. This resulted in a "spiral of overlapping patent claims in the hands

refined treatment recommendations. . . ."); *see generally* Ariad Pharms., Inc. v. Eli Lilly & Co., 560 F.3d 1366, 1371–77 (Fed. Cir. 2009); Petition for a Writ of Certiorari at 17, Ass'n for Molecular Pathology v. Myriad Genetics, Inc., 569 U.S. 576 (2013) (No. 1172517), 2012 WL 4502947, at *17; Lab. Corp. of Am. Holdings v. Metabolite Labs., Inc., 548 U.S. 124, 127 (2006) (Breyer, J., dissenting) ("The problem arises from the fact that patents do not only encourage research by providing monetary incentives for invention. Sometimes their presence can discourage research by impeding the free exchange of information, for example by forcing researchers to avoid the use of potentially patented ideas, by leading them to conduct costly and time-consuming searches of existing or pending patents, by requiring complex licensing arrangements, and by raising the costs of using the patented information, sometimes prohibitively so.").

[144] *See, e.g.*, Amgen v. Chugai, 927 F.2d 1200, 1203–04 (Fed. Cir. 1991). *Amgen* was a decision rendered under 35 U.S.C. § 102(g), and thus was not a question of obviousness. The case enabled the patentability of an adequately conceived DNA sequence. The Federal Circuit held that DNA sequences adequately defined in a manner sufficiently disclosing its actual structure and method of preparation would be considered as having been reduced to practice, even though an inventor may be unaware of its actual structure and nowhere near disclosing the actual structure. *Id.* at 1211; *see also* U.S. Patent No. 4,703,008.

[145] *In re* Deuel, 51 F.3d 1552, 1560 (Fed. Cir. 1995) (holding that obvious to try is not obvious); *see also* Srividhya Ragavan, Patent and Trade Disparities in Developing Countries 211–12 (2012).

[146] Sara DastgheibVinarov, *A Higher Nonobviousness Standard for Gene Patents: Protecting Biomedical Research from the Big Chill*, 4 Marquette Intell. Prop. L. Rev. 143, 165 (2000).

[147] *See* Anita Varma & David Abraham, *DNA Is Different: Legal Obviousness and the Balance Between Biotech Inventors and the Market*, 9 Harv. J.L. & Tech. 53, 78 (1996). ("On the one hand, based on prior art knowledge, the biotechnologist knows that sequencing around twenty amino acids is sufficient to obtain the cDNA sequence that codes for a particular protein, absent unforeseen difficulties. On the other hand, under current law, the expected product of this scientifically obvious manipulation is legally unobvious and thus patentable").

[148] Sara DastgheibVinarov, *A Higher Nonobviousness Standard for Gene Patents: Protecting Biomedical Research from the Big Chill*, 4 Marquette Intell. Prop. L. Rev. 143, 165 (2000).

of different owners."[149] The result was that basic research materials became inaccessible because of their private-property status and increased access costs, effectively slowing down the pace of innovation in this area.[150]

While these realities necessitated capping the free-for-all in biotechnology patent applications, they also highlighted a shift toward a system that greatly facilitated accumulating patent rights.[151] Disclosures steadily grew to occupy a central role in defining the rights and limits of patenting, obviating the need for broader discussions of the nature of information, especially from the perspective of public benefit and the constituents of the progress requirement.

Nonetheless, the biomedical industry is often regarded as the prime justification for patent rights. But in fact the costs of expansionist patent systems have severely impacted health-care access and affordability, with poorer countries often bearing the brunt.[152]

5. Conclusion: A New Framework for Socially Beneficial Innovation Rooted in Local Realities

This concluding section deals with the question of who will lead in the discussion for a new framework and the various paradigms that it should accommodate.

5.1 Prioritizing Socially Valuable Innovation

When market signals indicate that an innovation is economically valuable, does this necessarily identify a socially valuable innovation? Though economically valuable innovations are generally presumed to be socially valuable, lack of access tends to affect the social value of the innovation. What value should be ascribed to a wonder cancer drug when patients who need it die because they cannot access it? Though a patent may have a high market

[149] Michael A. Heller & Rebecca S. Eisenberg, *Can Patents Deter Innovation? The Anticommons in Biomedical Research*, SCI. MAG. May 1, 1998, at 698, 698.

[150] *Id.*

[151] Sara DastgheibVinarov, *A Higher Nonobviousness Standard for Gene Patents: Protecting Biomedical Research from the Big Chill*, 4 MARQUETTE INTELL. PROP. L. REV. 143, 165 (2000).

[152] Srividhya Ragavan & Amaka Vanni, *Can International Patent Law Help Mitigate Cancer Inequity in LMICs?*, 22 AMA J. ETHICS 102, 103–04 (2020).

value, the goal of the system should be to ensure that such patents have social value as well.

It is perhaps natural for the pharmaceutical industry to favor economically valuable innovation; nevertheless, it is time to reframe the issue of international health care, focusing on balancing economically valuable innovation with socially valuable innovation. Doing so will require more data on the losses in global productivity from a lack of socially valuable innovation. Any new framework should also appreciate that genuine innovation is and should continue to be a central objective.

Nevertheless, encouraging innovation along with unduly strong exclusion rights tends to cause overlapping research as multiple firms try to capture the rent incentive.[153] Thus, in order to reach an agreeable balance in the innovation spectrum, any new framework should include research, development, and grant costs with access.

5.2 Need for Dynamic Efficiencies

Instead of promoting static inefficiencies (best defined as necessary tradeoffs for an enhanced rate of innovation), perhaps a more dynamic model should be considered. Harold Demsetz referred to this as "the production of knowledge at efficient rates."[154] From a societal point of view, the innovator's contribution makes the knowledge available "earlier" in time.[155] Thus, what should be rewarded is the extent to which that knowledge was made available earlier than it otherwise would have been. Early availability for such purposes should be rewarded. "Economic efficiency requires that people's compensation be related to their marginal social returns."[156] This would effectively create dynamic efficiencies. The advantage of such dynamism is that its effectiveness will be systemic for a period of time, benefiting the public by making innovations available earlier.

[153] *See* Joseph A. DiMasi & Cherie Paquette, *The Economics of Follow-on Drug Research and Innovation: Trends in Entry Rates and the Timing of Development*, PHARMACOECONOMICS, Oct. 2004, at 1, 8–9. In a study done in 2004, DiMasi and Paquette find that research for "follow-on" drugs tend to relate to market trends and happen before the patent is granted and not as post-hoc imitation.

[154] Harold Demsetz, *Information and Efficiency: Another Viewpoint*, 12 J.L. & ECON. 1, 11–14 (1969).

[155] Joseph E. Stiglitz, *Economic Foundations of Intellectual Property Rights*, 57 Duke L.J. 1693, 1706–11 (2008).

[156] *Id.*

While static inefficiencies provide rewards, they do so to the detriment of those who may need the invention more by benefiting one or more of the inventors for a period of time. In other words, there cannot be dynamic efficiency when marginal private returns, represented by the deadweight loss, do not correspond to marginal social returns, represented by the enhanced rate of innovation or the value of bringing a product to the market.[157] Pharmaceuticals provide a great example of how static inefficiencies affect the system as a whole.

A calibrated trade-off, in which a balanced IP regime ensures that the losses from static inefficiencies do not outweigh the gains from a system that relies on dynamic efficiency, is a reasonable objective to pursue. Analysis from this lens could come in the form of increasing or decreasing the patentability criteria, breadth of patents, injunctions, and damages, or by implementing regulations external to patents, such as encouraging rational price discrimination to reduce static inefficiencies.[158]

5.3 Decentralized Patent Regime

Arguably, the current information signals for desired directions of innovation are expensive to generate in centralized innovation systems. Moreover, they do not always include all the necessary markers for a balanced regime. That is, market signals provide information as to what types of innovations society sees as desirable and therefore provide guidance on the types of innovative activity companies should engage in. But although this premise has become central to much of the contemporary economic analysis of patent law, in fields like health care and education a global conception of the "market" is typically an indicator of who has a stronger ability to express their preferences rather than a good indicator of what is socially desirable.

[157] *Id.*

[158] Theoretically, a patent holder can remove this deadweight loss by perfect price discrimination. Perfect price discrimination would allow the seller to charge each user based on his or her ability and willingness to pay. The seller would be able to sell the good to everyone at their ability (i.e., willingness) to pay above production cost without incurring any losses, as they would not be getting sales from the "deadweight" portion in their earlier scenario as well. However, for this to work, (1) sellers would have to ensure that buyers who would otherwise be paying at (or in case of perfect price discrimination, higher than) sale price are prevented from buying the goods at prices meant for the "deadweight" audience; and (2) methods of preventing arbitrage would be required. *See* SUZANNE SCOTCHMER, INNOVATION AND INCENTIVES 36 (2004).

Contemporary literature highlights the efficiency benefits that can arise from a more decentralized form of the patent regime, particularly because decentralization is more likely to address local issues relevant to a particular market.

Much of the impact of innovation implicates the need to consider local realities. In other words, where health-care access is an issue, it is necessary to create flexibilities within the trade regime to balance trade with welfare.[159] Such a balance specifically in the area of health care will necessarily implicate local conditions such as per capita income, insurance coverage, prevalence of a disease, and direct and indirect effects of lack of health-care access on productivity. Thus, differences in economic development have a direct and indirect bearing on how patents can be beneficial to the economy.

Moreover, any new framework for pharmaceuticals should engage with the question of distributional research, research that does not just focus on one type of market but may produce by-products that yield benefits to a larger global share of the market. This cannot be a burden on the pharmaceutical industry alone; instead, international, multilateral, regional, and other bodies need to take the lead in engaging with it.

5.4 Evidence-Based Rights-Duty Paradigm

Sometimes, the effectiveness of a medical treatment in either lengthening or improving a patient's quality of life is also a significant factor. The health-care industry uses a measure—Quality-Adjusted Life Years (QALYs)—to express the effectiveness of medical treatment in either improving a patient's quality of life or lengthening the patient's life.[160] For instance, a treatment resulting in two years of perfect health for the patient would have a QALY value of

[159] *See* Ellen 't Hoen, *TRIPS, Pharmaceutical Patents, and Access to Essential Medicines: A Long Way from Seattle to Doha*, 3 Chi. J. Int'l L. 27, 28–29 (2002); *see also* David K. Tomar, *A Look into the WTO Pharmaceutical Patent Dispute Between the United States and India*, 17 Wis. Int'l L.J. 579, 583–85, 601 (1999) (discussing India as a specific case study and noting that patent protection will decrease pharmaceutical availability and increase prices because the consumers will bear the cost associated with research and development); Michelle M. Nerozzi, *The Battle over Life-Saving Pharmaceuticals: Are Developing Countries Being "TRIPped" by Developed Countries?*, 47 Vill. L. Rev. 605, 605 (2002) (stressing that over 89 percent of the people living in poverty with HIV/AIDS reside in developing and least developed nations).

[160] *Cost-Effectiveness, the QALY, and the evLYG*, Inst. Clinical Econ. Rev. (2023), https://icer.org/our-approach/methods-process/cost-effectiveness-the-qaly-and-the-evlyg (last visited Oct. 20, 2025). Thus, QALYs is defined as the measure of "the product of duration of life and a measurement of quality of life."

2, whereas a treatment that provides a patient with two years of 50-percent perfect health would have a value of 1.[161] FDA clinical trial outcomes remain important indicators to determine a drug's QALY value.[162]

Alexander Yow asserts that QALYs can be used to compare treatment quality, to determine whether newer modifications of drugs show evidence of significant therapeutic benefit, and to determine whether a drug is worthy of further market-monopoly power.[163] If the QALY value is limited, there may not be much of a case for seeking a price increase for newer variations of existing medications, even medications that may represent some innovation.

Yow also asserts that this value can demonstrate whether such newly improvised versions of existing drugs deserve a separate patent, serving as an effective mechanism to curb the practice of obtaining patents for minimal improvements, which often results in evergreening.[164] By collaborating with regulatory agencies, patent offices can increase opportunities for regulators to verify the accuracy of a newly modified drug's QALY value and compare it to its patent's prior FDA trials, thereby increasing consistency in decision-making.[165]

5.5 Devising a Model for Pharma Pricing

In determining the prices of pharmaceutical products, factors should include the stages of investment in a product—such as whether public funds have already been heavily invested in the research—and the cost of future manufacturing, along with market size. Perhaps it is time to evolve a finite set of models for pricing lifesaving medications, especially in the post-Covid-19 world. Different models have been propounded based on cost, income in the market, market size (including R&D), type of diseases, and other such criteria.[166] It is imperative to establish protocols that suggest different models for considering some of these factors.

[161] *Id.*

[162] David S. Abrams & Bhaven N. Sampat, *Pharmaceutical Patent Citations and Real Value*, N.Y.U. https://www.law.nyu.edu/sites/default/files/upload_documents/David%20Abrams%20AND%20Bhaven%20Sampat.pdf (last visited Oct. 20, 2025).

[163] Alexander Yow, *Using Quality-Adjusted Life Years to Combat Patent Evergreening* 3–4 (Dec. 10, 2023) (unpublished comment) (on file with author and the Texas A&M Journal of Property Law).

[164] *Id.*

[165] *Id.*

[166] See also James Love, *Measures to Enhance Access to Medical Technologies, and New Methods of Stimulating Medical R & D*, 40 U.C. DAVIS L. REV. 679 (2007).

5.6 The Prevention Focus

A large chunk of the global disease burden could arguably be relieved by preventive measures rather than medicinal treatment options. In view of this, the pharmaceutical-innovation debate needs to adopt a completely different perspective, especially considering diseases with significant preventable factors. Any new framework should address allocation of resources between prevention and treatment. Again, this burden cannot be placed on the pharmaceutical industry; it is instead imperative that the new framework be conceived by international organizations. Ultimately, it is *policy* and not *poverty*.

That a new framework is needed seems clear. That such a framework will have to be worked out by international and regional bodies is also clear. The need for a framework is to not compromise on innovation, and yet evolving *policy* solutions has become imperative. At a global level, any such new framework should focus on sovereign nations having the ability to consider the need to balance larger innovation capabilities with appropriate use of limitations and flexibilities to improve national and global trade through productivity. Strong structural and internal policies addressing desired levels of protection, parallel importing, government subsidies, and price-control mechanisms would be a starting point for such a framework. Any such framework needs to be worked out with and through the WTO and related systems.

Essentially, the new innovation framework should empower the developing and least-developed countries with choices whereby to prioritize their national interest, based on their own local realities and emergent needs. In order to burst the innovation bubble created by presumption risks that assumes the number of patents as proxy for innovation, and thereby undermines the incentivizing efficiency of the innovation system as instrument of socio-economic development, the framework should be evidence-based, data-driven, and proactive.

International bodies could take the lead in formulating provisions on legal safeguards to ensure against presumption risks, by imposing the burden of proof regarding a patented invention's contribution to enhancement of innovation that benefits society on the patent-holder. Such safeguards should also clearly lay out the standard of proof expected from a claimant of exclusive patent rights, one that takes into account local social, economic, technological, and political realities.

International treaties need to accommodate enough flexibilities and exceptions so that sovereign nations can structure those flexibilities in a manner that generates maximum value—not just economic value but social value as well. The goal of an efficient patent system ought to be incentivizing innovation that is valuable not just economically but also socially, innovation that benefits the society and is grounded in local realities. Ushering in a virtuous cycle of local innovation could transform the global capacity to effectively deal with Covid-19-like pandemics in future.

3

Government as Guardians of Public Health

1. Introduction: Actors, Their Roles, and the Attribution Gap

1.1 Actors in the Innovation Landscape

This chapter discusses different actors and actions in order to better understand how their roles and policies, whether constitutional, statutory, or otherwise, play a role in ensuring health access globally. Because conventional studies on trade and innovation tend to focus on the impact of such policies on wealthier and more developed economies, in which the search for solutions has tended to favor the theoretical tenets of IP rights, the focus here will be mostly on the governments of developing countries. Developing countries have improved both their innovation metrics and general access to health care by instituting policies and mechanisms that go against conventional wisdom. Yet, even though fragile public health in lower-income countries has repeatedly affected global public health and trade, as it did during the SARS and Zika epidemics and the Covid-19 pandemic, the policy choices of these nations are rarely considered as viable solutions.

In appreciating the policy choices of developing countries and the roles of different actors in their pharmaceutical R&D and innovation landscape, this chapter highlights the nuances that are often conveniently forgotten when discussing drug innovators. Though drug innovation is largely the work of private pharmaceutical companies, issues relating to ensuring distribution, affordability, and other paradigms that are critical to health-care access usually implicate other entities and systems. This *attribution gap* creates blind spots in research, which can be best addressed by finding causes for the fragilities in the system by focusing on *local realities,* discussed more fully in chapter 2.[1] The chapter also focuses on the role of the judiciary, the

[1] *See* Rachael Ramirez, *Scientists Looked at More Than 100,000 Studies and Found the World Has a Giant Climate-Crisis Blind Spot*, CNN (Oct. 11, 2021), https://cnn.it/4pBUNyr (last visited Oct. 20, 2025).

Fractures in IP, Trade, and Health. Srividhya Ragavan and Swaraj Paul Barooah, Oxford University Press.
 DOI: 10.1093/9780197684085.003.0003

government, and NGOs, discussing the significance of their contribution to access outcomes.

Thus, the ensuing discussions delve into examples to help showcase how different entities, both governmental and nongovernmental, play a role in ensuring health access around the globe, focusing on how each type of entity, with its own objectives, strategizes to work alongside other entities that form part of the pharmaceutical food chain. For example, the goals of a pharmaceutical company will be completely different from those of an NGO, and the role of a diplomat will typically be different from that of a politician within the same government. The convergence of some of these different roles, and the strategies employed to find that point of convergence, may become critical to enabling the best outcome for health-care access.

1.2 Government Actions to Foster Innovation

In order to fully understand the role of different actors, this chapter slides between the past and present, discussing issues from various member states to identify significant government actions that have enhanced innovation without compromising health-care access. The discussion below uses examples of government actions in Brazil and India to demonstrate how governments can step in to balance international obligations with local realities.

The first example highlights how the Brazilian government effectively used IP norms to cater to national needs by constitutionalizing IP and embedding it within the overarching legal structure of the state, thereby leading to the coexistence of IP norms with public-health norms. The second, focusing on India, shows how IP norms and flexibilities can be framed in a balanced manner through a public-health lens, allowing stakeholders a structure within which patent-patient tensions could be constantly tested and resolved against each other.

A separate discussion focuses on how the United States enabled private rights through government intervention—thus, innovation using public funding. While the discussion acknowledges the limitations that this can cause for access to health care, it also highlights that governments can utilize such interventions to both enhance innovation and promote public-health goals in a complementary fashion.

The following discussion of India highlights an alternative model that uses government entities to further innovation while engaging in areas of R&D that private research has hesitated to engage in, such as tropical diseases. It details the Open-Source Drug Discovery (OSDD) model promoted through a government entity. The last two models are discussed as examples that work around structural limitations of the IP system, yet coexist with it. These two models provide interesting examples of government action driving pharmaceutical innovation, even in areas where private players have failed at a low cost.

National governments generally have enormous control over their domestic policies and are best positioned to address local issues while considering the ramifications and limitations of global influences and obligations. In order to align international obligations with policies that can achieve national targets, the role of the national government remains crucial and influential both in shaping innovation policy and in improving health-care access. It can also play an important role in advocating in international forums for needs that sync with local realities.[2]

National governments naturally have a presence as invested constituents.[3] Importantly, they are the main invested constituents bound by national constitutional mandates and legal precedents. This gives them the perfect vantage from which to consider local realities and how discharging international obligations by establishing policies can impact at the local level. Further, national governments are the one entity actively engaged in funding, facilitating, and protecting R&D; procurement and distribution; price negotiations; and shaping all the relevant legal and regulatory policies. Furthermore, national governments have a stake in providing health-care access not only to preserve public health but also to enhance the productivity of their labor capital. Thus, national governments occupy the best vantage

[2] *See* Srividhya Ragavan, *World Trade Organization: A Barrier to Global Public Health?*, *in* Intellectual Property Law and Access to Medicines: TRIPS Agreement, Health, and Pharmaceuticals 25 (Srividhya Ragavan & Amaka Vanni eds., 2021), https://scholarship.law.tamu.edu/facscholar/1534/ (last visited Oct. 20, 2025) (discussing the role and importance of local realities).

[3] *See* Srividhya Ragavan & Swaraj P. Barooah, *Historic Tensions Involving International Intellectual Property Protection of Medical Technology with Disastrous Public Health Consequences*, 54 Seton Hall L. Rev. 339 (2023), https://scholarship.law.tamu.edu/facscholar/1928/ (last visited Oct. 20, 2025).

from which to appreciate the broader ramifications of the innovation and access issues outside of a purely legal context.[4]

In democracies, oversight is to some extent naturally built-in, since the ability of national governments to deliver on these issues is critical to winning popular votes and staying in power. Consequently, the influence that national governments wield over the issue of health-care access is enormous, and it is national governments, given their stake in protecting the local public health, development, and innovation, that are best positioned to act.

Nevertheless, the framing of the debate on access does not always fully capture and often, even undermines the role of national governments, as maintained by Mariana Mazzucato and Rosie Collington. National governments are traditionally viewed as "self-interested" stakeholders, like private enterprises. Moreover, they are perceived as players interacting with other invested parties at several stages of the process and policy of access to patent innovation. As a result, the roles of national governments have frequently been defined by their constraints. But such a representation undermines and undervalues their role as a distinct and influential actor in the innovation ecosystem.

1.3 The Narrative of Free Trade

Indeed, national governments face many limitations, both external and internal, particularly the strong underlying narrative of "free trade" established under the auspices of the WTO and reflected in the harmonization of IP rights as outlined in the TRIPS Agreement. The narrative is further characterized by a prevailing normative belief that governments cannot and should not pick and choose winners, which is often the underlying theme behind this free-trade ideology.

However, this ideology is often viewed in a contextually insensitive manner, disregarding the geopolitical realities of countries and local regions.[5] These local realities and welfare issues are relegated to the background, while

[4] *See id.*

[5] *See* Michael Palmedo & Srividhya Ragavan, *The U.S. Posture on Global Access to Medication & the Case for Change* 11 Indian J. Intell. Prop. L. 76 (2020), https://scholarship.law.tamu.edu/facscholar/1512 (last visited Oct. 20, 2025) (providing data relevant to the material).

questions about international obligations occupy the forefront, and this is especially true regarding issues that relate to socioeconomically weaker sections.[6]

A consequence of this view is perhaps why international obligations, such as those in the TRIPS Agreement, do not provide sufficient flexibilities to permit national governments to act decisively even when there is an emergency. Srividhya Ragavan, Sean Flynn, and Brook Baker, in a submission to the ITC, assert the lack of "the right of WTO Members to take local realities into account and to adapt TRIPS's minimum standards pluralistically. . . ."[7] Ragavan also asserts that "TRIPS leaves no room for incremental development of patent policy; instead, in order to fulfill international obligations, it forces nations to make policy decisions that are unsynchronized with local realities."[8]

In contrast to the prevailing trend, the acclaimed free-trade thinker John Maynard Keynes, in a 1933 paper titled "National Self-Sufficiency,"[9] warned that contextual needs for government intervention to ensure national-interest priorities should not be left to the mercies of foreign economic fluctuations. Aditya Sinha contextualizes Keynes's essay in terms of industrial-policy requirements in the modern day, noting, "There's a shift in values towards prioritizing national interests and social goals, a trend of countries experimenting with various politico-economic systems to suit their unique contexts, a pursuit of economic resilience against global uncertainties, and a critique of international capitalist models perceived as inequitable and unsustainable."[10]

The following discussion focuses on the roles of three actors contextualized within specific types of actions. The first of these is the government, which is identified as a significant "architect" in defining the interactions between the two stakeholders: pharmaceutical innovators and patients. This chapter goes on to portray the impact of two other actors, the judiciary and NGOs, on pharmaceutical innovation and the health-care-access food chain.

[6] *See generally* Mariana Mazzucato, *Policy with a Purpose*, IMF (Sept. 2024), https://www.imf.org/en/Publications/fandd/issues/2024/09/policy-with-a-purpose-mazzucato (last visited Oct. 20, 2025).

[7] *See* Notice, 78 Fed. Reg. 69128 (Nov. 18, 2013).

[8] *See* Srividhya Ragavan, Patent and Trade Disparities in Developing Countries 140 (2012).

[9] *See* John Maynard Keynes, *National Self-Sufficiency*, 22 Yale Rev. 755 (1933).

[10] *See* Aditya Sinha, *Industrial Policy Is Not the Monster Under Your Economic Bed*, Khaleej Times (Mar. 24, 2024), https://www.khaleejtimes.com/opinion/industrial-policy-is-not-the-monster-under-your-economic-bed (last visited Oct. 20, 2025).

2. Brazil: A Shining Example of State Responsibility for Public Health

2.1 Pioneering the Coexistential Use of IP Norms

Brazil is one of the best and most studied cases of government action that challenges the myth of patent and public health as a two-stakeholder problem between pharmaceutical innovators and patients. The following discussion traces the changes Brazil has made historically to provide health-care access to its population, and showcases how government policies positively affected the ground realities by integrating IP norms to create a single public-health stakeholder. As a result, one stakeholder has benefited from government actions, and that was the general public.

A study by the Informational Society of Yale Law School notes that the Brazilian National Health System was driven by three principles of health-care access: (1) universal coverage, (2) equality of access, and (3) complete health-care coverage.[11] Consistent with these principles, in the midst of the biggest public-health crisis of its time, the HIV/AIDS crisis of the 1980s and 1990s, Brazil was a shining example of how a resource-constrained country could take care of its citizens by constitutionalizing a universal right to health and making access to medicines a state responsibility. In 1988, Brazil amended its Constitution to guarantee a right to health, and in the following year it established the "Sistema Único de Saúde," or Unified Health System, which describes itself as "the largest non-discriminatory government-run public health-care system."[12]

This radical tackling of public-health issues, especially those affecting patents, did not emerge from a vacuum. In 1809, Brazil became one of the first countries in the world to institute a patent policy, via a decree establishing exclusive privileges for inventors and first adopters of inventions.[13] In 1830, the

[11] *See* Monica Steffen Guise Rosina et al., *Access to Medicines: Pharmaceutical Patents and the Right to Health*, *in* ACCESS TO KNOWLEDGE IN BRAZIL 173 (Lea Shaver ed., 2008).

[12] *See* CONSTITUTION OF THE FEDERATIVE REPUBLIC OF BRAZIL art. 196 (stating that health is a right of all and a duty of the State, guaranteed by socioeconomic policies that aim at the reduction of the risk of illness and of other hazards and at the universal and equal access to the actions and services for its promotion, protection and recovery); *see also Health for All Toolkit: Brazil's Unified Health System*, CIV. SOC'Y ENGAGEMENT MECHANISM FOR UHC 2030, https://csemonline.net/brazil/ (last visited Oct. 20, 2025).

[13] *See* Roberto Mazzoleni & Luciano Martins Costa Póvoa, *The Evolution of Brazil's Regime of Intellectual Property Rights and the Accumulation of Technological Capabilities in the Pharmaceutical Industry*, ASSOCIAÇÃO BRASILEIRA DE PESQUISADORES EM HISTORIA (2009), https://www.abphe.org.br/arquivos/roberto-mazzoleni_luciano-martins-costa-povoa.pdf (last visited Oct. 20,

first Brazilian patent law came into being; among other things, it prohibited the patenting of foreign inventions.

With the introduction of the Paris Convention in 1883, of which Brazil was a founding member, the country started allowing foreign inventions to be patented, but kept a strict working requirement, failing which the rights could be forfeited or compulsorily licensed.[14] This period also saw the development of Brazil's pharmaceutical industry, which by 1907 would consist of sixty laboratories dedicated to the production and manufacturing of medicinal preparations.[15] As Roberto Mazzoleni and Luciano Martins Costa Póvoa note, the presence of several educational institutions offering pharmaceutical degrees facilitated this development.

Soon, several public laboratories began to focus on developing new serums and vaccines for such pressing public-health concerns as smallpox, yellow fever, and malaria.[16] The progress, especially on vaccines, quickly became renowned internationally, and it continued until the 1930s, when administrative changes stopped the assignment of profits to the institutions.[17]

In 1945 the working requirement was slightly modified, and in 1969 a bar on patenting of pharmaceutical inventions was introduced.[18] This was intended to promote public health while creating a robust domestic pharmaceutical industry. In 1971, Brazil abrogated the patents for pharmaceutical manufacturing processes.[19] The state-owned CdM was created to revive government laboratories. CdM's creation resulted in preferential treatment to local companies, thus enabling Brazil to manufacture pharmaceuticals domestically.[20] Shortly thereafter, a generic-drug industry developed in Brazil, and it soon accounted for approximately 15 percent of the local pharmaceutical market.[21]

2025) (stating that Brazil was the fourth country in the world to have a patent law, even preceding that of its colonial ruler Portugal, and would later become a founding member of the Paris Convention and WIPO).

[14] *See id.*
[15] *See id.*
[16] *See id.*
[17] *See* N. Stepan, *Beginnings of Brazilian Science*, WIPO Statistics Database (2008).
[18] *See* Roberto Mazzoleni & Luciano Martins Costa Póvoa, *Accumulation of Technological Capabilities and Economic Development: Did Brazil's IPR Regime Matter?*, *in* Intellectual Property Rights, Development, and Catch-Up: An International Comparative Study (Hiroyuki Odagiri et al. eds., 2010), https://academic.oup.com/book/9132/chapter-abstract/155741514?redirectedFrom=fulltext&login=false (last visited Oct. 20, 2025).
[19] *See* Ragavan, *supra* note 8, at 59.
[20] *See* Ragavan, *supra* note 8.
[21] *See id.*

2.2 Challenges and Winds of Change

This progress continued until major amendments were executed between 1994 and 1996,[22] when Brazil, having faced years of bilateral pressure from the United States on changing certain norms, consented to comply with the TRIPS Agreement, ten years earlier than it was required to do so.[23] Ragavan's discussion of Brazil provides an insight into the international issues that surrounded this change.[24] In 1987, US President Ronald Reagan authorized the imposition of trade sanctions on Brazil for failing to provide IP protection for American products.[25] One hundred percent tariffs were levied on specific goods, totaling US$39 million, a sum equivalent to the alleged loss suffered by the American pharmaceutical industry from Brazil's lack of patent protection.[26] Brazil requested that a GATT panel hear the dispute regarding the United States' use of §301 of its 1974 Trade Act, but settled the disagreement in 1990 by promising to enact patent legislation.[27] In 1991, in order to avert a second American trade sanction, Brazil promised to amend the 1971 Industrial Property Code.[28]

Note that, in addition to the evolution of patent-specific laws, Brazil during this time had a vibrant local pharmaceutical industry, which was essentially bought out by foreign firms in the 1950s and 1960s.[29] An inquiry commission later showed that this foreign takeover was a consequence of governmental policies that focused on incentivizing foreign firms, such as providing favorable exchange rates for firms importing capital goods for new factories.[30] It also showed that patent abuse had been taking place in

[22] *See* Mazzoleni & Póvoa, *supra* note 13.
[23] *See id.*
[24] *See* Ragavan, *supra* note 8, at 58–61.
[25] *See* Naomi A. Bass, *Implications of the TRIPS Agreement for Developing Countries: Pharmaceutical Patent Laws in Brazil and South Africa in the 21st Century*, 34 Geo. Wash. Int'l L. Rev. 191, 209 (2002) (detailing that Brazil responded to the sanctions imposed by the United States by increasing the price of pharmaceuticals); *see also* Am. Embassy to Brazil, Recent Developments In Brazilian Pharmaceutical Sector (1987), http://www.cptech.org/ip/health/c/brazil/cable051987.html (last visited Oct. 20, 2025).
[26] *See id*; *see also Reagan, Charging Patent Piracy, Imposes Sanctions on $39 Million of Brazilian Goods*, Int'l Trade Rep. (bna) 1415 (1988) (imposing tariffs at 100 percent ad valorem for $39 million worth of Brazilian non-benzenoid drugs, paper products, and consumer electronics).
[27] *See* O'Neal Taylor, *The Limits of Economic Power: §301 and the World Trade Organization Dispute Settlement System*, 30 Vand. J. Transnat'l. L. 209, 236 (1997).
[28] *See id.*
[29] *See* J. C. Cohen, *Expanding Drug Access in Brazil: Lessons for Latin America and Canada*, 96 Can. J. of Pub. Health 15, 15–17 (2006).
[30] *See id.* at 16 (concerning the formation of the Commission of Inquiry on the Pharmaceutical Industry in 1962).

the form of restrictive licensing practices and high royalties, including for expired patents.[31] Pushback against these abuses led to the 1969 amendments disallowing patents on pharmaceutical innovations. Additionally, together with Bolivia, Brazil submitted a draft resolution on the need for a development agenda.[32] Despite these efforts, the Brazilian pharmaceutical industry came to be dominated by foreign-owned firms, and by 1989 only three of its thirty major pharmaceutical firms were local firms.[33]

Following the changes in the wake of TRIPS Agreement and the Doha Declaration, and despite the government's industrial policies' successful "demand-pull," there was inadequate or insufficient "technological" industrial-policy support. As a result, local firms were unable to utilize the opportunities created by the local manufacturing policy,[34] and domestic manufacturers were once again acquired by or merged with foreign companies.[35]

Some commentators have traced this failure to take retaliatory action by the Brazilian state to its constitution.[36] Bruno Meyerhof Salama and Daniel Benoliel state that "[Brazil's] latest constitution of 1988 fragmented political power without creating a strong party system that is necessary to ensure programmatic coherence for long-run government actions. Weak parties and strong politicians act in a strong Congress, increasing the number of 'veto players' in the political process, so the transaction costs of law- and policy-making are high."[37] Ragavan asserts that national political uncertainty (a local reality for Brazil) coupled with economic pressures and a deteriorating

[31] *See* A. K. Menescal, *Changing WIPO's Ways: The 2004 Development Agenda in Historical Perspective*, 8 J. WORLD INTELL. PROP. 761 (2005).

[32] *See* Nneamaka Ifunanya Vanni, Narratives and Counter-Narratives in Pharmaceutical Patent Law Making: Experiences from 3 Developing Countries 82 (2016) (Ph.D. dissertation, University of Warwick).

[33] *See* Mazzoleni & Póvoa, *supra* note 13.

[34] *See* Vanni, *supra* note 32, at 84 (noting that even in the decades leading up to this point, the efforts were seen as insufficient, as the monetary policies continued to leave the local firms vulnerable to foreign capital).

[35] *See* Cohen, *supra* note 29; *see also* Vanni, *supra* note 32, at 88–90 (explaining the internal political struggles that shifted domestic policy more toward neoliberal prescriptions favored by the Washington Consensus); *see also* David Trubek et al., *New State Activism in Brazil and the Challenge for Law*, *in* L. AND THE NEW DEV. STATE: THE BRAZILIAN EXPERIENCE IN LATIN AM. CONTEXT (David M. Trubek et al. eds., 2012); *see also* Matthew Brian Flynn, Pharmaceutical Governance in Brazil: Globalization, Institutions and AIDS 54 (2010) (Ph.D. dissertation, University of Texas at Austin), https://repositories.lib.utexas.edu/items/23f40683-3ff4-40db-ae99-819a0f0c5dc3 (last visited Oct. 20, 2025); *see also* Thiago Caliari & Ricardo Machado Ruiz, *Brazilian Pharmaceutical Industry and Generic Drugs Policy: Impacts on Structure and Innovation and Recent Developments*, 41 SCI. AND PUB. POLICY 245 (2014).

[36] *See* Daniel Benoliel & Bruno Meyerhof Salama, Pharmaceutical Patent Bargains: The Brazilian Experience (Artigos Direito GV, Working Paper No. 51, 2010), https://papers.ssrn.com/sol3/papers.cfm?abstract_id=1856629 (last visited Oct. 20, 2025).

[37] *See id.*

diplomatic relationship with WTO nations with more bargaining parity, such as the United States, affected the success of some of Brazil's initiatives.[38]

Nevertheless, it remains true that the Brazilian government's handling of the HIV/AIDS crisis highlighted an alternative path to negotiating patent-patient tensions. Even before the amendments that came about in 1996 and subsequent changes that continued in that direction, the long history of Brazil in actively making patent policies focused on national priorities had ensured that it was more equipped in terms of experienced internal stakeholders than several other similarly resource-constrained countries. This approach has provided valuable lessons for many countries, offering insights that others could and did learn from.

2.3 Brazilian Response to the AIDS Crisis

The 1980s marked Brazil's movement toward democracy and economic growth. When the first Brazilian AIDS case was reported in 1982, the government provided subsidized drugs to minimize the effect of a potential AIDS epidemic on the economy.[39] The Ministry of Health created a health-care network under the National AIDS policy.[40] In 1986, two advisory committees forming part of the National AIDS Commission recommended free access to antiretroviral drugs (ARVs) through the public-health network.[41]

Rising to the challenges posed by the AIDS crisis to public-health access, the Brazilian government introduced a local working requirement in its patent legislation, allowing local companies to manufacture a product whose patent owner had failed to produce it in Brazil within three years of the patent grant.[42]

Going against the World Bank's recommendation and deciding to focus on treatment and prevention,[43] the CdM, together with the Ministry of Health,

[38] *See* RAGAVAN, *supra* note 8, at 104.

[39] *See* Mario Osava & Abraham Lama, *NGOs—The Driving Force Behind Public Policy and AIDS*, INTER PRESS SERVICE, http://www.ipsnews.net/aids/page_7.shtml (last visited Oct. 20, 2025) (reporting on AIDS for World AIDS Day, in collaboration with UNAIDS and PAHO).

[40] *See* GOVERNMENT OF BRAZIL, NATIONAL AIDS DRUG POLICY (2001), https://bvsms.saude.gov.br/bvs/publicacoes/41national_aids.pdf (last visited Oct. 20, 2025).

[41] *See* Charo Quesada, *The Fruits of Foresight—An Architect of Brazil's AIDS Program Describes the 'Critical and Innovative Vision' that Led to Success: IDB News*, 18 LATIN AME. REP. X, 47–48 (2002).

[42] *See U.S. Drops Brazil AIDS Drugs Case,* BBC NEWS (June 25, 2001), http://news.bbc.co.uk/2/hi/business/1407472.stm (last visited Oct. 20, 2025).

[43] *See* JANE GALVÃO, AIDS NO BRASIL: AN AGENDA DE CONSTRUÇÃO DE UMA EPIDEMIA 256 (2000) (stating that the World Bank at the time advised against this action, recommending a prevention-only program instead); *see also* Gabriela Costa Chaves et al., *Brazil: Patent Barriers*

distributed ARVs at no cost through a combination of government procurement and local manufacturing.[44] This two-pronged approach first required large-scale procurement of drugs for distribution under the SUS, which led to a large internal market demand, and this in turn spurred the development of domestic pharmaceutical manufacturing capacity for generics.[45] The government ensured that political and legal methods were explored at the procurement stage, including negotiating price discounts using the underlying threat that compulsory licenses would be required if prices remained unreasonable or for other reasons of public interest.[46]

This strategy of merely threatening to use a compulsory license was effective until May 2007, when a compulsory license was issued on public-interest grounds for the production of Stocrin, which had previously been manufactured by Merck under the brand name Efavirenz.[47] Brazilian patent law allowed such usage of flexibilities.[48] Drugs that could not be procured were locally manufactured.[49]

Soon, local pharmaceutical companies were manufacturing generic versions of eight out of the twelve AIDS drugs at 70 percent below the then-prevailing market price.[50] The government saved US$490 million from local production of AIDS drugs.[51] As a result, Brazil demonstrated a significant improvement in public health.[52] By 2002, fifteen ARVs were being distributed

and Access to Medicines Through the Public Health System, *in* Intellectual Property Law and Access to Medicines 154 (Srividhya Ragavan & Amaka Vanni eds., 2021); *see also* World Bank, Confronting Aids: Public Priorities In A Global Epidemic 353 (1997).

44 *See* Ragavan, *supra* note 8.

45 *See id.*

46 *See id.* (illustrating with an example of Merck).

47 *See* Maurice Cassier & Marilena Correa, *Nationalizing Efavirenz: Compulsory License, Collective Invention and Neo-Developmentalism in Brazil*, *in* Health Innovation and Social Justice in Brazil (Maurice Cassier & Marilena Correa eds., 2019), https://shs.hal.science/halshs-03975575v1/document (last visited Oct. 20, 2025).

48 *See* Presidencia Da Republica Casa Civil, Regula Direitos E Obrigacoes Relativos A Propriedade Industrial (1996), https://www.planalto.gov.br/ccivil_03/leis/l9279.htm (last visited Oct. 20, 2025).

49 *See* Ragavan, *supra* note 8.

50 *See* National AIDS Drug Policy, *supra* note 40 (stating that in 1993, the Laboratório do Estado de Pernambuco (LAFEPE) produced zidovudine (AZT), and by December 1996 protease inhibitors were also included within the program. Three of the drugs distributed by the Ministry of Health—amprenavir, efavirenz and nelfinavir—were patented abroad); *see also* Ragavan, *supra* note 8.

51 *See id; see also* Bass, *supra* note 25, at 209.

52 *See* Susan K. Sell, *Post-TRIPS Developments: The Tension Between Commercial and Social Agendas in the Context of Intellectual Property*, 14 Fla. J. Int'l L. 193, 201 (2002).

under the SUS via an Annual Operating Plan for distribution by local, state, and national agencies.[53] Of these, twelve were locally produced ARVs.[54]

Even as Brazil negotiated lower costs for its patients in need, it did not prevent pharmaceutical companies from selling their products at their regular full price. This combination of various aspects of government policy—creating demand, utilizing and spurring local capacity, and restraining patent holders from price gouging those who could not afford it—led to the prices of ARVs produced in Brazil falling on average by 82 percent between 1996 and 2001 and imported ARVs falling by 40 percent during this period.[55]

Thus, Brazil set an informed agenda regarding how it could best deal with the HIV/AIDS crisis in the face of high-priced patented medicines. Consequently, with an increasing patient population, was one wherein the government answered the question of "make or buy" by looking to its own prior experience to determine a way forward for its people.

2.4 An Amenable Brazilian Judiciary

Most importantly, judicial decisions in Brazil during this time seemed to synchronize with legislative objectives. For instance, lower courts tended to follow the trend of the Supreme Federal Court (Supremo Tribunal Federal, or STF), the highest court of appeals.[56] The STF has traditionally upheld all lower-court decisions regarding medicines.[57] The following passage from a STF decision of 1998 exemplifies its role in access to medicines:[58]

[53] *See id.*

[54] *See generally* MÉDECINS SANS FRONTIÈRES, UNTANGLING THE WEB OF PRICE REDUCTIONS (2005); *see also* Teixeira et al., *The Brazilian Experience in Providing Universal Access to Antiretroviral Therapy*, *in* ECONOMICS OF AIDS AND ACCESS TO HIV/AIDS CARE IN DEVELOPING COUNTRIES: ISSUES AND CHALLENGES 81 (Jean-Paul Moatti et al. eds., 2003) (stating that ARVs distributed by MOH in 2002 include Zidovudine (ZDV)*, Didanosine (ddI)*, Zalcitabine (ddC)*, Lamivudine (3Tc)*, Estavudine (d4T)*, Abacavir, Indinavir*, Ritonavir, Saquinavir, Nelfinavir, Amprenavir, Nevirapine*, Delavirdine, Efavirenz, and Lopinavir/r, where (*) denotes that a generic version was available); *see also* Constance Meiners et al., *Modeling HIV/AIDS Drug Price Determinants in Brazil: Is Generic Competition a Myth?*, 6 PLOS ONE (2011), https://www.ncbi.nlm.nih.gov/pmc/articles/PMC3156239/ (last visited Oct. 20, 2025).

[55] *See* Teixeira et al., *supra* note 54, at 69–88; *see also* Monica Steffen Guise Rosina et al., *supra* note 11, at 165–197.

[56] *See also* Monica Steffen Guise Rosina et al., *supra* note 11, at 173.

[57] *See id.*

[58] *See id.*, at 175.

> Forced to choose between protecting the essential right to life—an unalienable right assured by the Constitution (art. 5°)—or overruling it in favor of secondary or financial interests of the State, I understand, as this dilemma is set out, that judicial ethics dictate to the judge only one possible option: to decide in favor of the undeniable right to life.[59]

Similar studies of precedents from Brazil's second most important court, the Superior Court of Justice (Superior Tribunal de Justiça, or STJ), which hears appeals from the state courts, concluded that the state's obligation to provide medicines when needed for its citizens is firmly established.[60]

Similarly, the Superior Court of the state of São Paulo (Tribunal de Justiça de São Paulo, or TJSP), has held, in a record 85 percent of its decisions, that the provision of health care is an individual right, without any regard to further social and economic consequences, when considering questions concerning demands for HIV medication.[61] Thus, the Brazilian judiciary's endorsement of government's keen interest in prioritizing access to medication has had significant consequences for the country.

3. India: A Model of Strategic Use of TRIPS Flexibilities Under Domestic Laws

3.1 Ideological Foundation of India's Patent Policy

For several decades, India has been widely recognized as "The Pharmacy of the World."[62] This owes in large part to its role in the HIV/AIDS crisis, during which India supplied much of the developing world with low-cost generic alternative drugs.[63] At a time when branded AIDS/HIV medicines were being sold at US$10,000–15,000, Indian generic manufacturers, led by Cipla, started selling them at one thirtieth of that cost, and eventually for under US$100. How did India, another "developing" country, achieve this?

[59] *See also* Monica Steffen Guise Rosina et al., *supra* note 11.

[60] *See id.*, at 172.

[61] *See also* Monica Steffen Guise Rosina et al., *supra* note 11.

[62] *See Indian Court Ruling in Novartis Case Protects India as the Pharmacy of the Developing World*, Médecins Sans Frontières, https://www.msf.org/indian-court-ruling-novartis-case-protects-india-pharmacy-developing-world (last visited Oct. 20, 2025).

[63] *See* Brenda Waning et al., *A Lifeline to Treatment: The Role of Indian Generic Manufacturers in Supplying Antiretroviral Medicines to Developing Countries*, 13 J. Int'l AIDS Soc'y 1, 1–9 (2010).

The Indian government's journey on these issues exhibits some interesting similarities and divergences from the Brazilian approach. While Brazil focused on a series of active executive actions stemming from public-health-centric government bodies, India's actions seem to have changed over time. Government actions from India, as will be discussed below, show how IP norms and flexibilities are framed in a balanced manner through a public-health lens, allowing stakeholders a structure within which patent-patient tensions could be constantly tested and resolved.

Following India's independence in 1947, one of the first concerns of the newly formed government was the extent to which foreign interests controlled Indian markets. Pharmaceutical markets were of particular concern, since India had some of the highest drug prices in the world at the time,[64] and an average life expectancy of just thirty-two years.[65] The government commissioned two detailed reports to examine and make recommendations on the adequacy of the existing patent laws. While the 1948 Tek Chand Committee Report made some important observations related to patent abuse and patent working, it was the 1957 Ayyangar Committee Report that made a difference.[66]

With its excellent research and comparative studies, the Ayyangar Report paved the way for the revolutionary Indian Patent Act of 1970, which would be a major factor in the prospering of India's generic pharmaceutical industry.[67] Some of the important recommendations from the report included process (and not product) patents for food and drugs, an emphasis on local working of patents within a reasonable period, provisions for compulsory

[64] *See* Justice N. Rajagopal Ayyangar, Ministry of Commerce and Industry, Gov't of Ind., A Report on the Revision of the Law in India Relating to Patents for Inventions (1959), https://www.ipindia.gov.in/writereaddata/Portal/Images/pdf/1959-_Justice_N_R_Ayyangar_committee_report.pdf (last visited Oct. 20, 2025) [Ayyangar Report]; *see also* U.S. Senate Judiciary Committee, Report of the Subcommittee on Antitrust and Monopoly, S. Rep. No. 448, 87th Cong., 1st Sess. (June 27, 1961) (showing India with the highest prices out of the seventeen countries surveyed, which included the United States).

[65] *See* David G. Mandelbaum, *Population Problem in India and Pakistan*, 18(24) Far Eastern Survey 283–287 (1949).

[66] *See* Ayyangar Report, *supra* note 64; *see* Ministry of Industry and Supplies, Gov't of Ind., Report of the Patent Enquiry Committee (1948–1950), https://indianculture.gov.in/reports-proceedings/report-patents-enquiry-committee-1948-50 (last visited Oct. 20, 2025) [hereinafter Tek Chand Report].

[67] *See* Ayyangar Report, *supra* note 64; *see also* Tek Chand Report, *supra* note 66; *see also* Shamnad Basheer, *Trumping TRIPS: Indian Patent Proficiency and the Evolution of an Evergreening Enigma*, 18 Oxford U. Commonwealth L. J. 1, 7 (2018); *see also* V. K. Unni, *India's TRIPS-Complaint Patent Decade—The Tumultuous Journey in Search of a Pragmatic Equilibrium*, 50 Int'l Rev. of Intell. Prop. and Competition L. 161 (2019).

licensing and license revocation, and the establishing of a well-equipped patent office.[68]

As widely noted, India's prime minister, Indira Gandhi, who was at the helm when the 1970 Act came into being, had stated:[69]

> Medicines, which may be of the utmost value to poorer countries, can be bought by us only at exorbitant prices, since we are unable to have adequate independent bases of research and production. . . . My idea of a better-ordered world is one in which medical discoveries would be free of patents and there would be no profiteering from life or death.

These ideas, having propelled the growth of the domestic pharmaceutical industry in India while making pharmaceuticals dramatically more affordable, would continue to be influential.[70] Early on, India, much like Brazil, was focused on local working and limiting patents. However, since the introduction of TRIPS requirements, the domestic interactions with the patent-patient divide have been focused on structural measures to improve the quality of patents, the implied goal being to reduce the number of undeserving patents or minor innovations.

3.2 Evolution of India's Balanced Strategy for the Post-TRIPS World

Even as India would eventually sign on to the TRIPS Agreement, which required substantial harmonization of its laws with those of other countries, the government remained sensitive to the balance between innovation and affordability. To establish and implement this balanced approach, India markedly departed from similarly placed countries when it proceeded to deal with TRIPS-mandated changes to patent laws. For instance, India was one of the few developing countries that utilized the complete ten-year transition period allowed under the TRIPS Agreement to transition into the TRIPS-compliant patent regime.[71] This did not merely "delay the inevitable"; rather,

[68] *See* Ayyangar Report, *supra* note 64.

[69] *See* R. Ostergard, *Intellectual Property: A Universal Human Right?*, 21(1) Human Rights Quarterly 156–178 (1999).

[70] *See* Basheer, *supra* note 67, at 16–45.

[71] *See* George K. Foster, *Opposing Forces in a Revolution in International Patent Protection: The U.S. and India in the Uruguay Round and Its Aftermath*, 3 UCLA J. Int'l L. & Foreign Aff. 283, 312 (1998) (stemming apparently from the fact that India was also one of the reasons that

it also allowed for substantial discussion and debate regarding what should be the appropriate level of configuration for the newly required patent levers. Hence, the ten-year time frame allowed for complex preference formation and expression domestically. In fact, as Prashant Reddy has noted, contestations and changes to what would become the final amendments in 2005 continued until March 17, 2005, the day before the amendments were introduced in the Parliament.[72]

India had become a signatory to the WTO on January 1, 1995.[73] Meanwhile, at the end of the parliamentary session, on December 31, 1994, the president of India had promulgated the Patents (Amendment) Ordinance, 1994, to amend India's 1970 Patent Act.[74] The ordinance accepted interim applications and detailed application procedures, scope, and enforcement of exclusive marketing rights (EMR).[75] With a view to utilizing the full period of transition the country was permitted, the ordinance noted that the decision on patentability would be made when India completed the full transition on January 1, 2005.[76] The ordinance of 1994 lapsed on March 25, 1995, when both houses of Parliament failed to address the matter within six weeks of reconvening that year.[77]

this transitionary period was granted in the first place); *see also* Elijah Munyuki & Rangarirai Machemedze, *Implementation of the TRIPS Flexibilities by East and Southern African Countries: Status of Patent Law Reforms by 2010*, Equinet Discussion Paper 80 (2010); *see also* Omar Serrano & Mira Burri, *TRIPS Implementation in Developing Countries: Likely Scenarios to 2025*, *in* The Shifting Landscape of Global Trade Governance 275–294 (Manfred Elsig et al. eds., 2010); *see also* Ragavan, *supra* note 8, at 80–83.

[72] *See* Prashant Reddy, *Pages from History: The Mysterious Legislative History of §3(d)*, SpicyIP Open Gov't Project (Nov. 9, 2011), https://spicyip.com/2011/11/pages-from-history-mysterious.html (last visited Oct. 20, 2025); *see also* Department of Industrial Policy and Promotion, Ministry of Commerce and Industry, Gov't of Ind., Proposal for Amendment to the Patents Act, 1970, No. 12/14/2003-PP&C (2005), https://spicyip.com/docs/PMOapproval.pdf (last visited Oct. 20, 2025) (being notes exchanged between the DIPP and Cabinet Secretariat).

[73] *See India and the WTO*, World Trade Org., http://www.wto.org/english/thewto_e/countries_e/india_e.htm (last visited Oct. 20, 2025).

[74] *See* The Patents (Amendment) Ordinance, No. 13 of 1994 (Ind.) [Amendment Ordinance 1994]; *see also* Gov't of Ind., Notification No. IP/N/1/IND/1 (1995); *see also* Patents (Amendment) Ordinance, No. 7 of 2004 (Ind.); *see also* India Const. art. 123(1) (authorizing the president to legislate by passing ordinances, when Parliament is not in session and the president deems it necessary to take immediate action. In India, ordinances have the force of law provided both houses approve the ordinance within six weeks of beginning a new session of the Parliament.)

[75] *See* Amendment Ordinance 1994, *supra* note 74.

[76] *See* Panel Report, *India—Patent Protection for Pharmaceutical and Agricultural Chemical Products*, WTO Doc. WT/DS50/6 (adopted Sept. 5, 1997).

[77] *See* Shishir Mehta & Rajesh Chavda, *The Mail Box Dispute and Implications on Indian Patent Regime*, Student Advocate 40, 7 (1998); *see also* Shondeep Banerji, *The Indian Intellectual Property Regime and the TRIPS Agreement*, *in* Intellectual Property Rights in Emerging Markets 61 (Clarissa Long ed., 2000) (stating that a bill must be approved by a simple majority of both houses of Parliament—the Lower House or Lok Sabha, comparable to the House of Commons,

What the executive and the legislature did not do in this period is also significant. Following a presidential ordinance in 1994[78] to bring Indian patent law into compliance with the TRIPS articles 70.8 and 70.9, related to mailbox applications by introducing EMR, neither house of Parliament addressed this matter within the required time period, causing it to lapse.[79] Similarly, when a bill introducing some amendments was introduced around this time, with the objective of complying with the TRIPS mandate, the Lower House (Lok Sabha) of Parliament passed the bill but the Upper House (Rajya Sabha) got dissolved, causing the bill to lapse.[80]

This situation is not surprising, given the then-prevailing levels of domestic dissatisfaction with India's signing of the TRIPS Agreement. India's politically active civil society and industry both engaged in extensive lobbying to secure both anticipated and unexpected preferences.[81] This lobbying effort was partly due to India's positive trade balance and the globalization of the large Indian pharmaceutical firms from the late 1990s.[82] At the same time, there was an intense debate over the implications of patents on access to medicines in the developing world.

The perceived impracticality of the TRIPS Agreement, in the context of India's efforts to enhance access and affordability, spurred the emergence of a robust generic-drug industry. Thus was constructed a pharmaceutical pyramid in which generic drugs will always occupy a place in the future. During this period, the Indian drug manufacturer Cipla revolutionized the

and the Upper House or Rajya Sabha, comparable to the House of Lords—and signed by the president. The bill lapses if the Lok Sabha does not approve it. If approved in the Lok Sabha but not in the Rajya Sabha, a parliamentary committee is appointed to deliberate over the bill. The committee's report is passed to the Parliament and to the concerned departments. If the government agrees with the amendments suggested by the committee, the bill is sent for cabinet approval, after which it is again placed before the Lok Sabha.)

[78] *See* Amendment Ordinance 1994, *supra* note 74.

[79] *See* Agreement on Trade-Related Aspects of Intellectual Property Rights, art. 70.8, April 15, 1994, 1869 U.N.T.S. 299, 33 I.L.M. 1197 (1994) [TRIPS Agreement] (relating to what is sometimes called the "mailbox" provision. A metaphorical "mailbox" is created to receive and store the applications. The date of filing is significant, which is why the mailbox provisions were set up. It is used for assessing whether the application meets the criteria for patenting, including novelty or newness.); *see also* Basheer, *supra* note 67, at 18; *see also* RAGAVAN, *supra* note 8, at 107–8.

[80] *See* RAGAVAN, *supra* note 8; *see also* WTO APPELLATE BODY, INDIA—PATENT PROTECTION FOR PHARMACEUTICAL AND AGRICULTURAL CHEMICAL PRODUCTS, WTO Doc. WT/DS50/AB/R (1998) (being later challenged at the WTO DSU by the United States, wherein the latter was successful in establishing its case that India had violated its obligations under Article 70.8 and breached Article 70.9).

[81] *See* Anitha Ramanna, *Interest Groups and Patent Reform in India*, INDIRA GANDHI INST. OF DEV. RES. (2012) (discussing the unpredictable paths chosen by interest groups in this period).

[82] *See* Amy Kapczynski, *Harmonization and Its Discontents: A Case Study of TRIPS Implementation in India's Pharmaceutical Sector*, 97 CALIF. L. REV. 1571, 1583 (2009).

dynamics of the HIV/AIDS response globally. Incidentally, Cipla announced that it would, for the first time ever, provide generic versions of the US$10,000 ARVs at merely US$350, marking a significant shift in the international pharmaceutical landscape.[83] This transformed the conversations around what generic companies could contribute to public health and indirectly led to the Doha Declaration, which reaffirmed that TRIPS "can and should be interpreted in a manner supportive of WTO member nations' right to protect public health and, in particular, to promote access to medicines for all."[84]

The Doha Declaration was negotiated right after the United States faced its anthrax crisis.[85] The need for an immediate supply of anthrax drugs at an affordable cost caused the United States to consider significant steps to make the drugs available, including the option of buying generic versions of ciprofloxacin from India. Senator Charles Schumer approached the Indian generic-drug company Ranbaxy Ltd. to check the availability of the generic version of ciprofloxacin at a low cost.[86] Further, the US government considered federally appropriating Bayer's US patent on ciprofloxacin in order to locally manufacture the drug. Commentators wasted no time in highlighting the historic US stance against local manufacturing, as well as the federal appropriation of IP rights through compulsory licensing, which the developed nations seemed so opposed to during the TRIPS negotiations.[87] The Indian government pointed out that the steps taken by the United States and Canada during the crisis were comparable to policy options India had pursued to make medications available to its population.

[83] *See* Donald McNeil Jr, *Indian Company Offers to Supply AIDS Drugs at Low Cost in Africa,* N. Y. Times, Feb. 7, 2001, https://www.nytimes.com/2001/02/07/world/indian-company-offers-to-supply-aids-drugs-at-low-cost-in-africa.html (last visited Oct. 20, 2025).

[84] *See* World Trade Organization, Ministerial Declaration Fourth Session Doha, WTO Doc. WT/MIN(01)/DEC/1, 41 ILM 746 (2001) [Doha Declaration].

[85] *See* Helen Cooper & Geoff Winestock, *Poor Nations Win Global Trade Deal as U.S. Compromises,* Wall St. J., Nov. 15, 2001.

[86] *See* Mellinda T. Willis, *Officials Move Toward Doxycycline as First-Line Anthrax Treatment,* ABC News, Oct. 30, 2001 (noting that TV networks such as CNN in the United States advised people to take the affordable generic doxycycline rather than the patented Cipro. *See also CDC Considers Doxycycline over Cipro,* ABC News, Oct. 30, 2001, https://abcnews.go.com/Health/story?id=117149&page=1 (last visited Oct. 22, 2025); Lawrence K. Altman, *A Nation Challenged: The Treatments,* N. Y. Times, Oct. 26, 2001, https://www.nytimes.com/2001/10/26/us/nation-challenged-treatments-shift-agency-recommends-combinations-antibiotics.html (last visited Oct. 22, 2025); *Indian Pharmaceutical Companies Prepared to Provide Generic Cipro,* Infection Control Today (Oct. 25, 2001), https://www.infectioncontroltoday.com/view/indian-pharmaceutical-companies-prepared-provide-generic-cipro (last visited Oct. 20, 2025); *see also* Manu Joseph, *Indian Cipro Copies Don't Pay Off,* Wired (Nov. 8, 2001), https://www.wired.com/2001/11/indian-cipro-copies-dont-pay-off/ (last visited Oct. 20, 2025).

[87] *See* F. M. Abbott, *The Doha Declaration on the TRIPS Agreement and Public Health: Lighting a Dark Corner at the WTO,* J. Int'l Econ. L. 5, 469 (2002).

The Indian government gets the credit for highlighting the issues that countries representing a sizable percentage of the global population face to ensure that pharmaceuticals are accessible and affordable. The following three instances exemplify India's leadership role in international negotiations, voicing the unresolved concerns of developing and least-developed countries, especially regarding the deleterious impact of the TRIPS Agreement on access to public health and carve-outs in the form of negotiated flexibilities under TRIPS to address those concerns.

First, the Indian government, over the years, has been an advocate for and has taken leadership in negotiating flexibilities at the international level, as during the negotiations at Doha,[88] where India led the campaign to gain concessions from the WTO.[89] The role of Murasoli Maran, India's minister for commerce and industry, was widely viewed as pivotal in the resulting negotiations at the WTO. Mr. Maran's strong stance was in part a result of the government's keen sense of public sentiment in India, where rampant protests were organized days before the WTO session against protectionist measures envisaged under the TRIPS Agreement.[90]

Second, as discussed earlier in this chapter, India effectively made use of the existing flexibilities in the TRIPS Agreement, with the significant example being the compulsory licensing of Nexavar.[91] That this was strategic was not lost on Justice Prabha Sridevan, a point reflected in her judgment. In gist, the decision discussed a request by NATCO for a compulsory license, given Cipla's existing presence in the market. Ultimately, the decision weighed the balance of hardships: that is, balancing compulsory licensing of the patent which authorized third parties to produce or use a patented product or process without the owner's consent with the publics' need for the medication. For NATCO, this represented a huge strategic success. Ever since 2008, NATCO had been advocating for a compulsory license against Roche's anti-cancer drug Tarceva (erlotinib) for supply to Nepal, and later it would advocate for the manufacture and export of sunitinib (Sutent), also an anti-cancer drug.[92]

[88] *See* Doha Declaration, *supra* note 84.

[89] *See* Helen Cooper & Geoff Winestock, *Poor Nations Win Global Trade Deal as U.S. Compromises*, Wall St. J., Nov. 15, 2001, at A1.

[90] *See id.*

[91] *See* Bayer Corporation v. Natco Pharma Ltd. (2013), Order No. 45/2013 (Intellectual Property Appellate Board, Chennai).

[92] *See* Srividhya Ragavan et al., *Post-Hearing Submission to the Office of the United States Trade Representative*, United States Trade Representative, https://www.regulations.gov/document/USTR-2014-0020-0013 (last visited Oct. 20, 2025).

Third, India used the architectural power of law to gain legitimization of actions demanded by the countermovement groups for access to medicine, such as limiting the patent rights over such drugs.[93]

3.3 Consolidation of India's TRIPS-Compliant Patent Statute

Historically, India had opted for a process-patent-only regime for food and pharmaceuticals, with a short term of process protection of five years, in order to prioritize domestic issues such as access to health care and food security. TRIPS Agreement required a change in this approach, which had for decades helped India build its domestic generic pharmaceutical industry to eventually become the "pharmacy of the world." India duly fulfilled its international obligations under TRIPS Agreement by instituting a pharmaceutical product patent regime in 2005, in addition to its process-patent regime, as the TRIPS Agreement prevents discrimination against particular fields of technology. India also adopted the TRIPS-compliant international standard of patentability based on the requirements of novelty, inventive step, and industrial applicability. Consequently, India has used a number of flexibilities, as will be elaborated in the ensuing discussion, interpreting the TRIPS policy levers through the lens of its socioeconomic requirements and objectives.

3.3.1 Higher Standards on Patentability

India's definition of novelty or "new invention" includes a worldwide prior art standard. The term *prior-art* refers to knowledge available to the public before the patent application was filed. A world-wide prior-art standard requires the patent office to consider the application material as new *only* if there is no prior-art that has the same embodiments of the invention anywhere in the world. India's world-wide prior-art standard was broader than the requirement that prevailed under US patent statutes until 2011.[94] Under the US' earlier 1952 patent statute, *only* public use of the application material (within the United States) negated novelty.[95] Thus, something that was

[93] *See* Amy Kapczynski, *The Access to Knowledge Mobilization and the New Politics of Intellectual Property*, 117 YALE L.J. 804, 861–882 (providing Kapczynski's description of the gravitational power of the law, including architectural effects).

[94] 35 USC 1952, §102(b).

[95] *See* Srividhya Ragavan et al., *Justifying India's Patent Position to the United States International Trade Commission and Office of the United States Trade Representative*, 7 THE IND. J. OF INTELL. PROP. L. 1, 27 (2015).

used publicly outside the US would have still been considered new for the purposes for patenting, subject to other sub-sections of the provision. The United States moved to a world-wide prior art standard under the America Invents Act, 2011.[96]

The TRIPS Agreement also requires that patentable subject matter involve an inventive step. India's definition for invention step includes technical advancement, or, 'having economic significance', or both, which makes the invention not obvious to a person skilled in art.[97] That is, a patent eligible application material that is also considered *new* when compared with the prior-art, will pass the inventive step test if the application showed that the application material included some technical advancement, or had economic significance or both. The requirement for inventive step in India is a more stringent than the nonobvious requirement in the United States, which essentially means that India tried to be more stringent as a gate-keeper for granting patents.[98] Similarly, India's definition of industrial applicability is stronger than that under US statute. For instance, weaker standards on patentability in the United States have been accused of allowing the patenting of abstract inventions, whereas Indian statute specifically excludes such inventions that lack industrial applicability or utility.[99]

The Indian Patent Act of 1970 reflects some of the flexibilities outlined in TRIPS Article 27.3, which allows member nations exclusions from patentability. For example, the provision on exclusions from patentability, provided under §3 of the 1970 Indian Patent Act, outlines the categories of what are *not* inventions under Indian patent law. While these encapsulate a number of provisions, there are notable exceptions relevant for public health. Among these are discoveries of any living thing or nonliving substance occurring in nature (which in pertinent part excludes patent applications claiming important "discoveries" in the biotech and biologics sphere),[100] methods of medical treatments (which includes in vitro methods of diagnosis),[101] plants and animals (which in the Indian context are particularly relevant for traditional medicine),[102] biotechnology (such as genetically modified

[96] Leahy-Smith America Invents Act, enacted on September 16, 2011, is formally cited as Pub. L. No. 112-29, 125 Stat. 284.
[97] *See* Patents Act, No. 39 of 1970, §2(1)(ja) (Ind).
[98] *See* Ragavan et al., *supra* note 95.
[99] *See* Ragavan et al., *supra* note 95.
[100] *See supra* note 97, §3(c).
[101] *See supra* note 97, §3(i).
[102] *See supra* note 97, §3(j).

plant varieties and seeds),[103] immoral inventions,[104] traditional knowledge-related medicines,[105] mere admixtures (which ensure that only synergistic combinations showing properties beyond the mere aggregation of the properties of individual components are patentable),[106] and non-efficacious derivatives (which exclude structurally similar derivatives that do not demonstrate significant therapeutic efficacy over prior known substances).[107]

Exclusions from patentability exist in other legal systems. For instance, in *Mayo v. Prometheus*[108] a unanimous US Supreme Court struck down a method of medical treatment claim as being directed to a law of nature and thus, patent-ineligible. That is, materials that are considered to be part of the law of nature are not eligible for patent protection and hence, excluded from protection. Similarly, in Canada, methods of medical treatment are not patentable under §12.04.02 of the Manual of Patent Office Procedure.[109] Similarly, TRIPS Agreement leaves countries free to define patentability criteria, outline the scope of the term "invention" including exclusions therefrom, and determine the standards for nonobviousness or inventive step.

In instituting a higher patentability bar, a developing country like India would rightly avoid some of the excessive patenting problems that seem to plague the United States. Having a higher bar with standards is well within the rights of sovereign nations and well-established under the principles of the WTO. TRIPS Agreement allows for such a flexible approach, as outlined in its Article 1.1, which recognizes the right of member nations to take local realities into account and to adapt the minimum standards of TRIPS Agreement in a pluralistic manner.[110] Further, the Preamble of TRIPS Agreement, read in conjunction with Articles 7 and 8, clearly outlines the rights of sovereign nations to calibrate their IP laws by taking into consideration local developmental, technological objectives, social and economic welfare, and public-interest and/or public-health measures.[111]

[103] *See supra* note 97, §3(j).
[104] *See supra* note 97, §3(b).
[105] *See supra* note 97, §3(p).
[106] *See supra* note 97, §3(e).
[107] *See supra* note 97, §3(d).
[108] *See* Mayo Collaborative Services v. Prometheus Laboratories, 132 S.Ct. 1289 (2012).
[109] *See* GOVERNMENT OF CANADA, MANUAL OF PATENT OFFICE PRACTICE (MOPOP), https://manuels-manuals.opic-cipo.gc.ca/w/ic/MOPOP-en#!fragment/zoupio-_Toc185246039/BQCwhgziBcwMYgK4DsDWszIQewE4BUBTADwBdoAvbRABwEtsBaAfX2zgEYAOAVgCYALADYADAGYAnAEoANMmylCEAIqJCuAJ7QA5NpkRCYXAlXqtu-YeMgAynlIAhLQCUAogBlXANQCCAOQBhVxlSMAAjaFJ2KSkgA (last visited Oct. 20, 2025).
[110] *See* TRIPS Agreement, *supra* note 79, art. 1.1.
[111] *See* TRIPS Agreement, *supra* note 79, art. 7 & 8.

The struggles of the United States with a barrage of secondary patents on medicines have served as a lesson to other countries, including India.[112] In essence, India may have prevented issues that the United States faced, and continues to face, on account of unduly lowering the bar to facilitate more patents. In gist, lower patent standards can dangerously interfere with follow-on innovations and unjustly reward very low levels of innovation. For countries like India, such lowering of patenting standards for innovation can be onerous in its effects of pharmaceutical costs and untreated patients.

3.3.2 Anti-Evergreening

Of the exclusions from patentability prescribed under the 1970 Indian Patent Act, the last one, which is covered under §3(d), has garnered particular attention and scrutiny globally.[113] It is commonly known as India's anti-evergreening provision. As discussed in the previous chapter, the term *evergreening* refers to strategically patenting different forms or formulations of a medicine's active ingredients, specifying new uses, and staggering such protection so as to extend monopoly control over various forms or uses of the medicine beyond the twenty-year term of protection.[114]

After the Supreme Court of India's decision in *Novartis v. Union of India*, insofar as medicines were concerned, §3(d) of the Patents Act required structurally similar derivatives to demonstrate therapeutic efficacy.[115] In essence, the Supreme Court found, in a well-reasoned decision, that the beta-crystalline form of imatinib mesylate was revealed and claimed in a pre-TRIPS patent outside India and thus was time-barred from patentability in India unless it showed significantly enhanced efficacy.[116] The Court found that Novartis offered no evidence of increased efficacy of the relevant compound whatsoever, and that the patent was thus unmeritorious under § 3(d).[117]

Regardless of the judicial interpretation, the goal, as noted after the Novartis judgment by then-Minister of Commerce and Industry Kamal

[112] *See* Thomas A. Faunce & Joel Lexchin, *'Linkage' Pharmaceutical Evergreening in Canada and Australia*, Australia and New Zealand Health Pol'y (2007).
[113] *See id.*
[114] *See* Ragavan et al., *supra* note 92.
[115] *See* Novartis AG v. Union of India & Others, (2013) 6 SCC 1(Ind.).
[116] *See id.*
[117] *See id.*

Nath, was to ensure that "there is no question of evergreening."[118] To that extent, the strict requirement provided by §3(d), whether as a patent-eligibility threshold or a patentability test, ensures that trivial medical advances are not granted a patent.[119]

Interestingly, India's provision is styled along the exact lines of the opinion of the US Court of Appeals for the Federal Circuit (CAFC) in the case of *Pfizer v. Apotex*, involving Pfizer's patenting of the besylate form of amlodipine (salt form), which Apotex claimed was obvious in light of Pfizer's own patent on the base compound amlodipine.[120] The CAFC, in agreeing with Apotex that the patent on the besylate form was invalid, highlighted that the besylate form lacked adequate "unexpected superior results" from the base compound for the besylate form to be patented.[121] Further, the CAFC in several decisions has reiterated the requirement of "unexpected results" or "surprising effect" as tests to determine patentability of the new forms of known substances.[122]

Furthermore, secondary patents, which have a high correlation with evergreening, are a controversial issue not just in India but also in the United States.[123] The steady lowering of standards, especially for determining nonobviousness, has in turn contributed to strategic patenting, which later became and continues to be the subject of much scrutiny in the United States.[124] The resulting issues caused the US regulators to ensure that the Manual for Patent Examination Procedure under §716.02 and 2144.09 at Paragraph VII specifically memorializes "unexpected results" as a test, requiring the inventor to demonstrate "unexpected advantages" or "superior properties" in order to determine nonobviousness of structurally similar

[118] *See* Kamal Nath, Minister of Commerce and Industry, Response During Parliamentary Debates (stressing that Section 3(d) was introduced to prevent "ever-greening," in response to concerns by other Parliamentarians over its likely impact on prices).

[119] *See* Shamnad Basheer et al., Primer on Public Health and Intellectual Property Rights (IPR) 43-45 (2014), https://spicyip.com/wp-content/uploads/2014/08/Final-Report.pdf (last visited Oct. 20, 2025) (having been prepared for the WHO Country Office, India).

[120] *See* Pfizer v. Apotex, 488 F. 3d 1377 (Fed. Cir. 2007); *see also* Pfizer v. Apotex, 480 F.3d 1348 (Fed. Cir. 2007).

[121] *See* Pfizer v. Apotex, 480 F.3d 1348 (Fed. Cir. 2007); *see also In re Swain*, 33 C.C.P.A. 1266, 156 F.2d 246, 247–48 (1946).

[122] *See id.*

[123] *See* Federal Trade Comm'n, Generic Drug Entry Prior to Patent Expiration: An FTC Study (2002).

[124] *See generally* Srividhya Ragavan, *Correlative Obligation in Patent Law: The Role of Public Good in Defining the Limits of Patent Exclusivity*, 6 N.Y.U. J. Intell. Prop. & Ent. L. 47 (2016), https://scholarship.law.tamu.edu/facscholar/806 (last visited Oct. 20, 2025).

compounds like isomers and homologues.[125] These criteria are not measurably different from the *efficacy* requirement that India uses to assess patentability. Thus, India's standard is well within the lines of what has been allowed in the United States.

3.3.3 Compulsory Licensing

Other than patent exclusions, the Indian patent law has also ingrained public-health considerations in provisions that kick in after a patent has been granted. In §82-94 of the 1970 Indian Patent Act, India provides for compulsory licenses on patent abuse as well as for public interest.[126] Under §84 of the Act, compulsory licenses can be granted for reasons of patent abuse if, three years after the grant of patent, the reasonable requirements of the public have not been met, the patented invention has not been made available to the public at a reasonably affordable price, or the invention has not been worked in the territory of India.[127]

The 2005 amendment adds a requirement that applications for compulsory licensing of a patent should provide proof that the applicant had attempted to negotiate a license with the patentee for a minimum period of six months.[128] Another significant amendment, §90(1), allows for the export of compulsorily licensed products to use the flexibility provided under Article 31(*bis*) of TRIPS Agreement.[129] In order to aid such exports, §92A enables the exportation of pharmaceuticals to meet public-health emergencies in countries with insufficient or no manufacturing capacity in the pharmaceutical sector from countries possessing such manufacturing capacity, like India and Brazil.[130] The language in the Patent Amendment (Ordinance) of 2004, which allowed for the export of compulsorily licensed pharmaceuticals "provided compulsory license has been granted by such country," has been retained in the 2005 amendment.[131]

In gist, the Patent Act outlines four major grounds for compulsorily licensing a patent in India that are fully compliant under Article 31 of the

[125] *See* USPTO Manual of Patent Examination Procedure, §s 716, 2144 (2024), https://spicyip.com/wp-content/uploads/2014/08/Final-Report.pdf (last visited Oct. 20, 2025).
[126] *See supra* note 97, §s 82, 94 (referring to the law as amended in 2005).
[127] *See supra* note 97, §84(6)(iv); *see also* TRIPS Agreement, *supra* note 79, art. 31(b) (aligning the Indian law provided under §84(6)(iv) of the Indian Patent Act, 1970, with those under the Article 31(b) of the TRIPS Agreement as regard the requirements for efforts towards obtaining a license); *see supra* note 100 (interpreting the provisions of the 1970 Indian Patent Act).
[128] *See* Patents (Amendment) Act, No. 15 of 2005 (Ind.), §52.
[129] *See id.*, §90 & §90(1)(viii).
[130] *See supra* note 97, §92(A); *see also* Doha Declaration, *supra* note 84, at 6.
[131] *See supra* note 97, §92(A).

TRIPS Agreement, which allows countries to determine the grounds for issuing compulsory licenses.[132] These grounds are as follows:

First, under §84, third parties can seek a license on a patent after three years of the grant of patent, on the grounds that (a) the reasonable requirements of the public with respect to the patented invention have not been satisfied, or (b) that the patented invention is not available to the public at a reasonably affordable price, or (c) that the patented invention is not worked in the territory of India.[133]

Second, owners of improvements on existing patents who are unable to work the improvements can seek a license on the ground that, without such license, they are prevented or hindered from working the improvement efficiently or to the best advantage possible. Compulsory licenses under this provision are granted subject to the satisfaction of the controller that the applicant will be able to provide or generate a reasonable royalty to the patent owner and that the patent has "made a substantial contribution to the establishment or development of commercial or industrial activities in the territory of India."[134] The provision works only when there is a blocking patent.

Third, under §92, a compulsory license can be granted where the government certifies the existence of a national emergency, such as a public-health crisis.[135]

Fourth, under §92A, a compulsory license can be issued to facilitate export to countries that have insufficient or limited manufacturing capacity as required under Article 31(*bis*) of TRIPS Agreement.[136]

Indeed, authors Flynn, Baker, and Ragavan assert that India has one of the most sophisticated compulsory licensing provisions of any country and that it is fully compliant with Article 31 of the TRIPS Agreement, which permits compulsory licenses for any reasons, as clarified by the Doha Declaration.[137] The authors note that the grounds for issuing such licenses are fully in accord with traditional grounds for compulsory licenses dating back to the earliest patent laws and explicitly sanctioned under Article 5(A) of the Paris Convention.[138] Insufficient supply, excessive pricing, and lack of an adequate

[132] *See* TRIPS Agreement, *supra* note 79, art. 30.
[133] *See supra* note 97, §84.
[134] *See supra* note 97, §80.
[135] *See supra* note 97, §92.
[136] *See supra* note 97, §92A.
[137] *See* Srividhya Ragavan, *Justifying India's Patent Position to The United States International Trade Commission and Office of United States Trade Representative*, 9 THE IND. J. OF INTELL. PROP. L. 195 (2018).
[138] *See supra* note 97, §92.

market are all good reasons for invoking compulsory licenses, which are legally justified under international and national laws.[139] The authors also assert that these provisions help contextualize the cost of the drugs against the income inequalities within India.

Notably, the authors assert that, despite instituting such balancing provisions, US pharmaceutical exports to India had steadily increased in the period that immediately followed the reforms.[140] They add that, according to trade data from the WTO, US pharmaceutical exports to India rose sharply by 470 percent, from US$39 million to US$225 million, during the 2000–2012 period, as depicted in Figure 3.1. Further, the United States' total pharmaceutical exports to India during the 2000–2012 period grew at nearly double the pace of its exports to the world as a whole, as seen in Figure 3.1 below. In five out of seven years, the average annual growth rate of US pharmaceutical exports to India was higher than that of the world as a whole, as seen in Figure 3.2.

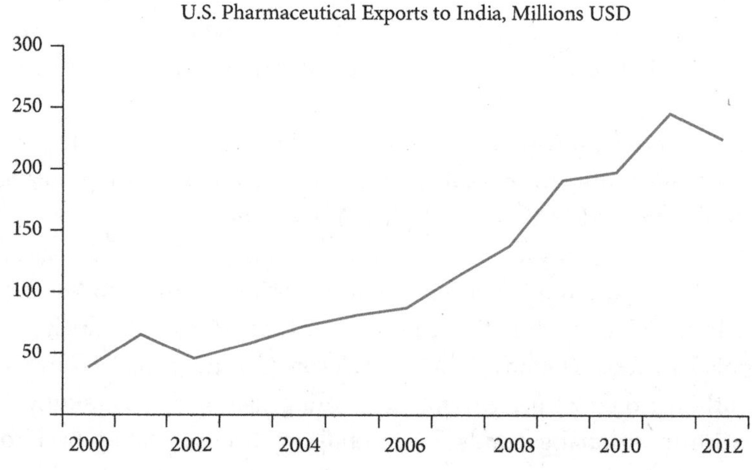

Figure 3.1 US pharmaceutical exports to India, in US$ millions. Reproduced from Mike Palmedo, Graphics on U.S. Pharmaceutical Exports to India, Patents, The Compulsory License, and Prices, InfoJustice, http://infojustice.org/wp-content/uploads/2014/02/US-Pharmaceutical-Exports-to-India.png. Under a Creative Commons Attribution 4.0 International Deed (CC By 4.0).

[139] *See* Michael Halewood, *Regulating Patent Holders: Local Working and Compulsory Licenses Under International Law*, 35 Osgoode Hall L.J. 243 (1997).

[140] *See* Ragavan et al., *supra* note 95, at 14–18 (being the post-hearing submissions of the authors to the USTR).

Table 3.1 US Pharmaceutical Exports to India and the World.

	Total Growth, 2000–2012	Average Growth over Prior Year
U.S. Exports to India	470%	18%
U.S. Exports to World	242%	11%

Reproduced from Mike Palmedo, Graphics on US Pharmaceutical Exports to India, Patents, the Compulsory License, and Prices, INFOJUSTICE, http://infojustice.org/wp-content/uploads/2014/02/US-Pharmaceutical-Exports-to-India.png. Under a Creative Commons Attribution 4.0 International Deed (CC By 4.0).

Figure 3.1 is further detailed in Table 3.1 above showing the sharp increase in US pharmaceutical exports to India by 470 percent (from US$39 million to US$225 million) in the period between 2000 to 2012.

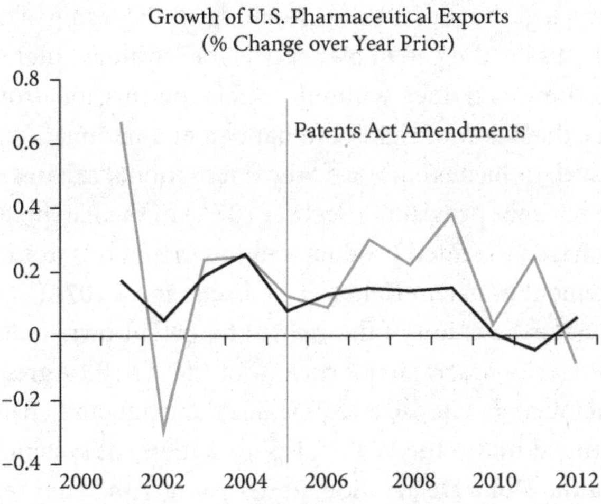

Figure 3.2 Growth rates of US pharmaceutical exports to India vs. the World. Reproduced from Mike Palmedo, Graphics on U.S. Pharmaceutical Exports to India, Patents, The Compulsory License, and Prices, INFOJUSTICE, http://infojustice.org/wp-content/uploads/2014/02/US-Pharmaceutical-Exports-to-India.png. Under a Creative Commons Attribution 4.0 International Deed (CC By 4.0).

Figure 3.2 complements the data provided in the previous table to reiterate that the average annual US pharmaceutical exports to India has steadily increased during the seven-year period.

3.3.4 Government Use

In addition to compulsory licenses, India includes one other form of non-authorized use of patents for public-emergency purposes: government-use provisions. These are outlined in §S99-103 and under §47(4) of the 1970 Indian Patent Act. These provisions envisage the government being able to use or acquire certain inventions upon the payment of a reasonable royalty, as well as to import the medicines for distribution through government channels.

3.3.5 International Exhaustion Regime

Other significant provisions in India's Patent Act respecting access to medicines include an international exhaustion regime.[141] The patent exhaustion doctrine, which is commonly known as the *first sale doctrine,* dictates that the authorized (legal) *first* sale of a patented item results in terminating further rights over that specific item. That is the patent owner cannot seek royalties from a legal buyer for using, reselling, or disposing of the purchased item. At the first sale, the patent owner gets the royalties, after which buyers can perform these activities without further permission from the patent holder. Such exhaustion of rights can happen at a national, regional, or international level. India has embraced the international exhaustion regime.

Under the relevant provision (Section 107A) of the Patents Actprocuring lawfully purchased patented product and importing it is not be considered as an infringement of patent rights.[142] In discussing § 107A(b) of India, and its international exhaustion of the rights of a patent owner, authors Flynn, Baker, and Ragavan assert that Article 6 of the TRIPS Agreement explicitly allows members to choose a regime of exhaustion and ensures that they can be challenged under the WTO dispute-settlement system.[143] They further note that the Doha Declaration, under paragraph 5, has reaffirmed that member states do have this right, stating that each member is free to establish its own regime for such exhaustion without challenge.[144]

[141] *See supra* note 97, §107A(b).
[142] *See* Basheer et al., *supra* note 119, at 63.
[143] *See supra* note 97, §107A(b).
[144] *See* Annex IC to the General Agreement on Tariffs and Trade, Apr. 15, 1994, 33 I.L.M 1981 (1994).

As a consequence of this provision, the sale or importation into India of a legally procured patented item from anywhere in the world will not amount to infringement.[145] In fact, even importation of a product acquired from sources other than the patent owner (or assignee)—for instance, from countries not yet recognizing product patent protection—would be covered by the provision.

3.3.6 Opposition and Revocation Proceedings

Additionally, Indian law contains a set of provisions that create more operational efficiency in patent prosecution. There are built-in safeguards that allow third-party intervention or assistance as necessary. This is achieved primarily through three mechanisms, as follows:

a) Pre-Grant Opposition Proceedings

Pre-grant opposition signifies the first instance at which a challenge can be made before the grant of a patent under the enactment.[146] As for the procedure, under §25 any third party can oppose a patent after publication of the patent application and before the grant of the patent on several grounds, including wrongful acquisition of patent, prior publication, prior public use,[147] obviousness,[148] lack of inventiveness,[149] lack of adequate application disclosures including a written description and specification requirements, and false information.[150] Such provisions are relatively uncommon globally.

A more effective process, though, is the reexamination procedure in the United States.[151] It specifies that "any person," as opposed to a "person interested," can challenge the patent application.[152] These safeguards not only encourage competition by opposing patents at the earliest stage but also allow patient groups and other third parties to submit objections prior to the grant of a pharmaceutical patent. Indeed, the TRIPS Agreement, under Article 62(4),

[145] *See supra* note 97, §107A(b).

[146] *See supra* note 97, §25(1) (providing for mechanism that very few countries have); *see also* Kapczynski, *supra* note 93, at 1571; *see also* Feroz Ali Khader, The Touchstone Effect: The Impact of Pre-Grant Opposition on Patents 40 (2009).

[147] *See supra* note 97, §25.

[148] *See supra* note 97, §25(c).

[149] *See supra* note 97, §25(e).

[150] *See supra* note 97, §25(h).

[151] *See* Khader, *supra* note 146, at 41; *see also* Patents Act of 1952 §302, 35 U.S.C. §390 (2006) (providing for US procedure on reexamination of patents).

[152] *See supra* note 97, §2(1)(t) (defining a person interested as a person "engaged in or in promoting research, in the same field as to which the invention relates").

explicitly references and thus indirectly condones the use of opposition procedures.

Indian law has taken an expansive view of the potential use of these proceedings, allowing any person to initiate them, keeping in mind the resource-constrained nature of the Indian patent office combined with the vast amounts of data and information that must be perused for each patent application. Permitting the submission of pre-grant opposition before the patent office saves administrative and judicial time by airing issues with the application at the earliest stage possible. The grant structure in India, with the in-built mechanism that allows for pre-grant opposition, circumvents one of the country's debilitating constraints, the backlog in the judicial system.[153] Hence, India's grant opinions seemingly have more economic value when compared to the USPTO's administrative opinions because of the influence of a combination of other factors, such as the time taken to resolve disputes in India.

b) Post-Grant Opposition Proceedings

This provision, while slightly narrower than the pre-grants opposition (being limited to "interested parties"), allows one more opportunity for third parties who can demonstrate that they have a direct interest—for example, patient groups and other stakeholders—to challenge undeserving patents.[154]

c) Revocation Proceedings

Direct revocation proceedings are safeguards available to stakeholders as well as via a counterclaim for an affected party in an infringement suit. Separately, under §66 of the Patent Act, India's central government is also empowered to invalidate any patent on public-interest grounds if it is of the opinion that a patent is being exercised in a way that is prejudicial to the public or the state.[155]

Revoking or weeding out patents helps preserve their quality by creating a process that establishes robust judicial or administrative scrutiny. While

[153] *See* Kapczynski, *supra* note 93, at 1571.

[154] *See supra* note 97, §25(2); *see also* Sandeep K. Rathod, *Examining Oppositions: Time for a Deeper Look*, SpicyIP (Jan. 18, 2023), https://spicyip.com/2023/01/examining-oppositions-time-for-a-deeper-look.html (last visited Oct. 20, 2025) (providing data on pre- and post-grant oppositions).

[155] *See supra* note 97, §64; *see also* Prashant Reddy, *Govt of India Follows Up on SpicyIP Reporting—Revokes Avesthagen Patent—First Indian Victory for TKDL*, SpicyIP (Oct. 27, 2012), https://spicyip.com/2012/10/govt-of-india-follows-up-on-spicyip.html (last visited Oct. 20, 2025).

there has been some criticism of this process, the level of judicial scrutiny envisaged under the Indian patent statute comports with the General Obligations to establish an independent judiciary consistent with the functioning of a sovereign government, outlined under Article(s) 41 to 61 of the TRIPS Agreement.[156] Flynn, Baker, and Ragavan's testimony to the ITC asserts that revoking patents, especially by invalidating claims, is not unknown in other countries such as the United States, citing a white-paper report that examines the number of patents invalidated by the CAFC from 2002 to 2012.[157] For instance, a study found that, between 2004 to 2012, the US Court of Appeals for the Federal Circuit invalidated between 10 and 25 percent of the patents it considered every year.[158] In any case, invalidation of patents does not violate TRIPS Agreement as long as such invalidation has a strong legal basis and is non-discriminatory.[159]

3.3.7 Transparency

In addition to these ex ante and post facto provisions, India has introduced creative legislative amendments, particularly as seen in two provisions. The first is the transparency requirements around the working of a patent,[160] to create an oversight mechanism that monitors the extent to which patents are being worked, if at all. There are provisions that also create a framework to challenge patents that are either undeserving or somehow prejudicial to the larger public interest.

3.3.8 Bolar Exception

Other important provisions that use flexibilities include non-market uses of a patent, including for experimental use,[161] which allow the use of a patent

[156] *See* Ragavan, *supra* note 137 (explaining that BIO's submission to the ITC (on page 4) raised complains about "counterfeiting, large backlogs and patent-office inefficiency; differing administrative, legal, and judicial standards for patentability; compulsory licensing; inadequate data protection; and a need for harmonization of substantive standards and processes across patent offices around the world. Issues unique to biotechnology include patentability of biotechnology inventions, double patent review systems, genetic-resource access and benefit-sharing regimes, and technology-transfer issues involving intellectual property").

[157] *See* Office of the United States Trade Representative, Notices: Federal Register, Vol. 79, No. 2, FR Doc. 2013-31487 (2014); *see also* Ragavan et al., *supra* note 95.

[158] *See* White Paper Report, United States Patent Invalidity Study, 2012, https://www.morganlewis.com/~/media/files/publication/presentation/speech/smyth_uspatentinvalidity_sept12 (last visited Oct. 20, 2025).

[159] *See* Ragavan, *supra* note 124, at 27.

[160] *See supra* note 97, §146(2).

[161] *See supra* note 97, §47(3); *see also* Shamnad Basheer & Prashant Reddy, *The "Experimental Use" Exception Through a Developmental Lens*, 50 Intell. Prop. L. Rev. 831, 832 (2010).

for (merely) experimenting for research. For instance, the Bolar exception (from a 1984 case involving Bolar Pharmaceuticals) allows third-party use of patents for obtaining regulatory approval for generic products.[162] This provision, codified under §107A of India's 1970 Patent Act, permits the use of patents for research, data gathering, and seeking regulatory approval, both domestically and abroad, which are exempt from being construed as infringement.[163] It allows the storage of patented material during the patent term to facilitate marketing immediately after the expiration of the patent term.[164]

This provision refers to the allowance for a research exemption. The provisions exempt the use of patented inventions for seeking regulatory approval "to market *any* product (not just drugs) in *any* country."[165] Thus, activities relating to data gathering and use of patented inventions for the purpose of seeking regulatory approvals anywhere in the world are all exempted. It is not clear whether the use must mandatorily result in the filing of an application. J. M. Mueller notes that the provision covers data-gathering activity to file for regulatory approvals abroad, considering that Indian companies now routinely seek approvals from the FDA to sell generic drugs in the US market.[166]

The provision falls within the ambit of Article 30 of TRIPS Agreement, which allows every country to consider the legitimate interests of third parties in structuring such exceptions. Indeed, Bolar exceptions have been considered in a WTO dispute opinion of a panel, "Canada—Patent Protection for Pharmaceutical Products" (adopted on 7 April 2000), upholding Canada's Bolar and regulatory exceptions, similar to those of India.[167] The 1970 Indian Patent Act has provisions that protect unfair commercial use of test data, but does not go so far as to implement a statutory mandate for data exclusivity.[168]

[162] *See supra* note 97, §107(A); *see also* Basheer & Reddy, *supra* note 161, at 832.

[163] *See supra* note 97, §107(A).

[164] *See supra* note 97, §107(A).

[165] *See* Drugs and Cosmetics Act, No. 23 of 1940 (Ind.), https://cdsco.gov.in/opencms/opencms/system/modules/CDSCO.WEB/elements/download_file_division.jsp?num_id=OTIyNw== (last visited Oct. 20, 2025).

[166] *See* J. M. Mueller, *The Tiger Awakens: The Tumultuous Transformation of India's Patent System and the Rise of Indian Pharmaceutical Innovation*, 68 Univ. Pittsburgh Law Rev. (2007); *see also supra* note 97, §107(A).

[167] *See* Bayer Corp. v. Union of India (2009), 41 PTC 634 (Ind.).

[168] *See supra* note 97, §107A(a) (including a Bolar provision which allows for the storage of patented material during the patent term to facilitate marketing immediately after the expiration of the patent term).

3.3.9 Creative Balancing and TRIPS Compliance

Thus, the Indian patent statutory framework is carefully designed to create a balance considering the local socioeconomic realities at each stage of the patent application's life cycle. As a result of this creative balancing for public-health considerations, the Indian statute includes unique patent provisions, whose distinctive feature is that they remain fully compliant with India's TRIPS obligations as detailed above.

4. Government Actions in Pharma R&D: Two Examples from the United States and India

4.1 The United States: Publicly Funded Research and Transparency Concerns

The importance of looking beyond the international IP regime and its influencing actors is perhaps best demonstrated in the context of the United States, which has consistently been the largest provider of publicly funded research in the world.[169] Significantly, this public funding has not been limited to basic research, but, as Marianna Mazzucato shows, has been distributed along the entire innovation chain, from basic to applied research to early-stage financing. Thus, despite the theory that government funding is used only for market "fixing," the reality has been that such funding has shaped and created markets for innovation landscapes.[170]

The Bayh-Dole Act of 1980 sought to govern the commercialization of academic research by facilitating the patenting of research by institutes that received public funds.[171] While public institutions had been engaged in patenting activity prior to 1980,[172] the Act introduced a number of

[169] *See* MARIANNA MAZZUCATO et al., UCL INSTITUTE FOR INNOVATION AND PUBLIC PURPOSE (UCL-IIPP), MISSION-ORIENTED INDUSTRIAL STRATEGY: GLOBAL INSIGHTS (2024).

[170] *See id.* (laying down the frameworks that help explain this dichotomy, such as mission-oriented innovation policy, development economics, techno-economic paradigm shifts, and the fundamental embeddedness of the state as a risk taker and investor in the economy).

[171] *See* Bayh-Dole Act of 1980 §203, 35 U.S.C §200-§212 (2018) (titled University and Small Business Patent Procedures Act, cited Pub. L. 96–517, Dec. 12, 1980, 94 Stat. 3015).

[172] *See generally* David C. Mowery & Bhaven N. Sampat, *University Patents and Patent Policy Debates in the USA, 1925–1980*, 10 INDUS. AND CORP. EXCH. 781 (1980) (providing evidence to suggest that most of the economic contributions stemming from public funds had historically occurred without patents); *see also* Anthony D. So et al., *Is Bayh-Dole Good for Developing Countries? Lessons from the US Experience*, 6 PLOS BIOLOGY 262 (2008); *see also* DAVID C. MOWERY et al., IVORY TOWER AND INDUSTRIAL INNOVATION: UNIVERSITY-INDUSTRY TECHNOLOGY TRANSFER BEFORE AND AFTER THE BAYH-DOLE ACT 241 (2004).

public-interest safeguards and controls, including most notably "march-in rights" and certain restrictions on licensing.[173] The effectiveness of the Act has received praise as well as criticism, but the focus here will be on the role it plays in the market.[174]

In the midst of the Covid-19 pandemic, the US government entered into federal contracts for subsidies or grants, for amounts up to almost US$6 billion, with several large pharmaceutical companies, including Johnson & Johnson, Sanofi, GSK, Merck, IAVI, Moderna, Novavax, Pfizer (BioNTech), and AstraZeneca (Cambridge).[175] Freedom of Information Act requests by Knowledge Ecology International have shown that more than 350 such contracts related to Covid-19 had been given out by the US government to various parties.[176] Under 35 U.S.C. §203 read with 37 C.F.R. §401.6, the government has the power to exercise "march-in rights" over contractors in situations involving:[177]

- Non-use (contractor has not taken steps within a reasonable time to achieve practical application of the invention),
- Health and safety (to alleviate reasonable health and safety needs),
- Public needs (to meet the requirements for public use), and
- Non-compliance with the preference for domestic manufacturing of the invention.

Traditionally, the National Institutes of Health (NIH) (where the majority of these contracts originated) has never exercised its march-in rights. There have been eight petitions seeking the exercise of march-in rights to date.[178] While it is true that the threat of exercising march-in rights has resulted in effective pricing or licensing negotiations in the past,[179] the NIH's absolute

[173] *See supra* note 171, 35 U.S.C at §203(a).

[174] *See* So *supra* note 187; *see also* Shamnad Basheer & Shouvik Kumar Guha, *Outsourcing "Bayh-Dole" to India: Lost in Transplantation?*, 23 Colum. J. Asian L. 270, 272 (2010).

[175] See Ragavan and Barooah, *supra* note 3.

[176] *See* Knowledge Ecology International, *COVID-19 Contracts*, www.keionline.org, https://www.keionline.org/covid-contracts (last visited Oct. 20, 2025).

[177] *See supra* note 171, 35 U.S.C at §203 read with 37 C.F.R. §401.6.

[178] *See* Alexander Kersten and Gabrielle Athanasia, *March-In Rights and U.S. Global Competitiveness*, Ctr for Strategic & Int'l Stud. (Mar. 24, 2022), https://www.csis.org/analysis/march-rights-and-us-global-competitiveness (last visited Oct. 20, 2025).

[179] *See* Knowledge Ecology International, *Several March-In and Royalty-Free Rights Cases, Under the Bayh-Dole Act*, www.keionline.org, https://www.keionline.org/cl/march-in-royalty-free (last visited Oct. 20, 2025).

neglect to use them has been widely noted. In December 2023, a renewed effort was made to examine and streamline the implementation of the march-in rights process, and the NIH accordingly released its "Draft Inter-Agency Guidance Framework for Considering the Exercise of March-In Rights," which was provided to the public for comments.

Inputs were sought from contractors on the use of funds, as well as disclosures on R&D investments, licensing agreements, and patent filings, to get a clearer picture of the value accruing to those contractors from the public funding, including through potential evergreening actions.[180] Importantly, formalized stakeholder inputs, especially from patient groups, NGOs, and other public-interest institutions, reflected an interest in maintaining the transparency of proceedings.

While the United States is still formalizing the approach, the introduction of clauses that emphasize the particular vulnerability of pharmaceutical inventions that have benefited from public funding will greatly help in keeping their prices reasonable.[181] Similarly, requiring disclosures related to the extent of government funding relative to the total cost of R&D, the extent of government funding relative to the sales projections, the nature of the disease treated by the invention, and the extent to which the country's populace has been or is likely to be affected by such diseases, can help create a balance between public funding and accountability for private rights created consequentially.[182]

Most importantly, publicly funded inventions that result in a related patent that has medical relevance should be subject to a *use* requirement. That is, governments should promote the utilization of inventions arising from federally supported R&D by requiring commercialization and public availability of such inventions, thus ensuring that the public is protected against nonuse or unreasonable use of such inventions and minimizing the costs

[180] *See* Shamnad Basheer and Rupali Samuel, SpicyIP, Bayer's Nexavar and the "Working" of Compulsory Licensing: Mind the Patent (Information) Gap! (2015), https://spicyip.com/wp-content/uploads/2015/04/Report-on-Bayer-for-writ-Finalized.pdf (last visited Oct. 20, 2025).

[181] *See generally* Shamnad Basheer, *Making Patents Work: Of IP Duties and Deficient Disclosures*, 7 Queen Mary J. Intell. Prop. 3 (2017); *see also* Pratyush Upreti, *Intellectual Property Responsibility: A Manifesto*, 55 IIC-Int'l Rev. of Intell. Prop. and Competition L. 595 (2024).

[182] *See generally*, Srividhya Ragavan, *Comment on Request for Information Regarding the Draft Interagency Guidance Framework for Considering the Exercise of March-In Rights*, Tex. A&M U. Sch. L. Legal Stud. Rsch. Paper 7–8 (2024) (focusing on government regulations vis-à-vis their domestic actions, and not discussing how these regulations could be clarified regarding international obligations, such as TRIPS Agreement, and price comparisons to similar countries).

of administering policies in this area. Those who benefit from government funding should be mandated to take steps within a reasonable time period to achieve the practice of the invention, whether through manufacturing or through licensing.[183]

Indeed, given the vast scale of public funding and the existing unrestrained use of such funding to further innovation, member nations should seek mechanisms to promote innovation, such as by providing private rights, but in a balanced manner consistent with public-health needs, especially when public funds are used.

4.2 India—Complementary Innovation Models

The narrative in the preceding section discussed how governments can utilize law and policy levers internal to IP law to safeguard public health. However, these are not the only interactions possible between the "innovation prerogative" and the "public health prerogative." The following discussion will highlight how governments, through law and policy mechanisms external to IP law, can also spur innovation that may be well aligned with their public-health priorities. An example of this is the government action to create a model using public entities to further innovation that is focused on the areas of pharmaceutical R&D that private research has hesitated to engage in, such as those related to tropical diseases. This discussion will highlight the Open-Source Drug Discovery (OSDD) model promoted by the government of India.

The OSDD project in India reflects the public-sector entity—the involvement of the Council of Scientific and Industrial Research (CSIR) in the larger, global, and open-source drug-discovery movement that continues to work with various models of innovation and implementation.[184] The commonly known example of the open-source innovation model is the Free and Open-Source Software (FOSS) movement. Other examples in the biotech

[183] *See* Palmedo and Ragavan, *supra* note 5, at 76; *see also* Pankhuri Agarwal, *India's Patent Working Disclosure Requirement Under Attack by US Govt and Big Pharma*, SpicyIP (May 9, 2018), https://spicyip.com/2018/05/indias-patent-working-disclosure-requirement-under-attack-by-us-govt-and-big-pharma.html (last visited Oct. 20, 2025) (interestingly, the USTR has not only taken a different view of such provisions when utilized by other countries but has also taken unilateral action for such provisions).

[184] *See* Stephen Maurer et al., *Finding Cures for Tropical Diseases: Is Open Source an Answer?*, 1 Pub. Libr. Sci. Med. 183 (2004).

and pharmaceutical sectors include the SNP consortium, the HapMap Project, and the BiOS.[185]

This approach bypasses some of the structural direction that guides patent incentives while also resulting in significant cost reductions due to decentralization, the prospect of continuous follow-on development, and a wider variety of perspectives provided by a diversity of contributors. Indeed, there are strong indications that such alternative approaches may especially be required in the pharmaceutical sector, where the structural "side effects" caused by patent incentives have serious real-world consequences for billions of people around the world, especially the vulnerable in the global South. Srividhya Ragavan and Jonathan Kimball assert that there has been an increase in the efficiency of clinical trials as a result of the application of AI technology, whose demonstrated benefits include reduced time and costs associated with drug development.[186] It is perhaps time to reassess the long periods of monopoly and exclusivity justified based on clinical-trials data in the pre-AI era.

The open-source movement is predicated on the perception that traditional patent and innovation mechanisms have viewed certain diseases, particularly tropical diseases, as unworthy of investing R&D resources. This market-based patent approach is based on the perception that patients in poorer nations are often unable to pay large sums for lifesaving medications.[187] The *commons* model, in sharp contrast to traditional understandings of incentives in patent theory, tries to use the concept of exclusionary rights to reverse or even deny them.[188]

Open access to drug development and community action to curb diseases have proven to be effective alternatives, improving existing efficiencies for drug development while creating newer efficiencies. Open-source models will increase efficiencies in areas where the populations requiring interventions against neglected tropical diseases are larger, typically in less-developed parts of the globe.[189] As one example, the Structural Genomics

[185] *See id.*

[186] *See* Jonathan Kimball and Srividhya Ragavan, *AI (Re)Defining Pharmaceutical Exclusivities*, 41 BIOTECHNOLOGY L. REP 23 (2022).

[187] *See id.*

[188] *See* Séverine Dusollier, *The Commons as a Reverse Intellectual Property—From Exclusivity to Inclusivity*, in CONCEPTS OF PROPERTY IN INTELLECTUAL PROPERTY LAW (Helena Howe ed., 2013).

[189] *See, for example,* Global Health Observatory, *NTD Interventions, People Requiring Interventions Against NTDs, Number,* WWW.WHO.INT, https://www.who.int/data/gho/data/indicators/indicator-details/GHO/reported-number-of-people-requiring-interventions-against-ntds (last visited Oct. 20, 2025).

Consortium (SGC), a GSK-led initiative using an open-access model, has contributed to the invention of the Bromodomain and Extra-Terminal (BET) motif inhibitors, with anti-cancer, immunosuppressive, and other medicinal effects."[190] Open-access work with relevant technology has already ensured a swift and smooth response to several disease outbreaks, examples of which are listed in Table 3.2 below.

As Table 3.2 shows, while most such initiatives in developed countries are an outcome of private-sector and personal-philanthropy efforts, in India such initiatives have resulted from the government's actions and involvement via the OSDD project.[191] This project was led by the CSIR to collaborate on therapies for neglected tropical diseases.[192] It was later subsumed into the India Tuberculosis Research and Development Consortium, led by the Indian Council of Medical Research (ICMR).[193] The crucial difference in this government-entity-led approach is that it enabled structured collaboration and sharing of information based on existing inherent incentives. The resulting drugs were not supposed to be patent-protected and were also likely to be affordable.

As an example of its potential as well as its partial success, the project has made progress on tuberculosis treatment. The project created a data repository for genome-level information regarding the *Mycobacterium tuberculosis* strain H37Rv by recruiting volunteers to gather, extract, and transcribe this information into a standardized format.[194] Following these initial successes, the OSDD project moved on to the more complex task of annotating the tuberculosis genome, including the computational extrapolation where required. Then it continued to the generation of eleven models for the prediction of anti-tuberculosis activity.[195]

[190] *See* Montserrat Pérez-Salvia and Manel Esteller, *Bromodomain Inhibitors and Cancer Therapy: From Structures to Applications*, 12 Epigenetics 323 (2017).

[191] *See* David C. Thompson and Jörg Bentzien, *Crowdsourcing and Open Innovation in Drug Discovery: Recent Contributions and Future Directions*, 25 Drug Discov. Today 2284 (2020) (noting that pharmaceutical companies, too, have started opening up to the engagement of "citizen scientists" to add on to their research).

[192] *See* Anshu Bhardwaj et al., *Open Source Drug Discovery—A New Paradigm of Collaborative Research in Tuberculosis Drug Development*, 91 Tuberculosis 479 (2011), https://www.who.int/data/gho/data/indicators/indicator-details/GHO/reported-number-of-people-requiring-interventions-against-ntds (last visited Oct. 20, 2025).

[193] *See* Jacob Koshy, *TB Drug Project Gets a Lease of Life*, The Hindu, Dec. 20, 2016, https://www.thehindu.com/sci-tech/health/TB-drug-project-gets-a-lease-of-life/article16907203.ece (last visited Oct. 20, 2025).

[194] *See generally* Chrisine Årdal and John-Arne Røttingen, *Open-Source Drug Discovery in Practice: A Case Study*, 6 plos neglected tropical diseases, 1827 (2012).

[195] *See id.*

Table 3.2 Open-Source Drug Discovery Projects Targeted Toward Neglected Tropical Diseases (NTDs).

Potential Case	Collaboration Efforts Viewable	Project Status	Timeframe of Data
Council for Scientific and Industrial Research Team India Consortium's Open Source Drug Discovery Project (CSIR OSDD)	Yes	Active	2008–Ongoing
Collaborative Drug Discovery	No	Active	2004–Ongoing
Cambia's Open Innovation	No	Inactive	2009
PATH's Malaria Vaccine Initiative	No	Active	1999–Ongoing
Structural Genomics Consortium	No	Active	2003–Ongoing
Pool for Open Innovation Against Neglected Tropical Diseases	No	Inactive*	2009-2011
Synaptic Leap's Malaria Project	Yes	Inactive**	2006–2008
Synaptic Leap's Schistosomiasis Project (TSLS)	Yes	Active	2006–Ongoing
Synaptic Leap's Toxoplasma Project	Yes	Inactive	2006–2007
Synaptic Leap's Tuberculosis Project	Yes	Inactive	2006–2007
Tropical Diseases Initiative	No	Active	2004–Ongoing
TDR Targets	No***	Active	2007–Ongoing

* This project has been transformed to the WIPO Re:Search project.

** This project has been restarted in 2012 with a considerable amount of activity.

*** TDR Targets does share posted lists. However, these are not collaboration efforts towards a designated goal.

Reproduced from Christine Ardel & John Rottingen, *Open Source Drug Discovery in Practice: A Case Study,* 6 PLOS NEGLECTED TROPICAL DISEASES, https://doi.org/10.1371/journal.pntd.0001827. Under a Creative Commons Attribution License.

While this alternative model of approaching the innovation of significant pharmaceuticals provides several potential upsides, it is not without disadvantages. Indeed, although the project started with much promise, it appears to have slowly fizzled out. The absence of incentives might be one factor; a lack of sustained government leadership could be another. Although the project received initial government funding, the guarantee of continued funding until completion remains uncertain.[196] The idea of completion too remains unclear. Nonetheless, it remains true that this model of pharmaceutical innovation relies on the "negative" spaces of patent law and, if developed thoughtfully, has the potential to create a balance between innovation and access.

While much has been written against the regulatory approach, Srividhya Ragavan and Feroz Ali Khader assert that federated levels of control via a government body can bring the benefits of decentralization without the loss of a supervisory superstructure in the context of including a high standard for non-obviousness.[197] The same argument can apply in this context as well. A model along these lines, combined with a long-term vision, has the ability to promote the needed and accessible pharmaceutical innovation.[198] Nevertheless, it is imperative for developing countries to create such alternative models that can work alongside negotiated international obligations in a manner positively affecting innovation and public health.

5. The Synergistic Role of Judiciary

5.1 The Judiciary as an Independent Actor

Of the several actors that play a critical role in shaping policy debates, one of the most impactful is the judiciary. While the judicial branch of the government does not directly formulate policy decisions, the role it performs in interpreting and evaluating policies is often significant. In every country, the role of the judiciary is balanced and circumscribed by the constitution's prescriptions and values. It is the mandate of the judiciary to sync constitutional ideals with national objectives. The national constitutional framework provides the basis for validating, challenging, or in some instances

[196] *See* Basheer et al., *supra* note 119; *see also* Thomas Vallianeth, *Spicyip Tidbit: Bureaucracy May Cost the OSDD a Year of Funding*, SpicyIP (Apr. 12, 2014), http://spicyip.com/?p=11257 (last visited Oct. 20, 2025) (noting that the government has not released the expected funds for this year).

[197] *See* Srividhya Ragavan and Feroz Ali Khader, *The Selection of Patents—The Choice Between Regulatory Reforms and Market Reliance to Weed Out Suspect Patents*, 46 IIC 38 (2015).

[198] *See generally*, Arti K. Rai, *Open and Collaborative Research: A New Model for Biomedicine*, *in* Intellectual Property Rights in Frontier Industries 131 (Robert W. Hahn ed., 2005).

interpreting, and thus engaging in policies. In any member nation, the values enshrined in the constitution provide and require oversight and draw sufficient limitations, subject to having a strong judiciary.

Especially when dealing with international obligations, such as with the TRIPS Agreement, whereby all member nations subscribe to minimum standards of protection, legislators may emulate laws or regulations from another country. However, "drafting similar laws d[oes] not necessitate making the same interpretative decisions."[199] In fact, case law in a given country can, despite any similarity to another country's underlying statutory construction and the borrowed influence of its jurisprudence, develop in wholly different ways from the case law in that country.[200]

In turn, the judicial wisdom and tenor outlined in precedents set the tone for government action. Judicial precedents often directly impact not just policy outcomes but also the future courses of legislative and executive actions. Judgments rendered with careful appreciation of the local realities would set the path forward.

Judicial interpretations are naturally influenced by the cultural, social, and economic norms of the nation the court resides in. Perhaps courts are government institutions that cannot shy away from confronting issues of local importance. National and international socioeconomic and political discourses influence judicial outcomes. Judgments rendered with due consideration to national social, cultural, and policy considerations thus tend to be naturally pragmatic and generally embrace an appropriate degree of realism to achieve national objectives.[201]

This section elucidates the substantial influence of the judiciary on the innovation and patent landscape, using case studies from the United States and India to demonstrate the judiciary's role in shaping the discourse.

5.2 The American Judiciary—Ushering in a New Era in Biotech Innovation

The role of the American judiciary in fostering innovation is perhaps best understood through the example of biotechnology law and policy. In the 1960s,

[199] *See* Matthias Kamber, *Coming Out of the Maze: Canada Grants the Harvard Mouse Patent*, 35 Geo. Wash. Int'l L. Rev. 761, 779 (2003).
[200] *See id.*
[201] *See generally,* Srividhya Ragavan, *Patent Judicial Wisdom,* 20 Nat'l L. Sch. India Rev. 165 (2008), https://scholarship.law.tamu.edu/facscholar/526 (last visited Oct. 20, 2025).

Europe grappled with the question of patenting modern biotechnology when a German pigeon breeder sought to patent a method of breeding a dove with "a considerably larger" red plumage.[202] The *Bundesgerichtshof* (West Germany's Federal Supreme Court) denied the patent on the grounds that there was no guarantee of "reproducibility."[203]

While Europe continued to struggle with the patentability of biotechnology during the 1970s and 1980s,[204] Ananda Mohan Chakrabarty, an Indian immigrant to the United States, genetically engineered a *Pseudomonas* strain of oil-eating bacterium.[205] His patent application claimed the *Pseudomonas* bacterium itself.[206] When the US Supreme Court considered the case in 1979,[207] commercial biotechnology was emerging as a significant area of research.[208] The Court's emphatic opinion confirming the patentability of living matter in 1980, by drawing a distinction between products of nature and human-made inventions, paved the way for the development of biotechnology industries and marked the beginning of a new era in biotechnology advances.[209]

The Supreme Court's decision created tremendous financial potential for biotechnology companies, which in turn encouraged biotech investors.[210] Lila Feisee, BIO's Director for Federal Government Relations and Intellectual Property, highlights that the Court decision in *Diamond*

[202] *See Rote Taube (Red Pigeon),* Bundesgerichtshof [BGH] [Federal Court of Justice], 52 BGHZ 74, 136, 137 (Ger. 1967) (regarding a single patent claim seeking protection for crossing an *Altdeutscher Kröpfer* with a *Rote Römertaube.* The doves resulting from the selection were crossed with a *Roter Hessenkröpfer* and then with an *Altdeutscher Kröpfer.*).

[203] *See id.* at 141 (explaining that German Patent Act § 2(2) explicitly denied patent protection for plant or animal varieties, or biological processes essential for the production of plants or animals. Arguably, the court's ruling implied that replicable biotechnological inventions can be patented; *see also* Andreas Schrell et al., *Biotechnology Patenting Policy in the European Union—as Exemplified by the Development in Germany,* 107 Adv. Biochem Engin/Biotechnol. 13–39 (2007).

[204] *See* Schrell, *supra* note 203, at 13.

[205] *See* Rebecca S. Eisenberg, *The Story of* Diamond v. Chakrabarty: *Technological Change and the Subject Matter Boundaries of the Patent System, in* Intellectual Property Stories 327–357 (Jane C. Ginsburg and Rochelle Cooper Dreyfuss eds., 2006).

[206] *See* Diamond v. Chakrabarty, 447 U.S. 303, 305 (1972).

[207] *See id; see also In re Bergy,* 596 F.2d 952 (1979) (relating to certiorari filed by the government in *Chakrabarty* and *In re Bergy,* a case that raised similar issues. After the petition was granted in *In re Bergy,* the applicant canceled his claims to the microorganism. Hence, the court merely considered the Chakrabarty issue.).

[208] See *In re Chakrabarty,* 571 F.2d 40 (1978); *see* Application of Chakrabarty, 596 F.2d 952 (1979) (being an appeal filed by the defendant against the USPTO's decision to the Court of Customs and Patent Appeals (CCPA). The CCPA's decision was vacated by a certiorari and then the case was remanded to the CCPA.).

[209] *See id.; see also* Geri Yonover, *What Hath (Not) Chakrabarty Wrought: From the Mouse That Roared to Hello Dolly and Beyond,* 32 Val. U.L. Rev. 349, 358 (1998).

[210] *See* Yonover, *supra* note 209.

v. Chakrabarty, along with the Bayh-Dole Act, propelled the biotechnology industry forward.[211]

Notwithstanding the key role played by the US Supreme Court in ushering in the biotechnology innovation, it is a fact that the Court of Appeals for the Federal Circuit has had an enormous influence on patent law and innovation policy, partly because of its specialized, near-exclusive jurisdiction over patent appeals.[212] However, the court has also faced criticism for being overly formalistic,[213] for being patent-friendly as opposed to innovation-friendly, for lacking a holistic appreciation of science, and for a "tendency to grab power precluding lower courts from adjusting patent law to account for differences among innovative industries."[214] Further, the court has been criticized for its exclusive focus on patent law, leading to patent holders dominating as an interest group over its appointment and other processes. As Gugliuzza notes, "The story of how the Federal Circuit developed its unusually expansive view of federal authority remains highly salient, for it introduces several institutional themes critical to understanding power dynamics in patent law."[215]

5.3 Indian Judiciary: A Tightrope Balancing Act

Notwithstanding the relatively recent trend of seeing an increase in IP litigations in India, the Indian judiciary has also demonstrated an admirable ability to rise to the challenge. Illustratively, the *Chakrabarty* buzz caused the Calcutta High Court in India to take the lead in the *Dimminaco A.G.* case (2002) to protect biotechnology inventions for the process of manufacturing a vaccine for infectious bursitis in poultry.[216] On appeal, the court held that

[211] *See* Lila Feisee, *Anything Under the Sun Made by Man*, BIOTECHNOLOGY INDUS. ORG. (Apr. 11, 2001), https://archive.bio.org/advocacy/letters/anything-under-sun-made-man (last visited Oct. 21, 2025) (discussing the patent's contribution to the development of biotechnology industry).

[212] *See id; see also* Federal Courts Improvement Act of 1982 §127(a), 28 U.S.C. §1295 (1982); *see also* Leahy-Smith America Invents Act of 2011 §19(b), 28 U.S.C. §1295(a)(1) (2011) (expanding the Federal Circuit Court's jurisdiction to include district-court cases concerning compulsory counterclaims arising under patent laws).

[213] *See* Lee Petherbridge, *Patent Law Uniformity?*, 22 HARV. J.L. & TECH. 421, 427–28 (2009).

[214] *See* Paul Gugliuzza, *The Federal Circuit as a Federal Court,* 54 WILLIAM & MARY L. REV. 1791, 1802 (2013); *see also* Dan L. Burk and Mark A. Lemley, *Policy Levers in Patent Law*, 89 VA. L. REV. 1575, 1674 (2003).

[215] *See* Gugliuzza, *supra* note 214, at 1804; *see also* Gunn v. Minton, 133 S. Ct. 1059 (2013).

[216] *See* Dimminaco A.G. v. Controller of Patents & Designs (2002), I.P.R.L. 255 (Ind.); *see also* *Patent Controller Order on Dimminaco Vaccine Quashed,* BUSINESS STANDARD, Feb. 2, 2013, 12:54

the definition of "manufacture" in §2 of the Indian patent legislation did not pose a statutory bar to the patentability of a living organism.[217] In so holding, *Dimminaco A.G.* opened India to the world of biotechnology patents.[218]

An example that characterizes the role of the Indian judiciary's role in shaping innovation policy outcomes and its ability to accommodate local realities involves a writ petition that Bayer Inc. filed in the Delhi High Court against the Union of India and Cipla. Bayer's writ sought to restrain the Drug Controller General of India (DCGI) from approving a generic version of Bayer's patented drug sorafenib tosylate, sold as Nexavar, at approximately ₹280,000 per month's treatment in India.[219] Bayer's counsel asserted that when the DCGI approved a generic version of a patented drug, it infringed in effect on the patentee's statutorily guaranteed monopoly rights under the patent statute.[220] Thus, Bayer's assertion was that the generic versions should be deemed spurious drugs under the 1940 Drugs and Cosmetics Act until otherwise proven in litigation.[221] A mechanism that links or connects a generic drug's marketing approval with the patent status of the originator drug is termed as patent linkage. It was meant to balance innovation with the onset of low-cost generic drugs. That is, in regimes that feature patent linkage, drug-approval statutes and regulations prevent an administrative body from approving a generic drug until it is clear that is either off-patent or, does not infringe the patent covering the branded medication.[222] Justice Ravindra Bhat declined to create such a linkage, considering the local realities, including the cost of Bayer's drug, which made the lifesaving drug

AM, https://www.business-standard.com/article/companies/patents-controller-order-on-dimminaco-vaccine-quashed-102021401045_1.html (last visited Oct. 21, 2025); *see also supra* note 234, at 259.

[217] *See* Dimminaco A.G. v. Controller of Patents & Designs, (2002) I.P.R.L. 255 (Ind.); *see also Manufacture Applies to Living Organism; HC—Boost to Biotech Patenting*, Business Line, http://www.patentmatics.com/news2002/news25.htm (last visited Oct. 21, 2025) (discussing how the patentability requirement of "novelty" was satisfied by the process for preparation, and that of "utility" was satisfied by the vaccine's protection against contagious bursitis infection in poultry).

[218] *See* Dimminaco A.G., *supra* note 216, at pp. 258–259, 293 (noting that Justice Ashok Ganguly quashed the Controller's order and directed a reconsideration of the application. The central government decided not to challenge the ruling; thus, the judgment of the Calcutta High Court is the authority in India on the issue of biotechnology patents.).

[219] *See* Bayer Corp. v. Union of India, (2009) WP(C) No.7833/2008 (Ind.).

[220] *See id.* at 2–4.

[221] *See* Shamnad Basheer, *Bayer vs Cipla: Attempting "Patent Linkage" in India*, spicy ip, (Feb. 28, 2009), https://spicyip.com/2009/02/bayer-vs-cipla-attempting-patent.html (last visited Oct. 21, 2025); *see also* Drugs and Cosmetics Act, 1940 *supra* note 165, §17(b).

[222] The Drugs and Cosmetics Act, No. 23 of 1940, *amended* by the Drugs (Amendment) Act, No. 2 of 1955, (Ind), Acts of Parliament, 1955, § 17(b), *available at* http://www.cdsco.nic.in/.

inaccessible to more than 99 percent of the Indian population. The decision notes that the 1970 Patents Act and the 1940 Drugs and Cosmetics Act have distinct and parallel objectives, and that it is the enterprise of the legislature and not the judiciary to link the statutes.[223] Deeming a generic-drug application "spurious" would, Justice Bhat held, result in all generics becoming spurious drugs, and this would also undermine the Bolar provisions of the patent statute.[224] A division bench of the Delhi High Court sustained the decision.[225]

In a separate case involving the same drug, Justice Prabha Sridevan's decision from the Intellectual Property Appellate Board (IPAB) in *Bayer v. Natco* was timely in ensuring access to the medication by refusing to grant an injunction preventing the compulsory licensing—and thus the availability—of a generic version of the drug for patients.[226]

It is important to appreciate that each country needs to promote trade while ensuring national safety and health. Toward that end, the judiciary substantially influences the shaping of the legal and policy framework, particularly by prompting and guiding the legislative branch to consider necessary amendments. From that perspective, some of the decisions from India drew essential lines to cater to national objectives. The Indian judiciary has shown a remarkable ability to draw the *welfare* lines where required and to stay within its constitutional mandate to balance economic values with social needs.[227] Much has been written by several scholars, including the authors, on how significant some of these judicial decisions have been in comprehending the tensions inherent in these areas.[228]

5.4 Other Judicial Systems

The biotechnology industry, particularly in the United States, was poised for radical changes after *Chakrabarty*, with several other judicial systems following suit. For instance, when considering the patentability of a genetically

[223] *See* Bayer, *supra n.* 219, at ¶ 38. *See also* SRIVIDHYA RAGAVAN, PATENT AND TRADE DISPARITIES IN DEVELOPING COUNTRIES (Oxford Univ. Press, 2012) at 232.
[224] *Id.* ¶ 44(iii), 49.
[225] *See* Bayer Corp v. Union of India, (2010) LPA 443/2009 (Ind.).
[226] *See supra* note 100.
[227] *See* INDIA CONST. Preamble.
[228] *See* Shayonee Dasgupta and Sakshi Agarwal, *Judicial Accountability and Independence: Exploring the Limits of Judicial Power*, 2 NUJS L. REV. 779, 779–809 (2009).

engineered mouse (*Harvard OncoMouse*) comprising an additional gene that makes the mouse more susceptible to cancer,[229] the appeal division in Canada granted the patent by specifically considering the *OncoMouse* patent granted in the United States and Europe.[230] At that time, Canada hosted the second-largest biotechnology industry in the world, and the lack of patent protection for biotechnology entailed the danger of hindering R&D and investment in the industry.[231]

6. The Emerging Role of Non-State Actors

6.1 Lobbyists: Traders in Influence

There is an extensive literature on the role and impact of varied and influential non-state actors (NSAs), including lobbyists, patient groups, corporations, and NGOs. Lobbyists on behalf of pharmaceutical and health products represent a huge and influential enterprise in the United States. The pharmaceutical industry spent a staggering US$378.6 million in federal lobbying in the year 2023 alone.[232] Health companies that year spent over US$739 million on federal lobbying, more than any other sector.[233] Of these, PhRMA, the main lobby group for US drug makers, alone spent US$27 million.[234]

The lobbying efforts of the industry tend to focus on the speed, procedure, and ease of the patent as well as regulatory approval process for both innovative and generic or biosimilar drugs; access to off-patent drugs by generic drugmakers; other regulatory standards; and the quantum of "user fee" paid by pharma companies to the FDA for drug/device approval. The user

[229] *See* Kamber, *supra* note 199, at 761.

[230] *See* President and Fellows of Harvard College v. Canada (Comm'r of Pats.) [2000] 4 F.C. 528 (Can.); *see also* Kamber, *supra* note 199.

[231] *See* Kamber, *supra* note 199, at 780.

[232] *See* Anna Massoglia, *State and Federal Lobbying Spending Tops $46 Billion After Federal Lobbying Spending Broke Records in 2023*, OpenSecrets (Jan. 26, 2024, 2:42 PM), https://www.opensecrets.org/news/2024/01/state-and-federal-lobbying-spending-tops-46-billion-after-federal-lobbying-spending-broke-records-in-2023?__cf_chl_rt_tk=NnT4tJfgIlADrFZxVnGHu6RFVv9HBmH9t_83UfSMARw-1713983557-0.0.1.1-1642 (last visited Oct. 21, 2025) (being a report published by a nonprofit organization based in Washington D.C. that tracks money in politics).

[233] *See id.*

[234] *See* Ahmed Aboulenein, *US Pharmacy Benefit Lobby Group Ramps up Spending as Lawmakers Close In*, Reuters (Jan. 25, 2024), https://www.reuters.com/business/healthcare-pharmaceuticals/us-pharmacy-benefit-lobby-group-ramps-up-spending-lawmakers-close-2024-01-25/ (last visited Oct. 21, 2025).

fee finances more than half of the FDA's budget, arguably affecting its independence and oversight, and forms a significant entry barrier for small drug manufacturers.[235]

6.2 The Office of the US Trade Representative: The State's Lobbyist

A prime example of non-state actors (NSAs) in the United States (principally lobbyists, patient groups, corporations, and NGOs) is the significant global influence that the office of the USTR wields. As Michael Palmedo and Srividhya Ragavan observe,

> The Trade Act, 1974,[236] under §301, unilaterally authorizes the office of the USTR to identify and pursue countries perceived as denying adequate and effective protection of IP rights or fair and equitable market access to US industries or entities that rely on IP protection. Every year, the USTR releases the Special 301 Report,[237] accusing various countries of having inadequate IP policies, and many of the alleged violations focus on pharmaceutical patent protection. Once identified, the USTR applies direct and indirect pressure through trade negotiations and preference systems in order to win policy changes favored by US IP-owning stakeholders in the identified countries. The USTR seeks IP policy changes, including action items such as amending laws, providing regulatory exclusivities, or directing the manner in which specific statutes or regulations should be implemented. These changes typically fall in line with the expectations of the USTR's goals governed by the Trade Act, 1974, which aim to promote US trade abroad. Thus, these requests and sought-after actions do not consider local realities or the TRIPS-based flexibilities that have been negotiated to balance with local conditions. Laws and amendments to ensure access to medication made in other countries form a huge part of the Special 301 Report, and developing countries typically assert that the

[235] *See* Christina Jewett, *F.D.A.'s Drug Industry Fees Fuel Concerns over Influence*, N.Y. TIMES, Sept. 15, 2022, https://www.nytimes.com/2022/09/15/health/fda-drug-industry-fees.html (last visited Oct. 21, 2025).

[236] *See* the Trade Act of 1974 §182, 19 U.S.C. §2242 (1974).

[237] *See Special 301*, OFFICE OF THE UNITED STATES TRADE REPRESENTATIVE, https://ustr.gov/issue-areas/intellectual-property/Special-301 (last visited Oct. 21, 2025).

> USTR works to take away the negotiated TRIPS flexibilities. The Special 301 Report is also faulted for routinely promoting the levels of IP protection that exceed what is required by the TRIPS Agreement, now termed as "TRIP-Plus" provisions.

Further, they note that a whopping 56 percent of the world's 8.3 billion population live in countries that were placed on the Special 301 List for including TRIPS flexibilities.[238] Thus, they add that, directly or indirectly, the USTR's actions have affected access to medication for over half of the world's population outside of the United States.[239] This underscores the significant impact of the USTR's actions.

6.3 Consulting Firms: Emerging Actors

Emerging research also shows that in the last few decades, *consulting firms* have contributed to shaping government actions, influencing government capacity and its policy direction.[240] In fact, Mariana Mazzucato and Rosie Collington argue that actions by a certain type of large consulting firm "weaken our businesses, infantilize our governments, and warp our economies."[241] They point to an example from the UK where, during the Covid-19 epidemic, more than £1 million per day was spent on consultants to deal with Covid-19 programs, with limited follow-up or oversight, causing NHS employees to decry that the ground realities they were dealing with were being ignored.[242]

7. Conclusion: Redefining the Innovation Landscape

As discussed in earlier chapters,[243] the Covid-19 pandemic unveiled the stark contrast in access to health care between the global North and South. The

[238] *See* Palmedo and Ragavan, *supra* note 5, at 76.
[239] *See* Palmedo and Ragavan, *supra* note 5, at 76.
[240] *See* Mariana Mazzucato and Rosie Collington, The Big Con: How The Consulting Industry Weakens Our Businesses, Infantilizes Our Governments, and Warps Our Economies (2003).
[241] *See id.*
[242] *See id.*
[243] *See* Shamnad Basheer, *The Invention of an Investment Incentive for Pharmaceutical Innovation*, 15 J. World Intell. Prop. 305 (2012).

WHO website notes that in 2022 there were 1.62 billion people who required treatment and care for neglected tropical diseases.[244] While this number has been gradually declining (from 2.19 billion in 2010), it is no coincidence that practically all of this population is in the global South. Hence, while the more-developed nations have focused on protecting incentives for pharmaceutical innovation, other countries have advocated for greater flexibility in patent policies to enhance access to essential medicines.[245]

While a multitude of factors remain involved in this matrix of decisions and conflicts, it does lead to the inevitable conclusion that, insofar as innovation and public health are concerned, there is an urgent need for striking workable solutions that promote innovation without compromising access.[246]

The drug discovery and development process in the United States is notoriously expensive, with costs ranging from US$400 million[247] to US$2 billion[248] per drug, a significant portion of which can be attributed to monopoly rents and other barriers inherent in the current system. In this context, public funding emerges as a crucial alternative, offering a means to mitigate these costs and promote more equitable access to medicines. Countries around the world have considered adopting versions of the Bayh-Dole Act.[249] As the National Institute of Standards and Technology leads discussions and considers potential amendments, there is a margin to redefine the role of government in pharmaceutical innovation. Such regulations will position governments as conscious creators, shapers, and facilitators of pharmaceutical innovation in the market.

[244] *See* Global Health Observatory, *Reported Number of People Requiring Interventions Against NTDs*, WWW.WHO.INT, https://www.who.int/data/gho/data/indicators/indicator-details/GHO/reported-number-of-people-requiring-interventions-against-ntds (last visited Oct. 21, 2025).

[245] *See* Donald W. Light and Rebecca Warburton, *Demythologizing the High Costs of Pharmaceutical Research*, 6 BioSocieties 34 (2011).

[246] *See Research and Development in the Pharmaceutical Industry*, Cong. Budget Off., https://www.cbo.gov/publication/57126 (last visited Oct. 21, 2025).

[247] *Id.* (noting that average R&D expenditures estimate for per new drug range from less than $1 billion to more than $2 billion, which include capital costs as well as expenditures on drugs that did not make it to market). *See also* Joseph A. DiMasi, Henry G. Grabowski, and Ronald W. Hansen, *Innovation in the Pharmaceutical Industry: New Estimates of R&D Costs*, 47 J. Health Econ. 25 (2016), https://doi.org/10.1016/j.jhealeco.2016.01.012. (The estimate reported in that study is $430 million in 2013.).

[248] *See* Research and Development in the Pharmaceutical Industry, *supra* note 246; *see also* National Science Foundation, "Business Enterprise Research and Development Survey" for current data (Feb. 25, 2023), https://www.nsf.gov/statistics/srvyberd/.

[249] *See* Michael S. Mireles, *The Bayh-Dole Act and Incentives for the Commercialization of Government-Funded Invention in Developing Countries*, 76 UMKC L. Rev. 525 (2007).

The historical and contemporary examples from Brazil, India, and the United States demonstrate that governments can effectively guide innovation and access through creative frameworks and strategic interventions. The response of South Africa to the AIDS crisis in recent years, ably led by its national government, is yet another instance of resolute government actions synergistically supported by NSAs in the face of devastating public-health challenges. As the South African government moved to incorporate TRIPS flexibilities in its patent statute through a proposed amendment to its patent statute, forty-one pharmaceutical companies in the country filed a lawsuit against the national government for its statutory move aimed at making medicines affordable and accessible to ordinary South Africans.[250] However, vehement popular mobilization across the country, led by NSAs such as civil society and media, forced the pharmaceutical companies to withdraw their suit and paved the way for the proposed amendments.[251]

While much has been achieved, these examples illustrate that much more could be accomplished if governments redefined their roles and responsibilities in the area. Governments should focus on streamlining their actions in the future to encourage an innovation landscape that not only accommodates public health but actively enhances it. Sovereign nations must establish and implement laws that comport with international obligations without compromising national health-care needs.

As Baker, Flynn, and Ragavan assert in their analysis of India, the country's demonstrated adherence to TRIPS Agreement in its legislation has been coupled with enactment of laws that are carefully calibrated to accommodate its national objectives while comporting with local realities.[252] In order to be successful, countries can and should tailor their IP laws and implementation to their domestic social, economic, and cultural needs—local realities—while trying to remain within the bounds of the TRIPS Agreement.

[250] *See* Srividhya Ragavan and Amaka Vanni, *Introduction: Access to Medicine and TRIPS Agreement: A Mapping of the Tradescape, in* Intellectual Property Law and Access to Medicines: TRIPS Agreement, Health, and Pharmaceuticals (Srividhya Ragavan and Amaka Vanni eds., 2021), https://scholarship.law.tamu.edu/facscholar/1535/ (last visited Oct. 21, 2025).

[251] *See id.*

[252] *See* Ragavan et al., *supra* note 92.

4
Pragmatic Multilateralism: Reimagining a Framework

1. Introduction: Covid-19 Unravels the Facade of Trade-IP Linkage

1.1 Unsustainable Policy Position

The previous chapter highlighted the background that led to the historic inclusion of IP in the trade regime, which resulted in an expansion of property rights and their eventual reframing for their inclusion in global trade. The reframing resulted in a rearrangement of global norm-setting for property generally and for IP specifically. Evolving power dynamics between member states resulted in policy positions that limited discourses on whether IP norms can or have become barriers to health-care access within the boundaries imposed by trade.

The emergence of this policy position seemed to largely divorce global policy discussions on health-care access and affordability from the local realities of member states. Meanwhile, the devastation left behind by the pandemic and other epidemics has caused many to question the narratives that "strong" IP is essential for global trade by instead highlighting the need for a "balanced" IP regime that accounts for public health as a requirement for promoting trade.

1.2 The Covid-19-Induced Public-Health Disruption

To appreciate the need for a new framework, it is important to recapitulate the circumstances under which Covid-19 spread. On January 30, 2020, when the WHO's director-general, Tedros Adhanom Ghebreyesus, following the recommendation of its International Health Regulations Emergency Committee, declared the then-newly discovered Covid-19 as a Public Health

Fractures in IP, Trade, and Health. Srividhya Ragavan and Swaraj Paul Barooah, Oxford University Press.
 DOI: 10.1093/9780197684085.003.0004

Emergency of International Concern (PHEIC), there were 7,818 confirmed cases worldwide, with only eighteen of those outside China.[1] By March 11, when the WHO declared that Covid-19 had achieved "pandemic" status, the virus had infected more than 118,000 people and killed more than 4,000 in 114 countries.[2] Within months, there would be millions of confirmed cases across the world.

The extremely virulent nature of the disease, combined with the lack of vaccines and treatment options, made the pandemic the most significant global health crisis since the 1918 influenza pandemic. As Covid-19 ravaged patient populations and health-care systems around the world, there was tremendous pressure for the creation of a vaccine as well as effective treatment options for the virus.[3] Several countries experienced mass shortages of treatment-related materials such as ventilators and personal protective equipment.

Even as there were some calls for a more collectivist approach to tackling Covid-19,[4] the much-touted benefits of international trade—that is, increased cooperation and deepening interdependence between nations—were turned on their head as richer nations turned inward, leaving poorer nations with dependencies hanging.[5] With domestic as well as international trade severely disrupted by the virus, heightened political rhetoric led to a rise of protectionist and hyper-nationalistic policies in many countries.[6] As fear and frustration grew, richer nations started stockpiling future supplies of

[1] *Archived: WHO Timeline—COVID-19*, World Health Org. (Apr. 27, 2020), https://www.who.int/news/item/27-04-2020-who-timeline---covid-19 (last visited Oct. 22, 2025).

[2] *WHO Director-General's Opening Remarks at the Media Briefing on COVID-19 – 13 March 2020*, World Health Org. (Mar. 13, 2020), https://www.who.int/dg/speeches/detail/who-director-general-s-opening-remarks-at-the-mission-briefing-on-covid-19---13-march-2020 (last visited Oct. 22, 2025); *see also* Mary Van Beusekom, *"Deeply Concerned" WHO Declares COVID-19 Pandemic*, Univ. Minn.: Ctr. for Infectious Disease Rsch. & Pol'y News (Mar. 11, 2020), https://www.cidrap.umn.edu/covid-19/deeply-concerned-who-declares-covid-19-pandemic (last visited Oct. 22, 2025).

[3] Rebecca Forman et al., *COVID-19 Vaccine Challenges: What Have We Learned So Far and What Remains to Be Done?, 125 Health Pol'y 553* (2021), https://doi.org/10.1016/j.healthpol.2021.03.013 (last visited Oct. 22, 2025).

[4] Divij Joshi, *CoViD-19 Pandemic Spurs Calls for 'Openness' in IP*, SpicyIP (Mar. 31, 2020), https://spicyip.com/2020/03/covid-19-pandemic-spurs-calls-for-openness-in-ip.html (last visited Oct. 22, 2025).

[5] For instance, several countries started indulging in export bans of vaccine supplies and related material. *See* Praharsh Gour, *A Recipe for Disaster: Export Bans, TRIPS Waiver and Hyper Nationalism*, SpicyIP (Apr. 25, 2021), https://spicyip.com/2021/04/a-recipe-of-disaster-export-bans-trips-waiver-and-hyper-nationalism.html (last visited Oct. 22, 2025).

[6] *See generally* Muhammad Zaheer Abbas, *Practical Implications of 'Vaccine Nationalism': A Short-Sighted and Risky Approach in Response to COVID-19*, South Centre (2020), https://www.southcentre.int/wp-content/uploads/2020/11/RP-124.pdf (last visited Oct. 22, 2025).

vaccines.[7] A report by Oxfam International showed that, by September 2020, wealthy nations representing just 13 percent of the world's population had struck deals for more than 51 percent of the promised doses of the leading Covid-19 vaccine candidates at the time.[8]

Even as the seriousness of the virus was making itself known, in October 2020 South Africa and India proposed a waiver of the TRIPS Agreement provisions that related to Covid-19 treatment (Covid-19 Waiver) for the duration of the pandemic.[9] Thus, the exigencies of Covid-19 have caused the world to reconsider the larger role of public health.

1.3 Global Rethinking for a Policy Reset

Matthew Boesler notes that "once ideas about how to manage the economy become entrenched, it can take generations to dislodge them. Historically, perceptions of IP rights are no different. Usually, something disruptive has to happen to jolt policy onto a different track."[10] In the context of the American economy, Boesler outlines how the Great Recession that followed the dark days of 2008 triggered a rethinking about dealing with the economy, causing the then-Federal Reserve chair, Paul Volcker, to steer US economic policies away from those of President Ronald Reagan in the 1980s.[11]

Covid-19 has been equally, if not more, disruptive in forcing a rethinking of alternatives to existing policies. Globally disruptive epidemics such as those of Ebola and SARS had already raised the issues of response and preparedness.[12] While pandemics present global challenges of enormous magnitude, chronic diseases such as diabetes and mental illness as well as acute

[7] Press Release, Oxfam Int'l, *Small Group of Rich Nations Have Bought Up More Than Half the Future Supply of Leading COVID-19 Vaccine Contenders* (Sept. 17, 2020), https://www.oxfam.org/en/press-releases/small-group-rich-nations-have-bought-more-half-future-supply-leading-covid-19 (last visited Oct. 22, 2025).

[8] *Id.*

[9] Press Release, *WHO and Costa Rica Preview Technology Pooling Initiative to Ensure Access to COVID-19 Health Products for All*, World Health Org. (May 15, 2020), https://www.who.int/news/item/15-05-2020-who-and-costa-rica-preview-technology-pooling-initiative-to-ensure-access-to-covid-19-health-products-for-all (last visited Oct. 22, 2025).

[10] *Id.*

[11] *Id.*

[12] Brendan Murray, *Slump in Global Goods Trade to Deepen with Coronavirus, WTO Says*, Bloomberg (Feb 17, 2020) https://www.bloomberg.com/news/articles/2020-02-17/slump-in-global-goods-trade-to-deepen-with-coronavirus-wto-says (last visited Oct. 22, 2025).

illnesses such as different forms of cancer also affect public health in varying magnitudes and can impact national productivity directly and trade indirectly. Such unexpected but impactful events often force an alignment of idealistic theories with existing realities.

Further, years of domination by the TRIPS Agreement over public-health policies from a trade vantage have left wealthy and impoverished countries alike open to discussing the health question from different perspectives, including those of access, safety, affordability, innovation, supply chains, IP laws, and regulations.

This chapter details how the global black-swan events involving public health have provided a rare and effective counter to an otherwise prevailing perception of a robust linkage between IP and trade. It is written from the vantage that public health has, over time, naturally regained its position as a top priority in the post-Covid globe. Taking the Covid pandemic as an example to discuss how the existing framework for health care failed at a critical juncture, this chapter highlights how an inflexible trade regime that was losing trajectory to begin with was further weakened by its inability to balance the needs of the public with private rights. Our goal in tracing this increasing fragility in the health-care system is to establish the need for a new framework whereby the WTO could continue its trajectory of leading with trade without compromising innovation in health care or access to it.

Beginning with a discussion of the pandemic, the chapter goes on to lay the foundation for a public-health treaty (PHT), to be discussed later in the book. It focuses on the issues countries faced in dealing with the pandemic, highlighting how the existing framework fell short during the emergency. After discussing the negotiated Covid-specific waiver of TRIPS Agreement and its deficiencies, it emphasizes the importance of a human-rights-centric approach above a diplomacy approach for addressing public-health concerns and offers suggestions for improving access and affordability (such as differential pricing). Its recommendations include calls for open innovation, sharing of resources and know-how, and provision of different types of licenses for this industry.

Finally, the chapter highlights the imminent need for a pragmatic multilateralism to enable global health-care equity. It calls for imagining a new framework that focuses on global public health without compromising the innovation paradigm and that allows flexibility for the local realities of member states.

2. The Covid-19 Waiver Proposal and the Global Response

2.1 The Proposal and Its Rationale

While there were many calls for action and proposals for ways forward in response to the unprecedented challenges posed by the Covid-19 pandemic, the unfolding of events at the WTO is of specific interest for the purposes of this chapter.[13] In October 2020, India and South Africa issued a joint statement before the WTO requesting the waiver of certain parts of the TRIPS Agreement relating to the prevention, containment, and treatment of Covid-19, as discussed above.[14] The Covid-19 Waiver proposal sought a waiver, for a limited duration with a possible termination period of no more than three years, of sections 1, 4, 5, and 7 of Part II of the Agreement—that is, the different IP-related provisions that could broadly impact vaccine production, distribution, therapeutics, and diagnostics.

The proposal noted that several countries, especially in the developing world, were likely to face institutional barriers in utilizing the negotiated flexibilities under the TRIPS Agreement, and that there were other related barriers, such as regulatory exclusivities, that prevented the efficient use of the existing flexibilities.[15] It also noted that the processes for importing and exporting pharmaceutical goods under Article 31*bis* were cumbersome and problematic, especially for countries with limited or no local manufacturing capacity.[16] While there was an imminent need to fill a growing supply-demand gap for all medical products, Covid-related products were urgently required in poorer nations to contain the pandemic. As many argued, the Covid-19 Waiver would be critical to removing these barriers and helping scale up global production so that a vaccinated globe could be back to business as before.

The stated purpose behind the proposal was to ensure that IP rights would not be a barrier to access to affordable medicines or to the R&D, manufacture,

[13] *See, e.g.*, Sudip Chaudhuri, *Making Covid-19 Medical Products Affordable: Voluntary Patent Pool and TRIPS Flexibilities*, 3 South Centre (2020), https://www.southcentre.int/wp-content/uploads/2020/06/SouthViews-Chaudhuri.pdf (last visited Oct. 22, 2025).

[14] *Waiver from Certain Provisions of the TRIPS Agreement for the Prevention, Containment and Treatment of COVID-19*: Communication from India and South Africa, WTO Doc. IP/C/W/669 (Oct. 2, 2020), https://docs.wto.org/dol2fe/Pages/SS/directdoc.aspx?filename=q:/IP/C/W669.pdf&Open=True (last visited Oct. 22, 2025).

[15] *Id.*

[16] *Id.*; *see generally Amendment of the TRIPS Agreement*, WTO Doc. WT/L/641 (Dec. 8, 2005), http://www.wto.org/english/tratop_e/trips_e/wtl641_e.htm (last visited Oct. 22, 2025).

and supply of medical products essential to fighting Covid. The Covid-19 Waiver was thus proposed as a tool to kick-start the prevention, containment, and treatment of the disease.

2.2 Legal Bases of the Proposal

The waiver had a legal basis in Article IX (3) of the Agreement Establishing the WTO, which allowed member nations to seek a waiver from certain provisions of the Agreement or any other multilateral trade agreements. Article IX (4) requires member nations to highlight the exceptional circumstances, along with the terms and conditions governing the waiver, including the date of its termination. The decision-making-by-consensus rule under Article IX(3)(a) requires that requests for waiver concerning the Agreement be submitted to the Ministerial Conference for review within ninety days, and that approval would require a three-fourths majority. Further, under Article IX(3)(b), the waiver request concerning the multilateral trade agreements was to be submitted to the Council for TRIPS. The Council, in turn, would, within ninety days, submit it for review to the Ministerial Conference (if the former is in session) or the General Council. In the current case, organizations including Health Gap asserted that the urgency triggered by Covid warranted simultaneous review by the WTO General Council for its independent consideration, as well as by the Council for TRIPS.[17]

Once the request was approved, the submitted body would review the request on a yearly basis until the termination date to determine if the exceptional circumstances that initially justified approval continue to warrant an extension, modification, or termination of the waiver. Alternatively, waivers would terminate if the underlying provision were amended through the established procedure.

Waivers are well-established in WTO precedents. For example, the first amendment to the TRIPS Agreement, dealing with compulsory licenses for the export of pharmaceutical products to countries lacking manufacturing

[17] Brook Baker, *Waive Recognition and Enforcement of Intellectual Property Rights for COVID-19 Medical Technologies Deserves Universal Support, but Countries Also Have to Take Domestic Measures*, Health Gap (Oct. 10 2020), https://healthgap.org/south-africa-and-indias-proposal-to-waive-recognition-and-enforcement-of-intellectual-property-rights-for-covid-19-medical-technologies-deserves-universal-support-but-countries-also-have-to/ (last visited Oct. 22, 2025).

capacity, under the Doha Declaration, which celebrated its twenty-fifth year in 2021, operated effectively as a waiver until being ratified by two-thirds of WTO member nations in 2017, sixteen years after the adoption of the Declaration.

2.3 Initial Reception of the Proposal

The Covid-19 Waiver proposal resulted in a much-needed debate and discussion across different vested groups around the world, including member nations, international institutions, NGOs, and academia, about the role of trade and IP in health care. In addition to the waiver, other responses addressing IP-related barriers included Costa Rica's patent pooling proposal[18] and open-source approaches to R&D for Covid.[19] Nonetheless, the proposal for the Covid-19 Waiver seemed to generate more interest, being supported by several governments of developing and least-developed countries, as well as members of civil society.[20] Initially, the waiver was intended as a response to a call from WTO member nations to ensure that IP rights did not hinder manufacturing, distribution, access to affordable medicines, or R&D, especially addressing the supply-related concerns for medical products essential to combating Covid.[21]

2.4 Unrealistic Opposition to the Proposal

While the proponents of the waiver supported it as a necessary step toward ensuring equitable access to lifesaving medicines and treatments, it was immediately opposed by a bloc of developed countries, including Switzerland, Norway, Australia, Canada, Japan, and the UK, as well as

[18] *Id.*

[19] *See, e.g.*, *COVID-19 Response*, OpenSource Pharma Found, https://www.ospfound.org/open-research-platform.html (last visited Oct. 22, 2025).

[20] *See generally* Praharsh Gour, *Wishful Thinking? Analyzing India and South Africa's Joint Statement to Waive Key Provisions of TRIPS—Part II*, SpicyIP https://spicyip.com/2020/10/wishful-thinking-analyzing-india-and-south-africas-joint-statement-to-waive-key-provisions-of-trips-part-ii.html (last visited Oct. 22, 2025).

[21] *See generally* Praharsh Gour, *Wishful Thinking? Analyzing India and South Africa's Joint Statement to Waive Key Provisions of TRIPS—Part II*, SpicyIP https://spicyip.com/2020/10/wishful-thinking-analyzing-india-and-south-africas-joint-statement-to-waive-key-provisions-of-trips-part-ii.html (last visited Oct. 22, 2025).

Brazil.[22] The United States eventually supported a limited waiver for Covid-19 vaccines,[23] but other nations such as the UK and Switzerland continued to oppose even that limited-purpose waiver.[24]

Biopharmaceutical companies maintained an unbending stance against the waiver, stating that supply constraints and technology transfer rather than patents were the real barriers and that to weaken patents would "send the wrong signal."[25] However, even assuming that know-how and technology transfer were more important than patents and other forms of IP in tackling Covid-related issues, this form of opposition remained unrealistic, considering that biopharmaceutical companies themselves were in the best position to share that know-how and to commit to negotiating viable technology transfers. In any event, the argument that it would send a "wrong signal" about weakening patents seemed to be a flimsy reason to oppose the waiver, in view of the cost of the pandemic to trade, human lives, and productivity—and also in view of the several billions of dollars of public money received in the development process of the various vaccines, the recoupment of which is generally considered the purpose of a patent.[26] Without meaning to minimize the role of biopharmaceutical companies in innovation, it seems fair to note that their corporate responsibility during exigencies has raised important questions.

Regrettably, as the debate around the waiver intensified over the next several months, millions more lives continued to be lost to the virus.[27]

[22] Thiru Balasubramanium, *WTO TRIPS Council (October 2020): South Africa Issues Clarion Call Urging Support for TRIPS Waiver Proposal*, Knowledge Ecology Int'l (Oct. 16, 2020), https://www.keionline.org/34235 (last visited Oct. 22, 2025).

[23] *Id.*

[24] *Id.*

[25] Press Release, Int'l Fed'n of Pharma. Mfrs. & Ass'ns, *IFPMA Statement on TRIPS Discussion Document* (Mar. 16, 2022), https://www.ifpma.org/resource-centre/statement-ifpma-trips-discussion-document/ (last visited Oct. 22, 2025); *see also* Press Release, PhRMA. Rsch. & Mfrs., *PhRMA Statement on WTO TRIPS Waiver Negotiations* (Mar. 15, 2022), https://www.phrma.org/resources/phrma-statement-on-wto-trips-waiver-negotiations (last visited Oct. 22, 2025).

[26] As examples, AstraZeneca's vaccine was developed at Oxford University with more than 90-percent public funding, the US government contributed $18 billion to Operation Warp Speed, and Moderna was funded by US taxpayers. *See, e.g.*, Michael Safi, *Oxford/AstraZeneca Covid Vaccine Research 'Was 97% Publicly Funded,'* Guardian (Apr. 15, 2021), https://www.theguardian.com/science/2021/apr/15/oxfordastrazeneca-covid-vaccine-research-was-97-publicly-funded (last visited Oct. 22, 2025); *see also* Adyasha Samal, *COVID-19 Vaccines: Patent Ownership and the Barriers to Equitable Access*, SpicyIP (Dec. 2, 2020), https://spicyip.com/2020/12/covid-19-vaccines-patent-ownership-and-the-barriers-to-equitable-access.html (last visited Oct. 22, 2025) (discussing ownership of patents, related public funding, and vaccine realities for the global South).

[27] Madhavi Sunder and Haochen Sun, *Intellectual Property and "The Lost Year" of COVID-19 Deaths*, Harv. Int'l L.J. (Nov. 8, 2023), https://journals.law.harvard.edu/ilj/2023/11/intellectual-property-and-the-lost-year-of-covid-19-deaths/ (last visited Oct. 22, 2025).

In the meantime, the Covid-19 Waiver proposal had morphed, through various rounds of negotiations, into a very different form from what was originally intended. This caused India to allege at the 12th WTO Ministerial Conference that the developed world was engaged in collusive tactics, diluting the waiver proposal while simultaneously feigning concern.[28] Even as these negotiations for global cooperation remained fraught with controversy, richer nations continued to sign bulky procurement orders in excess of their requirements, at a time when vaccine availability for many poorer countries around the world was uncertain.[29]

2.5 Subsequent Devolution of the Proposal

Despite the fierce opposition from vested interest groups, the heavily contested negotiations were finally concluded, nearly two years after the introduction of the Covid-19 Waiver proposal, with the adoption of a very limited form of the initially proposed waiver.[30] While the initial version of the waiver proposal was intended to apply to diagnostics, therapeutics, and medicines as well as to trade secrets, copyrights, and designs, the version eventually agreed upon excluded diagnostics and therapeutics and was limited to patented products only. Commentators observed that, in substance, it offered insignificantly more than what was already available to the WTO member nations under the existing rules.[31]

Moreover, those eligible to use the proposed solution under the Covid-19 Waiver had been narrowed down to include a few developing countries accounting for barely 10 percent of global exports of the Covid vaccine in 2021,

[28] Press Release, PIB Delhi, *Statement by Shri Piyush Goyal During the WTO 12th Ministerial Conference at the Meeting with Co-Sponsors of TRIPS Waiver* (June 14, 2022), https://pib.gov.in/PressReleasePage.aspx?PRID=1834066 (last visited Oct. 22, 2025).

[29] Carlos M. Correa, *Will the Amendment to the TRIPS Agreement Enhance Access to Medicines?*, South Centre policy brief no. 57 (Jan. 2019), https://www.southcentre.int/wp-content/uploads/2019/01/PB57_Will-the-Amendment-to-the-TRIPS-Agreement-Enhance-Access-to-Medicines_EN-1.pdf (last visited Oct. 22, 2025).

[30] Ministerial Decision on the TRIPS Agreement, WTO Docs. WT/MIN(22)/30, WT/L/1141 (June 22, 2022), https://docs.wto.org/dol2fe/Pages/SS/directdoc.aspx?filename=q:/WT/MIN22/30.pdf&Open=True (last visited Oct. 22, 2025); see also Roshan John, *The Quad Discussion Group's Compromise Falls Short of a Comprehensive TRIPS Waiver*, SpicyIP (Mar. 17, 2022), https://spicyip.com/2022/03/the-quad-discussion-groups-compromise-falls-short-of-a-comprehensive-trips-waiver.html (last visited Oct. 22, 2025).

[31] *Id.*; Andrew Green "*WTO Finally Agrees on a TRIPS Deal. But Not Everyone Is Happy*," devex, (June 17, 2022), https://www.devex.com/news/wto-finally-agrees-on-a-trips-deal-but-not-everyone-is-happy-103476 (last visited Oct. 22, 2025).

a year after the negotiations began. Additionally, restricting the waiver to patents alone left open the possibility of reduced access due to trade secrets and other IP-related barriers, as well as non-IP regulatory barriers such as data exclusivity[32] even if patent barriers were alleviated.[33]

Regardless of the specifics of the Covid-19 Waiver, the fact that such limited action required two years of protracted negotiation, despite the unprecedented urgency of the situation, demonstrates how public health has taken a back seat at the WTO, the forum that has been the playground for the trade–IP nexus for nearly three decades.

3. Diplomacy vs. Human-Rights Approach to Health-Care Access

3.1 The Diplomacy Approach and Its Failings

Contemporary discussions of public health implicate trade, globalization, access to medicines, and more.[34] The fragmentation of venues where IP norms and the norms of public health are shaped and influenced arguably has helped produce a power dynamic that favors powerful countries at the expense of weaker ones.[35] Unfortunately, public health has become a subset of the discourse on trade and innovation, and as a result, health has, over time, become a matter of "diplomacy."[36] As a constituent of the right to life, health should not be a matter of mere diplomacy without considered research on outcomes.

Health diplomacy efforts have produced an endless stream of literature even as the effort to evolve viable, practical solutions for improving public health remains ongoing. Meanwhile, the world has been ravaged by a slew

[32] *See, e.g.*, Srividhya Ragavan, *Data Exclusivity Is the New Way to Delay Generics*, 50 Conn. L. Rev. Online 1, 4 (2018).

[33] See Rohan Srivastava, *An Obituary to the TRIPS 'Waiver': Lessons from an Imperfect Response*, SpicyIP (Apr. 22, 2023), https://spicyip.com/2023/04/an-obituary-to-the-trips-waiver-lessons-from-an-imperfect-response.html (last visited Oct. 22, 2025).

[34] This section draws on an earlier article published by the authors titled *Historic Tensions Involving International Intellectual Property Protection of Medical Technology with Disastrous Public Health Consequences*, 54 (2) Seton Hall L. Rev. 339 (2023).

[35] Susan K. Sell, *TRIPS Was Never Enough: Vertical Forum Shifting, FTAS, ACTA, and TTP*, 18 J. Intell. Prop. L. 447, 451 (2011); *see also* Eyal Benvenisti and George W. Downs, *The Empire's New Clothes—Political Economy and the Fragmentation of International Law*, 60 Stan. L. Rev. 595, 597 (2007).

[36] *Id.*

of health-related issues which have highlighted the lacunae in health-diplomacy initiatives, some of which are captured below:

3.1.1 IP-Trade-Related Barriers to Health Overlooked in Policy Documents

Discussions on patent monopolies as barriers to health care access are limited in the right to health context. For instance, India's 2017 National Health Policy, which aims to prioritize the role of the government in shaping the health system in *all its dimensions*, with the aim of attaining the highest possible level of health and well-being for all, did not highlight the role of available patent or other IP flexibilities for the government to address public health issues.[37] The document supports a "right-based approach" to health care and advocates for an "enabling environment" in terms of adequate finances and infrastructure to meaningfully realize the right to health, and yet falls short of taking into account the salient role of IP and trade in shaping that environment.[38]

Similarly, a key policy document released by the WHO in 2025, entitled "A Global Health Strategy for 2025–2028," which cites the right to health as one of its key principles, ostensibly omits any reference to the barriers imposed by patents, the trade–IP linkage and its impact on access to medicines, or even the role of the WTO and TRIPS Agreement in impeding or strengthening health-care access.[39]

3.1.2 IP Policies Oblivious to the Right to Health

Second, even during the WTO era, national IP policies have not always cited the right to health. For example, India's 2016 National IP Policy, which was heavily influenced by unilateral pressure from the US Trade Representative (USTR), does not mention such a right,[40] even though it describe health care as one of the areas of national priority and specifies enhancement of access

[37] *See* National Health Policy, 2017, Ministry of Health and Family Welfare, https://mohfw.gov.in/sites/default/files/9147562941489753121.pdf (last visited Oct. 22, 2025).

[38] *Id.*

[39] *See A Global Health Strategy for 2025–2028*, World Health Org. (2025), https://cdn.who.int/media/docs/default-source/documents/about-us/general-programme-of-work/global-health-strategy-2025-2028.pdf (last visited Oct. 22, 2025).

[40] Srividhya Ragavan, Brook Baker, and Sean Flynn, *Comments on India's Draft National IPR Policy*, Am. U. Program Info. Just. & Intell. Prop.: Infojustice (2015), http://infojustice.org/wp-content/uploads/2015/02/ragavan-baker-flynn01302015.pdf (last visited Oct. 22, 2025).

to health care as one of its missions.[41] This contrasts with the IP policy of South Africa, which complements its constitutional guarantees of the right to health by recognizing the promotion of the right as one of the mandates of the Inter-Ministerial Committee on Intellectual Property (IMCIP), established following the recommendation of the Report of the United Nations Secretary General's High Level Panel on Access to Medicines (UNHLP).[42] However, even the highly progressive IP policy of South Africa goes no further than a mere nominal reference to the right to health, without providing any concrete recommendations on the role of IP, and patents in particular, in hindering or deepening health-care access and in the effective realization of the right.

Similarly, sociological discussions on health issues—such as high incidences of cancer or diabetes, as in India—rarely discuss the need for a right to health as a solution. To illustrate, the Operational Guidelines of the National Programme for Prevention and Control of Non-Communicable Diseases (2023–2030) do not offer a rights-based approach to health as a solution option to effectively deal with noncommunicable diseases.[43]

3.1.3 Non-Workable Flexibilities

Third, member nations have been unable to effectively use the inbuilt flexibilities of the TRIPS Agreement, since the WTO's interpretations are divorced from reality as a result of perceived ideological superiority. Over the years, member nations have realized that working TRIPS flexibilities was cumbersome and time-consuming and, importantly, that it left them in a defensive position against the globe while battling national public-health crises at home. Countries that used flexibilities found themselves endlessly defending their actions to bodies such as the USTR or the European Trade Commissioner. Several commentators have observed that the USTR's Special 301 process, in particular, has been a principal source of concern regarding

[41] *See National Intellectual Property Rights Policy*, Ministry of Commerce and Industry, Government of India (2016), https://ipindia.gov.in/writereaddata/Portal/Images/pdf/National_IPR_Policy_English.pdf (last visited Oct. 22, 2025).

[42] *See Intellectual Property Policy of the Republic of South Africa, Phase I*, Republic of South Africa (2018), https://www.gov.za/sites/default/files/gcis_document/201808/ippolicy2018-phasei.pdf (last visited Oct. 22, 2025).

[43] *See Operational Guidelines of the National Programme for Prevention and Control of Non-Communicable Diseases (2023–2030)*, Ministry of Health & Family Welfare, Government of India (2023), https://www.mohfw.gov.in/sites/default/files/NP-NCD%20Operational%20Guidelines_0.pdf (last visited Oct. 22, 2025).

the threat of unilateral retaliation against the use of TRIPS flexibilities.[44] Alternatively, the use of flexibilities historically has tended to leave member states dealing with the WTO's Dispute Settlement Body (DSB).

Notably, at the outset of the twenty-first century, while the United States considered the use of negotiated flexibilities—that is, the right to compulsory license medication—as a viable solution to deal with the epidemic of anthrax that caused a public-health scare in the country, over the years it has consistently objected to developing countries' use of such solutions to deal with the HIV/AIDS crisis.[45] As discussed in detail in previous chapters, India has been repeatedly placed on the USTR's Special 301's "priority watchlist" for using TRIPS-permitted flexibilities, such as utilizing its legislation to deny frivolous patents and issuing a compulsory license in 2013 with respect to Bayer's sorafenib, sold as Nexavar, a drug used to treat liver and kidney cancer, on the grounds that the patent owner was not catering to the demands of the Indian market.[46] The Special 301 Reports of the USTR issued in 2012, 2013, 2014, and as late as 2020 cited the decision of India's IPAB to grant a compulsory license for Nexavar as "concerning."

Similarly, when Brazil implemented a law in 1996 establishing a "local working" requirement that would have allowed compulsory licensing if a patent had not been adequately worked in the territory of Brazil, it was dragged by the United States into the DSB of the WTO merely for invoking TRIPS-permitted flexibilities in the public interest.[47] This pattern of hostility against the use of flexibilities was in evidence in May 2016 when the USTR threatened to withhold the funds intended for a peace accord with Paz Colombia in response to Colombia's legitimate exercise of TRIPS-permitted flexibilities under the Doha Declaration by issuance of a compulsory license to lower the price of Novartis's imatimib, a leukemia drug marketed as Glivec.[48]

[44] *See, e.g.*, Michael Palmedo, *United States: Unilateral Norm Setting Using Special 301*, *in* INTELLECTUAL PROPERTY LAW AND ACCESS TO MEDICINES: TRIPS AGREEMENT, HEALTH, AND PHARMACEUTICALS 274, 275 (Srividhya Ragavan and Amaka Vanni eds., 2021).

[45] Cecilia Oh, *U.S. Opposed to Moves to Address Public-Health Concerns About TRIPS*, THIRD WORLD NETWORK, https://twn.my/title/twr131f.htm (last visited Oct. 22, 2025); Divya Murthy, Comment, *The Future of Compulsory Licensing: Deciphering the Doha Declaration on the TRIPS Agreement and Public Health*, 17 AM. U. INT'L L. REV. 1299, 1302 n.12 (2002).

[46] *See Bayer Corp. v. Natco Pharma Ltd.*, OA/35/2012/PT/MUM (2013).

[47] *DS199: Brazil—Measures Affecting Patent Protection*, WTO, https://www.wto.org/english/tratop_e/dispu_e/cases_e/ds199_e.htm (last visited Oct. 22, 2025).

[48] *Excerpts from the August 24 Announcement of a Final Peace Accord Between the Colombian Government and the FARC: The Joint Communiqué*, COLOM. PEACE, https://colombiapeace.org/excerpts-from-the-august-24-announcement-of-a-final-peace-accord-between-the-colombian-government-and-the-farc/ (last visited Oct. 22, 2025).

Amidst this, the WTO has been hesitant to allow countries to deploy negotiated flexibilities, which have been cited as an important failure of the trade regime vis-à-vis health-care access.[49] Some commentators have argued that the economic interdependence encouraged by the WTO has been misused or even weaponized by some member nations, causing vulnerabilities that, in the health context, were exploited in the recent Covid pandemic to the detriment of the other member nations.[50]

Further, in a rush to push the flexibilities, WTO jurisprudence has not shown sufficient interest in using limitations (which would have been a good alternative to the use of a waiver and of flexibilities) which make it impossible to effectively use those flexibilities by requiring justifications with a high burden of proof for countries, even during exigencies.

3.1.4 An Inconsequential Diplomatic Tango

Fourth, the diplomatic tango between the WTO and the WHO personifies the failure of both organizations and has resulted in showcasing their limitations to the globe at a time when they need to work together synchronously. The gap caused by the disconnect between an ideologically posited institution (the WTO) and another institution based on realities on the ground (led by WHO) remains unbridged. The diplomatic tango seemed to manifest mostly because of the inability of a multilateral international regime and the hesitancy of international organizations, essentially the WTO, to enable quick access to vaccines and other health-related products when the globe truly needed such engagement.[51]

In contrast, the existing international framework was not conducive to facilitating this; rather, it was seen that a set of rich countries were able to unilaterally flex their muscles using trade to the detriment of national public health in other member nations. International organizations seemingly got tied down by their own policies, which prevented them from reacting expeditiously to a health-care crisis.[52]

[49] Srividhya Ragavan, *World Trade Organization: A Barrier to Global Public Health?*, *in* Intellectual Property Law and Access to Medicines: TRIPS Agreement, Health, and Pharmaceuticals 25, 31 (Srividhya Ragavan and Amaka Vanni eds., 2021).

[50] *See, e.g.*, Amrita Narlikar, *Holding Up a Mirror to the World Trade Organization: Lessons from the COVID-19 Pandemic*, Glob. Persps., at 1, 7, (2021); *see also* Henry Farrell and Abraham L. Newman, *Weaponized Interdependence: How Global Economic Networks Shape State Coercion*, 44 Int'l Sec. 42, 45 (2019).

[51] *Id.* at 29.

[52] Srividhya Ragavan, *World Trade Organization: A Barrier to Global Public Health?*, *in* Intellectual Property Law and Access to Medicines: TRIPS Agreement, Health, and Pharmaceuticals 25, 31 (Srividhya Ragavan and Amaka Vanni eds., 2021).

Perhaps it's time to formally institute a trilateral coordination between the WTO, the WHO, and the WIPO as a permanent inter-international body of sorts, with a mandate to oversee collaboration at the intersection of public health, trade, and IP, and an objective of ensuring availability, accessibility, and affordability of medicines for all, without compromising the need to support innovation in health technologies. Such cooperation has already begun with an unexpected impetus from the devastation caused by Covid, and after the adoption of the report titled "Global Strategy and Plan of Action on Public Health, Innovation and Intellectual Property," issued by the director-general of the WHO in 2021.[53] However, the need of the hour is to lend such trilateral cooperation the level of urgency that it deserves in view of the fragility of global public health confirmed during the Covid pandemic, by formalizing such cooperation as a permanent institution with a strong structure, a potent constitution, and an express mandate to secure and strengthen global public health as its top priority.

3.2 WTO—A Barrier to Health-Care Access?

The WTO has been accused of presiding over a steady downgrading of public health while simultaneously upgrading the role of private rights in the form of patents—a consequence of the marriage between IP and trade—by not sufficiently stepping up during global public-health crises such as the AIDS epidemic and the Covid pandemic. As a result, within the various IPs, patents—which can potentially encourage innovation—morphed into an important barrier to accessing medicines because of evergreening and the increasingly degrading quality of patented innovation.

The WTO has overseen—with few protests from other health diplomats—a regulatory regime, established on shaky legal grounds, that works to provide more money to the pharmaceutical industry for testing a drug, which may enjoy twenty years of monopoly to begin with.[54] Over time, the WTO rules, supposedly intended to bolster national regulatory regimes,

[53] *See* Global Strategy and Plan of Action on Public Health, Innovation and Intellectual Property, World Health Org. (2021), https://apps.who.int/gb/ebwha/pdf_files/EB148/B148_10-en.pdf (last visited Oct. 22, 2025).

[54] *See* Srividhya Ragavan, *World Trade Organization: A Barrier to Global Public Health?* 23 (Texas A&M Univ. Sch. of L., Legal Stud. Rsch. Paper No. 20-32, 2020).

actually came to endorse more private rights that seemed to impose additional barriers to health-care access.[55]

Furthermore, the disengagement of the TRIPS Agreement from local realities, when combined with the WTO's perceived lack of specific focus on the impact of those realities on welfare, caused real loss of human lives. It has arguably allowed the patent regime to become a barrier to access to medicines without ensuring commensurate benefits to innovation. In many member nations, opinion about the impact of the WTO on daily lives has become profoundly negative.

The WTO's vision of public health begs for a more realistic realignment. Such a realignment would pave the way for egalitarian solutions and acknowledge that policies pursued by developed countries based solely on their own eccentric economic realities have been inconsiderate and insufficient and have led to disastrous public-health consequences.

3.3 Pivot to the Human-Rights Approach

The 2016 Report of the United Nations High-Level Panel on Access to Medicines, while noting the "misalignment" between health as a right on the one hand, and as a subset of the IP and trade paradigm on the other, goes on to recognize that access to medicines is a human right.[56] A policy paper for the Global Health Justice Partnership notes that pursuing human-rights arguments in IP-related court cases at the national level is most likely to provide "real results" for access.[57]

Health is a matter of the right of people and the obligation of governments. The right to health finds support in a number of international instruments, such as Article 25 of the 1948 Universal Declaration of Human Rights (UDHR), and Articles 7, 11, and 12 of the 1966 International Covenant of Economic, Social, and Cultural Rights (ICESCR), as well as the preamble of the WHO's constitution. In addition, constitutions of several countries

[55] *Id.* at 35–36.

[56] U.N. Secretary-General, *Report of the United Nations Secretary-General's High-Level Panel on Access to Medicines*, at 16 (Sept. 14, 2016), https://static1.squarespace.com/static/562094dee4b0d00c1a3ef761/t/57d9c6ebf5e231b2f02cd3d4/1473890031320/UNSG + HLP + Report + FINAL + 12 + Sept + 2016.pdf (last visited Oct. 22, 2025).

[57] Brennan et al., *A Human Rights Approach to Intellectual Property and Access to Medicines* 11 (2013), https://law.yale.edu/sites/default/files/area/center/ghjp/documents/humanrightsapproachintellectualproperty.pdf (last visited Oct. 22, 2025).

protect the right to life, of which health has been considered a subset,[58] while some countries, several of which are members of the WHO as well as the WTO, promise universal health care within their socialist structure.

A study of the constitutions of several countries shows clear associations between constitutional rights and health outcomes, likely by creating a dialogue on the benefits of health policy to the national economy.[59] The national constitutions of more than half of the world's countries include some form of guaranteed specific right to public health and medical care for their citizens.[60] On the other hand, about eighty-six countries, including the United States, do not constitutionally guarantee any health protection.[61]

A 2010 study of 194 countries outlined several indicators of the right to health. These included access to essential medicines or technologies statutorily recognized as a right and further concretized through a national policy on health. Other indicators included price-control regimes, access to health-care facilities, access to health education, and per capita public expenditure on medicines.[62] Significantly, the study found that access and affordability are the two main components of health care.

A 2008 study by the WHO found that constitutions conceived before 1948—the beginning of the international discourse on health rights—were unlikely to include the right-to-health requirement.[63] Indeed, in 2013 a study of constitutional rights to health by Jody Heymann and others, examining 191 constitutions, found that only 30 to 40 percent of constitutions adopted before 1970 included a right-to-health provision; this increased to 80 to 90 percent of those adopted between 2000 and 2011 (see Figure 4.1).[64] Other

[58] *Id.*

[59] Hiroaki Matsuura, *Exploring the Association Between the Constitutional Right to Health and Reproductive Health Outcomes in 157 Countries*, 27 Sexual & Reprod. Health Matters 168, 177 (Apr. 25, 2019), https://www.tandfonline.com/doi/full/10.1080/26410397.2019.1599653 (last visited Oct. 22, 2025); *see generally* Hiroaki Matsuura, *The Effect of a Constitutional Right to Health on Population Health in 157 Countries*, PGDA Working Papers No. 10613, (1970–2007); *The Role of Democratic Governance*, https://cdn1.sph.harvard.edu/wp-content/uploads/sites/1288/2013/10/PGDA_WP_106.pdf (last visited Oct. 22, 2025).

[60] Mark Wheeler, *A Constitutional Right to Health Care: Many Countries Have It, but Not the U.S.*, ScienceDaily (July 19, 2013), https://www.sciencedaily.com/releases/2013/07/130719104927.htm (last visited Oct. 22, 2025).

[61] *Id.*

[62] S. K. Perehudoff et al., *Access to Essential Medicines in National Constitutions*, 88 Bulletin of the World Health Org. [WHO] 800, 800 (Nov. 1, 2010), https://www.ncbi.nlm.nih.gov/pmc/articles/PMC2971519/ (last visited Oct. 22, 2025); *see generally* Gunilla Backman et al., *Health Systems and the Right to Health: An Assessment of 194 Countries*, 372 Right to Health 2047 (2008).

[63] Jody Heymann et al., *Constitutional Rights to Health, Public Health and Medical Care: The Status of Health Protections in 191 Countries*, 8 Glob. Pub. Health 639, 650–51 (2013).

[64] *Id.*

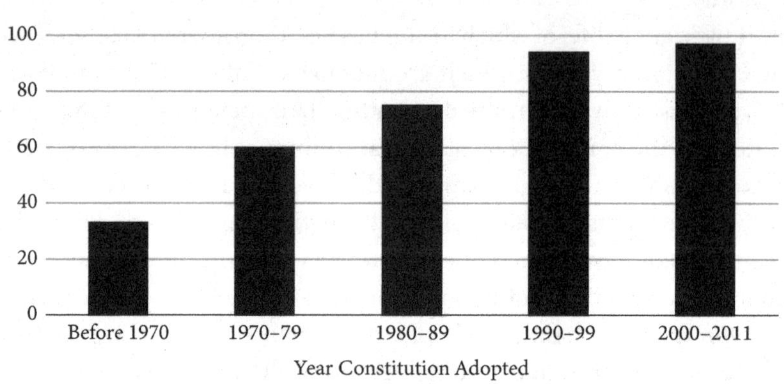

Figure 4.1 Percentage of world constitutions addressing health rights. *Adapted with permission from Jody Heymann et al., Constitutional Rights to Health, Public Health and Medical Care: The Status of Health Protections in 191 Countries, 8 Glob. Pub. Health 639, 650–51 (2013).*

studies have confirmed that constitutions adopted within the last sixty years have included more rights, duties, or entitlements related to health.[65] Similar conclusions on rights and duties pertaining to health were reached by other studies when evaluating the provisions in different constitutions.[66] However, to specifically show whether a constitutional right to health translates into better health-care outcomes, and if so, to what extent, will require additional studies.

Ideally, public health is a national objective that must not be compromised for the sake of international obligations. Poorer countries should not compromise the need to encourage foreign investment by promoting IP rights in lifesaving medication. The trade regime represents an opportunity for international organizations and regional entities to work together toward health equity by creating mechanisms wherein public health, the public good, or the public-benefit doctrine are treated as a limitation to IP rights, particularly patents.[67]

[65] S. Katrina Perehudoff, Health, Essential Medicines, Human Rights & National Constitutions 27 (2008).

[66] *See* Hiroaki Matsuura, *Exploring the Association Between the Constitutional Right to Health and Reproductive Health Outcomes in 157 Countries*, Sex Reprod. Health Matters (Dec. 2019) https://pmc.ncbi.nlm.nih.gov/articles/PMC7888040/ (last visited Oct. 22, 2025); *see also* Heymann et al., *supra* note 63.

[67] *See generally* Divya Murthy, *The Future of Compulsory Licensing: Deciphering the Doha Declaration on the TRIPS Agreement and Public Health,* 17 Am. U. Int'l L. Rev. 1299, 1327 (2003) (deciphering the definition of the term "public health").

3.4 Growing Disillusionment and the Call for Change

In the post-pandemic world, public health has taken over trade, with governments directly providing support to kick-start vaccinations. Policymakers have started to look beyond national boundaries to ensure global support for vaccinations. International institutions such as the WHO and UNICEF seem out of sync with the WTO's perceived exclusive vision of public health and have collectively called for a more realistic assessment.

The delayed response of international organizations in working to contain the Covid-19 pandemic and enabling quick access to vaccines lead to two important observations:

First, member nations dissatisfied with the existing framework of flexibilities to IP rules sought waivers from those rules. Indeed, this dissatisfaction is the stated purpose for seeking the Covid-19 Waiver discussed above. The protection regime outlined in TRIPS Agreement and the complete waiver from TRIPS-related IP provisions each represent opposing ends of a spectrum with limitations and flexibilities outlined in TRIPS falling in somewhere in the middle. But, WTO jurisprudence on limitations and on flexibilities disincentives the use of both of these accommodations even during a public health exigency, leaving countries with limited options.

Second, it has created an exigency to consider whether we need a new framework to address global health issues.

Meanwhile, much has been written about recommendations to preserve global and national public health. The following section examines some of these proposals before engaging with the question of whether we need a new framework.

4. Repositioning Health-Care Access Through a Public-Health Treaty

4.1 Reexamining the Needs of and Goals for a New Framework

In asserting that the historical structure of international trade agreements should be revisited to create global health equity, the authors endorse the view that there is a need for a separate treaty or international instrument that can integrate the strengths of the existing multilateral instruments. Any such instrument should rely on a careful examination of both the limitations and the achievements of ongoing multilateral processes at the global level. The framework would simultaneously take into account the limitations of a treaty as an instrument to solve global issues.

Additionally, the framework would need to determine how sovereign nations can deepen their cooperative frameworks to institute safeguards for preserving public health locally and consequently improving global public health. Importantly, this would require identifying and developing a greater understanding of the obstacles that competing international entities face when working together. Finally, contrary to existing practice, this framework should account for local realities in dealing with public health so as to sustain optimal levels of productivity along with optimal innovation.

The goal for such a public-health framework should be:

- to first identify the strengths and weaknesses of the various efforts so far undertaken to better address future pandemics, diseases, and related issues of global public health;
- to ensure that health-care access and health-related R&D are carefully positioned to balance demands for continued innovation in trade law with demands for the right to health from a perspective of human-rights law;
- to include policy proposals and provide options for members to weave a more transparent, inclusive, and holistic approach to managing public health broadly; and
- to create a multilateral framework within which public health can and should work in a symbiotic fashion.

Though meeting these goals will not be easy, in view of the strong vested and contrarian interests of the involved parties, accomplishing them could create a framework for effective multilateralism.

4.2 Coexistential Multilateralism with Local Pragmatism

One such approach is "pragmatic multilateralism"—that is, multilateralism (whether regional or global) that takes account of local realities, allowing for local authorities room to use flexibilities and/or limitations of patent rights (which under the TRIPS Agreement is different from negotiated flexibilities) by prioritizing health-care access.

The underlying assumption for such coexistential multilateralism would be prioritizing robust public health as a prerequisite rather than a negotiable trading chip vis-à-vis international trade. Examining the causes that impact local public health and its effects on global trade can help create a framework that will consider existing literature on a public-health treaty (PHT), patent pledges, and other impactful international-law materials. Knowledge and expertise about local realities, as opposed to theoretical frameworks unconnected to local realities, will be critical to providing operationally realistic suggestions. This approach, while not dismissive of theoretical frameworks, seeks a deeper appreciation of where realities might intersect in a manner that could derail theoretical approaches.

Enabling pragmatic multilateralism should also draw from existing theories to enunciate strong legal policies and address the existing impediments without compromising innovation. Legal academics, economists, and management pundits have discussed different models for enabling access by providing a workable paradigm. Recognizing that the great variety of ground realities globally includes different types and natures of diseases, different populations affected, and different levels of health-care access, the discussion below captures some solution options that have proved effective.

4.3 Existing Proposals to Enable Global Health Access

We believe that the proposed new framework, perhaps implemented through a new treaty that focuses on public health, should include a non-exhaustive list of existing solutions, various options that could be made available to nations facing a future health crisis. Though these options and solutions may not be infallible, either individually or collectively, presenting such options to member nations will alert them to the breadth of flexibilities that are available for use if needed.

Thus, we conceive of an alternative framework that addresses public health as a broader document encompassing a repertoire of flexibilities and solution options. Considering the variety of options, we, the authors, favor a PHT that would present some or all of these options to the signatory countries.

4.3.1 Differential Pricing

The concept of differential pricing allows for the pricing of pharmaceuticals at a lower level in poorer nations, or in targeted poorer sections within middle-income countries, while maintaining higher price levels with large profit margins elsewhere. Under this model, pharmaceutical pricing would be adjusted to correspond to the per capita income and affordability of different patient populations.[68]

The TRIPS Agreement neither expressly allows nor disallows differential pricing. As one of its basic principles, Article 8 of the Agreement provides member nations with the liberty to adopt measures necessary to protect public health and nutrition, and to promote the public interest in sectors of vital importance to their socioeconomic and technological development. This liberty is subject to the single caveat that such measures should be consistent with the provisions of the Agreement. Certainly, accessibility to and affordability of essential medicines is in the public interest, and securing public health is of vital importance to the socioeconomic and technological development of member nations. Hence, any measure adopted to enhance access to health care, including differential pricing, falls within the purview of the principle enunciated under Article 8.

With respect to consistency of differential pricing measures with the provisions of TRIPS Agreement, the Most-Favored Nation (MFN) Treatment under Article 4 could be particularly relevant. The provision spells out that, with regard to protection of IP, any advantage, favor, privilege, or immunity granted by a member to the nationals of any other country shall be accorded immediately and unconditionally to those of all other members. Thus, a differential pricing regime under which relatively lower prices are charged to the nationals of lower- and middle-income countries (LMICs) in comparison to those of developed ones could be regarded as inconsistent with the MFN provisions.

When a differential pricing regime charges relatively lower prices to its own nationals than to the nationals of other countries, it could violate the National Treatment provision under Article 3 of the TRIPS Agreement, which requires each member to accord to the nationals of other members

[68] Heinz Redwood, *Advantages and Risks of Differential Pricing for Prescription Drugs*, WTO (Apr. 9, 2001), https://www.wto.org/english/tratop_E/trips_e/hosbjor_presentations_e/14redwood_e.pdf (last visited Oct. 22, 2025); *see also* Patricia M. Danzon and Adrian Towse, *Differential Pricing for Pharmaceuticals: Reconciling Access, R & D and Patents*, 3 Int'l J. Health Care Fin. & Econs. 183, 200–1 (2003) (highlighting that perhaps differential pricing is better than compulsory licensing).

treatment no less favorable than that it accords to its own nationals with regard to protection of IP. However, when such a differential pricing regime charges relatively lower prices for drugs from certain vulnerable sections of population *within the same country*, such measures cannot be regarded as inconsistent with either the MFN provision (as it does not grant any advantage, favor, privilege, or immunity to the nations of "any other country") or the National Treatment provision (as not all "own nationals" get the benefit or favor of lower prices). Moreover, such intranational differential pricing intended to ease access to essential medicines for certain disadvantaged populations of a country could be regarded as falling well within the ambit of the principle outlined in Article 8, as discussed above.

The Doha Declaration addressed some of the concerns expressed above with regard to differential pricing by providing under Article 31 and 31*bis* for compulsory licensing of drugs and allowing the export of such compulsorily licensed drugs by countries with manufacturing capacity to countries that lack such capacity. This has allowed for the emergence and growth of generic-drug companies, which can now apply for compulsory licenses based on certain stated criteria with respect to local working of the patent and subject to fulfilling certain conditions, and can export those drugs to countries lacking manufacturing capacity, without infringing patents on those inventions. Moreover, differential pricing based on legitimate socioeconomic differential criteria also finds justification under Article 7 of the TRIPS Agreement, which provides for the objectives of the TRIPS: that is, that protection and enforcement of IP rights should contribute to the promotion of technological innovation and to the transfer and dissemination of technology in a manner conducive to social and economic welfare.

The benefit of this model, unlike compulsory licensing, is that the patent owner can continue to benefit from the market,[69] recovering R&D expenditure from richer markets while simultaneously selling directly or licensing for local production in low-income countries.[70] Further, in poorer nations, there is often a very small population of insured patients,[71] so, if prices are fixed high, the high elasticity of the market condition in those nations will

[69] *See* Danzon and Towse, *supra* note 68, at 195.

[70] *See id.*; *see also* Helene Bank, *Differential Pricing and Politics of Health Development*, Third World Network (Apr. 25, 2001), https://twn.my/title/politics.htm (last visited Oct. 22, 2025) (search for "Helene Bank" in the page's search bar; select the article from the results).

[71] Brady Hooley et al., *Health Insurance Coverage in Low-Income and Middle-Income Countries: Progress Made to Date and Related Changes in Private and Public Health Expenditure*, 7(5) BMJ Glob Health (2022), https://doi.org/10.1136/bmjgh-2022-008722 (last visited Oct. 22, 2025).

act to the detriment of product sales. Instead, adopting differential pricing models can allow pharmaceutical companies to enable their own presence for wider market access while creating a conduit for patient access to essential medicines and also benefiting from the patent either by way of licensing or through increased overall sales volume.[72]

Moreover, differential pricing would comport with the objectives of the trade regime without compromising the access/welfare paradigm of trade.[73] Differential pricing, if calculated well, can increase health-care access while preserving incentives for pharmaceutical R&D.[74] Thus, this recommendation has the benefit of enabling the presence of the patent holder in the market in return for agreeing to charge a price that those individual markets can bear.

Member nations need to consider whether pharmaceuticals can be priced differently for different groups of people within a country based on the dual criteria of income and affordability. The fact is, differential pricing is not alien to the system in many countries; in countries such as India, for example, government-funded hospitals are more affordable than private ones. Such differential-pricing regimes may also be worked through technology-transfer arrangements by engaging other member nations regionally or globally, consistent with their per capita income and other measures that can impact the prices.

Different economic models have also been proposed to determine the optimal levels of differentiated prices. One suggestion is that pricing in poorer countries should account for the cost on R&D but discount the extent of funding from the government or other sources as well as voluntary overheads such as the cost of marketing.[75] Other models, including the Ramsey Pricing Model, require that the minimum price charged in elastic markets such as poorer nations be equal to or very close to the marginal

[72] Kalipso Chalkidou et al., *Value-Based Tiered Pricing for Universal Health Coverage: An Idea Worth Revisiting*, NAT'L LIBR. MED. (2020), https://pmc.ncbi.nlm.nih.gov/articles/PMC7059551/ (last visited Oct. 22, 2025).

[73] *See* Danzon and Towse, *supra* note 68, at 186–189.

[74] Frank R. Lichtenberg, *Pharmaceutical Companies' Variation of Drug Prices Within and Among Countries Can Improve Long-Term Social Well-Being*, 30 HEALTH AFFAIRS 1539, 1539–1544 (2011); Patricia M. Danzon, *Differential Pricing of Pharmaceuticals: Theory, Evidence and Emerging Issues*, 36 PHARMACOECONOMICS 1395 (2018).

[75] For a glimpse at various models, *see generally* James Love and Tim Hubbard, *Prizes for Innovation of New Medicines and Vaccines*, 18 ANN. HEALTH L. (2009); *see also* Danzon and Towse, *supra* note 68, at 184 (including in the R&D expenses the cost of testing plus the cost of the FDA application).

cost.[76] The Ramsey Pricing Model has been commended for having the potential to successfully address some of the issues that currently plague access to health care.[77] However, the pharmaceutical industry has expressed concerns that the model does not adequately take into account the issue of parallel importation.[78]

One of the main objections against differentially pricing pharmaceuticals is a fear of parallel importation, which occurs when lower-priced drugs from markets of low per capita countries find their way into rich-country markets where the same commodities are priced higher.[79] The patent owner's fear of parallel importation is not without merit. The fear is that exporters from low-priced markets can export them to richer nations, causing the same drug to be sold at two prices, which will eventually create a parallel market for that drug in the importing country. It is a fact that counterfeit pharmaceuticals find their way into markets at a very high rate. Technological developments have made such parallel importation difficult to tackle while making the importing itself relatively easier. Even the United States has repeatedly faced issues with cheaper imports of medicines from Mexico and Canada.[80]

All of this makes it imperative that any public-health framework be considered alongside obligations imposed on national governments to ensure that discounted pharmaceutical products stay in their intended market as key to the successful working of a differential pricing regime.[81] Thus, it may be necessary to impose strong caveats and restrictions preventing parallel importation as a precondition for patented drugs to enter a market with the government, for the transfer of technology with private entities within the nation, and for importing accessible medicines with importing governments.

[76] David W. Opderbeck, *Patents, Essential Medicines, and the Innovation Game*, 58 VAND. L. REV. 501, 531 (2005); *see also* Danzon and Towse, *supra* note 68, at 184 (asserting that drugs marketed in developed countries should be differentially priced in poorer nations to reconcile patents with affordability).

[77] Danzon and Towse, *supra* note 68 at 201 (arguing that Ramsey pricing "is consistent with the criterion of economic efficiency" and "standard norms of equity").

[78] Opderbeck, *supra* note 76.

[79] *Id.*; *see also* Lana Kraus, *Medication Misadventures: The Interaction of International Reference Pricing and Parallel Trade in the Pharmaceutical Industry*, 37 VAND. J. TRANSNAT'L L. 527, 542 (2004).

[80] *See id.* at 308; *see also* Simon R. Rabinovitch, *On the Legitimacy of Cross Border Pharmacy*, 43 ALTA. L. REV. 327, 343 (2005) (discussing cross-border pharmacy sales of prescription drugs to US patients by Canadian Internet pharmacies).

[81] Markus Nolff, *Paragraph 6 of the Declaration on the TRIPS Agreement and Public Health and the Decision of the WTO Regarding Its Implementation: An "Expeditious Solution?"* 86 J. PAT. & TRADEMARK OFF. SOC'Y 291, 307 (2004).

Member nations, in their contracts with pharmaceutical companies, could agree to prevent parallel importation in exchange for either pricing differently or investing within the country simply to create access by working with local entities through appropriate licenses.[82] After all, countries such as India and Brazil have manufactured generic versions of medicines for more than a decade within the contours of Article 31*bis* of the TRIPS Agreement[83] without exporting them to developed nations.[84] Ultimately, creating global competitiveness in poorer nations complies with the TRIPS Agreement's objective of enabling members to "[c]reate a sound and viable technological base."[85]

In devising a solution, the experience of the video and computer industries can serve as a good example. They demonstrate that the reimportation of spurious products can be curtailed without resorting to outright deprivation. Had several software companies, such as IBM, Texas Instruments, Microsoft, and Intel, decided to shun the Indian market because of copyright issues, the mutually beneficial relationship that has since evolved to enhance the competitive potential of the Indian software industry would have been lost to the world.[86] The companies' entry into the Indian market in fact resulted in an explosion of talent and production and has actually helped the local industry tackle software piracy.[87] As some have pointed out, the larger impact of increased capacity and imitative ability has had several positive network effects that are often overlooked in the black-and-white discussion

[82] Some of the world's poorest countries are in no economic position to even produce enough drugs for their national needs, let alone export them to developed nations. *See generally* William Fisher, Ruth L. Okediji, and Padmashree Gehl Sampath, *Fostering Production of Pharmaceutical Products in Developing Countries*, 43 MICH. J. INT. LAW 1 (2022).

[83] SHUBHA GHOSH AND IRENE CALBOLI, EXHAUSTING INTELLECTUAL PROPERTY RIGHTS: A COMPARATIVE LAW AND POLICY ANALYSIS (2018).

[84] Patricia M. Danzon, *Differential Pricing of Pharmaceuticals: Theory, Evidence and Emerging Issues*, 36 PHARMACOECONOMICS 1395 (2018).

[85] *See* TRIPS Agreement, Preamble, recital 6; *See also generally* Peter K. Yu, *The Objectives and Principles of the TRIPS Agreement*, *in* THE REGULATION OF SERVICES AND INTELLECTUAL PROPERTY (2013).

[86] *See $245 M Lost in 2001 from Software Piracy: IDC Report,* HINDU BUS. LINE (Jun. 26, 2002), https://web.archive.org/web/20090221043616/http://www.thehindubusinessline.com/bline/2002/06/27/stories/2002062700400700.htm (last visited Oct. 22, 2025) ("[I]ndependent Software Vendors (ISVs) such as Microsoft, Oracle and Adobe are fighting individually, as well as through industry alliances such as Nasscom, to combat piracy." Nasscom is the National Association of Software and Services Companies in India, representing the voice of the Indian software industry.).

[87] *See Software Piracy: Understanding the Larger Picture,* EXPRESS COMPUTER (Jul. 21, 2003), https://web.archive.org/web/20100703060317/http://www.expresscomputeronline.com/20030721/indtrend1.shtml (last visited Oct. 22, 2025); *see also* Salman Saeed, *China & India—Major Global Economic Players by 2025,* SOUTH ASIAN.COM (Jan. 2002), http://www.the-south-asian.com/Jan2002/Technology-&-Investments-Foreign-Investments-in-India.htm (last visited Oct. 22, 2025) (discussing the extent of foreign investment in software technology in India).

of "piracy."[88] Meanwhile, these effects contained piracy and enabled these corporations to benefit from India's large talent pool. It has helped those companies to tap mutually beneficial synergies and competitive potentials.[89] The consequential explosion of talent helped develop the software industry in India, which in turn encouraged the government to model legal norms in a manner that encouraged the local capacity to innovate.[90]

Several other policy options have been suggested for incentivizing or enforcing differential pricing across countries, even by LMICs. A 2015 study[91] identified several such policy options already present and in use across various LMICs. These broadly include:[92]

- Pricing techniques, including external reference pricing, internal reference pricing, pharmaco-economic evaluation for value-based purchasing, cost-plus pricing, and profit ceilings
- Pricing policies, including fixing maximum retail prices, maximum wholesale prices, ex-manufacturer and importer level prices, limiting price increases, price freezes, price cuts, margin cuts, different approaches to markups, fixed dispensing fees, and prohibition on discounts
- Purchasing policies, including positive lists, negative lists, price volume agreements, health-outcome guarantees, public tenders, and pooled procurements
- Other methods, including co-payments, safety nets, independent pricing policies, and generic substitution

The effectiveness of each of these options can vary depending on the context and national priorities. Nevertheless, it remains true that for LMIC

[88] *See, e.g.*, Shivam Kaushik, *A Game of Software Piracy: The Network Effect*, 46 Euro. Intell. Prop. Rev. Issue 2, Thomson Reuters (2023).

[89] *You're Killing Jobs if You're Using Pirated Software*, Econ. Times (Mar. 28, 2005), https://economictimes.indiatimes.com/youre-killing-jobs-if-youre-using-pirated-software/articleshow/1063679.cms?from=mdr (last visited Oct. 22, 2025) ("Independent Software Vendors (ISVs) such as Microsoft, Quark and i-flex are fighting individually as well as through industry alliances such as [NASSCOM], to combat piracy.").

[90] *See* K. J. Joseph, *Growth of ICT and ICT for Development: Realities of the Myths of the Indian Experience*, World Inst. for Dev. Econs. Rsch. [Wider] discussion paper no. 2002/78, 13 (2002), https://www.wider.unu.edu/sites/default/files/dp2002-78.pdf (last visited Oct. 22, 2025).

[91] Tuan Anh Nguyen et al., *Policy Options for Pharmaceutical Pricing and Purchasing: Issues for Low- and Middle-Income Countries*, 30 Health Pol'y & Plan. 267 (2015), https://academic.oup.com/heapol/article/30/2/267/618341 (last visited Oct. 22, 2025).

[92] *Id.*

governments, national-level approaches or policies still do not exhaust the aforementioned list of alternative models.

While differential pricing strategies[93] may reduce the burden of disease, issues relating to arbitrage should be addressed to ensure that prices are affordable while maintaining reasonable—as opposed to higher-than-needed—levels of protection for pharmaceutical products.[94] Meanwhile, scholars like Kevin Outterson conclude that some forms of pharmaceutical arbitrage remain beneficial, as they deliver lower prices to consumers without harming innovation.[95] As Shamnad Basheer points out, this "concern" may have been rooted in worries that lower prices in poorer countries would lead to demands for lower prices in the home markets of the United States and the EU.[96] Indeed, there has been much criticism and controversy over the high prices of drugs especially in the United States.[97] So, whatever is gained or lost by this trade-off of differentially pricing health-care products is an open question. This means that, for the most part, patients have been "priced out" from accessing drugs sold by multinational pharmaceutical companies, even if it had been possible to lower prices to a more reasonable level (which may still be higher than the prices required to recoup investments).[98]

A particular species of patent pledges or pooling model prevalent in the context of standardized products is Fair, Reasonable, and Non-Discriminatory (FRAND) licenses, under which participants often agree to license their patents to producers of such standardized products on terms that either are royalty-free or that specify royalties that are fair, reasonable and non-discriminatory.[99] Jorge Contreras and Anne Layne-Farrar define

[93] F. M. Scherer, *A Note on Global Welfare in Pharmaceutical Patenting*, 27 World Econ. 1127, 1127–28 (2004). Perfect price discrimination could eliminate this deadweight loss but is not expected in practice.

[94] *See* Kevin Outterson, *Pharmaceutical Arbitrage: Balancing Access and Innovation in International Prescription Drug Markets*, 5 Yale J. Health Pol'y, L. & Ethics 193, 196 (2005).

[95] *Id.*

[96] Shamnad Basheer, *Merck vs Roche: Towards Differential Pricing in India*, SpicyIP (May 7, 2008), https://spicyip.com/2008/05/merck-vs-roche-towards-differential.html (last visited Oct. 22, 2025).

[97] *See, e.g.*, Samuel F. Ernst, *The Pharmaceutical Industry's Corrupt Price Discrimination System: A Single Solution?*, 51 U. Pac. L. Rev. 475, 482 (2021) (discussing Robin Feldman's work on pharmacy benefit managers "who collaborate with the branded drug companies to raise prices and create economic pressure and perverse incentives for other health care system actors to also facilitate price increases").

[98] On the other hand, it is indeed theoretically possible that, since it does not make a difference to their returns, pharmaceutical firms could sell them at cost price in developing markets and receive non-tangible benefits, such as enhancing of their reputation.

[99] *See* Jorge L: Contreras, *The New Extraterritoriality: FRAND Royalties, Anti-Suit Injunctions and the Global Race to the Bottom in Disputes over Standards-Essential Patents*, 25 B.U. J. Sci. & Tech. L., (2) (2019), https://www.bu.edu/jostl/files/2019/10/1.-Contreras.pdf (last visited Oct. 22, 2025).

"discrimination," which is antithetical to the concept of FRAND, as treating different parties differently, and prohibition on discrimination could be interpreted to prohibit any such differential treatment.[100] However, they caution that not every form of differential treatment is prohibited by the definition of discrimination, and that nondiscrimination does not require that every potential licensee be offered identical terms, but only that similarly situated parties should be offered comparable terms.

In other words, offering discriminatory terms only to similarly situated parties would amount to discrimination and go against the basic tenets of FRAND.[101] By inference, FRAND could allow for differential royalty pricing among parties that are not similarly situated, such as those facing different commercial realities and other market conditions, without violating nondiscrimination criteria. Further, Contreras and Richard Gilbert propose that there are sound economic reasons to allow for a nonuniform royalty schedule under a FRAND license by including terms such as volume discounts and taking account of the nature of the devices that employ the licensed technology.[102]

Hence, even those most standardized patents allow for differential pricing to take account of variations in economic and commercial realities and varying market conditions, and such pricing models cannot be regarded as discriminatory. Merely treating unequally placed parties on different terms with regard to price or royalties is not by itself considered discriminatory.

4.3.2 Patent Pledges and Patent Pools

Similarly, the idea of a patent pledge, originally framed as such and proposed by Professor Contreras, is to identify specific concerns that are likely to arise in the acquisition of IP rights.[103] Economists such as Jean Lanjouw suggest that an inventor from a developed nation should relinquish the right to sue for patent infringement in certain markets for technologies involving essential

[100] *See* Jorge L. Contreras and Anne Layne-Farrar, *Non-Discrimination and FRAND Commitments*, Univ. of Utah Coll. of L. Rsch. Paper No. 251 (Mar. 16, 2018), https://papers.ssrn.com/sol3/papers.cfm?abstract_id=3138578 (last visited Oct. 22, 2025).

[101] *Id.*

[102] *See* Jorge L. Contreras and Richard J. Gilbert, *Non-Discrimination—FRAND's Last Stand?*, CPI Antitrust Chron. (2020), https://www.competitionpolicyinternational.com/wp-content/uploads/2020/12/2-Non-Discrimination---FRAND's-Last-Stand-By-Jorge-L.-Contreras-Richard-J.-Gilbert.pdf (last visited Oct. 22, 2025).

[103] Jorge Contreras, *Patent Pledges*, Ariz. St. L.J., 543 (2015); *see also* Jesse Reynolds, Jorge L. Contreras, and Joshua D. Sarnoff, *Solar Climate Engineering and Intellectual Property: Toward a Research Commons*, 18 Minn. J.L. Sci. & Tech. 1, 85–89 (2017).

life-threatening diseases.[104] In gist, it gives the inventor the ability to exercise a choice in enforcing the patent; should the inventor choose to patent or enforce it in a developed nation, he or she should relinquish the right to sue for infringement in certain markets for certain types of technologies.[105] Such a system could preserve the benefit of generic competition in developing-country markets.

The formation of "research commons" that will permit research institutions, both public and private, to share and act as a repository of research data has been proposed.[106] Member institutions would pledge any patent or trade secret to the research commons in order to minimize unnecessary barriers to R&D and to facilitate the safe and effective use of the technologies protected by those patents or trade secrets. Although the discussion has a specific focus on solar climate engineering and FRAND licenses, such patent pledges can also be easily replicated for biotechnology and biomedical research.[107] Indeed, some of the benefits and issues of using such patent pools were addressed by the Eco-Patent Commons (EcoPC) in relation to the promotion of green/clean technologies.[108]

The EcoPC was an innovative, philanthropic, industry-led initiative with the goal of pledging "green technology" patents for broad, royalty-free use to accelerate diffusion and adoption of such technologies in addressing environmental challenges.[109] A total of 248 green-technology patents were contributed by thirteen EcoPC participants to the patent pool between EcoPC's formation in 2008 and its discontinuation in 2016.[110]

Jorge Contreras, Bronwyn Hall, and Christian Helmers analyzed the impact of such technological diffusion, its advantages, and the issues that caused its demise in 2016.[111] The issues identified included lack of significant interest by third parties in the technologies covered by the patents contributed to the patent pool; lack of government support and incentives; the purely philanthropic orientation of the pool, with uncertain potential

[104] Jean O. Lanjouw, *A New Global Patent Regime for Diseases: U.S. and International Legal Issues*, 16 Harv. J.L. & Tech. 85, 91–93 (2002).
[105] *Id.*
[106] Reynolds et al. *supra* note 103 at 101.
[107] Jorge L. Contreras, *A Market Reliance Theory for FRAND Commitments and Other Patent Pledges*, 2 Utah L. Rev. 479, 542 (2015).
[108] *Id.*
[109] *Id.*
[110] *Id.*
[111] Jorge L. Contreras, Bronwyn H. Hall, and Christian Helmers, *Pledging Patents for the Public Good: Rise and Fall of the Eco-Patent Commons*, 57 Hous. L. Rev. 61, 70–71 (2019).

for monetary gain (a factor considered central to many pooling decisions); flawed implementation without consulting the demand side or the potential users of the patents or technologies contributed; lack of technical assistance on utility of those technologies; absence or lack of coordination among the contributors regarding the technologies covered by the pledged patents, resulting in loss of synergies from contribution of multiple patents covering selected technologies; the voluntary (and free-of-cost) nature of the initiative, without any scope for provision of value-added services against payment of fees; low membership due to the high cost of internal patent analysis; changing corporate priorities; reluctance of participants to lend potentially valuable patents; and failure to track patent utilization, which made it impossible to assess the impact of the initiative.[112]

Notwithstanding the above, the experimental run of the EcoPC and its eventual demise provide crucial lessons and have made a signal contribution to the study of patent commons and pledges. Numerous lessons have been learned from EcoPC's failure to ensure that future initiatives on patent commons and pledges succeed in their goals of technology transfer and diffusion for the common benefit of humanity, regarding issues such as government support in the form of incentives for contributors of key patented technologies, tracking of utilization of pledged patents for cost-benefit analyses and impact assessments of such initiatives, factoring in inputs from key stakeholders such as potential technology users, provision of value-added services for a fee, and ensuring the financial sustainability of the initiative.

4.3.3 The Game-Theory Approach

Other commentators, such as David W. Opderbeck, prefer a game-theory approach based on the variation in elasticity of demand in the developing and developed world.[113] The game-theory solution asserts that demand for pharmaceuticals in the developed world is inelastic because a change in price does not affect demand.[114] On the contrary, because demand for pharmaceuticals is highly elastic in the developing world, notwithstanding the level of patent protection, higher levels of patent protection with consequentially higher cost of medication are unlikely to stimulate R&D on

[112] *Id.*
[113] Opderbeck, *supra* note 76, at 535.
[114] *Id.* at 503.

diseases unique to such nations.[115] Lowering the level of patent protection in one or more countries—say, by using flexibilities or limitation to address a public-health crisis—is unlikely to affect the equilibrium of the innovation game.[116] Under such circumstances, pharmaceutical companies will continue to derive monopoly rents from other jurisdictions (except when there is a pandemic) and thus should be in a position to continue comparative or adjusted levels of commitment for R&D.[117]

4.3.4 Government-Funded R&D

To stimulate pharmaceutical R&D, governments of member nations have also created different models, such as government-funded health-care innovations, some of which are discussed below. A variation on the theme of differential price control is government price control, whereby the respective governments control pharmaceutical prices by setting a maximum sale price while leaving enough room for profits;[118] another is the US model of indirect price control, which entails federal negotiation of prices for certain high-cost essential drugs under Medicare and the provisions of the Inflation Reduction Act of 2022.[119]

Governments of many other member nations also fund pharmaceutical R&D and innovation. The question of whether publicly funded R&D should allow private benefits to accrue from patent protection, a private property right, has been a central question in contemporary times. This question has resonated especially in view of the level of public funding that private corporations received during Covid-19, as shown in Table 4.1 below.

[115] *Id.*

[116] *Id.* at 553.

[117] *Id.* at 554.

[118] *See* Shondeep Banerji, *The Indian Intellectual Property Regime and the TRIPS Agreement, in* Intellectual Property Rights in Emerging Markets 47, 84 (Clarissa Long ed., 2000); *see also* India Const. 1950, preamble. The preamble of the Indian constitution opts for a "socio-economic" model of development, asserting that "social" (societal) needs in India cannot be constrained for economic benefits. *See* Rahul Mukherji, *The State, Economic Growth, and Development in India*, 8 India Rev. 81 (2009) (discussing how economic development in India has been moderated by societal actors).

[119] *See, e.g.*, Me. Rev. Stat. Ann. tit. 22, § 2681 (West, Westlaw through 2023 2d. Reg. Sess. 131st Leg.); Fla. Stat. Ann. §§ 409.91195, 409.912(5)(a)(7) (West, Westlaw through Jun. 13, 2024); *see also* Pharm. Rsch. and Mfrs. of Am. v. Walsh, 538 U.S. 644, 649 (2003) (discussing the Maine Rx program, which is intended to provide discounted prescription drugs to Maine's uninsured citizens); *see generally* Patricia Danzon, Price Comparison for Pharmaceuticals: A Review of US and Cross National Studies (1999) (arguing that, at least in the United States, there is no guarantee that a pharmacist will pass on any discount in prices to the retail customer).

Table 4.1 Level of public funding received by private corporations during the Covid-19 pandemic.

S. No.	Vaccine Sponsor	Amount
1.	Johnson & Johnson	$2 billion
2.	Sanofi and GSK	$2.35 billion
3.	Merck and IAVI	$38 million
4.	Moderna	$5.95 billion
5.	Novavax	$1.66 billion
6.	Pfizer (BioNTech)	$5.97 billion
7.	AstraZeneca (Oxford)	$1.6 billion

Adapted with permission from Chad P. Bown and Thomas J. Bollyky, *Here's How to Get Billions of COVID-19 Vaccines to the World*, PETERSON INST. FOR INT'L ECONS. (Mar. 18, 2021), https://www.piie.com/blogs/trade-and-investment-policy-watch/heres-how-get-billions-covid-19-vaccine-doses-world.

Hence, what caveats, if any, would help achieve appropriate publicly funded R&D, and whether such R&D should be susceptible to private property rights, are questions that a public-health framework needs to address. Arguably, considering that what falls within the public domain cannot be protected by IP rights, it makes limited sense to argue that what is funded essentially by public funds should be protected by private rights.

Other suggestions for enabling access without compromising innovation include incorporating incentives such as subsidies to stimulate R&D in technologies where demand is highly elastic—on diseases unique to developing nations.[120] Another alternative would be to create an "innovation tax,"[121] collected from upper-income groups, that could be deployed to fund government R&D in the country.

4.3.5 Transparency in Pharmaceutical R&D

Pharmaceutical companies have been notoriously opaque with regard to their R&D investments, even while highlighting the high R&D costs they

[120] *Market Reliance Theory*, *supra* note 107 at 544; *see* Danzon and Towse, *supra* note 68, at 184 (asserting that external subsidies can be used to fund the research for drugs that cater to purely developing-country diseases).

[121] *See generally* Ted Sichelman, *Patents, Prizes and Property*, 30 HARV. J.L. & TECH. 279, 285-90 (2017) (looking at taxation as a complementary system to the patent system); *see also* Mark A. Lemley, Lisa Larrimore Ouellette, and Rachel E. Sachs, *The Medicare Innovation Subsidy*, 95 N.Y.U. L. REV. 75 (2020) (examining the expansion of tax subsidies in health care).

need to recuperate through patent protection, and researchers have called for more transparency in the companies' operations.[122] Others have called for more transparency in the use of patents in developing countries, hoping to determine whether multinational pharmaceutical companies were merely filing patents without actually serving the patient population that required those patented medicines.[123]

Scholars have also proposed several alternative pharmaceutical innovation mechanisms external to the IP system, although these will not be explored in this chapter.[124]

5. Conclusion: Call for a Tectonic Transformation in IP Law

More than four years later, the lessons from the contested negotiations around the Covid-19 Waiver and misaligned priorities of different countries continue to be discussed.[125] Experts have also pointed out that, regardless of the Covid-19 Waiver, nations should be pursuing the various flexibilities already offered through the TRIPS Agreement.[126] It remains to be seen how the WTO can enable a workable solution to deal with future pandemics or global health emergencies, whether through the Covid-19 Waiver or any other method.

[122] Nora Frazen et al., *Affordable Prices Without Threatening the Oncological R&D Pipeline—An Economic Experiment on Transparency in Price Negotiations*, 2 CANCER RSCH. COMMC'NS 49, 54 (2022); *see also* Donald W. Light and Rebecca Warburton, *Demythologizing the High Costs of Pharmaceutical Research*, 6 BIOSOCIETIES 34, 44 (2011).

[123] Shamnad Basheer and Rupali Samuel, *Bayer's Nexavar and the "Working" of Compulsory Licensing: Mind the Patent (Information) Gap!, 16* SPICYIP (2015), https://spicyip.com/wp-content/uploads/2015/04/Report-on-Bayer-for-writ-Finalized.pdf (last visited Oct. 22, 2025).

[124] *See, e.g.*, Michael B. Abramowicz, *Prize and Reward Alternatives to Intellectual Property, in* RESEARCH HANDBOOK ON THE ECONOMICS OF INTELLECTUAL PROPERTY LAW 350–375, 351 (Ben Depoorter and Peter S. Menell eds., 2019).

[125] Brook Baker, *Bad Faith from Big Pharma, Rich Countries and the WTO Poison WTO TRIPS Waiver Negotiations*, HEALTH GAP (June 14, 2022), https://healthgap.org/bad-faith-from-big-pharma-rich-countries-and-the-wto-poison-wto-trips-waiver-negotiations%EF%BF%BC/ (last visited Oct. 22, 2025) (demonstrating similar arguments for the waiver); *see also* Brook K. Baker, *TRIPS-Compliant Alternatives for Overcoming Intellectual Property Barriers to COVID-19 Countermeasures*, INFOJUSTICE (June 30, 2022), https://infojustice.org/wp-content/uploads/2022/07/TRIPS-Compliant-Alternatives-for-Overcoming-Intellectual-Property-Barriers-to-COVID-19-Countermeasures.pdf (last visited Oct. 22, 2025); Jamie Love, *The Quad WTO Proposal on COVID 19 and TRIPS Proposal Is Tied for the 5th Best Option for Exports*, JAMES LOVE BLOG (Mar. 20, 2022), https://jamie-love.medium.com/the-quad-wto-proposal-on-covid-19-and-trips-proposal-is-tied-for-the-5th-best-option-for-exports-dd8f165efdee (last visited Oct. 22, 2025).

[126] Prashant Reddy, *The Need for an IP Policy to Build a Strategic Stockpile for Pandemics*, SPICYIP (Mar. 26, 2020), https://spicyip.com/2020/03/the-need-for-an-ip-policy-to-build-a-strategic-stockpile-for-pandemics.html (last visited Oct. 22, 2025).

The current state of global health causes the authors to assert that trade cannot be an excuse for countries, especially poorer ones, to compromise their public-health initiatives. Achieving public health through access to health care should be an important objective for every nation that seeks to function as a productive member of the global trading community. Public health cannot be sacrificed at the altar of international obligations to the detriment of a few member nations. Health-care access should not become a luxury.[127]

The trade regime represents an opportunity for the developing world to metamorphose into innovators.[128] Nevertheless, encouraging R&D and furthering innovation cannot be at the cost of human lives, the saving of which should be the principal objective of pharmaceutical R&D. Although patents should form a part of the future R&D agenda of the pharmaceutical industry, the principle that pharmaceutical R&D should ultimately benefit humanity and contribute toward global productivity must lie at the core of that agenda.[129]

All of this leads us to one conclusion: In order for a trade regime to make access to health care more egalitarian, a tectonic transformation of many aspects of IP law, particularly pharmaceutical patents and regulatory exclusivities, will be needed. Such a transformation will require us to seek viable and sustainable alternatives to ingrained theories. This chapter has attempted to engage with the question of whether we need a new framework to effectuate that radical transformation. To do so, it has taken into account the realities of health-care access in the post-Covid-19 globe and peeked into existing frameworks to suggest that it is time to take a more comprehensive approach. Believing that a new framework is needed, we suggest, as a possible working model, a treaty that would incorporate the framework.

Such a framework should not shun innovation or IP rights but should carefully calibrate the need for health-care access by positioning it as the focal point. Ultimately, a medley of viable solutions that focus on reforming the

[127] *See generally* Peggy B. Sherman and Ellwood F. Oakley III, *Pandemics and Panaceas: The World Trade Organization's Efforts to Balance Pharmaceutical Patents and Access to AIDS Drugs*, 41 Am. Bus. L.J. 353, 411 (2004).

[128] *See* Frederick M. Abbott, *The WTO Medicines Decision: World Pharmaceutical Trade and the Protection of Public Health*, 99 Am. J. Int'l L. 317, 343 (2005).

[129] *See generally* Sherman and Oakley, *Pandemics and Panaceas: The World Trade Organization's Efforts to Balance Pharmaceutical Patents and Access to AIDS Drugs*, 41 Am. Bus. L.J. 353, 404 (2003–2004); *see also* Steven Shavell and Tanguy van Ypersele, *Rewards Versus Intellectual Property Rights*, 44 J.L. & Econ. 525, 534–39 (2001).

patent system's interaction with public health has been offered by different commentators and authors, all of which could inform the new framework.

Thus, this chapter proposed a new framework, which, if implemented in the form of a treaty, should be in the form of a broader public-health treaty rather than the narrower pandemic treaty approach that is currently on-going. Such a PHT would be premised on the assumption that public health should be a global issue, in that it is conceived along the same lines as the current discussions for a pandemic treaty.[130] No institution whose central goal is not public health, such as the WTO, should dictate the boundaries of addressing global public health.

Policies should stimulate innovation without compromising health equity. The role of intellectual property policies is discussed in the next chapter. The discussion will focus on patents with an emphasis on how the impact of patents specifically, and IP generally can vary with the differences in local realities.

The objectives and the development of patent policies, will be analyzed to see determine whether contemporary patent law can accomplish its objectives of incentivizing innovation with the differences presented from local realities of each member state and without becoming a barrier to health-care access.

[130] This is dealt with in more detail in chapter 6 of this book.

5

A Globalist Approach to Harmonizing Health

1. Introduction: Evolution and Devolution of the Global Consensus on Public Health

1.1 The Pre-Covid-19 International-First Approach

Public-health law has traditionally been framed with respect to infectious diseases and externalities with significant health impacts, such as pollution.[1] The WHO, now seventy-eight years into its existence, has normatively been the foremost authority for negotiating and utilizing international legal instruments to advance global health governance. Yet, as Lawrence Gostin and others point out,[2] only two major legally binding instruments have been adopted in these seventy-eight years—the International Health Regulations (IHR) and the Framework Convention on Tobacco Control (FCTC).

During pre-Covid times, coordinated actions on global public health were a by-product of not just the severity for those affected or the countries impacted but also the effect of infectious diseases on trade.[3] Access to good health care in different parts of the world, especially for preventing and controlling infectious diseases, seemed to be the one solution to preventing

[1] Richard A. Epstein, *In Defense of the "Old" Public Health: The Legal Framework for the Regulation of Public Health*, 69 Brook. L. Rev 1421, 1421–22 (2004), https://brooklynworks.brooklaw.edu/blr/vol69/iss4/8/ (last visited Oct. 20, 2025).

[2] Lawrence O. Gostin et al., *The World Health Organization Was Born as a Normative Agency: Seventy-Five Years of Global Health Law Under WHO Governance*, Global Public Health (2013), (Abstract, ¶ 2), https://journals.plos.org/globalpublichealth/article?id=10.1371/journal.pgph.0002928 (last visited Oct. 20, 2025).

[3] *See generally* Srividhya Ragavan, *World Trade Organization: A Barrier to Global Public Health?*, *in* Intellectual Property Law and Access to Medicines: TRIPS Agreement, Health, and Pharmaceuticals 25 (Srividhya Ragavan and Amaka Vanni eds., 2021) (discussing the relation between public health and trade).

Fractures in IP, Trade, and Health. Srividhya Ragavan and Swaraj Paul Barooah, Oxford University Press.
 DOI: 10.1093/9780197684085.003.0005

global social, political, and economic impacts with potentially devastating impacts on national and global productivity. Many of these issues were viewed through the lens of international obligations, and whether and to what extent carving flexibilities from such international obligations in the national interest would affect the seamless operation of the international trade regime.

Arguably, the lack of bargaining parities of the member states skew the outcome of these negotiations. The juridical equality notwithstanding, it is difficult to get an equitable outcome. Over time, established patterns of power equations also characterize international relations. Interestingly, an international-first approach, which prioritized international obligations, the dominant theme of the pre-Covid globe.[4] Nevertheless, the reality of a nation-first approach was what stood out amidst the unprecedented global crisis resulting from the Covid-19 pandemic.

1.2 Global Skepticism and the Post-Covid-19 Nation-First Approach

Gordon Brown, former prime minister of the UK, has astutely noted that the Covid-19 crisis unfortunately unfurled the lack of global consensus to a public health crisis. Mr. Brown characterized the outcome as being in opposite of what the WHO intended. The WHO's ability to coordinate the global response was stymied as the pandemic unfolded. Even as the role of the WHO gained more relevance and became central to maintain global public health of the post-Covid globe, systematic concerns and questions about the organization's ability to deal with large scale public health crisis remained.[5] To observers of the WTO system, this result was not particularly surprising, as "global health governance" had strong influences from a confluence of trade and IP regimes.

Thus, the onset of the pandemic caused the world to view international institutions and international coordination mechanisms with skepticism. An

[4] It would be apt to note here that, while the "international-first" approach was dominant in rhetoric, this coincided largely with the narrative given to developing countries when they had various health crises. For example, as described in an earlier chapter, when the United States had its own health scare over anthrax, it immediately took a nation-first approach in its actions.

[5] Gordon Brown and Daniel Susskind, *International Cooperation During the COVID-19 Pandemic*, 36 Oxford Rev. Econ. Pol'y S64, S64-65 (2020), https://academic.oup.com/oxrep/article/36/Supplement_1/S64/5863407 (last visited Oct. 20, 2025).

article by Anne Bucher and others captured succinctly why such a view is especially concerning:

> [P]ublic health is a global common and should have been an easy area for successful collective action: incentives to cooperate are strong; cooperation practices are rooted in history; there exists a strong epistemic community; and last but not least, collective action can rely on a long-established multilateral institution with a strong mandate, a proven track record and the tools needed—at least in principle—to tackle pandemics. And yet the initial response to the emergence of the virus was dramatically slow, and fragmentation rather than coherence and coordination prevailed after the pandemic outbreak. The very institution that should have promoted cooperation ended up as a battlefield.[6]

The resultant *nation-first approach* was neither surprising nor illogical. Nevertheless, it highlighted the one paradigm that is often ignored when discussing international obligations: local realities. Thus, during and after the pandemic, it was clear that the future would present three simultaneous challenges for addressing some of the global health-related inequities: (1) appreciating the role of local realities, as discussed in the previous chapters; (2) prioritizing public-health-related norms in a structural fashion along with economic goals; and (3) adjusting "global" health norms in a manner that comports with national sovereignty. In other words, health norms for countries will have to be seen through a lens that structurally encourages appropriate fragmentation consistent with international obligations, so as to benefit global welfare and productivity without compromising national welfare and productivity from issues of health-care access. Such a framework would indeed be a tall order.

As promised, this chapter hopes to present an alternative framework. To do so effectively, at the outset it will discuss efforts that are currently ongoing in the form of a PHT, and then delve into the pandemic-agreement approach to determine its potential for addressing the need to secure global public health.

[6] Anne Bucher et al., *The Failure of Global Public Health Governance: A Forensic Analysis*, Bruegel, at 2 (Feb. 17, 2022), https://www.bruegel.org/system/files/wp_attachments/PC-03-170222-2.pdf (last visited Oct. 20, 2025).

1.3 From Good Intentions to Restrained Outcomes

Before considering alternative models for such a framework, this chapter will examine whether the pandemic-agreement approach is consistent with that framework. Tracing how the World Health Organization Pandemic Agreement (WHOPA) came into being will help lay out this journey from good intentions to disappointing outcome.

The initial Covid-19 wave produced a strong momentum for cooperation in building an effective global health strategy. In March 2021, a joint statement by heads of state and the WHO was issued calling for a new instrument, such as a treaty, and stating, "COVID-19 shows why united action is needed for a more robust international health architecture."[7] That was the first step leading to the birth of the WHOPA.

In his opening statement at the Special Session of the World Health Assembly (WHA) in November 2021, Dr. Tedros Adhanom Ghebreyesus, WHO's director-general, specifically noted that more than 80 percent of the world's vaccines had gone to G20 countries, with low-income countries receiving just 0.6 percent of all vaccines, and went on to note that "Vaccine equity is not charity; it's in every country's best interests."[8] The WHA would take the initial steps in the process of creating the WHOPA.[9]

The process of negotiating and concluding the WHOPA was expected to culminate in May 2024.[10] Initial statements and positions took a strong globalist stance, incorporating existing conceptions of a mix of *rights*, *equity*, *solidarity*, *development*, and *shared goals* for the universal citizen. A joint statement from members conceived of a "shared responsibility" by a "global community" of juridically equal state actors working alongside international organizations, the private sector, and NGOs.[11]

[7] *COVID-19 Shows Why United Action Is Needed for More Robust International Health Architecture*, World Health Organization (Mar. 30, 2021), https://www.who.int/news-room/commentaries/detail/op-ed---covid-19-shows-why-united-action-is-needed-for-more-robust-international-health-architecture (last visited Oct. 20, 2025).

[8] Dr. Tedros A. Ghebreyesus, Director-General, World Health Organization, Opening Remarks at the Special Session of the World Health Assembly (Nov. 29, 2021), https://www.who.int/director-general/speeches/detail/who-director-general-s-opening-remarks-at-the-special-session-of-the-world-health-assembly---29-november-2021 (last visited Oct. 20, 2025).

[9] *Id.*

[10] Nina Schwalbe et al., *The Pandemic Treaty: A Forensic Review of Process and Pitfalls*, 20 Global Public Health, no. 1, 2025, at 1, 2, https://www.tandfonline.com/doi/full/10.1080/17441692.2025.2522916 (last visited Oct. 20, 2025).

[11] *See* Clare Wenham et al., *The Futility of the Pandemic Agreement: Caught Between Globalism and Statism*, 98 Int'l Aff. 837, 842 (2022), https://academic.oup.com/ia/article/98/3/837/6549855 (last visited Oct. 20, 2025).

Despite these initial expressions and worldwide support in the wake of the Covid-19 pandemic, the draft agreement and its associated negotiations failed to achieve the required consensus on time, and the final text of the agreement was released only in May 2025. However, announcing the text as final could be seen as strategic move, since one of the most contentious parts of the negotiations, relating to pathogen access and benefit-sharing (PABS), had been moved out of the main text into an appendix, which has been given another year's extension for completion.[12]

The PABS issues have already been, in fact, extremely contentious ones for the three years of the WHOPA negotiations, so it is to be seen whether a single year will be sufficient to complete these. The "final text" of the WHOPA won't actually be signed till the PABS appendix has been negotiated.[13]

The final text (minus the PABS issues) was agreed upon in May 2025 by the WHO's 194 member nations, with the notable exception of the United States, which under President Trump had withdrawn from the WHO. Notwithstanding the United States' withdrawal and the transfer of PABS to the appendix, many hailed the consensus as a victory for multilateralism.

Note that this was not the first international instrument aimed at addressing infectious diseases. That title would go to the IHR, which had been in place since 1969.[14] Its regulations were revised in 2005 and amended as of June 2024.[15] On paper, the IHR actually deals with much of what was needed during the Covid-19 outbreak, including what to do when an outbreak is detected and how and to whom to report it, as well as guidelines on how states should coordinate, communicate, and respond. However, it did not actually play any significant role when Covid-19 broke out.[16]

Before discussing the instrument that would go on to be negotiated, it is pertinent to note that, despite the 2024 amendments, commentators have

[12] *See* Report by the Director-General, *Intergovernmental Negotiating Body to Draft and Negotiate a WHO Convention, Agreement or Other International Instrument on Pandemic Prevention, Preparedness and Response*, A78/10, May 14, 2025, World Health Organization, https://apps.who.int/gb/ebwha/pdf_files/WHA78/A78_10-en.pdf (last visited Mar. 2, 2026).

[13] *Id.*

[14] Schwalbe, *supra* note 10, at 2.

[15] *See generally* Cong. Research Serv., *International Health Regulations Amendments* (IF12139) (2024), https://www.congress.gov/crs-product/IF12139 (last visited Oct. 20, 2025).

[16] *See generally* Gian L. Burci, *The Legal Response to Pandemics: The Strengths and Weaknesses of the International Health Regulations*, 11 Journal of International Humanitarian Legal Studies 204 (2020), https://brill.com/view/journals/ihls/11/2/article-p204_204.xml (last visited Oct. 20, 2025) (discussing the role of IHR in the international Covid-19 response).

attributed the failure of the IHR to address the Covid-19 pandemic, *inter alia*, to the lack of consequences for not following it, as well as the limited scope regarding fundraising and provisions regarding sharing of vaccines and related technologies.[17] Interestingly, a WHO review committee had issued similar findings in the previous decade when identifying reasons for the failures in the response to Ebola, noting lack of implementation, insufficient funding, and insufficient coordination between states, among other reasons.[18]

2. The WHOPA: The Theory-Practice Gap

Despite these and more such interventions, the final text of the WHOPA seemed a far cry from what might have been expected in view of the spirit in which it had been undertaken. Concerningly, it does not seem to have addressed the reasons why earlier initiatives such as the IHR were unable to function usefully in the pandemic situation. Once again,[19] these shortcomings seem to be rooted in coordinating international responses within a system grounded in national sovereignty.

And yet, as Siddarth Jain aptly notes,[20]

> the proponents of the WHOPA argue that it signifies a substantial conceptual advancement from the Doha Declaration, primarily due to its proactive, forward-looking framework for pandemic preparedness. [. .] Indeed, its framing explicitly acknowledges historical inequities and incorporates aspirational terms such as "equitable access," "solidarity," "pathogen

[17] David P. Fidler, *The Amendments to the International Health Regulations Are Not a Breakthrough*, Think Global Health, June 7, 2024, https://www.thinkglobalhealth.org/article/amendments-international-health-regulations-are-not-breakthrough (last visited Oct. 20, 2025).

[18] *See generally Report of the Review Committee on the Role of International Health Regulations (2005) in the Ebola Outbreak and Response*, World Health Organization (May 13, 2016), https://iris.who.int/items/11a7a263-4ad3-4ba6-aa9f-d700988d0b34 (last visited Oct. 20, 2025) (discussing the flaws of IHR in relation to the Ebola outbreak).

[19] *See* Dr. Suerie Moon et al., *Will Ebola Change the Game? Ten Essential Reforms Before the Next Pandemic. The Report of the Harvard-LSHTM Independent Panel on the Global Response to Ebola*, 386 Lancet 2204, 2206 (2015), https://www.thelancet.com/journals/lancet/article/PIIS0140-6736(15)00946-0/fulltext (last visited Oct. 20, 2025).

[20] *See* Dr. Siddarth Jain, *The WHO Pandemic Agreement: A Contested Step Beyond Doha*, SpicyIP (July 17, 2025). https://spicyip.com/2025/07/the-who-pandemic-agreement-a-contested-step-beyond-doha.html (last visited Oct. 20, 2025) The authors have gone on to highlight Mr. Jain's arguments in this section with his permission.

> benefit-sharing," and "genomic sovereignty." Its vision and vocabulary mark a commendable step in global health discourse, as it ventures into previously uncharted territory by acknowledging genomic sequence data, particularly related to pathogens, and the role of knowledge infrastructures, concepts that were beyond the scope of the TRIPS [Agreement] and the Doha Declaration. It broadens the governance conversation from merely pharmaceutical end products to encompass critical upstream elements like biological samples, genomic data, and manufacturing platforms.

However, as seen later in this chapter, there remains a significant gap between these theoretical progressive movements and the practical possibilities of enforcement.

2.1 The Equity Question

An instructive example of the gradual dilution of the WHOPA proposal is that of how "equity" has been negotiated and how the use of the term has changed over the rounds of negotiations. This is particularly interesting considering that all countries had agreed on equity as a principle, and its changing scope became more apparent as the negotiations progressed. Article 3 of the draft of the WHOPA released in October 2023 states:

> Equity is at the center of pandemic prevention, preparedness and response, both at the national level within States and at the international level between States.[21]

This draft defines equity as the

> Unhindered, fair, equitable, and timely access to safe, effective, quality and affordable pandemic-related products and services, information, pandemic-related technologies and social protection.[22]

[21] World Health Org., *Draft: Negotiating Text of the WHO Convention, Agreement, or Other International Instrument on Pandemic Prevention, Preparedness and Response (WHO Pandemic Agreement)*, at 6 (Oct. 16, 2023), https://healthpolicy-watch.news/wp-content/uploads/2023/10/advance-DRAFT_Negotiating-Text_INB-Bureau_16-Oct-2023.pdf (last visited Oct. 20, 2025).
[22] *Id.*

By April 2024, this text had morphed into:

> a goal and outcome of pandemic prevention, preparedness and response, striving for the absence of unfair, avoidable or remediable differences among and between individuals, communities and countries.[23]

A few months later, the revised September 2024 draft[24] of the WHOPA retained equity as a goal and outcome but contextualized it by adding an optional term, "principle." The final text utilizes this combination of words in the Article, along with some minor changes, and refers to it as follows:

> Equity as a goal, principle and outcome of pandemic prevention, preparedness and response, striving in this context for the absence of unfair, avoidable or remediable differences among and between individuals, communities and countries.

The initial dilution of the term "equity," when positioned alongside "principle," seems to confirm the expressed concerns that equity had morphed from being an objective to a guiding principle within a short period of time and was no longer a core outcome.[25] While the semantics of this raise serious concerns and its impact on bargaining parties are significant, the pressing need at this time is to institute a framework that is equitable whether or not it is semantically appropriate.

Critics compared this process of slow dilution of a core and central tenet of the WHOPA with the historic negotiations that culminated in the TRIPS Agreement.[26] In May 2024, following an impasse at the negotiations at the

[23] World Health Org., *Proposal for the WHO Pandemic Agreement*, at 7 (Apr. 16, 2024), https://healthpolicy-watch.news/wp-content/uploads/2024/04/DRAFT_WHO-Pandemic-Agreement_16-April-2024.pdf (last visited Oct. 20, 2025).

[24] World Health Org., *Intergovernmental Negotiating Body to Draft and Negotiate a WHO Convention, Agreement or Other International Instrument on Pandemic Prevention, Preparedness and Response*, at 10 (May 27, 2024), https://healthpolicy-watch.news/wp-content/uploads/2024/09/Draft-WHO-Pandemic-Agreement_19-Sept_17.30.pdf (last visited Oct. 20, 2025).

[25] *See generally* Haytham A. Sheerah et al., *Navigating Hurdles: A Review of the Obstacles Facing the Development of the Pandemic Treaty*, 14 J. Epidemiology and Glob. Health 580, 582 (2024), https://link.springer.com/article/10.1007/s44197-024-00233-5 (last visited Oct. 20, 2025); *see* Richard Horton et al., *The Pandemic Treaty: Shameful and Unjust*, 403 The Lancet 781, 781 (2024), https://www.thelancet.com/journals/lancet/article/PIIS0140-6736(24)00410-0/fulltext (last visited Oct. 20, 2025).

[26] *See generally* World Trade Org., The Making of the TRIPS Agreement: Personal Insights From the Uruguay Round Negotiations (Jayashree Watal and Antony Taubman eds., 2015), https://www.wto.org/english/res_e/booksp_e/trips_agree_e/history_of_trips_nego_e.pdf (last visited Oct. 20, 2025) (see views expressed by negotiators of India and other developing countries).

WHA, a body of civil-society organizations categorically highlighted the move from equity to primacy of trade goals at the expense of health.[27]

Perhaps the concern that equity will be relegated to the sidelines became pronounced with the deletion of an envisaged "Peace Clause." Originally inserted as Article 11.4*bis* in the March 27, 2024, draft text, the clause stated the following:

> [4bis. The Parties shall not challenge, or otherwise exercise any direct or indirect pressure on the Parties that undermine the right of WTO Members to use TRIPS flexibilities at any multilateral, regional, bilateral, judicial or diplomatic forum. . . .][28]

The principles in the text are akin to those outlined in Article 1.1 of the TRIPS Agreement, as well as the 2001 Doha Declaration, to explicitly permit and encourage the usage of TRIPS flexibilities.[29] It remains a fact, though, that any developing or least-developed countries that are seen to be considering taking advantage of such flexibilities face immense pressure, often in the form of trade pressure, to reconsider.[30] As discussed in earlier chapters, the USTR's Special 301 Report is notorious for exerting this type of pressure.[31]

The WHOPA would have been a great opportunity, following the devastating effects of the Covid-19 pandemic, to indicate renewed global solidarity to affirm the primacy of human health and prosperity using the Peace Clause. However, this text was removed in the later drafts, confirming the fears of some of the member nations.

[27] Knowledge Ecology Int'l et al., *Constituency Statement of Knowledge* (May 28, 2024), https://www.keionline.org/40035 (last visited Oct. 20, 2025).

[28] "At the WHO pandemic agreement negotiations, the proponents of the peace clause in the WHO Pandemic Accord include: Brazil, Colombia, Guatemala, El Salvador, Nicaragua, Tunisia, Argentina, the African Group + Egypt, Bangladesh, Fiji, Philippines, Pakistan, and Indonesia. The opponents of a peace clause are: the European Union, Japan, the United States of America, the United Kingdom of Great Britain and Northern Ireland, Canada, and Switzerland." *See* Thiru Balasubramaniam, *The WHO Pandemic Agreement: The Peace Clause and Its Discontents*, Knowledge Ecology Int'l (Apr. 3, 2024), https://www.keionline.org/39585 (last visited Oct. 20, 2025).

[29] Medics. L. & Pol'y Notes, *Pressure from European Countries Related to the Use of TRIPS Flexibilities,* Who Tracker (May 8, 2024), https://who-track.phmovement.org/pressure-european-countries-related-use-trips-flexibilities (last visited Oct. 20, 2025).

[30] *See* Carlos M. Correa, *Interpreting the Flexibilities Under the TRIPS Agreement,* in Access to Medicines and Vaccines 1, 5 (Carlos M. Correa and Reto. M. Hilty eds., 2022), https://link.springer.com/chapter/10.1%20007/978-3-030-83114-1_1 (last visited Oct. 20, 2025).

[31] Michael Palmedo and Srividhya Ragavan, *The U.S. Posture on Global Access to Medication & The Case for Change,* 11 Indian J. Intell. Prop. L. 76, 81 (2020), https://scholarship.law.tamu.edu/facscholar/1512 (last visited Oct. 20, 2025).

2.2 Reconfiguring Local Realities

The preamble of the WHOPA addresses fundamental concerns relevant to the current debate. In paragraph 7 it rightly acknowledges systemic global health inequities, stating that "the parties are deeply concerned by inequities at national and international levels that have hindered timely and equitable access to health products to address Covid-19." In a similar vein, the WHOPA language recognizes the need for the "widest possible international and regional collaboration, cooperation and solidarity" for an "effective, coordinated, appropriate, comprehensive and equitable international response."[32] Further, paragraph 15 recognizes that "intellectual property protection . . . does not and should not prevent Member States from taking measures to protect public health, and . . . provides flexibility to protect public health, as recognized in the Doha Declaration on the TRIPS Agreement and Public Health."[33]

This approach, while valuable, would have been more meaningful if the WHOPA also recognized the existence of disparate disease burdens, differing health infrastructures, and other distinguishing factors such as human capital, and how each of these in turn imposes unique burdens variously on different sections of the global population. Doing so would have helped acknowledge the presence of local realities that result in different impacts from the same disease in different parts of the globe based on the unique social, economic, or cultural conditions of member nations and allowed those nations to structure flexibilities to address them appropriately.

As aptly described by Priti Patnaik and Nishant Sirohi,[34]

> Far from perfect, this legal instrument tries to seek a balance between the interests of 193 member states of WHO (sans United States). Given the vast inequalities between countries, a balanced agreement, however, may not necessarily mean an equitable outcome.

[32] World Health Org., *WHO Pandemic Agreement*, WHA78.1, at 7 (May 20, 2025), https://apps.who.int/gb/ebwha/pdf_files/WHA78/A78_R1-en.pdf (last visited Oct. 20, 2025) [Pandemic Agreement].

[33] *Id.* at 8.

[34] Priti Patnaik and Nishant Sirohi, *Countries Choose Consensus on Pandemic Agreement, G7 Fait Accompli on Caveated Terms of Tech Transfer Compromises Policy Space for Developing Countries*, Geneva Health Files (Apr. 16,2025), https://genevahealthfiles.substack.com/p/countries-choose-consensus-on-pandemic-agreement-geneva-tech-transfer-compromise-inb-may-world-health-assembly-2025-european-union-africa-group (last visited Oct. 20, 2025).

Any holistic plan must reconfigure how local realities, which can be akin to moving parts, fit with each other. Recognizing local realities would have helped to better structure the universal scheme that was originally contemplated. Conversely, without meaningful and systemic response objectives and plans built into the architecture of the WHOPA, it became merely a shield with which some countries could protect themselves from diseases originating from poorer countries.

2.3 The Human-Rights Perspective

Along the same lines and much like the equity principles, the early days of the pandemic saw some very appreciable centering of the larger human-rights paradigm when discussing a pandemic response.[35] Specialist bodies such as the International Commission of Jurists (ICJ) noted that there was a lack of certainty of "scope, meaning and implementation of international human rights obligations," which led to the inadequate public-health response.[36] Such a framework was seen as capable, in theory, of disrupting the existing matrix of factors, which has traditionally resulted in a systemic breakdown of health-care access.[37]

Indicatively, the ICJ, together with the Global Health Law Consortium and in consultation with a wide range of experts, built upon the widely known 1984 Siracusa Principles,[38] aimed at ensuring that emergency-response imperatives integrate human rights rather than treat them as

[35] *See generally* Dr. Tedros A. Ghebreyesus, director-general, World Health Organization, WHO Director-General's Opening Remarks at the Mission Briefing on COVID-19 (Mar. 12, 2020), *in* https://www.who.int/director-general/speeches/detail/who-director-general-s-opening-remarks-at-the-mission-briefing-on-covid-19---12-march-2020 (last visited Oct. 20, 2025).

[36] Roojin Habibi et al., *Harmonizing Global Health Law and Human Rights Law to Develop Rights-Based Approaches to Global Health Emergencies*, Int'l Comm'n of Jurists (Mar. 20, 2023), https://www.icj.org/resource/harmonizing-global-health-law-and-human-rights-law-to-develop-rights-based-approaches-to-global-health-emergencies/ (last visited Oct. 20, 2025).

[37] Arguably, current international human-rights organizations have worked with existing structural frameworks. *See, e.g.*, Shanta Devarajan and Jishnu Das, *Improving Access to Drugs: Fitting the Solution to the Problem*, World Bank Blogs (Oct. 23, 2012), https://blogs.worldbank.org/en/africacan/improving-access-to-drugs-fitting-the-solution-to-the-problem (last visited Oct. 20, 2025) (explaining that money "leaks" before it reaches the ultimate beneficiary, health-care workers spend less than an hour per day counseling patients, and doctors fail to adequately diagnose and treat patients).

[38] *The Siracusa Principles on the Limitation and Derogation Provisions in the International Covenant on Civil and Political Rights*, Int'l Comm'n of Jurists (1985), https://www.icj.org/wp-content/uploads/1984/07/Siracusa-principles-ICCPR-legal-submission-1985-eng.pdf (last visited Oct. 20, 2025).

expendable.[39] This later turned into the Civil Society Alliance for Human Rights in the Pandemic Accord (CSA), which came together to enunciate ten human-rights principles that were presented before the negotiating parties.[40] While the draft of the WHOPA mentions and acknowledges human rights in its Preamble as well as in Article 3, "Principles and Approaches," it arguably could have included more meaningful human-rights principles in its substantive provisions.[41]

2.4 The One Health Perspective

The One Health perspective is a central principle in the WHOPA, which recognizes the interconnectedness of human health, animal health, and environmental health. This emphasizes that pandemics often arise from zoonotic diseases. Zoonotic diseases result from pathogens that jump from animals to humans and are typically influenced by environmental and sometimes cultural factors such as deforestation, climate change, and agricultural practices. Therefore, the One Health perspective emphasizes that addressing pandemics requires a holistic, multisectoral approach that integrates human, animal, and environmental health.

Several elements have been key to the One Health perspective in the WHOPA. The first of these is the interdisciplinary collaboration between human health, animal health, and environmental sectors with a view to proactively prevent, detect, and respond to pandemics. Such a collaboration is envisaged through shared surveillance systems and data exchange across the different sectors.

The second aims to prevent zoonotic diseases by addressing factors such as wildlife trade, land-use changes, and agricultural practices in order to address issues that cause zoonotic spillovers. The goal here is to institute stronger regulations and monitor high-risk interfaces between humans, animals, and ecosystems.

[39] *See generally supra* note 30.

[40] These include principles on "Consultation and Participation," "Human Rights Protection," "Health Systems," "Diagnostics, Medications, Vaccines and Therapeutics," "Human Rights-Based Responses to Public Health Emergencies," "Equality & Non-Discrimination," "Accountability and Access to Justice," "Economic, Social and Cultural Rights," "Solidarity/International Cooperation," and "Information, Technology and Data."

See Human Right Principles for the Pandemic Treaty, INT'L COMM'N OF JURISTS (Apr. 11, 2022), https://www.icj.org/wp-content/uploads/2022/04/11-April-2022-Human-Rights-Principles-for-a-Pandemic-Treaty-.pdf (last visited Oct. 20, 2025).

[41] *Draft "Pandemic Treaty" Fails to Protect Rights*, HUMAN RIGHTS WATCH (Nov. 7, 2023), https://www.hrw.org/news/2023/11/07/draft-pandemic-treaty-fails-protect-rights (last visited Oct. 20, 2025).

The third seeks to detect and prevent emerging zoonotic threats early by requiring countries to establish integrated surveillance systems that monitor human, animal, and environmental health.

All of these elements are meant to embrace two important principles, namely, environmental sustainability and equity. The presumption here is that environmental degradation, biodiversity loss, unsustainable farming practices, and lifestyle choices that contribute to climate change create a framework of pandemic risks.

Hence, the WHOPA advocates for policies that protect ecosystems and promote sustainable development. The goal of the WHOPA, as discussed earlier, is for such One Health interventions to be equitable, ensuring that low- and middle-income countries have adequate access to resources, technology, and capacity-building to implement One Health strategies through R&D and innovation.

The surveillance and monitoring within all countries was seen as having the potential to result in better international cooperation. Nevertheless, there is concern that the WHOPA in its current form has the potential to disproportionately burden member countries, especially those that lack the requisite infrastructural architecture.

2.5 R&D, Local Production, and Tech-Transfer

The WHO has made clear, despite its multilateralist mission, that states are bound only by their own domestic decisions, with no international mandates coming from the WHOPA.

Ideally, achieving the benefits from harmonization via an instrument like the WHOPA will require structural mechanisms to create clear cofinancing requirements, incentives for regional cooperation, and monitoring frameworks to track these mechanisms. Thus, Article 9 of the WHOPA relates to R&D, participation, and the need for cooperation between parties to build and strengthen diverse capacities and institutions, particularly in developing countries, with a view to rapidly sharing information and results, particularly during pandemics.[42] The language of the provision, however, is vague in important respects.

[42] *World Health Org., Report by the Director-General: WHO CA + for the Consideration of the World Health Assembly*, at 14–16, (May 27, 2024), https://apps.who.int/gb/ebwha/pdf_files/WHA77/A77_10-en.pdf (last visited Oct. 20, 2025).

Some backtracking from earlier drafts was seen in the next related provision relating to sustainable and geographically diversified local production. In the October 2023 draft, Article 10(d) encouraged nonexclusive and royalty-free licenses to manufacturers from other countries for certain products, to facilitate sustainable production and distribution of prepandemic products. The goal was to encourage production, technology transfer, and know-how, although based on "mutually agreed terms." Article 10(c) of that draft also provided that parties shall strengthen coordination with the UN and other international organizations on issues related to public health, IP, and trade, including timely matching of supply to demand and mapping of manufacturing capacities and demand.

Once again, the language in the final text was diluted significantly, with the focus shifting to encouraging international organizations to establish "arrangements" for pandemic-related health products[43] with "a view to promoting the sustainability of such geographically diversified production facilities."[44] The reference to international organizations such as the UN on issues related to public health, IP, and trade was deleted altogether and replaced with more general language referencing only the WHO technology, skills, knowledge transfer, and local production programs.[45]

Despite heavy negotiations over one of the most contentious provisions of the WHOPA, language regarding vital transfer of technology and knowledge provision ultimately fell along the same old lines as well. Developing countries had hoped for concrete commitments in this realm in particular, and this was reflected in the earlier drafts. In the October 2023 draft, Article 11 required patent holders to waive patent rights and required holders of undisclosed information to disclose it. Such agreed time-bound waivers in the face of global public-health exigencies were commendable. As such, the commitments in this Article would have been important, even if still insufficient, since in order to be effective, the instances at which a recommendation or an encouragement translates into a mandatory requirement suggested by the WTO and carried forward by the national government needed to be clarified for better implementation. However, this passage too was changed completely, and the present text essentially hinges upon rights holders regardless of pandemic emergency requirements.

[43] *Pandemic Agreement*, *supra* note 32, Article 10(2)(e).
[44] *Id.* at Article 10(2)(a).
[45] *Id.* at Article 10(2)(c).

The IP provisions within the WHOPA are characterized by vague and diplomatic language. Instead of creating new, binding IP waivers or flexibilities, they largely reaffirm existing TRIPS flexibilities. Critically, high-income countries have strongly resisted any mandatory commitments to share technology or waive IP rights in real time during pandemics, as elaborated in previous chapters.[46] This stands in stark contrast to the demands from the Global South negotiators, who argue that voluntary mechanisms proved insufficient during Covid-19 and that binding commitments are essential for genuine equity.[47]

Similarly, James Love of Knowledge Ecology International (KEI) pointed out in an open letter[48] to Anne Yu, Director for Global Pandemic Preparedness at the National Security Council, that even as the EU proposed domestic regulation on compulsory licensing that would mandate and make technology transfer within the EU possible,[49] it continued demanding, together with the United States, that technology transfer provisions under the WHOPA be much narrower. Mr. Love adds that aside from the EU's proposed regulations, it is also relevant to note that the United States itself, despite its international history of clamping down on the use or potential use of TRIPS flexibilities by developing countries, has historically taken steps akin to compulsory licensing domestically for medical technologies.[50]

The process through which these changes took place could be seen over the years of negotiation. While civil-society groups as well as pharmaceutical companies launched declarations regarding their respective positions,[51] the

[46] *See* Richard Clements, *The WHO Pandemic Agreement: Equity for Developing States or Business as Usual?*, Eur. J. of Int. L. (May 8, 2025), https://www.ejiltalk.org/the-who-pandemic-agreement-equity-for-developing-states-or-business-as-usual/ (last visited Oct. 20, 2025).

[47] *See* Greta Cranston, *Understanding the Expectations, Positions and Ambitions of LMICs During Pandemic Treaty Negotiations, and the Factors Contributing to Them*, PLOS Global Public Health at 6-7 (Mar. 12, 2025), https://journals.plos.org/globalpublichealth/article?id=10.1371/journal.pgph.0003851 (last visited Oct. 20, 2025).

[48] James Love, *Letter to Anne Yu, Director for Global Pandemic Preparedness, NSC, on Negotiations for WHO Pandemic Agreement*, Knowledge Ecology International (May 1, 2024), https://www.keionline.org/39776 (last visited Oct. 20, 2025).

[49] *European Parliament Legislative Resolution of 13 March 2024 on the Proposal for a Regulation of the European Parliament and of the Council on Compulsory Licensing for Crisis Management and Amending Regulation No 816/2006*, recitals 32a-b, COM (2023) 0224 final (Mar. 13, 2024).

[50] *See generally Compulsory Licensing in the Context of U.S. Injunction Cases Involving Medical Technologies*, Knowledge Ecology Int'l, https://www.keionline.org/us-injunction-medical (last visited Oct. 20, 2025) (a collection of decisions discussing compulsory licenses to medical technology granted in patent infringement and trade-secret litigation).

[51] For example, the Civil Society Alliance for Human Rights in the Pandemic Accord (CSA) submitted ten recommendations to the Intergovernmental Negotiating Body; *see supra* note 34. Similarly, the International Federation of Pharmaceutical Manufacturers & Associations

submissions by civil-society groups were largely ignored. Despite the strong early drafts, the positions of countries such as the United States, the EU, Israel, Japan, and Australia ultimately succeeded in changing technology-transfer provisions to voluntary commitments rather than mandatory ones.[52]

To that extent, Articles 13 and 14, dealing with supply-chain logistics, procurement, and distribution, are relatively less problematic. Article 13 establishes a Global Supply Chain and Logistics Network (GSCL Network) to be convened by the WHO with state and non-State partners and ultimately under the oversight of a Conference of Parties (COP). The COP is required to develop guidelines and modalities for collaborating with the GSCL Network. The GSCL Network calls for establishing accountability, transparency, and inclusiveness in its functioning and governance and allowing for equitable representation of WHO regions.[53] It is important that this provision incentivizes stakeholder participation to engage with the GSCL Network,[54] especially in the presence of sanctioning measures that otherwise may exist.[55]

Lastly, Article 14 focuses on procurement and distribution. Once again, the parts of the provision with meat in them are subjective or nonbinding. For example, the provision had the opportunity to disallow excessive stockpiling and has even stated that states "should not" do this, but does not mention any threshold. Similarly, it only asks parties "to consider" setting aside portions of their procurement or making procurement arrangements for use in countries that are facing challenges in meeting public-health needs and demands. Also, it only requires states to "consider" including provisions in their pandemic-related publicly funded agreements for the promotion

(IPFMA) also made their position clear in their "Berlin Declaration." *See* INT. FEDERATION OF PHARMACEUTICAL MANUFACTURERS & ASSN., BERLIN DECLARATION—BIOPHARMACEUTICAL INDUSTRY VISION FOR EQUITABLE ACCESS IN PANDEMICS (2022), https://www.ifpma.org/wp-content/uploads/2023/01/i2023_IFPMA_Berlin-Declaration_Biopharmaceutical-industry-vision-for-equitable-access-in-pandemics-1.pdf (last visited Oct. 20, 2025).

[52] Schwalbe, *supra* note 10, at 8.

[53] *Pandemic Agreement*, *supra* note 28, at Article 13(2)(e).

[54] *See generally* Willy C. Shih, *Global Supply Chains in a Post-Pandemic World*, HARV. BUS. REV., Sept.–Oct. 2020, https://hbr.org/2020/09/global-supply-chains-in-a-post-pandemic-world (last visited Oct. 20, 2025) (discussing the need for stakeholders to build more resilient supply-chain networks and rethink global-supply-chain strategies).

[55] KEI, for instance, argues that the treaty should have overriding effect on any such sanctions, along with the presence of certain exceptions to deal with emergency situations. It does, however, also acknowledge that Articles 13(4) and 13(5) address this to some extent. *See generally*, *supra* note 44.

of timely and equitable access, especially for developing countries, such as provisions regarding donations, licensing, and global-access plans.[56]

2.6 The Pathogen-Access and Benefit-Sharing Mechanism

The last set of issues relating to areas of clear disagreement were, in turn, slated to be resolved within the very optimistic timeline of one year from May 2025. The issue of access- and benefit-sharing (ABS) with regard to "materials and sequence information on pathogens with pandemic potential," along with rapid, timely, fair, and equitable sharing of benefits from use of such materials, remains a significant point of disagreement between developed and developing nations. The current text establishes a framework with some promise. However, the operational details have been left to be negotiated and entered as an annexure within a period of one year.

During the WHOPA negotiation, the United States advocated for benefit-sharing "options" that manufacturers could select from. Conversely, developing countries have emphasized the need for meaningful benefit-sharing that is proportionate to the obligation of sharing biological materials and sequence information. They have also stressed the importance of ensuring certainty and predictability in the timely provision of vaccines, therapeutics, and diagnostics to address public-health emergencies of international concern (PHEICs) and pandemics.[57]

Some observers, however, view this as potentially irreconcilable in its current form. It has been noted that pathogen access and benefit-sharing (PABS) tries to combine "two separate public-health resource-allocation problems: (1) pathogen and data sharing, and (2) pharmaceutical supply and distribution."[58] Some of the tensions are already seen in the existing draft text. For example, Article 12 of the draft stipulates that in the event of

[56] *Pandemic Agreement*, *supra* note 28, at Article 14(2); *see also WHO Pandemic Agreement: A Win for Multilateralism, A Missed Opportunity for Public Health?*, Third World Network (May 16, 2025), https://www.twn.my/title2/health.info/2025/hi250502.htm (last visited Oct. 20, 2025) (critiquing in the Agreement's reliance on non-binding "consider including" language in publicly funded procurement obligations and its equity implications).

[57] *The Pandemic Agreement Negotiations: A Reset is Needed*, Third World Network (Sept. 14, 2024), https://twn.my/title2/health.info/2024/hi240903.htm (last visited Oct. 20, 2025).

[58] Abbie-Rose Hampton et al., *'Equity' in the Pandemic Treaty: The False Hope of 'Access and Benefit-Sharing,'* 72 Int'l and Comparative L. Quarterly 909, 931 (2023), https://www.cambridge.org/core/services/aop-cambridge-core/content/view/EDDC7C190807F992643129ADD476955B/S0020589323000350a.pdf/equity-in-the-pandemic-treaty-the-false-hope-of-access-and-benefit-sharing.pdf (last visited Oct. 20, 2025).

a pandemic, the WHO would have access to 20 percent of pandemic-related products. An editorial in *The Lancet* characterized it as follows:

> The other 80%—whether vaccines, treatments, or diagnostics—would be prey to the international scramble seen in COVID-19 that saw vital health technologies sold to the highest bidder. Most of the world's people live in countries that might not be able to afford these products, but 20% seems to be all that high-income countries were willing to agree to. *This is not only shameful, unjust, and inequitable, it is also ignorant.* Creating and signing up to a strong and truly equitable set of terms on access and benefit sharing is not an act of kindness or charity. It is an act of science, an act of security, and an act of self-interest.[59]

Moreover, key issues continue to remain for generating consensus between member states.[60] These include defining the scope (negotiations have focused only on human samples versus zoonoses; similarly, the challenges of resolving contradictions with the Access and Benefit Sharing regime of the Convention on Biological Diversity and its associated protocols that govern use of genetic resources and Digital Sequence Information, determining the criteria for allocating benefits, issues of contract transparency, feasibility of tracking and tracing the use of PABS materials and sequential information, and unclear interactions between the Convention on Biological Diversity (CBD) and the WHOPA.[61]

3. Going Forward: A Systemic vs. Fragmented Framework

3.1 Progress over or Retreat from Doha?

While the WHOPA text does go further than the IHR, such as the proposed multilateral mechanism for PABS,[62] several commentators have pointed

[59] Horton, *supra* note 21, at 781.

[60] *See* Hampton, *supra* note 54, at 912.

[61] *See* Mark Eccleston-Turner et al., *Fate Unknown: The Pandemic Agreement's Pathogen Access and Benefit Sharing*, Think Global Health (May 20, 2025), https://www.thinkglobalhealth.org/article/fate-unknown-pandemic-agreements-pathogen-access-and-benefit-sharing (last visited Oct. 20, 2025).

[62] Pedro A. Villareal et al., *The Proposed Pandemic Agreement: A Pivotal Moment for Global Health Law*, 53 J. L. Med. Ethics S1, 55, 56 (2025), https://www.cambridge.org/core/services/aop-cambridge-core/content/view/5E6923A2D72B651C82631165156E9D14/S1073110525000221a.pdf/the-proposed-pandemic-agreement-a-pivotal-moment-for-global-health-law.pdf (last visited Oct. 20, 2025).

out that, though it may have marked a big moment for multilateralism, it is still essentially nonbinding, especially in areas like technology transfer, local production, financing, equity, and access.[63] Table 5.1 below succinctly compares the key attributes and provisions of the WHOPA with the Doha Declaration.

Overall, there is some consensus that the WHOPA, despite its shortcomings, has been a victory for multilateralism. Be that as it may, it does raise the question of whether, aside from symbolism, it has brought about any tangible progress in the sphere of global public health.

Table 5.1 A Comparative Analysis of Key Provisions of the Doha Declaration (2001) and the Draft WHOPA.

Issue	Doha Declaration (2001)	Pandemic Treaty (2023–2025 Drafts)
Trigger Context	HIV/AIDS, chronic diseases, access to medicines	Covid-19 acute outbreaks, equitable response in emergencies
Focus	Right to issue compulsory licenses, affirm TRIPS flexibility	Pre-agreed access and benefit-sharing, coordination during pandemics
Scope	IP law in general (medicines and generics)	Broad: samples, genomic sequence data/DSI, countermeasures, knowledge, supply chains
IP Flexibilities	Affirms right to use TRIPS flexibilities in health crises	Suggests IP waiver mechanisms pre-crisis, but lacks enforcement teeth
Benefit-Sharing	Not addressed	Introduces Access and Benefit-Sharing (ABS) model for pathogens (PABS)
Infrastructure	Not part of the IP model	Mentions technology transfer, local production, genome-access platforms
DSI and Genomic Data	Not relevant in 2001	Directly tackles DSI equity, though still unresolved

Reproduced with permission from Dr Siddarth Jain, *The WHO Pandemic Agreement: A Contested Step Beyond Doha,* July 17, 2025, SpicyIP, *available at* https://spicyip.com/2025/07/the-who-pandemic-agreement-a-contested-step-beyond-doha.html.

[63] *See, e.g., supra* note 52; *see also* Eccleston-Turner, *supra* note 57; Clements, *supra* note 42.

In this regard, Dr. Siddarth Jain has astutely addressed the question of whether the WHOPA has even taken us forward from the 2001 Doha Declaration:

> The treaty attempts to establish pre-defined rules for pandemic preparedness rather than responding to post-crisis situations, distinguishing its very main scope from that of the Doha Declaration on the TRIPS Agreement and Public Health (2001). However, the extent to which it genuinely builds upon Doha's legacy remains a deeply contested issue, particularly when viewed from the perspective of the Global South.[64]

The current WHOPA aims to address inequities highlighted by the Covid-19 pandemic through binding commitments on access, technology transfer, and benefit-sharing, as viewed by many Global South negotiators and civil-society actors. However, from the perspective of science and technology studies, the WHOPA represents a reframing of biopolitical control within genomic governance, moving from the Doha Declaration's focus on "access to medicines" to the broader concept of "access to biology," including pathogen samples, genetic sequences, and surveillance data. While it may suggest a global knowledge commons, it does not fundamentally redistribute epistemic power structures or ensure infrastructural capacities in the Global South. Therefore, equity, rather than merely serving as a procedural ideal, necessitates a structural mandate for tangible changes in global dynamics and resource allocation.

All of this raises the question of whether a new framework is required. This important question will be addressed in chapter 6.

3.2 Proposed Outlines of a Broader "Public Health" Framework

With this background, any pandemic agreement or PHT discussions ought to flow as a proposal for an alternative framework in the form of a broader instrument that holistically covers global public health rather than merely pandemics and epidemics. As we envisage the form of the new framework,

[64] Dr. Siddarth Jain, *The WHO Pandemic Agreement: A Contested Step Beyond Doha*, SpicyIP (July 17, 2025) https://spicyip.com/2025/07/the-who-pandemic-agreement-a-contested-step-beyond-doha.html (last visited Oct. 20, 2025).

it could be an instrument that will work within the trade regime complex of which IP is an integral part. The chief goal of such an instrument should be to position health at front and center while also fostering innovation, so that IP ceases to be a barrier to global public health either directly or indirectly.

Thus, the need for a broader and more unified framework cannot be ignored. Whether such a framework would best be created by treaty or through some other instrument needs to be closely considered. The following sections explore the key features, objectives, and expected outcomes of a framework that could establish minimum standards for a robust system of global public health and pandemic response.

3.2.1 Inter-International Institutional Cooperation

The WHOPA showcases the importance of global public health as an agenda. That agenda implicates the WTO, which is currently at the intersection of an opportunity to remain as a trade organization per se or to undertake a more pragmatic approach to major global issues such as global public health, alongside the efforts of the WHO. Such pragmatism could result in a more responsible and realistic outcome for both global trade and global public health.

For instance, the lack of proper benefit-sharing conflicts was one of the initial reasons for which a WHOPA was first discussed. Initial discussions included introducing a mechanism to persuade, if not require, high-income countries and large-capability companies to act in a fair manner, so as not to repeat the lopsided stockpiling and gatekeeping of lifesaving knowledge and products.[65]

In theory, the goal was for the WHO to take stronger leadership in this regard by implicating the supporting roles of the WTO and the WIPO. The Trilateral Cooperation[66] envisaged between the three international organizations could enable coordination in addressing concerns of countries with limited resources. Whether the WHO and its member nations can implicate the WTO and the WIPO remains uncertain. However, the WHO's leadership as a member of the Trilateral Cooperation could potentially maximize efficiency by enabling the sharing of R&D and data about the impact of IP on

[65] *See* Eccleston-Turner, *supra* note 54.

[66] *See generally Trilateral Cooperation on Global Health*, World Intell. Prop. Org., https://www.wipo.int/policy/en/global_health/trilateral_cooperation.html (last visited Oct. 20, 2025) (overview of WHO–WIPO–WTO trilateral cooperation on public health).

areas that affect development in health-related goods and services, and identify the best practices for the use of IP in those areas.

For instance, the Trilateral Cooperation could be critical to ensure that trade and IP norms contribute to achieving sustainable development by promoting more locally contextualized and calibrated norms for innovation, economic growth, and access to essential goods and services. A functional benefit-sharing arrangement would also acknowledge that improved public health will be an important factor in achieving the sustainable-development goals of the trade regime.

3.2.2 Focus on Local Realities

Any comprehensive instrument that deals with health care—whether under pandemic circumstances or as a whole—should structurally be able to respond to at least the following factors simultaneously: (a) local realities of different member nations, (b) limitations and capacity building of individual nations, and (c) estimation of potential benefits with potential costs viewed in relation to their respective socioeconomic realities. Unfortunately, the WHOPA provisions that relate most closely to these factors—the provisions on financing, PABS, IP rights and technology transfer, and common but differentiated responsibilities—appear to be among the most contested ones, as discussed earlier.[67]

The nationalist-versus-globalist conundrum of the WHOPA needs a balancing approach to be resolved in a manner that compromises neither faction. A nuanced understanding and articulation of individual and joint priorities that focus on reasons and instances for international, regional, national, and even local action enmeshed in international cooperation may be required. Otherwise, the WHOPA risks becoming merely a set of directorial rules and facing the same eventual outcome as the IHR.

Moreover, in order for the WHOPA provisions to be effective, it is imperative that the WHO, through the WHOPA or otherwise, create educational opportunities to encourage other countries to institute regulations commensurate with the level of development of those engaged. This could perhaps

[67] For commentary on these aspects of the negotiations, *see generally* Sheerah, *supra* note 21 (discussing the challenges in the development and implementation of WHOPA); *see also* Josh Michaud et al., *The "Pandemic Agreement": What It Is, What It Isn't, and What It Could Mean for the U.S.*, KFF (Apr. 1, 2024), https://www.kff.org/global-health-policy/the-pandemic-agreement-what-it-is-what-it-isnt-and-what-it-could-mean-for-the-u-s/ (last visited Oct. 20, 2025) (discussing US objections to the Pandemic Agreement).

be done by commissioning policy studies at a regional or national level with a view to appreciating approaches that may be suggested to institute mechanisms that can protect global public health while preserving innovation. Thus, studies on types of flexibilities, limitations of such flexibilities, and outcome expectations would all comport well with the objectives of helping member nations institute systems that are consistent with their local realities of development and creating a more efficient role for them in the global public-health governance.

3.2.3 Global Knowledge Commons

Any solution, be it in the form of a treaty, accord, agreement, or other instrument, must consider public health at large as a primary goal and must structurally recognize that the distribution of power is central to achieving that goal. Access to robust health care and health technologies is critical if global populations as a whole are to develop, and ensuring the wide dissemination of these technologies should be the goal of both innovation and health-care policy.

For instance, digital sequencing information (DSI), which refers to the genetic information derived from genomic databases, can be crucial for developing diagnostics, vaccines, and therapeutics. But without binding obligations for equitable benefit-sharing from the use of DSI, the Global South countries, which often share pathogen samples leading to the generation of this data, fear continued exploitation without commensurate benefits. Inclusive DSI governance connected with the PABS mechanism represents an opportunity to establish a global knowledge commons rooted in equity.

The Intergovernmental Negotiating Body (INB) draft CTO in May 2024 introduces the term "genomic sequence data" (GSD), but only in bracketed text, and clearly separates it from broader "digital sequences" (akin to DSI)—which are still placeholders. It makes no binding references to DSI, focusing instead on PABS.[68]

3.2.4 Implementation Is the Key

While the WHOPA includes mechanisms for ABS of pathogens and related information, or PABS, these mechanisms are largely decoupled from binding

[68] Pierre Walckiers et al., *A Roadmap to Equity in Pandemic Preparedness, Prevention and Response*, 14 J. Glob. Health 03031, 4–5 (2024), https://jogh.org/2024/jogh-14-03031 (last visited Oct. 20, 2025).

commitments to deliver essential vaccines, diagnostics, or therapeutics during pandemics. This means that even if pathogen samples are shared, there are no guaranteed mechanisms to ensure that the resulting health products are made available to countries in need at affordable prices.[69] Minus the requirement of mandates or minimum commitments, the WHOPA once again, in essence, reverts to a situation where progress is dependent on voluntarism and charity rather than robust, reliable and resilient action and cooperation.[70] Moreover, unlike the TRIPS Agreement, which is legally binding and enforced through the WTO's dispute-settlement mechanism, the current draft of the WHOPA lacks strong and mandatory enforcement mechanisms for ABS. This absence of robust and actionable commitments raises concerns about its ability to compel compliance when future crises demand immediate action.

In fact, the much contested "as mutually agreed" terminology, which essentially converts any obligation into a voluntary action, occurs repeatedly in the footnotes of the final text, and is specifically explained as "willingly undertaken and on mutually agreed terms, without prejudice to the rights and obligations of the Parties under other international agreements."[71]

The dynamic political climate of the last few years will no doubt be a major factor in the next round of PABS negotiations as well. The state-centric approach has been made clear yet again. And this time it may carry even more significance than it did in previous situations under IHR. Earlier in 2025, immediately after his inauguration, President Trump withdrew the United States from the WHO. The United States having been the WHO's largest donor, the country's withdrawal reduced the WHO's annual budget by US$1 billion dollars. Simultaneously, the United States, while blaming the WHO for helping China cover up the origins of the pandemic, has called upon other countries to cooperate outside of the WHO.[72] Nonetheless, there are

[69] *See* Seema Prasad, *Agreement on Sharing Pathogen Access Unlikely at World Health Assembly, May Delay Pandemic Treaty,* Down To Earth (May 29, 2024), https://www.downtoearth.org.in/health/agreement-on-sharing-pathogen-access-unlikely-at-world-health-assembly-may-delay-pandemic-treaty (last visited Oct. 20, 2025).

[70] *See* Riddhi Yogesh Bhutada, *Preparedness Without Power? Analysing IP and Access in the WHO Pandemic Agreement,* SpicyIP, https://spicyip.com/2025/06/preparedness-without-power-analysing-ip-and-access-in-the-who-pandemic-agreement.html (last visited Oct. 20, 2025).

[71] *See Pandemic Agreement, supra* note 28, (noting "For the purposes of the WHO Pandemic Agreement, 'as mutually agreed' means 'willingly undertaken and on mutually agreed terms, without prejudice to the rights and obligations of the Parties under other international agreements,'" and cross-referencing *supra* note s 11, 12, 13, 16, and 17).

[72] Carmen Paun, *RFK Jr. Calls for Global Health Cooperation Outside the World Health Organization,* Politico (May 20, 2025), https://www.politico.com/news/2025/05/20/rfk-jr-pandemic-covid-china-un-00358464 (last visited Oct. 20, 2025)

some who say that the US withdrawal may actually have galvanized support for finalizing the WHOPA text, as if to prove that multilateralism is "alive and well."[73]

The statement put out by the United Nations Programme on HIV/AIDS (UNAIDS), even though perhaps on the optimistic side, points to where the WHOPA leaves us today:

> This is an agreement with human rights at its heart, prioritising community engagement and whole-of-society and whole-of-government approaches to pandemic preparedness, prevention and response. But, while the agreement supports equitable access to lifesaving vaccines, tests, and medicines, *it falls short of what developing countries called for, particularly regarding obligations to transfer technology*.
>
> The Pandemic Agreement is not a panacea. If adopted by the World Health Assembly, a fairer response to future health crises *will depend on member states taking concrete steps to implement the agreement. Governments will need clear implementation frameworks, including timelines* for ensuring that all can benefit from affordable access to scientific innovation."[74]

3.2.5 Systems-Thinking Framework

Countries all around the world suffer from high incidences of diseases, including treatable diseases such as cancer, diabetes, mental-health issues, and other conditions that clearly affect the population at both the individual and the national or regional level. For instance, vulnerable populations relying on cancer medications, preventive medications, and other health-care technologies that are critical to prevent and treat disease conditions must not be deprived of such treatments in order to properly equip them for a pandemic, as is increasingly occurring today.

If health care is viewed solely through the lens of a pandemic, it becomes unclear how other existing health-care concerns will be dealt with. For example, one study in Italy showed that there was a concerning drop in

[73] Kai Kupferschmidt, *Global Pandemic Treaty Finalized, Without U.S., in "A Victory for Multilateralism,"* SCIENCE (Apr. 16, 2025), https://www.science.org/content/article/global-pandemic-treaty-finalized-without-us-victory-multilateralism (last visited Oct. 20, 2025).

[74] *UNAIDS Reacts to WHO Member States Reaching Pandemic Agreement Consensus*, UNAIDS, https://www.unaids.org/en/resources/presscentre/pressreleaseandstatementarchive/2025/april/20250416_PR_pandemic_agreement (last visited Oct. 20, 2025).

admissions for certain types of diseases, including cardiac and neurologic diseases, and noted that "Those patients postponed medical attention, possibly with fatal consequences, just for fear of exposure to Covid-19, leading to unnecessary morbidity and mortality."[75]

Indeed, a clear framing for what exactly is happening may help highlight the limitations of such an approach. The current approach of viewing specific emergency situations as ones that demand the most attention takes a fragmented approach to a situation that needs integrated solutions. A *systems-thinking framework* asks that, instead of reducing problems to their individual parts ("reductionism"), it is more useful to view problems through the lens of "expansionism (the belief that a system is always a subsystem of some larger system) and analysis (gaining knowledge of the system by understanding its parts) with synthesis (explaining its role in the larger system of which it is a part)."[76] This approach allows for the recognition that problems may have several links in other parts of a system and focuses on fundamental drivers rather than symptoms.

Hence, although any lasting regime must effectively contextualize important global events on health, focusing on a unique agenda in a multifaceted world is no longer an option. Rather, long-term sustainability accounting for the inequities of global trade should be the goal. The objective should be to view health care holistically instead of as specific problems that arise only in siloed contexts, and therefore to include access to health care and pharmaceuticals at large, as opposed to limiting it to pandemic-related responses and materials.[77]

4. Conclusion—Toward a Public-Health Treaty

The earlier parts of this chapter have discussed the shortcomings in the form and structure of the WHOPA. Like its predecessors, the WHOPA can be faulted for dealing with the health issue in a piecemeal manner. By limiting

[75] Veronica Ojetti et al., *Non-COVID Diseases During the Pandemic: Where Have All Other Emergencies Gone?* 56 Medicina, Oct. 2020 no. 512, at 1 (2020), https://www.mdpi.com/1648-9144/56/10/512 (last visited Oct. 20, 2025).

[76] John Pourdehnad et al., *Integrating Systems Thinking and Design Thinking*, The Systems Thinker, https://thesystemsthinker.com/integrating-systems-thinking-and-design-thinking/ (last visited Oct. 20, 2025).

[77] Srividhya Ragavan et al., *The World Intellectual Property Organization*, *in* The International Law of Economic Integration 193 (Julian Chaisse and Christoph Herrmann eds., 2025).

its scope to pandemics, WHOPA perhaps inadvertently treats measures for addressing a "pandemic" as distinct from rather than as part of a larger public-health concern.

Because of the narrow scope of the WHOPA, some of the pressing global issues of public health and access to medicine fail to be addressed as part of this effort. While there is clear intent by the WHO to build a framework that may ease the burden of future pandemics, there is no reason that health-care access could not have been treated as a singular framework while also taking into account why the existing approaches failed or had such limited success.[78]

The difficulty in achieving a "successful" equitable treaty only for pandemics need not be a dissuading factor in adoption of a broader "public health" approach. In fact, the One Health approach in the WHOPA may have already laid the groundwork for such an approach. Further, the interdependence of global public health, economy, welfare, trade, and geopolitics would, if anything, strengthen the case for an equitable path forward, as compared to taking just one emergency situation as the model around which to construct such instruments.

To construct an instrument in a manner that is not amenable to easy displacement by individual powers, be it nation-states or supranational entities such as transnational corporations or large philanthropic organizations, is a difficult exercise.[79] Nonetheless, a broad and unified approach to dealing with health care, consistent with the systems thinking framework as outlined in the previous section, would comprehensively consider provisions needed for countries to provide for public-health-related exigencies, including anchoring "flexibilities," appreciating local realities, and being cognizant of other countervailing forces as required.[80]

With these objectives, the chapter proposes that international entities work together in a complementary fashion on such an instrument. The challenge is to provide policy tools that will empower sovereign nations with

[78] As another example, when the "first full application" of IHR 2005 was attempted in response to H1N1 (Influenza A) in 2009, it was seen as valuable but still latent in its potential as a framework to address the disease across borders. *See* Inst. of Med. (US) Forum on Microbial Threats, Infectious Disease Movement in a Borderless World (2010).

[79] *See, e.g.*, Tim Schwab, The Bill Gates Problem: Reckoning with the Myth of the Good Billionaire (2023) (describing Bill Gates's influence over global-health governance priorities through little-understood philanthro-capitalistic moves).

[80] Srividhya Ragavan and Swaraj Paul Barooah, *Historic Tensions Involving International Intellectual Property Protection of Medical Technology with Disastrous Public Health Consequences*, 54 Seton Hall L. Rev. 339, 340, 358–59, 363–64, 376–77, 380–81 (2023).

sufficient flexibilities to institute safeguards to preserve public health locally and ultimately to improve global public health. In contrast to the existing rubric of normative and operational harmonization, this framework, in accounting for local realities, will deal with public health at regional and national levels in a manner that sustains optimal levels of productivity along with optimal innovation. Such an instrument or framework, which could be termed a "public-health treaty," will be discussed more fully in the final chapter.

6

Imagining Public Health as the Fulcrum of Global Trade

1. Introduction—Failure of the New International Economic Order

1.1 A Faulty International-Trade Approach

Experts have repeatedly decried the global public-health system, and Covid-19 has become the easy example of its failings. During the Covid crisis, when various governments refused to acknowledge the realities of a global health crisis or declined to take bold actions, many others lacked vaccines with which to protect their population in a timely manner.

The responses by various governments to Covid-19 displayed an international-trade approach, with the WTO taking a back seat even amidst the pandemic. The challenges in obtaining the Covid-19 Waiver showcased how international treaty obligations were used as an excuse to prevent reasonable national exemptions, even as powerful developed countries actively pursued nation-centric actions. Consequently, poorer countries were unable to provide Covid-related treatments by waiving select IP obligations. The challenge they faced was reminiscent of the HIV/AIDS crisis, when poorer nations were prevented from using IP waivers even when millions of people were dying.[1]

For instance, by September 2022 advanced economies had 75 percent vaccine coverage, with booster shots rolled out, even though a significant percentage of their populations subscribed to anti-vaccine theories, leaving many of these nations with excess vaccines. Meanwhile, in developing countries, where the need for vaccines surged because of a denser population,

[1] A different version of this chapter has been accepted for publication as a book chapter with the title *Accountable Approaches for Better Global Public Health in the Post-Pandemic Era*, in A HUMAN-CENTERED APPROACH TO HEALTH INNOVATIONS (Lisa Biersay et al. eds., 2025).

Fractures in IP, Trade, and Health. Srividhya Ragavan and Swaraj Paul Barooah, Oxford University Press.
 DOI: 10.1093/9780197684085.003.0006

only 32 percent of the population had vaccine coverage.[2] The global access to Covid-19 vaccines was far below the 70 percent target that the WHO set for mid-2022, and below even the 40 percent target previously set for the end of 2021.[3] The failure to meet WHO targets remains significant, especially considering that the targets were embraced by and announced in a joint statement involving the heads of the International Monetary Fund (IMF), the World Bank, and the WTO, after "high-level consultations" with UNICEF and the vaccine alliance Gavi.[4]

Unfortunately, health exceptions to WTO's patent norms existed during this time, raising the question of why so many governments were unwilling to use negotiated solutions such as compulsory licensing. Arguably, member states were reluctant to cooperate and coordinate to effectively tackle the pandemic.[5] One theory proposed by Jumee Barooah is that international organizations and intergovernmental bodies have become dependent on charity and goodwill to fulfill global public-health goals, to the point of making internal processes functionally redundant. A dependency on charity and goodwill instead of strong policies connected with local realities foreshadows a failure to enable global access to health care.

The history of these international institutions making a mark can arguably be traced from the more recent history when a "Group of 77" countries (G77), as they are now known, successfully advocated for a UN "Declaration on the Establishment of a New International Economic Order" (NIEO) in 1974. Interestingly, the United States was one of the first governments to reject the NIEO, just as it would be the first to reject public-health flexibilities in the WTO TRIPS Agreement. While the G77 countries passed the declaration in the UN, it has had few if any practical implications and little or no impact in policy terms. Muchkund Dubey, a former foreign secretary for the government of India, specifically notes one of the G77's achievements as preventing the introduction of TRIPS Agreement into the 1982 GATT

[2] *See IMF-WHO COVID-19 Vaccine Tracker*, INT'L MONETARY FUND (Sep. 8, 2022), https://www.imf.org/en/Topics/imf-and-covid19/IMF-WHO-COVID-19-Vaccine-Tracker (last visited Oct. 22, 2025).

[3] *See* WORLD HEALTH ORG., STRATEGY TO ACHIEVE GLOBAL COVID-19 VACCINATION BY MID-2022, 9 (2021), https://cdn.who.int/media/docs/default-source/immunization/covid-19/strategy-to-achieve-global-covid-19-vaccination-by-mid-2022.pdf (last visited Oct. 24, 2025); *see also International Organizations Discuss How to Improve Access to COVID Vaccines, Countermeasures*, WORLD TRADE ORG. (Dec. 22, 2021), https://www.wto.org/english/news_e/news21_e/covid_22dec21_e.htm (last visited Oct. 22, 2025) [hereinafter *COVID Vaccines, Countermeasures*].

[4] *See COVID Vaccines, Countermeasures*, *supra* note 3.

[5] *See* Norihiro Kokudo & Haruhito Sugiyama, *Call for International Cooperation and Collaboration to Effectively Tackle the COVID-19 Pandemic*, 2 GLOB. HEALTH & MED. 60, 60 (2020).

Ministerial Meeting's agenda.[6] He goes on to state, "It was only eight months later when India gave up its position, which was a major factor accounting for G77 as a whole yielding under pressure and accepting substantive negotiations on TRIPS."[7]

1.2 WHOPA: A Missed Opportunity

As the previous chapter showed, the ongoing WHOPA negotiations reveal serious concerns about how global health inequities are being addressed. Peeling back the layers of these negotiations exposes an approach that may be structurally deficient.[8] The concern is that such a structure with an arguably narrow vision risks repeating historical patterns of neglecting the global public-health priorities as a single unit. The fear is that the WHOPA, even if concluded, may not only represent a missed opportunity for necessary reform that considers global public health at large but may also risk cannibalizing political will toward addressing these challenges in the future.[9]

Indeed, the biggest flaw of the WHOPA may be the fact that, notwithstanding the various health-centric articulations, it has insufficiently focused on global public-health issues as a whole and instead has emphasized a narrow objective of dealing with certain situations arising from pandemics and epidemics at the center of policymaking. This approach is reminiscent of the Covid-19 Vaccines Global Access (COVAX) initiative, which was established under the mistaken assumption that it could take on the burden of dealing with the pandemic without fully addressing the larger issues affecting global public health. Thus, although the initiative dealt with health in the pandemic context, it can perhaps be faulted for not placing global public health front and center.

[6] *See* Muchkund Dubey, *The Historic Importance of G-77*, THE UN CHRONICLE (May 16, 2014), https://www.un.org/en/chronicle/article/historic-importance-g-77 (last visited Oct. 22, 2025).

[7] *See id.*

[8] *See* WORLD HEALTH ORG., PROPOSAL FOR NEGOTIATING TEXT OF THE WHO PANDEMIC AGREEMENT (2023) (being a proposal made under the auspices of the WHO and discussed at the seventh meeting of the intergovernmental negotiating body to draft and negotiate a WHO convention, agreement, or other international instrument on pandemic prevention, preparedness, and response).

[9] *See* Srividhya Ragavan, *Agreement or Other International Instrument on Pandemic Prevention, Preparedness and Response Submitted to Dept of Health & Human Resources,* TEXAS A&M UNIVERSITY SCHOOL OF LAW LEGAL STUDIES RESEARCH PAPER (2024), https://papers.ssrn.com/sol3/papers.cfm?abstract_id=4736051 (last visited Oct. 22, 2025).

1.3 A Structural Shift from Form to Substance

While it is true that the WHOPA holds promise for addressing global health emergencies, it needs to evolve beyond the shortcomings already displayed in historically utilized frameworks. Furthermore, public-health obligations, whether of nations or of the globe at large, need not falter in addressing two separate issues—global frameworks such as harmonization and individual limitations, and exceptions such as compulsory licensing—which seem to be at perpetual odds.

Thus, to create a more balanced framework structural responsiveness needs to be reevaluated considering critical factors such as:

a) requirements of each member state,
b) respective capabilities, and
c) potential social and economic benefits weighed alongside estimated costs.
   Provisions on financing, PABS, IP rights and tech transfer, and common but differentiated responsibilities should also be closely considered although they seem to be amongst the most contentious.[10]

This book asserts a strong substantive structural framework will greatly further the evolution of global public health as a norm. While acknowledging that clear IP systems and laws are important to further innovation and trade, we assert the need to redefine those norms in a manner that promotes robustness in public health by establishing a framework that holistically takes into account local realities of individual member states.[11]

We further assert that any future framework should recognize health care as an important public good that deserves immediate, significant, and necessary attention. In imagining a new framework, this chapter utilizes terms such as "right to health," "public health," and "global health" to address the normative interplay and interdependence of these concepts. Other scholars, including

[10] *See* Haytham A. Sheerah et al., *Navigating Hurdles: A Review of the Obstacles Facing the Development of the Pandemic Treaty,* 14 J. Epidemiol. & Global Health 580 (2024), https://link.springer.com/article/10.1007/s44197-024-00233-5 (last visited Oct. 22, 2025); *see also* Josh Michaud et al., *The "Pandemic Agreement": What It Is, What It Isn't, and What It Could Mean for the U.S.*, KFF (Apr. 1, 2024), https://www.kff.org/global-health-policy/the-pandemic-agreement-what-it-is-what-it-isnt-and-what-it-could-mean-for-the-u-s/ (last visited Oct. 22, 2025).

[11] *See* Srividhya Ragavan & Swaraj P. Barooah, *Historic Tensions Involving International Intellectual Property Protection of Medical Technology with Disastrous Public Health Consequences*, 54 Seton Hall L. Rev. 339, 352, 350–355 (2023), https://scholarship.shu.edu/shlr/vol54/iss2/1 (last visited Oct. 22, 2025).

Jonathan Mann, Lawrence Gostin, and Audrey Chapman, have used a similar approach to highlight the issues more succinctly.[12] For simplicity, we borrow the following articulation from John Tobin and Damon Barrett:

> [T]he normative content of the right to health now provides a foundation for state obligations to respect, protect, and fulfill the right to health; limitations on other rights for public health goals; the right's essential attributes of availability, accessibility, acceptability, and quality; the minimum core obligations of the right to health; and the progressive realization of health-related human rights.[13]

Hence, this chapter will discuss the need for global public health to embody a different international framework. To do so, it first identifies the prevailing systemic and structural deficiencies that may be addressed through a new framework, posing the following question: *How do we think about public health in a world where international institutions have consistently failed it?*

While we call for the establishment of a new PHT, our emphasis here is on the substance, not the form, of this framework. Hence, while asserting that the new framework can take any form, from a treaty to a declaration, the chapter does not go into granular details regarding the framework, reserving that question for future work.

2. Deficiencies Impeding Global Public Health

2.1 Systemic and Structural Deficiencies

In the global public-health system, systemic and structural deficiencies arise from a combination of unrealistic ideals that translate into IP norms affecting global access to health care. The chapter uses the term "systemic deficiencies" to denote deficiencies that affect global public health either directly or indirectly by limiting access to medication particularly and to health care more

[12] *See* Audrey R. Chapman, *The Right to Health: Then, Now, and a Call to Arms*, 22 HEALTH & HUM. RTS. J. 331 (2020), https://pmc.ncbi.nlm.nih.gov/articles/PMC7348420/ (last visited Oct. 22, 2025).

[13] *See* John Tobin & Damon Barrett, *The Right to Health and Health-Related Human Rights, in* FOUNDATIONS OF GLOBAL HEALTH & HUMAN RIGHTS (Lawrence O. Gostin & Benjamin Mason Meier eds., 2020), https://academic.oup.com/oxford-law-pro/book/32071/chapter-abstract/267884217?redirectedFrom=fulltext (last visited Oct. 22, 2025).

generally. An example of a deficiency that has an indirect impact is the lack of a distribution network, which is the case in various parts of the globe.

"Structural deficiencies," on the other hand, are inherent to the market-centric mandates of the international trade regime, and are further defined by the role played by international institutions, governments, norms, and policies. This role, in turn, adversely affects one or more localities by limiting access to health care, consequently affecting global public health.

One such structural deficiency, the cost of disparity in bargaining power among states, has resulted in discussions on public health being dominated by funding questions, much to the detriment of access to health care and regardless of prevailing global health crises. For instance, during the HIV/AIDS epidemic, multinational pharmaceutical companies sued the South African government for using TRIPS flexibilities to reduce the cost of medication and increase the supply of ARVs.[14] In the late 2000s, amidst the bird-flu scares, the one entity that was manufacturing the relevant vaccines entered into licensing agreements with only a handful of corporations (whose identities were kept secret) in order to keep costs high and maintain market control.[15] Similarly, one of the arguments against the Covid-19 Waiver was that the instrument would weaken incentives for pharmaceutical companies to invent and manufacture vaccines, despite projections that companies that could do so were bound to make billions of dollars in sales.[16] Vaccines for Zika, a relatively obscure virus prior to 2015, received little to no attention, because the virus largely affected poorer nations and there was no concern that it might become an epidemic affecting the global North.[17] Similarly, R&D for Ebola languished for almost a decade without funding.[18]

[14] *See* William W. Fisher III & Cyrill P. Rigamonti, *The South Africa AIDS Controversy: A Case Study in Patent Law and Policy*, Harv. L. Sch. (Feb. 10, 2005), https://cyber.harvard.edu/people/tfisher/South%20Africa.pdf (last visited Oct. 22, 2025).

[15] *See* Dawn Dziuba, *TRIPS Article 31*bis *and H1N1 Swine Flu: Any Emergency or Urgency Exception to Patent Protection?*, 20 Ind. Int'l & Compar. L. Rev. 195, 205 (2010).

[16] *See* Bryan Mercurio, *WTO Waiver from Intellectual Property Protection for COVID-19 Vaccines and Treatments: A Critical Review*, 62 Va. J. Int'l L. Online 9, 16 (2021); *see also* Julia Kollewe, *From Pfizer to Moderna: Who's Making Billions from COVID-19 Vaccines?*, The Guardian (Mar. 6, 2021, 11:55 AM), https://www.theguardian.com/business/2021/mar/06/from-pfizer-to-moderna-whos-making-billions-from-covid-vaccines (last visited Oct. 22, 2025).

[17] *See* U.N. Dev. Programme, Inequality in Access to Essential Health and Medicine: COVID-19 Vaccines 10 (2021), https://www.undp.org/sites/g/files/zskgke326/files/2023-02/UNDP-Inequality-in-Access-to-Essential-Health-and-Medicine-COVID19-Vaccines-2021.pdf (last visited Oct. 22, 2025); *see also* Anthony S. Fauci & David M. Morens, *Zika Virus in the Americas—Yet Another Arbovirus Threat*, New Eng. J. Med. 601, 601 (2016).

[18] *See* Steven M. Jones et al., *Live Attenuated Recombinant Vaccine Protects Nonhuman Primates Against Ebola and Marburg Viruses*, 11 Nature Med. 786, 786 (2005) (describing the efficacy of the rVSV-ZEBOV vaccine in nonhuman primates); *see also* U.N. Dev. Programme, *supra* note 17, at 30.

Each of these cases is an example of a barrier to access to medication created by a power disparity. Over time, the ideal of upward harmonization of IP rights, currently featured in international agreements, lacks a realistic appreciation of ground realities. In turn, embracing such an ideal has precluded a required focus on global public health from a care, cost, and access perspective. It has emphasized other critical values such as innovation and trade, but in a manner ignorant of global public health needs. A quotation from the BBC aptly summarizes this wrongheaded prioritization: "Clinging to . . . ideology, far removed from the reality . . . , exemplifies to perfection what it means to go against common sense when steering . . . politics."[19]

There is, therefore, an imminent need to review and assess the status quo to remedy prevailing policy incoherencies that have resulted in deprioritizing public-health concerns.[20] Unfortunately, structural deficiencies have become systemic and continue to remain disconnected from local realities. Allowing the *denormalization* of the prevailing wisdom, which perpetuates a siloed or unique focus on trade and IP, can weed out some of the existing structural factors that can set out guideposts for imagining an alternative framework, as will be discussed later.

2.2 Globalist, Aspirational, Reactive Approaches

International instruments that focus on trade embody health care as an aspirational rather than an achievable goal. For instance, the preamble of the International Health Regulations (IHR) expressly declares an aspiration for revising the epidemic response. These regulations repeatedly emphasize preparedness without outlining a state obligation to develop and protect core public-health facilities and resources.[21] In sum, the aspirational approaches, while well intended, remain disconnected from the on-the-ground realities implicating health-care access. Instead, addressing global

[19] *See "Liz Truss the Brief?" World Reacts to UK Political Turmoil*, BBC (Oct. 17, 2022), https://www.bbc.com/news/world-63285480 (last visited Oct. 22, 2025).

[20] *See* U.N. Dev. Programme, *supra* note 17, at 17.

[21] *See* International Health Regulations, May 23, 2005, WHA58.3, World Health Org., art. 40–42 (describing the core capacity requirements, which focus on capacity regarding "surveillance, reporting, notification, verification, response and collaboration activities").

health emergencies should involve substantive improvements in healthcare access.[22]

Unfortunately, the post-pandemic responses have been reminiscent of those we saw after the HIV/AIDS, Zika, and Ebola crises—that is, aspirational and trade-centric, without embodying the operational realities of the affected member states. The responses in each instance were reactive in nature and showcased how public-health issues had been sidelined. In effect, the responses posited global health along pre-drawn lines, where territoriality and harmonization formed bright-line thresholds that facilitate trade and IP protection without taking full account of their effects on global public health. Each of these reactions focused on trade outcomes, when they should have focused on health outcomes instead.

While existing institutions have been faulted for being reactive, the WHO's ongoing attempts to negotiate a pandemic treaty provide another example of this reactive approach, which remains both narrow and shallow.[23] Hence, we assert that the WHO's proposed WHOPA suffers from the same flaw in *aspiring* to foster an approach to strengthening capacities and resilience, which will be discussed further below.[24] To a large extent, the proposal for a pandemic treaty was a defensive or reactive approach to the failure of the international health regime to provide meaningful guidance during the initial stages of the Covid-19 pandemic. The pandemic showcased gaping problems of ineffective monitoring and enforcement mechanisms, including those involving the trilateral cooperation between the WHO, the WIPO, and the WTO.[25]

[22] *See* Stéphanie Dagron, *Going Beyond the Rhetoric: Taking Human Rights Seriously in the Post-COVID-19 New Paradigm*, VERFASSUNGSBLOG (Mar. 27, 2021), https://verfassungsblog.de/going-beyond-the-rhetoric-taking-human-rights-seriously-in-the-post-covid-19-new-paradigm/ (last visited Oct. 22, 2025) (noting the link between poverty and access to health care during the Covid-19 pandemic).

[23] *See* Press Release, World Health Org., World Health Assembly Agrees to Launch Process to Develop Historic Global Accord on Pandemic Prevention, Preparedness and Response (Dec. 1, 2021), https://www.who.int/news/item/01-12-2021-world-health-assembly-agrees-to-launch-process-to-develop-historic-global-accord-on-pandemic-prevention-preparedness-and-response (last visited Oct. 22, 2025).

[24] *See* World Health Org., REPORT OF THE SECOND MEETING OF THE INTERGOVERNMENTAL NEGOTIATING BODY TO DRAFT AND NEGOTIATE A WHO CONVENTION, AGREEMENT OR OTHER INTERNATIONAL INSTRUMENT ON PANDEMIC PREVENTION, PREPAREDNESS AND RESPONSE (2022), https://apps.who.int/gb/inb/pdf_files/inb2/A_INB2_5-en.pdf (last visited Oct. 22, 2025).

[25] *See* Nasiya Daminova & Shisong Jiang, *The First Working Draft of the WHO's "Pandemic Treaty": Attempting to Cover Normative Gaps Indicated by the COVID-19 Pandemic?*, EJIL: TALK! (Oct. 13, 2022), https://www.ejiltalk.org/the-first-working-draft-of-the-whos-pandemic-treaty-attempting-to-cover-normative-gaps-indicated-by-the-covid-19-pandemic/ (last visited Oct. 22, 2025).

In our view, the fundamental concern with the WHOPA is not with negotiating useful treaty language. Instead, it is the WHOPA's *globalist* approach, which tries to address the next pandemic without acknowledging or attempting to address the presence of systemic health inequities that undermine global public health as well as the breadth of its pervasiveness across the world. A globalist approach falls in line with the existing conceptions of "rights, equity, solidarity and shared goals" for universal citizens, where a "shared responsibility" is undertaken by the "global community" consisting of international organizations, governments, philanthropists, the private sector, and NGOs.[26] Such an approach is characterized by a lack of consideration for disparate disease burdens, differing health infrastructures, and other distinguishing factors such as varying human capital.

Typical of a globalist approach, the WHOPA, as currently considered, is unlikely to foster accountability consistent with differences in local realities that will affect both the availability and affordability of medication. The proposal continues to aim for a harmonized treaty with standardized application or implementation. This is perhaps why the effort has been criticized for placing disparate obligations on LMICs by imposing stronger implementation and reporting requirements, such as those for sharing data and reporting health threats, while being weaker on medical countermeasures, such as those on international stockpiling of health-care materials for emergency use or on voluntary participation in technology sharing.[27] Thus, even when the WHOPA imposes unique burdens on member states by focusing on select issues, it ignores unique local conditions that need to be addressed in member states before international norms can be imposed.

2.3 Overemphasis on Preparedness

Arguably, the WHOPA's prime emphasis is on preparedness, with a focus on cooperation and the development of resilient supply chains.[28] Thus,

[26] *See* Clare Wenham et al., *The Futility of the Pandemic Treaty: Caught Between Globalism and Statism*, 98 Int'l Affs. 837 (2022).

[27] *See* Mark Eccleston-Turner, *Future-Proofing Global Health Governance Through the Proposed Pandemic Treaty*, Verfassungsblog (Aug. 18, 2022), https://verfassungsblog.de/future-proofing-global-health-governance-through-the-proposed-pandemic-treaty/ (last visited Oct. 22, 2025) (discussing the successes and shortcomings of the Pandemic Treaty).

[28] *See* Patrick Butchard & Bukky Balogun, What is the WHO Pandemic Treaty?, House Commons Lib. (May 20, 2025), https://researchbriefings.files.parliament.uk/documents/CBP-9550/CBP-9550.pdf (last visited Oct. 22, 2025).

the WHOPA provides significant emphasis on surveillance, alerts, and response mechanisms. Although these issues are arguably necessary for this type of treaty, they are insufficient if one takes a *health-first* perspective. The assumption that preparedness alone qualifies as an adequate response is pervasive in public-health discussions. After all, inadequate preparedness aggravated the crisis during the Covid-19 pandemic. Nevertheless, prevention, access to treatment, and availability of public resources facilitated in a realistic manner are also important aspects that deserve immediate attention.

While the emphasis on preparedness may help mitigate future public-health crises, the WHOPA overwhelmingly, and perhaps inadvertently, shifts the focus to ensuring that trade-focused countries do not get burdened with infectious diseases, rather than addressing the larger issue of actually preventing a crisis while also improving health-care access to populations around the world. Notably, the ideal of preparedness was largely absent during the decades when infectious diseases were the predominant cause of deaths in poorer nations. In the post-Covid-19 environment, even when noncommunicable diseases have become predominant globally, many countries are considering the WHOPA largely because of the realization that infectious diseases can eventually cross borders to adversely affect international trade and global supply chains.

2.4 Perverse Incentivization and Market Fundamentalism

Admittedly, the key advantage of market-based incentives is that they use market signals to decide what progress is socially optimal. However, in the health-care arena, the ability to express a preference on the market does not equate to optimal health outcomes. Issues relating to access, IP rights, and directions of R&D have encountered market barriers, leaving lower resource availability per person for public-health needs.

To some extent, trade and IP norms provide perverse incentives that can cause systemic problems at the global level, such as a patent-induced monopoly over lifesaving drugs during a local health crisis that can lead to a global public-health issue. As far as existing international instruments go, the internal gaps between norms and allowed exceptions and the external gaps between norms and countervailing forces weaken the ability of these instruments to adequately counteract market fundamentalism.

The fundamentally market-centric political economy erects further constraints, with legal idealism and formalism often provided as a front. An example of the former is IP protection in economies with welfare constraints, and an example of the latter is the interpretation of treaty provisions by the WTO's DSB with no room for flexibility to accommodate local realities and constraints.

Arguably, a market with rewards for impactful innovations, such as the Nobel Prize, would not have the same problem and might be better aligned with public-health goals. However, such a market would still encounter issues such as government intervention and might not always fulfill public-health needs, just as Nobel Prizes have not achieved human solutions such as world peace or environmental protection.

2.5 Systemic Problems and Band-Aid Responses

While the TRIPS Agreement and subsequent bilateral and multilateral agreements have resulted in upward harmonization of IP norms across the world, these legal instruments have especially failed to institute sufficient flexibilities or exceptions to promote global public health. Moreover, as the WTO experiences its own existential crisis over its appellate process, new trade norms are likely to be developed through bilateral or multilateral agreements or through contractual exercises of power by multinational pharmaceutical companies.

Moreover, the lack of sufficient flexibility for member states undermines public health while exacerbating the inadequacy of sufficient tools in international treaties for enabling access to available health care. International organizations and their member states should therefore focus on preparedness by creating equitable access and addressing larger structural failures, which have been discussed in this chapter.

Arguably, the lack of a solution with sufficient flexibilities for member nations to account for local realities has resulted, *inter alia,* in increased local surveillance and/or implementation requirements, which in turn increase the overall global and national health burdens. For example, the increased use of pre-purchase agreements has created an additional layer of barriers to access to medication, resulting in inflating pharmaceutical prices.

In addition, the provision of regulatory exclusivities tends to block critical information, preventing faster entry of generics or biosimilars. In turn, such exclusivities have increased delays in poorer nations' gaining access to medication—and, in some cases, to enabling these nations to develop local (generic) pharmaceutical production. Unequal technological prowess has left a few powerful nations or multinational investors controlling the supply of treatments.

Against this background, the exigency of the Covid-19 pandemic showcased the immense challenges of creating a standard to embrace a global solution, such as a uniform TRIPS waiver, which India and South Africa proposed at that time, as well as the difficulties of effectively instituting previously negotiated flexibilities, such as compulsory licensing locally.

During the pandemic, countries had lost faith in the use of flexibilities, causing their proponents and supporters to seek an explicit waiver from select IP provisions as an alternative, temporary framework. In response to the Covid-19 Waiver proposal, traditional supporters of global frameworks and harmonization, typically the more powerful, developed countries, pivoted toward using negotiated TRIPS flexibilities, such as compulsory licenses, on a territorial basis, despite having formerly repeatedly opposed the idea of providing member states with the ability to loosen the protection of certain forms of IP rights in order to address their local public needs.

In fact, public-health obligations, whether of the globe or individual nations, repeatedly wavered between instituting uniform or harmonized global frameworks and providing flexibilities to sovereign member states to develop individualistic national solutions consistent with their local public-health needs. The resulting tension has pushed the globe further away from what we believe ought to have been the core purpose of a global framework—that is, improving the overall status of global public health. Such improvement should have been the lowest common denominator for all member states. At a minimum, access to health care as a means to improve productivity demands our attention.

We believe that the current calls for reforms, including the Pandemic Treaty, discount local realities. In the process of developing these reforms, a host of interactive and impactful issues are left out of consideration. What is needed, therefore, is a structural realignment of factors to remove some of the systemic and structural deficiencies explored above.[29] Therefore, in

[29] *See* Shanta Devarajan & Jishnu Das, *Improving Access to Drugs: Fitting the Solution to the Problem*, World Bank Blogs (Oct. 23, 2012), https://blogs.worldbank.org/en/africacan/improving-access-to-drugs-fitting-the-solution-to-the-problem (last visited Oct. 22, 2025) (explaining that money "leaks" before it reaches the ultimate beneficiaries, health-care workers spend less than an hour per day counseling patients, and doctors fail to adequately diagnose and treat patients).

the next section, we will discuss the possibility of developing a new global public-health framework.

3. Addressing Global Public-Health Inequities Within the Innovation Framework

The framework we discuss below aims to change how public health is framed internationally. Such a change should account for the existing power imbalances by using a human-centric approach as the basis for this new framework. Such a framework, which we hope to develop in the form of a public-health treaty (PHT), should be broader than the WHOPA currently in discussion at the WHO. We hope that our proposed treaty will include creating access to the prevention of and treatment for not only infectious diseases but also non-infectious diseases such as cancer that are not individualized.

The objective of this instrument should be to recognize and respond to the existing systemic and structural deficiencies by providing viable alternatives with adequate sovereign flexibilities to deal with health exigencies. Thus, we enlist below the core values that a treaty focused on public health, termed a "Public Health Treaty," should embody, although we are open to consideration of other similarly effective frameworks. A detailed description of our proposed treaty and its related framework is beyond the scope of this book.

3.1 Primacy for Health

Historically, terms of trade have repeatedly relegated public health to a mere exception, notwithstanding international principles such as sovereignty. Such relegation has resulted in enormous resources being deployed to prioritize the protection of private rights at the expense of fulfilling the states' welfare obligations, such as those relating to promoting access to health care to ensure productivity. Significant efforts and resources have been invested in trying to achieve a goal that fits within an existing paradigm of trade and IP protection, built over an ideology that is far removed from on-the-ground realities.

Placing public health repeatedly as a subset of secondary rights often compromises welfare-based objectives and exacerbates systemic concerns.

Tying health care with trade and other issues has had persistent detrimental effects on the access paradigm of global public health. Even within countries that have considerable resources per capita, an increasing number of vulnerable people have been left behind as health benefits have been steadily redistributed upward.

Given the underlying premise of global development, the tendency is to treat trade norms as sacrosanct *in and of themselves*. However, it is time to question why trade norms are treated as justified normative bases for public-health outcomes. Jurisprudentially and theoretically, this question has not been satisfactorily addressed, apart from general claims that such norms lead to overall global development. The national cost of such global development has been disparate, and the linkage between trade norms and overall global development remains empirically ambiguous. A public-health narrative would provide an important context that is not sufficiently weighed within the larger trade paradigm.

Arguably, health is the fulcrum on which trade rests, not the other way around. Even if we instead assume that public health is a subset of trade, productivity and trade are affected whenever global public health is. The supply-chain issues following the Covid-19 pandemic illustrated how trade can grind to a halt as a consequence of global health issues. Similarly, the distribution failures involving vaccines during the pandemic symptomatized the monumental failures of international institutions in recognizing the limits of national systems. National systems and international organizations need to be insulated from the flow of power that has allowed global health inequities to expand.

The strength of our proposed treaty would derive from putting global public health front and center. To achieve this goal, we believe that the current paradigm should be inverted—that is, that public-health outcomes should not be viewed from the lens of trade but rather that trade should be viewed through the lens of public-health realities of individual countries. This alternative framing would recognize that public health and trade norms are not contradictory, nor do they function as exceptions to the other set of norms.

Our underlying assumption is that the proposed treaty should be stronger than the TRIPS Agreement from the standpoint of health-care access. We need to view global public health as separate from and competing with trade, while recognizing the substantial overlap between the two. We believe that global public health must be engaged independently and prior to deciding questions of reconciliation or exceptionalism. Viewed through this lens, we consider it timely to discuss whether terms for trade and IP rights should be disengaged from public health or should have a more limited and defined engagement.

Hence, any new framework should be based on an underlying premise that a certain standard of public health is not just a desirable norm but a requisite for trade that aspires to deliver its promised developmental goals. The objective should be to frame policies in a way that would weave in sufficient sovereign flexibilities to accommodate national realities with a view to enabling access to health care. The difficult part of this new paradigm is to institute appropriate border measures and safeguards, where required, to avoid impeding innovation.

3.2 Alternative Innovation and Incentive Models

Even after a PHT has been established, innovation will remain a necessary, albeit insufficient, element that must be incentivized. Historically, drugs resulting from the IP–based innovation mechanism are legally positioned to be scarce, rivalrous, and resource-intensive in nature.[30] Over time, experts have examined the IP system more closely to evaluate the extent to which it can serve as a tool for innovation.

For public health to be the focus, one of the starting points should be a reexamination of the existing incentive mechanisms with which the IP system is ideologically linked in the pharmaceutical area. The goal is to determine how best IP policy levers can help innovation without becoming a barrier to access to those innovations. It is also imperative to reexamine the existing reliance factors for drug development for signals of desirable innovation.[31] Delinking drug price from drug R&D cost may be required, and global sales volume may turn out to be a better indicator of market needs. Alternatively, publicly funded innovation can refocus on the therapeutic use of a drug rather than its profitability.[32] Government-funded projects

[30] *See* Antony Taubman, *A Typology of Intellectual Property Management for Public Health Innovation and Access: Design Considerations for Policymakers*, 4 OPEN AIDS J. 4, 5 (2010).

[31] *See* William Fisher & Talha Syed, *Global Justice in Healthcare: Developing Drugs for the Developing World*, 40 US DAVIS L. REV. 581 (2006), https://lawcat.berkeley.edu/record/1120730?v=pdf (last visited Oct. 22, 2025).

[32] *See* Swaraj Paul Barooah, *Mainstreaming Delinkage*, SPICYIP (Jun. 27, 2014), https://spicyip.com/2014/06/mainstreaming-delinkage.html (last visited Oct. 22, 2025).

in particular can be restructured to include provisions obligating the beneficiary to engage in more-inclusive research collaborations. Public funding can also entail requirements for open-access publication or different models for access.

Although IP rights are typically associated with large efficiency costs—such as deadweight losses—the determinants of efficiency in the health-care area should focus on health-care access and considerations beyond innovation norms. Distributive justice, welfare obligations of states, and self-sufficiency are among the values that should play a central role. Important considerations in this mix are the question of cost and the balance of cost with innovation. Hence, any solution should be based on a variety of policy and operational considerations, including cost and access; but cost alone should not dominate policy discussions.

Moreover, for innovation to continue unabated, market- and IP-based models should be placed alongside non-market-centric innovation models, such as OSDD, pledges, health alliances, and local manufacturing. These options should be available to countries when they choose how to address issues related to health-care access. The motivation behind these models should be to further the scientific advances for a society with wider access to health care. Importantly, none of these models need to be seen in isolation, as they can be combined in various permutations, which should be the basis of flexibility afforded in a public-health framework that takes account of local health realities.

Significantly, for such flexibility to operate effectively, a public-health framework should emphasize each member state's ability to manufacture the needed drugs locally. Manufacturing locally would result in more overall efficiency from a perspective of health care access. Such a move would likely steer away from the current framework of the international trade regime, under which critical lifesaving innovations emanate in one part of the world for mere consumption in others.

In cases where there is insufficient manufacturing capacity, the framework should target potential markets and set clear operational milestones. This arrangement can be effective in addressing the unmet demand for medication and other treatments that have been historically seen as unprofitable.[33]

[33] *See* Mark Eccleston-Turner, *The Economic Theory of Patent Protection and Pandemic Influenza Vaccines: Do Patents Really Incentivize Innovation in the Field?*, 42 Am. J.L. & Med. 572, 575 (2016) (assuming that drugs will be brought from developers and then disseminated to the public, thus resulting in demand for the drugs); *see also* Praharsh Gour, *Guest Post: Understanding Organization of Islamic Cooperation's Involvement in the Gambia v. Myanmar Case at the ICJ*, Ind. Blog Int'l L.

Similar arrangements can also assist in collectively voicing the need for establishing manufacturing hubs within countries to serve identified regions (not necessarily limited by national borders).[34]

Similarly, in order to maintain readiness of regional facilities, policy frameworks that remove export-import barriers should be drafted and made available to be used in the event of a health exigency in any country. Other medical countermeasures, such as training and education on the involved technologies through the WHO system, styled along the lines of the WIPO Academy, could also promote innovation.

Encouraging participation efforts to promote global supply-chain networks through grants and other mechanisms will also greatly help to address issues of health-care access. Examples include studies to promote R&D on innovation in supply-chain management to improve distributional or logistical efficiencies during health exigencies, and studies on issues that affect infrastructure and other distributional networks that can affect the supply chain in developing countries.

3.3 Ushering in Transparency and Accountability in Publicly Funded Research

R&D remains integral to innovation. While a systemic global change to R&D may be the ultimate goal, several steps along the way should be interim goals. For example, member states must have sufficient policy space and flexibility for conditional public (government) funding of innovation. It is thus imperative that concrete rather than aspirational steps be included in any way forward.

Thus, publicly funded projects can consider inclusive research collaborations, which should be more fully and comprehensively defined in the funding agreement to support public sharing of actions against pathogens with the potential to become infectious diseases, epidemics, and pandemics.

(May 3, 2020), https://allaboutil.wordpress.com/2020/05/03/guest-post-understanding-organization-of-islamic-cooperations-involvement-in-the-gambia-v-myanmar-case-at-the-icj/ (last visited Oct. 22, 2025) (noting that this model is already applied by the Organization of Islamic Cooperation, which has funded its members to resolve problems faced by the Muslim community).

34 *See* Amy Maxmen, *South African Scientists Copy Moderna's COVID Vaccine*, NATURE (Feb. 3, 2022), https://www.nature.com/articles/d41586-022-00293-2 (last visited Oct. 22, 2025) (noting that some initiatives along these lines, such as South Africa's mRNA hub, have already commenced).

Universities that benefit from federal funding on pandemic-related products should be obliged to educate students from the poorer nations of the world. Instituting measures toward ensuring transparent and public sharing of clinical trial protocols could enable more innovation. At regional levels, separate funding mechanisms could be created whereby universities could mentor laboratories and other research systems established in poorer countries lacking local manufacturing facilities, such as in parts of Africa.

At a more granular level, funding agreements should also carefully include the second generation of licensees or beneficiaries. In other words, if a university benefits from a grant, the university should have an obligation to bind a licensee of any resulting patent with some terms and conditions that comport with the public-access objectives. Whether through regional or national funding, any public funding must be conditioned on provisions such as:

a) disclosure, including publication of the invention information as well as terms of the licensing agreement for products that fall within the scope of the treaty under Article 10;
b) deposit of certain materials, along the lines of the Budapest Treaty, perhaps a requirement that certain types of inventions will be licensed voluntarily by the patent holder;
c) creation of a repository to store certain types of data involving clinical trials;
d) either voluntary licensing agreements or waivers of certain rights in specific jurisdictions in the event of a public-health crisis;
e) management of royalties on the use of the technologies for the production of pandemic-related products and promotion of voluntary licensing and transfer of technology and related know-how for such products; and
f) encouragement to private rights holders to establish regional or global technology-transfer hubs or other multilateral mechanisms or networks.

Additionally, funding sources should include sufficient opportunities to conduct disease-burden studies relevant to pathogens with pandemic potential and studies on pandemic-response outputs, as well as pandemic-response cooperation at national, regional, and international levels. Having such instruments ready could help ensure future deployment in a timely manner.

Further, in order to encourage sustainable production and exchange of information, including IP, technology, products, and know-how, it is important that beneficiaries of public funding be notified and educated in advance about their duties, their obligations, and their innovations' market potential.[35] In turn, national governments or regional bodies could maintain a register wherein funding information is made available transparently so as to encourage scrutiny and accountability.

Furthermore, when providing details such as the nature of funding provided and the type of IP output generated from such funding, a listing of patents or other type of IP rights, licenses, and their market price should be included. Doing so could promote sustainable production by imposing obligations in exchange for receiving public funding.

3.4 Empirical Basis for Interpretive Clarity

Because the normative approach of the current trade and IP regimes is divorced from local realities, the functioning of these regimes often trivializes considerable public-health harms into "invisible" negative externalities, which are often difficult to quantify empirically if not actually assumed away. Therefore, any new framework should involve and rely on a multi-governmental public-health impact assessment, perhaps for specific time periods. This arrangement would overcome the interpretive limitations that frequently undermine the ability of international trade and IP norms to address public-health problems to which they have arguably contributed. The debate around different interpretations of various provisions would be reduced as a result.

Fundamentally, prevention, health innovations, and access to health care should be considered from the perspective of meeting health goals and guided by the public-health impact assessment, as mentioned above. This arrangement would comport with the 2002 report of the WHO Commission on Macroeconomics and Health entitled *Global Public Goods for Health*,

[35] *See* Knowledge Ecology International, KEI Comments on the Implications of Access and Benefit Sharing (ABS) Commitments/Regimes and Other Proposed Commitments in the WHO Pandemic Agreement (2024), https://www.keionline.org/wp-content/uploads/KEI-Comments-HHS-WHO-pandemic-negotiations-29Jan2024.pdf (last visited Oct. 22, 2025).

which states that public health is deeply connected to government action and other classic public goods.[36]

3.5 Health Care as a Public Good

Since the 1970s, human-rights norm-setting has risen as an international tool of status equalization.[37] While the international human-rights movement has been responsible for many successes, their criticisms of distributional concerns—especially those caused by trade and IP norms—have been guarded at best. Despite focusing on material insufficiency, this movement, perhaps inadvertently, has not adequately addressed the steady increase in material inequality over the decades, including inequality caused by a lack of access to health care.[38]

We believe that the solution lies in framing flexibilities within a larger human-rights or human-centric paradigm. Such a framework would replace the existing matrix of factors, which has historically resulted in a systemic breakdown of health-care access. Arguably, current international human-rights organizations have worked with—rather than disrupted—existing structural frameworks.

To enable public health to be the central focus, it should be viewed through the lens of a public good in order to recognize the structural, social, and political forces affecting the health of the world's population.[39] At a basic level, a public-goods approach to global public health recognizes that countries can benefit from collaboration and the sharing of technology, knowledge, and policy choices. Sociopolitical realities also make it clear that the prevailing disparities between countries compel a strong public-goods approach to public health at the domestic level,[40] so as to enable countries to make unconstrained policy choices on public health to fit their needs.

[36] *See* World Health Org., Global Public Goods for Health: The Report of Working Group 2 of the Commission on Macroeconomics and Health, 1 (2002), https://iris.who.int/server/api/core/bitstreams/40fb972f-ec8b-4771-a588-8e599f43ca35/content (last visited Oct. 22, 2025).

[37] *See* Samuel Moyn, Not Enough: Human Rights in an Unequal World 176 (2019).

[38] *See id.*

[39] *See* Sandro Galea, *Public Health as a Public Good*, Bos. Univ. Sch. of Health (Jan. 10, 2016), https://www.bu.edu/sph/news/articles/2016/public-health-as-a-public-good/ (last visited Oct. 22, 2025).

[40] *See* Sourindra Mohan Ghosh & Imrana Qadeer, *Public Good Perspective of Public Health: Evaluating Health Systems Response to COVID-19*, Econ. & Pol. Wkly., Sept. 5, 2020, at 40, https://www.epw.in/journal/2020/36/special-articles/public-good-perspective-public-health.html (last visited Oct. 22, 2025).

Over time, IP norms, notwithstanding their stated public objectives, have established large swaths of private rights. Thus, at a minimum, the public-goods approach will clarify the role of public health as a countervailing policy priority. Even within the international trade regime, it is important to recognize that health care is a public good, and that neglecting it anywhere can lead to significant and adverse impacts on global trade. Sovereign nations should therefore have greater latitude to assure the availability of pharmaceuticals essential to public health.

Recent discussions at the WTO public forum have included a proposal by Knowledge Ecology International (KEI) to initiate a trading framework for several "global public goods" modeled after the General Agreement on Trade in Services (GATS). This proposal would enable countries to voluntarily pledge medical resources or know-how in exchange for reduced tariffs in another trade sector.[41]

The past few decades have also seen a growing literature on alternative mechanisms that could increase access to medicines. These mechanisms include patent pools, patent pledges,[42] restructuring logistics and supply-chain requirements, and more collaborative approaches to expertise sharing and technology transfer.[43] By elevating health care as a public good, many of these viable solutions would become available as part of the flexibilities that nations have.

3.6 Aid vs. Ability

Poorer nations have decried the use of international aid as a debt trap or merely a vehicle for multinational pharmaceutical companies to increase

[41] *See* John Heilprin, *Advocates Mount New Initiative for WTO to Recognize "Public Goods" in Trade Agreements—from Medicines to Forests*, Health Policy Watch (Sept. 30, 2022), https://healthpolicy-watch.news/a-push-for-public-goods-to-fight-pandemics/ (last visited Oct. 22, 2025).

[42] *See* Jorge L. Contreras, *Patent Pledges*, 47 Ariz. St. L. J. 543, 543 (2016).

[43] *See* OPEN COVID PLEDGE, https://opencovidpledge.org (last visited Oct. 22, 2025) (illustrating patent pledges, in the form of Open Covid Pledge, which enabled large-scale pledging of patent for Covid-19 response, with estimated pledges of 500,000 patents. Patent pledges are voluntary statements made by innovators who agree to refrain from exercising their rights on patents); *see also* Medicines Patent Pool, https://medicinespatentpool.org/ (last visited Oct. 22, 2025) (illustrating patent pools in the field of medicine. Patent pooling refers to agreements between at least two rights holders to cross-license their patents for a common purpose. Notable examples include the UNITAID-backed Medicines Patent Pool, which has signed agreements with seventeen patent holders for thirteen HIV antiretrovirals, one HIV/AIDS technology platform, three direct-acting antivirals for hepatitis C, a tuberculosis treatment, four long-acting technologies, three oral antiviral treatments for Covid-19, and twelve Covid-19 technologies).

their sales.[44] Often, such foreign aid is highly inefficient, as the providers lack the knowledge needed to effectively traverse cultural and social barriers. Thus, aid providers are viewed suspiciously.

Foreign aid, whether through such providers or through national governments, is perceived as charity that tends to discount local talent while reducing a country's ability to manufacture or distribute medication efficiently using local means. Historically, countries that have taken care of their national needs are best positioned to graduate into the innovation and trade spectrum as informed players.[45] Such aid, perceived more as charity, can also be a disservice to countries wanting to graduate to the next level of health equity.

Graduating to the next level, whether by instituting policies that promote local pharmaceutical manufacturing capacity or enabling more transfer of technology to achieve targeted national objectives in this area to enable more health-care access, may be the most important step toward ultimately achieving increased productivity and innovation, which is ultimately the objective of the international trade regime. Therefore, any public-health framework should clarify the roles and limitations of aid providers.

3.7 Mechanism for the Engagement

Coalition formation and the creation of informal groups have traditionally been common in multilateral negotiations, and such coalitions can play an

[44] *See* M. Asif Ismail, *PEPFAR Policy Hinders Treatment in Generic Terms*, Int'l Consortium of Investigative Journalists (Dec. 13, 2006), https://www.icij.org/investigations/divine-intervention/pepfar-policy-hinders-treatment-generic-terms/ (last visited Oct. 22, 2025) (noting that PEPFAR initially refused to buy HIV/AIDS drugs from generic pharmaceutical manufacturers, thus reducing the number of people who could benefit from these drugs, while also ensuring that Big Pharma increased its turnover. This process came under severe criticism and was later amended to include more generic drugs); *see also* Harinder Singh Chahal et al., *The US Food and Drug Administration's Tentative Approval Process and the Global Fight Against HIV*, 20 J. Int'l AIDS Soc'y (2017) (noting that the nature of private control over public-policy decisions via this medium is discussed most widely in the context of the Bill & Melinda Gates Foundation. With the Foundation's growing influence and control in various global public-health contexts, there is growing criticism of the risks of philanthro-capitalism due to the "asymmetric distribution of power, which is sufficient to produce dependence, and that is uncontrolled insofar as its use either rests on the will of powerful agents or on terms of social cooperation beyond contestation"); *see also* Gwilym David Blunt, *The Gates Foundation, Global Health and Domination: A Republican Critique of Transnational Philanthropy*, 98 Int'l Affs. 2039 (2022) (noting that the Gates Foundation spends more on global health than most countries and is also instrumental as the largest private contributor in different international intergovernmental organizations); *see also* Sophie Harman, *The Bill and Melinda Gates Foundation and Legitimacy in Global Health Governance*, 22 Global Governance 349 (2016).

[45] *See* Srividhya Ragavan, *Of the Inequals of Uruguay*, 10 Marq. Intell. Prop. L. Rev. 273 (2006).

important role. Notoriously, though, the opinions of these groups on contentious trade issues are often faulted for being formally or informally "guided" by bilateral discussions held in private with developed countries. In these circumstances, the balance of power skews in favor of richer member states that are far removed from the local realities of poorer countries. Calculations and harmonization of public health through the trade lens tend to ignore those realities and the related socioeconomic cost.[46]

Thus, ensuring a Global South focus group, rather than a global one, would help mitigate some of the systemic disregard of issues that are important to countries where public-health issues are common. Importantly, such an approach would also allow member states needing to improve access to national health care to scrutinize different strategies before accepting a standardized arrangement. This approach, in turn, could help some nations frame and structure internal policies such as the desired or undesired levels of parallel importation, government subsidies, and price-control mechanisms, which would be a starting point for many nations.

There are policy flexibilities available inherent in the WTO's TRIPS Agreements as well as in other treaties such as the Convention on Biological Diversity and it is imperative for member states to coalesce and determine how these flexibilities can best be instituted into their national laws. Bilateral or multilateral agreements are also be effective means to address and negotiate flexibilities for better public health outcomes. Using available flexibilities to their maximum potential can also help member states expose the practical challenges involved in operationalizing them. These member states are best positioned to determine the effective means or mechanisms to overcome these challenges and to improve healthcare access.

We believe that formalized discussions between developing countries and least-developed countries, which currently lack a common forum, would represent the first step forward. These member states should determine:

(a) existing "solutions" within treaties that they are already a part of;
(b) consider varying local realities within each member state;

[46] *See* Mayur Patel, New Faces in the Green Room: Developing Country Coalitions and Decision-Making in the WTO (Univ. of Oxford, Glob. Econ. Governance Programme, Working Paper No. 2007/33, 2007), https://www.peio.me/wp-content/uploads/2014/04/Conf1_Patel_Developing.Countries.Coalitions.WTO_.pdf (last visited Oct. 22, 2025); *see also* John S. Odell, Negotiating Trade Developing Countries in the WTO and NAFTA 85–114 (2006).

(c) consider varying realities between different similarly positioned member states; and
(d) determine policy options by appreciating their effects on access to health care, focusing on ensuring availability.

International organizations involved in public health sometime seem to have conflicting goals. For example, the trilateral cooperation between the WHO, the WIPO, and the WTO does not provide a mechanism to fully resolve the competing issues affecting member states. If country A refuses to either license a patent in or export drugs to country B in the wake of a public-health crisis in the latter, it remains, at best, unclear whether and how the roles and interpretations of these organizations will change in the trilateral arrangement.

For instance, in the context of the Covid-19 pandemic, the failure of COVAX highlighted the inability of the entities running it in the face of the world's most pressing public-health need and missed opportunities for pressing alternative solutions.[47] As mentioned earlier, even the COVAX initiative did not place global public health front and center.

Positing public health as the central agenda would make it more viable to generate the cooperation needed to address a health crisis, whether local or global. Thus, in order for cooperation (trilateral or otherwise) to work, we envisage that the PHT should put global public health at the forefront by clearly aligning the roles of these international organizations with the unique purpose of ensuring health equity.

To achieve the benefits from the possibilities of harmonization via an international instrument focused on health, there must be structural mechanisms in place. These should enable innovation and access by creating sufficient cofinancing requirements, incentives for regional cooperation, and monitoring frameworks to track instituted mechanisms. This is not new for the WHO. Resolution WHA 59.24 by the WHO, on May 27, 2006, for the first time called for the establishment of an intergovernmental working group focusing on setting objectives and priorities in R&D. Further, a proposal by a Consultative Expert Working Group on Research and Development: Finance and Coordination (CEWG) in 2012 stated that the treaty would require member states to spend at least 0.01 percent of their

[47] *See* Olivia Goldhill, *'Naively Ambitious:' How COVAX Failed on Its Promise to Vaccinate the World*, Stat News (Oct. 8, 2021), https://www.statnews.com/2021/10/08/how-covax-failed-on-its-promise-to-vaccinate-the-world/ (last visited Oct. 22, 2025).

GDP on R&D that addresses the special health needs of developing countries, and to spend at least 20 percent of that funding through a single pooled funding mechanism.[48] The proposal also stated that R&D under the convention should focus on the development of health technologies for Type II and Type III diseases, as well as the specific needs of developing countries related to Type I diseases. The report also suggested alternative methods of funding, which included an indirect tax that, aside from generating revenue, would also help reduce consumption of products that harm health (alcohol, tobacco, etc.). The report also committed 15 percent of government expenditure to Africa, 2 percent of national health expenditure to R&D, and 5 percent of development assistance for health to health R&D.[49]

3.8 Other Considerations

Supply chains and logistics—including training, technology transfer, collaboration, and local manufacturing—should become a part of any calculus for a global way forward. A state's ability to contribute to innovation—whether in terms of supplies, logistics, or resources—would not only enhance infrastructure and supply-chain resilience but also identify areas of concern that are currently underserved across nations.

Outside of "tensions" between IP and trade on the one hand and public health on the other, regulatory concerns such as market exclusivities should be carefully addressed. For example, the issue of substandard or spurious drugs is often raised regarding developing countries.[50] If public health is

[48] *See* Sixty-Fifth World Health Assembly, Report of the Consultative Expert Working Group on Research and Development: Financing and Coordination (2012), https://apps.who.int/gb/CEWG/pdf_files/A65_24-en.pdf (last visited Oct. 22, 2025).

[49] *See id.*

[50] *See* Vinti Agarwal et al., *A Failure of Regulatory Diligence: A Case Study of Ranbaxy Laboratories Ltd*, *in* Fifteenth AIMS International Conference on Management 126 (Omprakash K. Gupta & Shiv Prakash Agrawal eds., 2018), https://www.aims-international.org/aims15/15ACD/PDF/A228-Final.pdf (last visited Oct. 22, 2025) (indicating that the international investigations into Ranbaxy Laboratories (India) were eventually initiated after Dinesh Thakur, an employee turned whistleblower, persistently insisted that the US Food and Drug Administration examine Ranbaxy's manufacturing processes for drugs exported to the United States. It was found that bioequivalence data for drugs being made at Ranbaxy's facilities either did not exist or had been made up. Thakur's similar attempts at getting India's drug-regulatory body to investigate did not result in any substantive action); *see also* Roger Bate et al., *Poor Quality Drugs and Global Trade: A Pilot Study*, 2 Am. J. Health Econ. 373 (2017) (noting that the drugs manufactured in India are a source for several developing and least-developed countries, and some studies have shown that poorer markets may be receiving substandard drugs from these manufacturing sites).

seen as an overarching concern, the integrity of test-data quality, regulatory examinations, and manufacturing processes require significantly more attention to ensure that the poorest nations are not treated as dumping grounds by multinational pharmaceutical companies. Thus, transparency of clinical-trial test data, for example, could not only assist in monitoring for safety and efficacy but also contribute to developing local practices and knowledge dissemination.[51]

Lastly, sufficient flexibility to account for sociopolitical realities will ensure that international treaty obligations do not constrict permissible sovereign behavior of the kind seen during both the HIV/AIDS crisis and the Covid-19 pandemic.[52]

4. Conclusion—A Human-Centric, Health-First Approach Is the Way Forward

To conclude, we reiterate that resolving issues of health equity requires addressing global public health as a concern in its own right and one that is separate from the power dynamics that have worked to its detriment thus far. Public health should be treated as a significant challenge with its own separate framework, without creating barriers to the free flow of trade otherwise. Hence, we call for the development of a new framework focusing on global public health, untethered to trade and IP norms. Such a framework would also provide a mechanism to respond to public-health exigencies.

In sum, while this chapter does not focus on advancing a human-rights–based approach, it recognizes access to health care as a human right that can lead to improved productivity. A human-centric approach may be critical to leading us away from market-led knowledge generation, especially so as to ensure better global public health. We believe that a treaty would be the preferred framework for such a human-centric approach to posit public health as a larger concern front and center, partly because an international treaty is more likely to generate the needed consensus than any other type of instrument or framework.

[51] *See* Jonathan Kimball et al., *Reconsidering the Rationale for the Duration of Data Exclusivity*, 51 U. Pac. L. Rev. 525, 536 (2020).

[52] *See* Srividhya Ragavan & Amaka Vanni, Intellectual Property Law and Access to Medicines: TRIPS Agreement, Health, and Pharmaceuticals, Routledge Press (2021).

While we call for the development of a new PHT, based on the assumption that it would be the best instrument for generating international consensus, the focus of the public-health framework needs to be a health-first approach. Thus, any framework that delivers access to health care efficiently and effectively is desirable. Embracing such an approach in all norm-setting exercises would strengthen the promotion of public health, although we believe such a norm-setting approach will ultimately wind up creating a treaty of some sort.

Index

For the benefit of digital users, indexed terms that span two pages (e.g., 52–53) may, on occasion, appear on only one of those pages.

Tables are indicated by an italic *t* following the page number.